SUICIDE RESEARCH: SELECTED READINGS

Volume 12

May 2014 – October 2014

A. Sheils, J. Ashmore, K. Kõlves, D. De Leo

Australian Institute for Suicide Research and Prevention

Griffith
UNIVERSITY

WHO Collaborating Centre for
Research and Training in Suicide Prevention

National Centre of Excellence in Suicide Prevention

First published in 2014
Australian Academic Press
18 Victor Russell Drive,
Samford QLD 4520, Australia
Australia
www.australianacademicpress.com.au

ISBN: 978 1 9221 1738 0

Book and cover design by Maria Biaggini — The Letter Tree.

Contents

Citation list

Foreword

This volume contains quotations from internationally peer-reviewed suicide research published during the semester May 2014 – October 2014; it is the twelfth of a series produced biannually by our Institute with the aim of assisting the Commonwealth Department of Health in being constantly updated on new evidences from the scientific community.

As usual, the initial section of the volume collects a number of publications that could have particular relevance for the Australian people in terms of potential applicability. These publications are accompanied by a short comment from us, and an explanation of the motives that justify why we have considered of interest the implementation of studies' findings in the Australian context. An introductory part provides the rationale and the methodology followed in the identification of papers.

The central part of the volume represents a selection of research articles of particular significance; their abstracts are reported *in extenso*, underlining our invitation at reading those papers in full text: they represent a remarkable advancement of suicide research knowledge.

The last section reports all items retrievable from major electronic databases. We have catalogued them on the basis of their prevailing reference to fatal and non-fatal suicidal behaviours, with various sub-headings (e.g. epidemiology, risk factors, etc). The deriving list guarantees a level of completeness superior to any individual system; it can constitute a useful tool for all those interested in a quick update of what is most recently published on the topic.

Our intent was to make suicide research more approachable to non-specialists, and in the meantime provide an opportunity for a *vademecum* of quotations credible also at the professional level. A compilation such as the one that we provide here is not easily obtainable from usual sources and can save a considerable amount of time to readers. We believe that our effort in this direction may be an appropriate interpretation of one of the technical support roles to the Government that the new status of National Centre of Excellence in Suicide Prevention — which has deeply honoured our commitment —entails for us.

The significant growth of our centre, the Australian Institute for Suicide Research and Prevention, and its influential function, both nationally and internationally, in the fight against suicide, could not happen without the constant support of Queensland Health, Queensland Mental Health Commission and Griffith University. We hope that our passionate dedication to the cause of suicide prevention may compensate their continuing trust in our work.

Diego De Leo, DSc
Director, Australian Institute for Suicide Research and Prevention

Acknowledgments

This report has been produced by the Australian Institute for Suicide Research and Prevention, WHO Collaborating Centre for Research and Training in Suicide Prevention and National Centre of Excellence in Suicide Prevention. The assistance of the Commonwealth Department of Health in the funding of this report is gratefully acknowledged.

Introduction

Context

Suicide places a substantial burden on individuals, communities and society in terms of emotional, economic and health care costs. In Australia, about 2000 people die from suicide every year, a death rate well in excess of transport-related mortality. At the time of preparing this volume, the latest available statistics released by the Australian Bureau of Statistics[1] indicated that, in 2012, 2,535 deaths by suicide were registered in Australia, representing an age-standardised rate of 11.2 per 100,000.

Despite the estimated mortality, the prevalence of suicide and self-harming behaviour in particular remains difficult to gauge due to the often secretive nature of these acts. Indeed, ABS has acknowledged the difficulties in obtaining reliable data for suicides in the past few years[4, 5]. Without a clear understanding of the scope of suicidal behaviours and the range of interventions available, the opportunity to implement effective initiatives is reduced. Further, it is important that suicide prevention policies are developed on the foundation of evidence-based empirical research, especially as the quality and validity of the available information may be misleading or inaccurate. Additionally, the social and economic impact of suicide underlines the importance of appropriate research-based prevention strategies, addressing not only significant direct costs on health system and lost productivity, but also the emotional suffering for families and communities.

The Australian Institute for Suicide Research and Prevention (AISRAP) has, through the years, gained an international reputation as one of the leading research institutions in the field of suicide prevention. The most important recognition came via the designation as a World Health Organization (WHO) Collaborating Centre in 2005. In 2008, the Commonwealth Department of Health DoH appointed AISRAP as the National Centre of Excellence in Suicide Prevention. This latter recognition awards not only many years of high-quality research, but also of fruitful cooperation between the Institute and several different governmental agencies.

As part of this mandate, AISRAP is committed to the creation of a databank of the recent scientific literature documenting the nature and extent of suicidal and self-harming behaviour and recommended practices in preventing and responding to these behaviours. The key output for the project is a critical bi-annual review of the national and international literature outlining recent advances and promising developments in research in suicide prevention, particularly where this can help to inform national activities. This task is not aimed at providing a critique of new researches, but rather at drawing attention to investigations that may have particular relevance to the Australian context. In doing so, we are committed to a user-friendly language, in order to render research outcomes and their interpretation accessible also to a non-expert audience.

In summary, these reviews serve three primary purposes:

1. To inform future State and Commonwealth suicide prevention policies;
2. To assist in the improvement of existing initiatives, and the development of new and innovative Australian projects for the prevention of suicidal and self-harming behaviours within the context of the Living is for Everyone (LIFE) Framework (2008);
3. To provide directions for Australian research priorities in suicidology.

The review is presented in three sections. The first contains a selection of the best articles published in the last six months internationally. For each article identified by us (see the method of chosing articles described below), the original abstract is accompanied by a brief comment explaining why we thought the study was providing an important contribution to research and why we considered its possible applicability to Australia. The second section presents the abstracts of the most relevant literature — following our criteria — collected between May 2014 and October 2014; while the final section presents a list of citations of all literature published over this time-period.

Methodology

The literature search was conducted in four phases.

Phase 1

Phase one consisted of weekly searches of the academic literature performed from May 2014 to October 2014. To ensure thorough coverage of the available published research, the literature was sourced using several scientific electronic databases including: PubMed, ProQuest, Scopus, Safetylit and Web of Science, using the following key words: *suicide OR suicidal OR self-harm OR self-injury OR parasuicide.*

Results from the weekly searches were downloaded and combined into one database (deleting duplicates).

Specific inclusion criteria for Phase 1 included:

- Timeliness: the article was published (either electronically or in hard-copy) between May 2014 and October 2014;
- Relevance: the article explicitly referred to fatal and/or non-fatal suicidal behaviour and related issues and/or interventions directly targeted at preventing/treating these behaviours.
- The article was written in English.

Articles about euthanasia, assisted suicide, suicide terrorist attacks, and/or book reviews, abstracts and conference presentations were excluded.

Also, articles that have been published in electronic versions (ahead of print) and therefore included in the previous volume (Volumes 1 to 11 of *Suicide Research: Selected Readings*) were excluded to avoid duplication.

Phase 2

Following an initial reading of the abstracts (retrieved in Phase 1), the list of articles was refined down to the most relevant literature. In Phase 2 articles were only included if they were published in an international, peer-reviewed journal.

In Phase 2, articles were excluded when they:
- were not particularly instructive or original
- were of a descriptive nature (e.g. a case-report)
- consisted of historical/philosophical content
- were a description of surgical reconstruction/treatment of self-inflicted injuries
- concerned biological and/or genetic interpretations of suicidal behaviour, the results of which could not be easily adoptable in the context of the LIFE Framework.

In order to minimise the potential for biased evaluations, two researchers working independently read through the full text of all articles selected to create a list of most relevant papers. This process was then duplicated by a third researcher for any articles on which consensus could not be reached.

The strength and quality of the research evidence was evaluated, based on the *Critical Appraisal Skills Programme (CASP) Appraisal Tools* published by the Public Health Resource Unit, England (2006). These tools, publically available online, consist of checklists for critically appraising systematic reviews, randomised controlled trials (RCT), qualitative research, economic evaluation studies, cohort studies, diagnostic test studies and case control studies.

Phase 3

One of the aims of this review was to identify research that is both evidence-based and of potential relevance to the Australian context. Thus, the final stage of applied methodology focused on research conducted in countries with populations or health systems sufficiently comparable to Australia. Only articles in which the full-text was available were considered. It is important to note that failure of an article to be selected for inclusion in Phase 3 does not entail any negative judgment on its 'objective' quality.

Specific inclusion criteria for Phase 3 included:
- applicability to Australia
- the paper met all criteria for scientificity (i.e., the methodology was considered sound)
- the paper represented a particularly compelling addition to the literature, which would be likely to stimulate suicide prevention initiatives and research
- inevitably, an important aspect was the importance of the journal in which the paper was published (because of the high standards that have to be met in order to obtain publication in that specific journal); priority was given to papers published in high impact factor journals

- particular attention has been paid to widen the literature horizon to include socio-logical and anthropological research that may have particular relevance to the Australian context.

After a thorough reading of these articles ('Key articles' for the considered timeframe), a written comment was produced for each article detailing:

- methodological strengths and weaknesses (e.g., sample size, validity of measurement instruments, appropriateness of analysis performed)
- practical implications of the research results to the Australian context
- suggestions for integrating research findings within the domains of the LIFE framework suicide prevention activities.

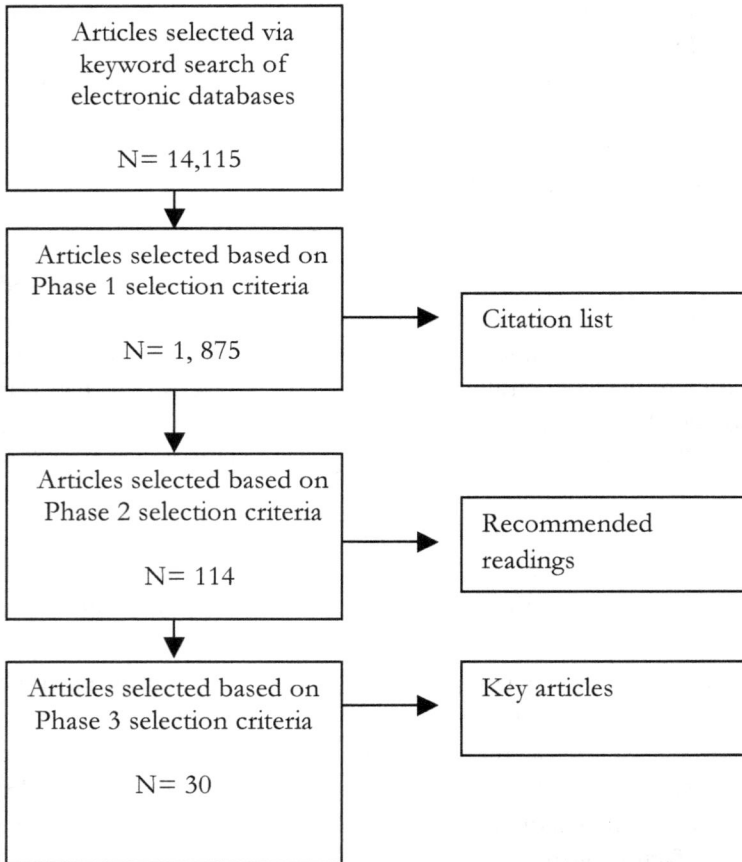

Figure 1

Phase 4

In the final phase of the search procedure all articles were divided into the following classifications:

- *Fatal suicidal behaviour* (epidemiology, risk and protective factors, prevention, postvention and bereavement)

- *Non-fatal suicidal/self-harming behaviours* (epidemiology, risk and protective factors, prevention, care and support)

- *Case reports* include reports of fatal and non-fatal suicidal behaviours

- *Miscellaneous* includes all research articles that could not be classified into any other category.

Allocation to these categories was not always straightforward, and where papers spanned more than one area, consensus of the research team determined which domain the article would be placed in. Within each section of the report (i.e., Key articles, Recommended readings, Citation list) articles are presented in alphabetical order by author.

Endnotes

1 Australian Bureau of Statistics (2014). *Causes of death, Australia, 2012. Suicides.* Cat. no. 3303.0. Canberra: ABS.

Key Articles

Are suicidal behaviours contagious in adolescence? Using longitudinal data to examine suicide suggestion

Abrutyn S, Mueller A (USA)

American Sociological Review. Published online: 31 March 2014. doi: 10.1177/0003122413519445, 2014

Durkheim argued that strong social relationships protect individuals from suicide. We posit, however, that strong social relationships also have the potential to increase individuals' vulnerability when they expose people to suicidality. Using three waves of data from the National Longitudinal Study of Adolescent Health, we evaluate whether new suicidal thoughts and attempts are in part responses to exposure to role models' suicide attempts, specifically friends and family. We find that role models' suicide attempts do in fact trigger new suicidal thoughts, and in some cases attempts, even after significant controls are introduced. Moreover, we find these effects fade with time, girls are more vulnerable to them than boys, and the relationship to the role model — for teenagers at least — matters. Friends appear to be more salient role models for both boys and girls. Our findings suggest that exposure to suicidal behaviors in significant others may teach individuals new ways to deal with emotional distress, namely by becoming suicidal. This reinforces the idea that the structure — and content — of social networks conditions their role in preventing suicidality. Social ties can be conduits of not just social support, but also antisocial behaviors, like suicidality.

Comment

Main Findings: Social integration and regulation are often emphasised as the primary social forces that either protect an individual or put individuals at risk of suicide[1]. Some research indicates that social ties are not just mechanisms for social support but also potential conduits for the spread of suicidal behaviours via suicide suggestion[2]. This longitudinal study, conducted in the USA, aimed to address four major gaps in the literature: 1) whether suicide suggestion is associated with the development of suicidal thoughts among individuals who reported no suicidal thoughts at the time a role-model attempted suicide; 2) whether the effects of suicide suggestion fade with time; 3) whether the relationship between the role model and respondent matters; and 4) whether there are differences between boys and girls. Data from a preliminary in-school survey with follow-up interviews at three different wave periods were used. The analytic sample comprised of 9,309 USA adolescents in grades 7 through 12 across 132 middle and high-schools.

Findings from this study suggest that social relationships are not always protective against suicide, at least not when significant others exhibit suicidal tendencies. Role-model suicide attempts (primarily friends) were in fact associated with adolescents' development of suicidal thoughts and, in some cases, attempts. This suggests that exposure to role models is a powerful way that drastic and deviant behaviours, like suicide, become normalised. This finding is in line with a study conducted in Australia which concluded that the strongest predictor of deliberate self-harm in adolescents was exposure to self-harm in family and friends[3]. The effect of a friend's or family member's suicide attempt lasted at least one year. By six years, the effect appeared to fade significantly. However, among adolescent girls, a friend's suicide attempt may continue to shape their suicidal thoughts even six years later. A significant gender difference was found indicating that girls were more vulnerable to suicide suggestion than boys. Finally, findings also indicated that peers may be more meaningful than family to adolescents, for both boys and girls. Friends' suicide attempts were more influential than family members' suicide attempts in adolescents' lives.

Implications: This study has important policy implications for public health officials attempting to prevent adolescent suicide. Policies and practitioners need to be sensitive to the importance of suicide attempts, particularly among peers and for girls. The increased risk of suicidality associated with friends' suicide attempts may last a year or more, which is longer than previously thought[4]. For adolescents, whether these social ties integrate adolescents into society with positive repercussions for their emotional well-being, or whether they promote feelings of alienation, depends in part on the qualities embedded in those ties. For a full understanding of how social integration works in individuals' lives to shape their life chances, we must consider not only the support that social ties provide but also the emotions, behaviours and values inherent in those social relations.

Endnotes

1. Wray M, Colen C, Pescosolido B (2011). The sociology of suicide. *Annual Review of Sociology* 37, 505-528.
2. Gould MS (2001). Suicide and the media. *Annals of the New York Academy of Sciences* 932, 200-224.
3. De Leo D, Heller TS (2004). Who are the kids who self-harm? An Australian self-report school survey. *Medical Journal of Australia* 181, 140-144.
4. Phillips DP (1974). The influence of suggestion on suicide: Substantive and theoretical implications of the Werther effect. *American Sociological Review*, 340-354.

How many times and how many ways: The impact of number of nonsuicidal self-injury methods on the relationship between nonsuicidal self-injury frequency and suicidal behavior

Anestis MD, Khazem LR, Law KC (USA)

Suicide and Life-Threatening Behavior. Published online: 16 September 2014. doi: 10.1111/sltb.12120, 2014

Several variables have been proposed as heavily influencing or explaining the association between nonsuicidal self-injury (NSSI) and suicidal behavior. We propose that increased comfort with bodily harm may serve as an incrementally valuable variable to consider. We sought to indirectly test this possibility by examining the moderating role of number of NSSI methods utilized on the relationship between NSSI frequency and lifetime number of suicide attempts, positing that increased variability in methods would be indicative with a greater general comfort with inflicting harm upon one's own body. In both a large sample of emerging adults (n = 1,317) and a subsample with at least one prior suicide attempt (n = 143), results were consistent with our hypothesis. In both samples, the interaction term was significant, with the relationship between NSSI frequency and suicidal behavior increasing in magnitude from low to mean to high levels of NSSI methods. Although frequency of NSSI is robustly associated with suicidal behavior, the magnitude of that relationship increases as an individual engages in a wider variety of NSSI methods. We propose that this may be due to an increased comfort with the general concept of damaging one's own body resulting from a broader selection of methods for self-harm.

Comment

Main findings: Although there is no apparent conscious intention to die, nonsuicidal self-injury (NSSI) has been repeatedly associated with suicidal ideation and future suicide attempts. No single comprehensive explanation for this relationship has been found; however, a number of potential mechanisms have been put forward, including depression, emotion dysregulation, and acquired capability for suicide. Frequency of NSSI has previously been associated with severity of suicidal behaviour; this study found that repeated engagement in a variety of methods of NSSI is associated with a lifetime history of suicidal behaviour. The results showed that NSSI clearly differentiated those with and without a prior history of suicidal behaviour; only 2.5% of those with no prior history of NSSI had ever attempted suicide, compared with 33.6% of individuals with a prior history of NSSI. NSSI methods appeared to impact upon suicidal behaviour differently than frequency; in the subsample of suicide attempters, NSSI frequency was only a significant predictor of suicidal behaviour at high levels of NSSI methods. While use of one NSSI method, such as cutting, may result in comfort only with that particular method, it is suggested that versatility of methods may reinforce comfort with the general infliction of self-harm, and may be a contributing factor to suicidal behaviour.

Implications: Deliberate self-harm without conscious suicidal intent has increasingly been studied as a clinical phenomenon[1]. Self-injurious behaviour places a considerable burden on the Australian economy, as people who self-injure may frequently access public emergency and psychiatric health services[2]. While it can occur at any age, adolescents and young adults are at a greater risk[1]. A recent Australian study surveyed nearly 2,000 secondary school students (years 9 and 10) across two time points one year apart; 12% of participants reported a history of NSSI at the second time point, with a cumulative incidence of 3.8%[3]. NSSI studies of adolescents in Australia have typically shown lower prevalence rates compared to international rates; lower incidence may partly be due to limited research participation by students experiencing emotional difficulties[3]. Past research on deliberate self-harm has focused on risk factors, but a lack of consistency in defining self-injurious behaviour has made comparison of findings difficult, particularly as suicidal intent is very difficult to determine[1]. The conceptualisation of NSSI as a distinct diagnostic category is particularly problematic. Suicidal intention is a multidimensional variable which may be categorised by differing degrees of intensity; reducing it to a dichotomous category may have misleading implications, especially if clinical attention is reduced as a result[4]. Future investigations of the complex relationship between self-injury and suicidal behaviour should seek to refine conceptualisations and measurements of suicidal behaviours, including the basis of the experience an individual has undergone.

Endnotes

1. Fliege H, Lee J-R, Grimm A, Klapp BF (2009). Risk factors and correlates of deliberate self-harm behavior: A systematic review. *Journal of Psychosomatic Research* 66, 477-493.
2. Steenkamp M, Harrison J (2000). *Suicide and hospitalised self-harm in Australia.* Canberra: Australian Institute of Health and Welfare.
3. Andrews T, Martin G, Hasking P, Page A (2014). Predictors of onset for non-suicidal self-injury within a school-based sample of adolescents. *Prevention Science* 15, 850-859.
4. De Leo D (2011). DSM-V and the future of suicidology. *Crisis* 32, 233-239.

Near-term predictors of the intensity of suicidal ideation: An examination of the 24h prior to a recent suicide attempt

Bagge CL, Littlefield AK, Conner KR, Schumacher JA, Lee HJ (USA)
Journal of Affective Disorders 165, 53-58, 2014

Background: The extent to which acute exposures such as alcohol use (AU) and negative life events (NLE) are uniquely associated with intensity of suicidal ideation during the hours leading up to a suicide attempt is unknown. The main aim of the current study was to quantify the unique effect of acute exposures on next-hour suicidal ideation when adjusting for previous hour acute exposures and suicidal ideation. An exploratory aim of the current study was to examine the effect of non-alcohol drug use (DU) on suicidal ideation.

Methods: Participants included 166 (61.0% female) recent suicide attempters presenting to a Level 1 trauma hospital. A timeline follow-back methodology was used to assess acute exposures and intensity of suicidal ideation within the 24 h prior to the suicide attempt.

Results: Findings indicated that acute AU (b=.20, p<.01) and NLE (b=.58, p<.01) uniquely predicted increases in next-hour suicidal ideation, over and above previous hour suicidal ideation, whereas acute DU did not.

Limitations: The current study's methodology provides continuous hourly snapshots prior to the suicide attempt, quite close to when it happened, but is retrospective and causality cannot be inferred.

Conclusions: Understanding that, within a patient, AU and NLE predict near-term increases in suicidal ideation has practical utility impacting providers clinical decision-making, safety concerns, and ultimate determination of level of risk for suicide.

Comment

Main Findings: From a preventative perspective, it is critical to understand what acute exposures may intensify the risk of suicidal ideation that precedes suicidal behaviour. The aims of this study were to examine whether the presence of near-term factors (acute alcohol use [AU], negative life events [NLE], and non-alcohol drug use [DU]) predict the intensification of suicidal ideation during the 24 hours prior to a recent suicide attempt and to determine whether these relations hold after adjusting for previous hour suicidal ideation. Patients were individuals aged between 18 and 64 years, who presented to hospital with Level 1 trauma (i.e. self-inflicted behaviour with some intent to die) within 24 hours after a suicide attempt between October 2008 and December 2012. A total of 166 participants were included with complete data (61% females, mean age 36.61 years). A two and a half-hour assessment of questionnaires and semi-structured interviews was undertaken. Within 24 hours prior to a suicide attempt, 32.5, 27.1 and 47.0% of participants reported experiencing at least one AU, DU or NLE respectively. Number of hours between when the event was experienced and attempt ranged from 0-14 (AU), 0-13 (DU) and 0-8 (NLE). Notably, apart from DU, these results held even after the additional adjustment for previous hour suicidal ideation. This indicates that AU and NLE predict subsequent increases in suicidal ideation in the near term, above and beyond a patient's current level of suicidal ideation, over a time frame (24 hours prior to attempt) with practical significance for clinical decision-making and safety concerns.

Implications: Taken as a whole, the methodology of this study allowed for a unique insight into the events and behaviours that predict increases in the intensity of suicidal thinking during the hours leading up to a suicide attempt. The knowledge that both AU and NLE increase short-term risk for suicidal ideation prior to a suicide attempt has practical implications for both suicide research and clinical work. It is important for future researchers to model the dynamic nature of suicidal ideation and its correlates within an individual. A single rating of suicidal ideation will not accurately capture changes in an individual's state, particularly for time periods of critical importance for clinicians (hours or days preceding a suicide attempt) when the determination of imminent risk is key.

Given that the majority of suicide attempters report formulating a plan and deciding to act within three hours prior to their attempt and that suicidal thoughts and acute predictors are episodic, clinicians are faced with the challenging task of determining whether a patient is at imminent risk of suicide[1]. Thus, they should consider employing individualised distress safety plans for high-risk people and also those who do not presently have suicidal thoughts. Such plans should focus on inventing strategies to prevent or cope with future NLEs or AU with the overall intention of thwarting subsequent suicidal ideation and potential for imminent risk. AU may proximally influence suicidal thoughts and behaviours[2] through alcohol-related increases in acute psychological distress, self-directed aggression, constricted attention involving the inability to produce reasons for living and adaptive coping strategies, and suicide-specific alcohol motives[3]. Furthermore, NLEs may produce enhanced states of burdensomeness and decreased belongingness, contributing to increased suicidal thoughts within an individual. However, direct empirical research testing such mechanisms is lacking, and should be considered in future research.

Endnotes

1. Bagge CL, Littlefield AK, Lee HL (2013).Correlates of proximal premeditation among recently hospitalized suicide attempters. *Journal of Affective Disorders* 150, 559–564.
2. Hufford MR (2001). Alcohol and suicidal behavior. *Clinical Psychology Review* 21, 797–811.
3. Bagge CL, Sher KJ (2008). Adolescent alcohol involvement and suicide attempts: Toward the development of a conceptual framework. *Clinical Psychology Review* 28, 1283–1296.

Adverse childhood experiences and associations with health-harming behaviours in young adults: Surveys in eight eastern European countries

Bellis MA, Hughes K, Leckenby N, Jones L, Baban A, Kachaeva M, Povilaitis R, Pudule I, Qirjako G, Ulukol B, Raleva M, Terzic N (UK, Romaina, Russian Federation, Lithuania, Latvia, Albania, Turkey, the former Yugoslav Repulic of Macedonia, Montenegro)
Bulletin of the World Health Organization 92, 641-655, 2014

Objective: To evaluate the association between adverse childhood experiences — e.g. abuse, neglect, domestic violence and parental separation, substance use, mental illness or incarceration — and the health of young adults in eight eastern European countries.

Methods: Between 2010 and 2013, adverse childhood experience surveys were undertaken in Albania, Latvia, Lithuania, Montenegro, Romania, the Russian Federation, The former Yugoslav Republic of Macedonia and Turkey. There were 10 696 respondents — 59.7% female — aged 18-25 years. Multivariate modelling was used to investigate the relationships between adverse childhood experiences and health-harming behaviours in early adulthood including substance use, physical inactivity and attempted suicide.

Findings: Over half of the respondents reported at least one adverse childhood experience. Having one adverse childhood experience increased the probability of having other adverse childhood experiences. The number of adverse childhood experiences was positively correlated with subsequent reports of health-harming behaviours. Compared with those who reported no adverse experiences, respondents who reported at least four adverse childhood experiences were at significantly increased risk of many health-harming behaviours, with odds ratios varying from 1.68 (95% confidence interval, CI: 1.32-2.15), for physical inactivity, to 48.53 (95% CI: 31.98-76.65), for attempted suicide. Modelling indicated that prevention of adverse childhood experiences would substantially reduce the occurrence of many health-harming behaviours within the study population.

Conclusion: Our results indicate that individuals who do not develop health-harming behaviours are more likely to have experienced safe, nurturing childhoods. Evidence-based programmes to improve parenting and support child development need large-scale deployment in eastern European.

Comment

Main findings: Adverse childhood experiences, including abuse and neglect, are known to be associated with poorer health and behavioural outcomes, such as attempted suicide. Countries with relatively low per-capita incomes have been reported to have a higher incidence of child abuse; within the European region of the World Health Organization (WHO), levels of child mortality and morbidity appear to be higher in the east than in the west. This large scale study surveyed young adults in secondary or higher education in eight Eastern European countries seeking information about adverse childhood experiences such as physical, sexual and emotional abuse, parental divorce or separation, and experiences of other household members who may have been depressed or suicidal, incarcerated, or are experiencing problematic use of drugs or alcohol. Possible outcomes of respondents' health-harming behaviours included attempted suicide, problematic sexual behaviour and problematic drug and alcohol use. Respondents in Turkey were not asked about attempted suicide, and relatively large numbers of respondents failed to answer questions about sexual abuse and partners. Amongst those reporting no adverse childhood experiences, 0.7% reported attempted suicide and this rate increased as number of adverse experiences increased. Amongst those reporting four or more adverse childhood experiences, 23.6% reported attempted suicide. More than 18% who had lived with someone who was depressed or suicidal reported attempting suicide themselves, compared to just 2.5% of other respondents. Other adverse experiences most highly correlating with attempted suicide were incarceration by a household member (23%), drug abuse by another household member (22%), emotional abuse (16%), and sexual abuse (12.9%). Family environment is known to be greatly influenced by economic pressure[1]; in this study, parental educational achievement was used as a proxy for childhood economic status. However, adverse childhood experiences were associated with health-harming behaviours, including attempted suicide, independently of respondents' parental education level. Many respondents were in higher education and it is possible that this introduced bias against more disadvantaged groups.

Implications: These findings are in line with other studies finding increased risk of suicidal behaviours amongst young people who have experienced adverse childhood experiences, and highlight child vulnerability to changes within family conditions[1]. In Australia, suicide is a major contributor to child and adolescent death, with clearly related psychosocial and environmental factors. A Queensland study found that 34.4% of children and 39.3% of adolescents who died by suicide between 2004 and 2012 had experienced physical, sexual or emotional abuse during their lifetimes. More than 50% of the children and 35.7% of the adolescents had experienced familial problems as a precipitating event to suicide[2]. Adverse experiences in childhood are also linked to suicide behaviours much later in life. Another Australian study linked 2,759 victims of child sexual abuse between 1964 and 1995 with Victorian coronial records up to 44 years later; they found that female sexual abuse victims had a risk of suicide 40 times higher than that in the general population, with a risk of fatal overdose 88 times higher than rates in the general population. Respective rates for males were 14 times and 38 times higher than the general population[3]. Current adverse economic conditions in Australia leading to higher unemployment and decreased family income are likely to exacerbate risk of suicidal behaviours for children and young people already vulnerable to changes within their family systems. The consequences of current adverse childhood experiences may impact on society for many years into the future; however, little is yet known about how risk and protective factors impact on risk for individual children, and which issues should be addressed in future suicide prevention programs[1].

Endnotes

1. Kõlves K (2010). Child suicide, family environment, and economic crisis (editorial). *Crisis* 31, 115-117.
2. Soole R, Kõlves K, De Leo D (2014). Factors related to childhood suicides: Analysis of the Queensland Child Death Register. *Crisis* 35, 292-300.
3. Cutajar MC, Mullen PE, Golf JRP, Thomas SD, Wells DL, Spataro J (2010). Suicide and fatal drug overdose in child sexual abuse victims: A historical cohort study. *Medical Journal of Australia* 192, 184–187.

Perceptions of Australian emergency staff towards patients presenting with deliberate self-poisoning: A qualitative perspective.

Chapman R, Martin C (Australia)

International Emergency Nursing 22, 140–145, 2014

Introduction/Background: Attitude of staff towards patients who present to the emergency department following deliberate self-poisoning may be integral to the outcome of these events. There is little in-depth understanding of emergency staff perceptions about this vulnerable group.

Aim: Explore staff perceptions about caring for patients who present to the emergency department following deliberate self-poisoning.

Design: Qualitative descriptive study.

Methods: Two open-ended questions enabled 186 clinicians to describe their perceptions about caring for people who present to the emergency department following deliberate self-poisoning. Data were analysed using qualitative data analysis procedures.

Results: Three themes emerged from the data representing staff perceptions about caring for patients who deliberately self-poisoned and included depends on the patient, treat everyone the same, and skilled and confident to manage these patients.

Conclusion: Staff reported mixed reactions to patients presenting with deliberate self-poisoning. These included feelings of empathy or frustration, and many lacked the skills and confidence to effectively manage these patients.

Relevance to Practice: Health networks are required to ensure that emergency staff have specialist support, knowledge, skills, and guidelines to provide effective care for this vulnerable population.

Comment

Main findings: Patients that present with deliberate self-poisoning (DSP) can add to the burden on Emergency Departments (ED). Although accounting for a relatively small percentage (0.5-2%) of ED attendees in Australia[1], DSP patients are at increased risk of discharging themselves from the hospital before treatment or against medical advice and can be perceived to increase staff workload overall[2]. Only a few studies have explored the attitudes and perceptions of doctors and nurses towards patients who present following self-poisoning. The current paper presents the results of an Australian survey, distributed to three EDs in one health care network in Melbourne's south eastern suburbs to investigate their attitudes towards patients who present with DSP. Two open-ended questions were provided to staff asking how they felt when caring for a patient who deliberately self-poisoned, and any additional thoughts, feelings or perceptions regarding these patients. From the 186 surveys returned, 169 included written responses to the two open-ended questions. The majority of the respondents were female nurses aged between 27 and 55 years.

The first theme to emerge was that ED staff experienced mixed emotions toward DSP patients depending on the patient's reason for admission and the situation within the department. Participants reported feeling empathetic, compassionate and concerned towards patients who they considered had made an actual suicide attempt. ED staff also identified feeling frustrated by admission of patients who were thought to have overdosed to gain attention or to access the psychiatric ward, or those patients who had been admitted to the department before following a prior DSP attempt. The second theme to emerge was staff reporting that they treated all patients the same regardless of their reasons for admission, stating that they had a duty of care and a job to do. The third theme to emerge was frustration occurring in ED staff who believed they lacked the skill and confidence to care for these patients. Those who believed they acquired adequate skills enjoyed the challenge and gained satisfaction managing DSP patients. Participants acknowledging a lack of skills highlighted the need for continuing education and training to have a communication focus, be aimed across the lifespan and cover all aspects of DSP.

Implications: This Australian research study allowed a more in-depth understanding about ED staff perceptions of caring for people who present following DSP. Staff experience of negative feelings of frustration, powerlessness and failure can result in these patients being ignored or marginalised[3]. An earlier study conducted in Western Australia found that patients are conscious of these negative attitudes, reporting that they felt judged as being attention seekers and time wasters, were unworthy of care and were not treated like other patients who present to the ED[4]. Staff attitudes are important, considering that some patients report avoidance of the ED when they self-harm if they had experienced previous negative behaviour from staff. Staff who lack knowledge and skills to confidently manage patients presenting to the ED with DSP may hinder the provision of optimal care to these patients. Hospital and department managers and educators are required to provide staff with access to specialised staff resources, education and training, and evidence-based clinical guidelines[5].

Previous research has found systematic challenges both within and external to acute care settings that limit the ability to translate guidelines and processes into the most positive possible outcomes for patients at high/imminent risk of suicide. A key challenge was ensuring that sufficient resources were available (i.e. resources relating to staffing) to effectively implement care policies and processes[6]. In addition, a study that attained data from 10 of 15 Australian medical schools demonstrated the importance and need for 'specific skills-based' suicide prevention education, more precisely at a tertiary level, including assessment, intervention and management of suicidal persons[7]. Such training will assist ED staff to ensure consistent and equitable practice and better outcomes for this vulnerable group and increase their own satisfaction when caring for DSP patients. To ensure that these interventions and strategies are effective, it is essential that further research in this area be conducted.

Endnotes

1. Rahman A, Martin C, Graudins A, Chapman R (2014). Deliberate self-poisoning presenting to an emergency medicine network in South-East Melbourne: A descriptive study. *Emergency Medicine International*. Published online: 12 June 2014. doi:10.1155/2014/461841.

2. Anderson M, Standen P, Noon J (2003). Nurses' and doctors' perceptions of young people who engage in suicidal behaviour: A contemporary grounded theory analysis. *International Journal of Nursing Studies* 40, 587–597.

3. Conlon M, O'Tuathail C (2012). Measuring emergency department nurses' attitudes towards deliberate self-harm using the Self-Harm Antipathy Scale. *International Emergency Nursing* 20, 3-13.

4. Strevens P, Blackwell H, Palmer L, Hartwell E (2008). Better services for people who self-harm: *Aggregated report – Wave 3 baseline data*. London: Royal College of Psychiatrists.

5. National Institute for Clinical Excellence, 2012. *Self-harm: Longer-term management. NICE clinical guideline 133*. Manchester: National Institute for Clinical Excellence.

6. McPhedran S, De Leo D (2013). *Pathways to care: to examine the mechanisms in place across Australia to respond to and provide care to people at imminent risk of suicide: Summary*. Brisbane: Australian Institute for Suicide Research and Prevention.

7. Hawgood JL, Krysinska KE, Ide N, De Leo D (2008). Is suicide prevention properly taught in medical schools? *Medical Teacher* 30, 287-295.

Predictors of suicides occurring within suicide clusters in Australia, 2004-2008

Cheung YTD, Spittal MJ, Williamson MK, Tung SJ, Pirkis J (Australia, Hong Kong-China)
Social Science and Medicine 118, 135-142, 2014

A number of studies have investigated the presence of suicide clusters, but few have sought to identify risk and protective factors of a suicide occurring within a cluster. We aimed to identify socio-demographic and contextual characteristics of suicide clusters from national and regional analyses of suicide clusters. We searched the National Coroners Information System for all suicides in Australia from 2004 to 2008. Scan statistics were initially used to identify those deaths occurring within a spatial-temporal suicide cluster during the period. We then used logistic regression and generalised estimation equations to estimate the odds of each suicide occurring within a cluster differed by sex, age, marital status, employment status, Indigenous status, method of suicide and location. We identified 258 suicides out of 10,176 suicides during the period that we classified as being within a suicide cluster. When the deceased was Indigenous, living outside a capital city, or living in the northern part of Australia (in particular, Northern Territory, Queensland and Western Australia) then there was an increased likelihood of their death occurring within a suicide cluster. These findings suggest that suicide clustering might be linked with geographical and Indigenous factors, which supported sociological explanations of suicide clustering. This finding is significant for justifying resource allocation for tackling suicide clustering in particular areas.

Comment

Main findings: Suicide clusters can be defined as occurrence of an exceptionally greater number of deaths than would be expected in a location over a particular time period. Detection of suicide clusters is an important means of identifying areas of high suicide risk, but the mechanisms causing clusters are still being debated. Some evidence suggests that imitation occurs when there are links between members of the cluster, with communication occurring across social networks. Previous Australian research has identified suicide clusters in individual states and territories[1]; this study further examines common characteristics among members of these clusters. Analysis of suicides that occurred within a cluster found that exceptionally high proportions of clustered suicides occurred amongst those younger than 20 years (5.6%), Aboriginal and Torres Strait Islanders (16.4%), living in the Northern Territory (18%), Queensland (5.7%), remote centres (12.6%) and other remote areas (21.2%). Examining interactions between variables showed that the odds of Aboriginal and Torres Strait Islander deaths having been in a suicide cluster varied by state or territory, but not by remoteness. The odds of an Aboriginal or Torres Strait Islander person being in a cluster was greater in Western Australia (odds ratio [OR] = 1.16 vs. 16.80 for other Australians and Aboriginal and Torres Strait Islanders respectively) and lower in the

Northern Territory (OR = 33.30 vs. 12.09). There were no significant differences between odds for other Australians and Aboriginal and Torres Strait Islanders in the other states.

Implications: Identification of common characteristics within suicide clusters may assist to determine where targeted suicide prevention efforts are most urgently needed. The findings of this study show that suicide clusters are more likely to occur in remote or rural areas, in the Northern Territory, Queensland, South Australia and Western Australia. Aboriginal and Torres Strait Islander suicides in the Northern Territory, Queensland and Western Australia have a heightened risk of being clustered. In rural and remote areas, groups most vulnerable to suicide appear to be males, young people, farmers and Aboriginal and Torres Strait Islanders. These findings are supported by past research; for example, Queensland Suicide Register data has shown that male suicide rates in remote areas are approximately twice as high as those in non-remote areas[1]. Factors put forward to explain high suicide rates in rural and remote areas have included social isolation, economic stressors, a lack of available services, occupational issues relating to farming, stressors relating to changing climactic conditions, problematic use of alcohol and drugs, and access to lethal suicide methods such as firearms[2]. In the Northern Territory, the gap between suicide rates of Aboriginal and Torres Strait Islanders and non-Indigenous people is believed to have increased over the past three decades in direct correlation to increasing social and economic gaps[3]. In Queensland, suicide rates are approximately 2.2 times higher amongst Aboriginal and Torres Strait Islanders than amongst other Australian people, particularly among young people[4]. It is possible that greater exposure to suicidal behaviour of others may create higher risk of imitative suicide, mainly due to the dense social networks and complex interpersonal relationships within Aboriginal and Torres Strait Islander communities[3]. Further research to enable a better understanding of the mechanisms of suicide clustering and contagion would assist to inform policy and resource allocation.

Endnotes

1. Austin AE, van den Heuvel C, Byard RW (2011). Cluster hanging suicides in the young in South Australia. *Journal of Forensic Sciences* 56, 1528-1530.
2. Kõlves K, Milner A, McKay K, De Leo D (2012). *Suicide in rural and remote areas of Australia.* Brisbane: Australian Institute for Suicide Research and Prevention.
3. Hanssens L (2011). "Suicide (echo) clusters" – Are they socially determined, the result of a pre-existing vulnerability in Indigenous communities in the Northern Territory and how can we contain cluster suicides? *Aboriginal and Islander Health Worker Journal* 35, 14-23.
4. De Leo D, Sveticic J, Milner A (2011). Suicide in Indigenous people in Queensland, Australia: Trends and methods, 1994-2007. *Australian and New Zealand Journal of Psychiatry* 45, 532-528.

Deaths by suicide and their relationship with general and psychiatric hospital discharge: 30-year record linkage study

Dougall N, Lambert P, Maxwell M, Dawson A, Sinnott R, McCafferty S, Morris C, Clark D, Springbett A (Scotland, Australia)

British Journal of Psychiatry 204, 267-273, 2014

Background: Studies have rarely explored suicides completed following discharge from both general and psychiatric hospital settings. Such research might identify additional opportunities for intervention.

Aims: To identify and summarise Scottish psychiatric and general hospital records for individuals. who have died by suicide.

Method: A linked data study of deaths by suicide, aged >= 15 years from 1981 to 2010.

Results: This study reports on a UK data-set of individuals who died by suicide (n = 16 411), of whom 66% (n = 10 907) had linkable previous hospital records. Those who died by suicide were 3.1 times more frequently last discharged from general than from psychiatric hospitals; 24% of deaths occurred within 3 months of hospital discharge (58% of these from a general hospital). Only 14% of those discharged from a general hospital had a recorded psychiatric diagnosis at last visit; an additional 19% were found to have a previous lifetime psychiatric diagnosis. Median time between last discharge and death was fourfold greater in those without a psychiatric history. Diagnoses also revealed that less than half of those last discharged from general hospital had had a main diagnosis of 'injury or poisoning'.

Conclusions: Suicide prevention activity, including a better psychiatric evaluation of patients within general hospital settings deserves more attention. Improved information flow between secondary and primary care could be facilitated by exploiting electronic records of previous psychiatric diagnoses.

Comment

Main Findings: Contact with healthcare providers offers the opportunity to engage in suicide prevention and there has been considerable interest in establishing predictive information on which individuals accessing healthcare services are most at risk. This study used records of suicides from the National Records of Scotland (NRS) death register from 1981 to 2010 to analyse patterns after last discharge by hospital type (general or psychiatric). Hospital records were ascertained from a digitalised National Health Service (NHS) that is linkable by unique patient identification numbers. A total of 16,475 deaths by suicide occurred during this 30-year period. Of those, 10,907 had a hospital record and were discharged alive (i.e. did not die in hospital). Individuals with hospital records who died by suicide were predominantly male (72%), with a mean age of 43 years and were more frequently living alone. Males were significantly younger than females at death and also accessed secondary-care services less often. A total of 66,188 psychiatric and general hospital records were collected for the 10,907 patients who died by suicide. Significantly more people who died by suicide were last discharged from general (76%) rather than psychiatric hospitals (21%). A total of 16% of all deaths by suicide had occurred within three months of last discharge from any hospital (n = 2,575/16,411). This amounted to about a quarter of all deaths among previous hospital patients (24%) in the same period (n = 2,575/10,907). Less than half (38%) of those last discharged from a general hospital had received a diagnosis of 'injury or poisoning', with more than half of these being younger men. The patients who produced the shortest median time until death (seven months) after they were discharged from hospital were those who had a recorded comorbid psychiatric diagnosis at their last hospital visit (14%), followed by those who did not have a recorded comorbid psychiatric diagnosis at their last hospital visit but did have a diagnosis at some point in their life (nine months; 19%). This was in contrast with those who had no (hospital) psychiatric diagnosis (33 months; 67%).

Implications: The findings from this study further highlight the importance of engaging in suicide prevention within the general hospital setting. There is a need to follow up people admitted to general hospital with self-harm (in particular younger men); screening for psychological problems in those where there has been either a history of self-harming or any psychiatric condition along the life course would be beneficial. It is important to ensure that all hospital staff engage in some first-line mental health screening of these 'at risk' patients. Many of those who died by suicide in this study had no hospital records at all, which also highlights the need for adequate community and primary care mental health resources in order to reach those who do not present to general or psychiatric hospitals. A study conducted at the Gold Coast Hospital, Queensland, compared the difference between patients receiving Intensive Case Management (ICM) following discharge, featuring weekly face-to-face contact with a community case manager and outreach phone calls from counsellors, versus those who received Treatment As Usual (TAU)[1]. At the end of the twelve-month treatment phase, people in the ICM condition had significant improvements in depression and suicide ideation scores, improved quality of life, more contacts with mental and allied health services, better relationships with therapists, and were more satisfied with the services they received. In conclusion, this highlights the importance of implementing appropriate care strategies post-discharge for those patients who present to hospital with self-harm history or psychiatric comorbidity, past or present, and of utilising appropriate methods to identify those at high risk of suicide.

Endnotes

1. De Leo D, Heller T (2007). Intensive case management in suicide attempters following discharge from inpatient psychiatric care. *Australian Journal of Primary Health* 13, 49-59.

Impact of a major disaster on the mental health of a well-studied cohort

Fergusson DM, Horwood J, Boden JM, Tulder, RT (New Zealand)
JAMA Psychiatry 71, 1025-1031, 2014

Importance: There has been growing research into the mental health consequences of major disasters. Few studies have controlled for prospectively assessed mental health. This article describes a natural experiment in which 57% of a well-studied birth cohort was exposed to a major natural disaster (the Canterbury, New Zealand, earthquakes in 2010-2011), with the remainder living outside of the earthquake area.

Objective: To examine the relationships between the extent of earthquake exposure and mental health outcomes following the earthquakes-net of adjustment for potentially confounding factors related to personal circumstances, prior mental health, and childhood family background.

Design, Setting, and Participants: Data were gathered from the Christchurch Health and Development Study, a 35-year longitudinal study of a birth cohort of New Zealand children (635 males and 630 females). This general community sample included 952 participants with available data on earthquake exposure and mental health outcomes at age 35 years.

Exposures: A composite measure of exposure to the events during and subsequent to the 4 major (Richter Scale > 6.0) Canterbury earthquakes during the years 2010-2011.

Main Outcomes and Measures: DSM-IV symptom criteria for major depression; posttraumatic stress disorder; anxiety disorder; suicidal ideation/attempt; nicotine dependence; alcohol abuse/dependence; and illicit drug abuse/dependence. Outcomes were measured approximately 20 to 24 months after the onset of exposure to the earthquakes and were assessed using DSM-IV diagnostic criteria and measures of subclinical symptoms.

Results: After covariate adjustment, cohort members with high levels of exposure to the earthquakes had rates of mental disorder that were 1.4 (95% CI, 1.1-1.7) times higher than those of cohort members not exposed. This increase was due to increases in the rates of major depression; posttraumatic stress disorder; other anxiety disorders; and nicotine dependence. Similar results were found using a measure of subclinical symptoms (incidence rate ratio, 1.4; 95% CI, 1.1-1.6). Estimates of attributable fraction suggested that exposure to the Canterbury earthquakes accounted for 10.8% to 13.3% of the overall rate of mental disorder in the cohort at age 35 years.

Conclusions and Relevance: Following extensive control for prospectively measured confounding factors, exposure to the Canterbury earthquakes was associated with a small to moderate increase in the risk for common mental health problems.

Comment

Main findings: The sequence of more than 10,000 recorded earthquakes that struck the Canterbury province, New Zealand, between September 2010 and mid-2012 included four major earthquakes with Richter scale values exceeding 6.0. The devastating earthquake on 22 February 2011 caused 185 deaths and substantial damage to the city. Amongst members of a surviving longitudinal birth cohort, 543 (57%) had reported varied levels of exposure to the earthquakes. Cohort members with high level of exposure to earthquake impact and consequences had rates of mental disorder 1.4 times higher than those not exposed, with significant increases in mental disorders including major depression and posttraumatic stress disorder. The study did not report significant increases in suicide attempt or ideation amongst those exposed. Of four levels of exposure representing quartiles of consequences, higher percentages of suicide attempt and ideation were found among those with lowest level of exposure (n=137; 3.7%) and highest level of exposure (n=135; 3.0%), compared to those with no exposure (n=409; 1.5%), the second quartile of exposure (n=135; 1.5%) and third quartile (n=136; 2.2%). The study, while well-controlled for confounding factors, was limited to a population aged in the mid-30s. Other studies have found that suicide rates in middle-aged males were more impacted by earthquakes than in other age groups; this may be related to economic conditions found to correlate with suicide of middle-aged men[1]. The findings demonstrate the importance of targeting services to those who experience the greatest impact of natural disaster. The strong community-based response to support those impacted by the earthquakes may have been a protective factor for those experiencing high levels of adversity.

Implications: Australia experiences a range of natural disasters, including cyclone, fire, flood and drought, estimated to cost an average of $1.14 billion annually. As population and living density continue to grow, the potential impact of a natural disaster increases[2]. A growing body of empirical literature on psychological problems brought on by natural disasters has found that disaster victims can be more vulnerable due to factors such as cultural, social and economic background, psychopathology, threat to life, extent of loss, coping skills, and availability of social support[1]. Among survivors of large-scale disasters, suicide can be attributed to serious disruption of daily life due to bereavement, property loss and destruction of interpersonal and social networks[3]. However, there has been a lack of research specifically analysing suicidal consequence of natural disasters. Previous and current mental health problems have been linked to mortality and non-suicidal behaviours following natural disasters, as well as a drop in non-fatal suicidal behaviours in the initial post-disaster period, with some studies reporting delayed increases in suicidal behaviours[1]. Given the increase in mental health disorders of those with high exposure to the Canterbury earthquakes, future cohort assessments reviewing longer-term suicide ideation and behaviour may be of interest. A 2013 systematic literature review of suicide mortality and non-suicidal behaviours across a range of international natural disasters reported contradictory findings, which may be partly explained by different methodological limitations and limited validity of comparison between studies, including differences in registration and reporting of mortality data by countries, relocation of vulnerable people, and use of single-item scales. This highlights the need for consistency in further studies with sound designs to create models which include vulnerability factors[1]. Given the ongoing impact of natural disasters on Australian communities, it is important that disaster preparedness plans include mobilisation of mental health professionals to meet population needs[3]. There is clearly a need to monitor mental health and suicidal behaviours for several years after the disaster, not only for those directly affected, but indirectly affected by economic circumstances, such as those who lose their jobs[1].

Endnotes

1. Kõlves K, Kõlves KE, De Leo D (2013). Natural disasters and suicidal behaviours: A systematic literature review. *Journal of Affective Disorders*. Published online: 20 March 2013. doi: 10.1016/j.jad.2012.07.037
2. Middelman M (2008). Understanding natural hazard impacts on Australia. In Australian Bureau of Statistics, *Year Book Australia, 2008*. Cat. no. 1301.0. Canberra: ABS.
3. Yang C-H, Xirasagar S, Chung H-C, Huang Y-T, Lin H-C (2005). Suicide trends following the Taiwan earthquake of 1999: Empirical evidence and policy implications. *Acta Psychiatrica Scandinavica* 112, 442-448.

A systematic review of evaluated suicide prevention programs targeting indigenous youth

Harlow AF, Bohanna I, Clough A (Australia)

Crisis 35, 310-321, 2014

Background: Indigenous young people have significantly higher suicide rates than their non-indigenous counterparts. There is a need for culturally appropriate and effective suicide prevention programs for this demographic.

Aims: This review assesses suicide prevention programs that have been evaluated for indigenous youth in Australia, Canada, New Zealand, and the United States.

Method: The databases MEDLINE and PsycINFO were searched for publications on suicide prevention programs targeting indigenous youth that include reports on evaluations and outcomes. Program content, indigenous involvement, evaluation design, program implementation, and outcomes were assessed for each article.

Results: The search yielded 229 articles; 90 abstracts were assessed, and 11 articles describing nine programs were reviewed. Two Australian programs and seven American programs were included. Programs were culturally tailored, flexible, and incorporated multiple-levels of prevention. No randomised controlled trials were found, and many programs employed ad hoc evaluations, poor program description, and no process evaluation.

Conclusion: Despite culturally appropriate content, the results of the review indicate that more controlled study designs using planned evaluations and valid outcome measures are needed in research on indigenous youth suicide prevention. Such changes may positively influence the future of research on indigenous youth suicide prevention as the outcomes and efficacy will be more reliable.

Comment

Main findings: Australia shares a colonial history in common with the USA, Canada and New Zealand, along with significantly higher suicide rates among Indigenous peoples, particularly young people. However, information about evaluation of existing suicide prevention or reduction programs is scarce. Of the nine peer-reviewed published program evaluations identified by this systematic review, two Australian evaluations were included which related to a suicide prevention pamphlet[1] and community gatekeeper training[2]. Although all studies reviewed reported favourable outcomes, most of the evaluation designs were not rigorous enough to yield reliable evidence of intervention effect. Most of the evaluations were non-randomised, non-controlled designs using outcome measures such as non-validated surveys, questionnaires, assessments and interviews. Conducting randomised control trials in suicide prevention may be challenging due to ethical considerations of withholding treatment to the control group; however, it is important that controlled designs are used to be confident that positive effects observed are due to the intervention. Most of the programs involved could have benefited from process evaluations to determine how effectiveness was achieved and whether the program would be successful in other settings and contexts. Programs were generally time and labour-intensive, and faced difficulties such as low participation and consent rates, and attrition. However, the interventions used creative and suitable approaches to develop culturally appropriate content.

Implications: Effective programs targeting young Aboriginal and Torres Strait Islanders are urgently needed. In Australia between 2001 and 2010, the suicide rate for young Aboriginal and Torres Strait Islander females aged 15-19 was 5.9 times higher than those for non-Indigenous females, and the rate for young Aboriginal and Torres Strait Islander males was 4.4 times higher than for their non-Indigenous counterparts. The highest age-specific rate of suicide in the Aboriginal and Torres Strait Islander population was by males between 25 and 29 years of age (90.8 deaths per 1000,000 population); for females it was amongst 20-24 year olds (21.8 deaths per 100,000 population)[3]. The paucity of rigorous evaluation of suicide prevention programs for Aboriginal and Torres Strait Islanders is not limited to those targeting young people[4], and applies to health research in general[5]. Several of the US program evaluations reviewed in this paper may involve some useful aspects which could be applied in Australian settings, particularly the use of mixed-methods designs including quantitative and qualitative designs which collected more convincing evidence for the effectiveness of their prevention strategies. Time and labour intensity may be reduced by use of age appropriate frameworks which can be transferred to other locations or contexts by tailoring with culturally specific and locally appropriate activities and information. Effective partnerships between Aboriginal and Torres Strait communities and research agencies may assist to design robust evaluations which can provide much needed evidence of effectiveness, so that findings can be applied in design of prevention strategies in other communities[6]. Overcoming any mistrust of empirical research among Aboriginal and Torres Strait Islander communities and researchers is vital to achieve this goal, while allowing communities to have control in choice of implementation activities[5].

Endnotes

1. Bridge S, Hanssens L, & Santhanam R (2007). Dealing with suicidal thoughts in schools: Information and education directed at secondary schools. *The Royal Australian and New Zealand College of Psychiatrists* 15, 58-62.

2. Capp K, Dean FP, & Lambert G (2001). Suicide prevention in Aboriginal communities: Application of community gatekeeper training. *Australian and New Zealand Journal of Public Health* 25, 315-321.

3. Australian Bureau of Statistics (2012). Aboriginal and Torres Strait Islander suicide deaths. In Australian Bureau of Statistics. *Suicide, Australia, 2001-2010*. Cat. no. 3303.0. http://www.abs.gov.au/ausstats/abs@.nsf/Products/3309.0~2010~Chapter~Aboriginal+and+Torres+Strait+Islander+suicide+deaths?OpenDocument

4. Clifford AC, Doran CM, & Tsey K (2013). A systematic review of suicide prevention interventions targeting indigenous peoples in Australia, United States, Canada and New Zealand. *BMC Public Health*. Published online: 13 May 2013. doi: 10.1186/1471-2458-13-463.

5. Walter, M (2005). Using the 'power of the data' within Indigenous research practice. *Australian Aboriginal Studies* 2, 27-34.

6. LaFramboise, T (2008). The Zuni life skills development program: A school/community-based suicide prevention intervention. *Suicide and Life-Threatening Behavior* 38, 343-353.

Determinants of suicidal ideation and suicide attempts: Parallel cross-sectional analyses examining geographical location

Inder KJ, Handley TE, Johnston A, Weaver N, Coleman C, Lewin TJ, Slade T, Kelly BJ (Australia)
BMC Psychiatry. Published online: 23 July 2014. doi: 10.1186/1471-244X-14-208, 2014

Background: Suicide death rates in Australia are higher in rural than urban communities however the contrib utors to this difference remain unclear. Geographical differences in suicidal ideation and attempts were explored using two datasets encompassing urban and rural community residents to examine associations between socioeconomic, demographic and mental health factors. Differing patterns of association between psychiatric disorder and suicidal ideation and attempts as geographical remoteness increased were investigated.

Methods: Parallel cross-sectional analyses were undertaken using data from the 2007 National Survey of Mental Health and Wellbeing (2007-NSMHWB, n = 8,463), under-representative of remote and very remote residents, and selected participants from the Australian Rural Mental Health Study (ARMHS, n = 634), over-representative of remote and very remote residents. Uniform measures of suicidal ideation and attempts and mental disorder using the World Mental Health Composite International Diagnostic Interview (WMH-CIDI-3.0) were used in both datasets. Geographic region was classified into major cities, inner regional and other. A series of logistic regressions were undertaken for the outcomes of 12-month and lifetime suicidal ideation and lifetime suicide attempts, adjusting for age, gender and psychological distress. A sub-analysis of the ARMHS sample was undertaken with additional variables not available in the 2007-NSMHWB dataset.

Results: Rates and determinants of suicidal ideation and suicide attempts across geographical region were similar. Psychiatric disorder was the main determinant of 12-month and lifetime suicidal ideation and lifetime suicide attempts across all geographical regions. For lifetime suicidal ideation and attempts, marital status, employment status, perceived financial adversity and mental health service use were also important determinants. In the ARMHS sub-analysis, higher optimism and better perceived infrastructure and service accessibility tended to be associated with a lower likelihood of lifetime suicidal ideation, when age, gender, psychological distress, marital status and mental health service use were taken into account.

Conclusions: Rates and determinants of suicidal ideation and attempts did not differ according to geographical location. Psychiatric disorder, current distress, employment and financial adversity remain important factors associated with suicidal ideation and attempts across all regions in Australia. Regional characteristics that influence availability of services and lower personal optimism may also be associated with suicidal ideation in rural communities.

Comment

Main findings: Suicide death rates in Australia have been consistently higher in rural areas than urban areas, particularly amongst men; however, depression (the strongest predictor of suicidal ideation) has been found to have a similar prevalence in urban and rural areas[1]. Past research into suicidal behaviour and geographical location has been limited by representing location as a dichotomous concept, made up of 'urban' and 'rural' areas[2]; this study used a broader classification of locality to ensure better representation of remote and very remote residents. Findings did not support the hypothesis that 12-month and lifetime rates of suicidal ideation and lifetime suicide attempt would be higher in more remote residents; no difference was found in the rates or key determinants of suicidal ideation or attempts across geographical location. Understanding rural-urban disparities may require analysis which goes beyond analysis of disorder rates, and explores distribution of personal, social and community level factors which may have a bearing on trajectory and impact of mental illness, and its social and personal impact. Further investigation is required to understand the possibility that psychological distress, suicidal ideation and mental disorder are similar across geographical location, but suicide death is not.

Implications: The outcomes of this study illustrate the complexity involved in differences impacting on suicidal behaviour in urban, rural and remote areas. Past research has indicated that while geographical location alone may not be a risk factor, life events more likely to occur in rural environments may increase vulnerability to suicide. It appears that there are interconnected risk and protective factors which can potentially impact upon individual people and communities in rural and remote Australia, which may not be unique to non-urban areas, but when combined may greatly increase vulnerability within certain groups of non-urban residents such as Aboriginal and Torres Strait Islanders and farmers[3]. District level socio-economic status, and other population-specific factors may affect long-term health outcomes but not be well represented in geographical categorisation. These include isolation, indigeneity, increased numbers of people working in high health-risk occupations such as primary industries, decreased access to health services, increased vulnerability to adverse environmental impacts such as drought, vulnerability to population shifts, and other adverse social and economic events. While various suicide prevention strategies have been implemented in rural Australia, there are some gaps in the current non-urban suicide prevention framework which should be addressed by evidence-based research[3].

Endnotes

1. Slade T, Johnston A, Teesson M, Whiteford H, Burgess P, Pirkis J, Saw S (2009). *The mental health of Australians 2. Report on the 2007 National Survey of Health and Wellbeing.* Canberra; Department of Health and Ageing.
2. Smith KB, Humphreys JS, Wilson MGA (2008). Addressing the health disadvantage of rural populations: How does epidemiological evidence inform rural health policies and research? *Australian Journal of Rural Health* 16, 56-66.
3. Kõlves K, Milner A, McKay K, De Leo D (2012). *Suicide in rural and remote areas of Australia.* Brisbane: Australian Institute for Suicide Research and Prevention.

Are immigrants responsible for the recent decline in Australian suicide rates?

Kõlves K, De Leo D (Australia)

Epidemiology and Psychiatric Sciences. Published online: 2 May 2014. doi: 10.1017/S2045796014000122, 2014

Aims: This study aims to examine Queensland suicide trends in the Australian-born population and in the overseas born populations over the past 2 decades.

Methods: All suicide cases for the period 1991–2009 were identified in the Queensland Suicide Register. Age-standardised suicide rates were calculated. Join-point regression and Poisson regression were applied.

Results: A significant decline in suicide rates of young (15–44 years) overseas-born males was reported over the past 2 decades. Australian-born young males showed significant increase until 1996, followed by a significant decline; furthermore, their suicide rates were significantly higher when compared to overseas-born (RR = 1.36, 95%CI: 1.15; 1.62). Contrary older Australian-born males (45+ years) had significantly lower suicide rates than overseas-born males (RR = 0.90, 95%CI: 0.83; 0.98). Despite the convergence of the suicide trends for older males, changes were not significant. While Australian-born females had a significant increase in suicides, overseas-born females had a decline in 1991–2009.

Conclusion: Significantly declining suicide rates of migrants have contributed to the declining in suicide trends in Queensland. Potential reasons for significantly lower suicide rates among young migrants might include the change in the nature of migration from involuntary to voluntary.

Comment

Main findings: Australia's population includes an increasingly high proportion of people born overseas. According to Australian Census figures, this proportion increased from 22% in 1991 to 27% in 2011. In Queensland, the overseas born population aged 15 years and over has almost doubled from 435,000 in 1991[1] to 816,000 in 2001. Australia has particularly experienced a marked increase in overseas-born populations from Asian and African countries[2] Given the potential social, cultural[3] and genetic[4] influences originating from country of birth, this study sought to examine whether increasing numbers of overseas born migrants had influenced changes in suicide trends over the last two decades. The study focused on Queensland, where the Queensland Suicide Register (QSR) provides high-quality suicide data. In total, 10,058 suicides were recorded in the QSR for the study period of 1991 to 2009. Suicide rates for the study were calculated using the population aged 15 years and over, excluding those whose country of birth could not be identified (3.03%).

Results for the study period showed that overall Queensland suicide rates for those aged 15 years and over significantly increased until 1996, followed by a significant decline. The figures were particularly influenced by suicide rates for younger males (those aged 15 to 44 years). Suicide rates of young Australian-born males increased significantly until 1996, followed by a significant decline. However, young overseas-born men had significantly lower rates than young Australian-born males (average rates of 27.92 and 36.17 per 100,000 respectively), with a significant decrease in suicide rates for the overseas-born group during the whole period. Older males (45 years and over) had significantly lower rates overall than the younger group. Unlike younger males, Australian-born males aged 45 and over had lower suicide rates than the overseas-born group (average rates of 27.65 and 29.97 per 100,000 respectively). Suicide rates for overseas-born females decreased during the study period, while rates for Australian-born females rose significantly. In addition, significantly higher rates were observed in Australian-born females aged between 15 and 44 years compared to those born overseas (average rates of 8.71 and 7.39 per 100,000 respectively). The study was limited by the relatively short time period and inability to distinguish between specific countries of birth.

Implications: Current analysis in Queensland showed a significant increase in suicide rates until 1996, followed by a significant decline for all people aged over 15 years. This could be explained by the contribution of declining suicide rates of overseas-born populations in Queensland since 1991. The change in composition of first-generation migrants could also be an important factor in the decrease in suicide rates of young overseas-born migrants; Asian, Middle-Eastern and African-born people show significantly lower suicide rates than those born in Australia[5]. The same effect may have been exerted on a national level, considering a reported 17% decrease in suicide rates in Australia over the past decade[6]. The concurrent change in the nature of migration from involuntary to voluntary may be a potential reason for lower suicide rates among young migrants[7], although this concept requires further study. Despite the reported decreases in overseas-born suicide rates, it is important to note that immigrant populations are highly diverse. Suicide rates vary by country of birth, gender, age and reason for immigration; for example, high rates have been found for men from various European countries and New Zealand[3]. Further investigation is needed to identify those minority groups at risk in order to introduce evidence-based prevention strategies.

Endnotes

1. Australian Bureau of Statistics (1993). *Census characteristics of Australia, 1991 census of population and housing*. Canberra: ABS.

2. Australian Bureau of Statistics (2012). *Reflecting a nation: Stories from the 2011 census, 2012-2013*. Canberra: ABS.

3. Ide N, Kõlves K, Cassaniti M, De Leo D (2012). Suicide of first-generation immigrants in Australia, 1974–2006. *Social Psychiatry and Psychiatric Epidemiology* 47, 1917–1927.

4. Voracek M, Loibl LM (2008). Consistency of immigrant and country-of-birth suicide rates: A meta-analysis. *Acta Psychiatrica Scandinavica* 118, 259–271.

5. Burvill PW (1998). Migrant suicide rates in Australia and in country of birth. *Psychological Medicine* 28, 201–208.

6. Australian Bureau of Statistics (2006). *2006 Census non-response rates fact sheets.* Canberra: ABS.

7. Kwan YK, Ip WC (2007). Suicidality and migration among adolescents in Hong Kong. *Death Studies* 31, 45–66.

Suicide rates in children aged 10-14 years worldwide: Changes in the past two decades.

Kõlves K, De Leo D (Australia)

British Journal of Psychiatry 205, 283-285, 2014

Background: Limited research is focused on suicides in children aged below 15 years.

Aims: To analyse worldwide suicide rates in children aged 10-14 years in two decades: 1990-1999 and 2000-2009.

Method: Suicide data for 81 countries or territories were retrieved from the World Health Organization Mortality Database, and population data from the World Bank data-set.

Results: In the past two decades the suicide rate per 100 000 in boys aged 10-14 years in 81 countries has shown a minor decline (from 1.61 to 1.52) whereas in girls it has shown a slight increase (from 0.85 to 0.94). Although the average rate has not changed significantly, rates have decreased in Europe and increased in South America. The suicide rates remain critical for boys in some former USSR republics.

Conclusions: The changes may be related to economic recession and its impact on children from diverse cultural backgrounds, but may also be due to improvements in mortality registration in South America.

Comment

Main findings: Although relatively rare compared with other age groups, child suicide is a leading cause of death in children under 15 years worldwide[1]. Although research has found that by the age of 10 years, children understand the concept of death and suicide[2], only a few studies have focused specifically on time trends of suicide in children. This paper analysed suicide rates in children aged 10-14 years in two decades, 1990-1999 and 2000-2009, using absolute numbers of suicides in 81 countries or territories sourced from the WHO Mortality Database; as population data were not given for several countries, the population numbers for the same age group were obtained from the World Bank data-set. In these two decades, the average suicide rate of children showed a small decline for boys (from 1.61 to 1.52 per 100,000) and a slight increase for girls (from 0.85 to 0.94 per 100,000).

Australian rates were lower than the world averages, and showed slight insignificant declines for boys (from 0.90 to 0.82 per 100,000) and girls (0.48 to 0.46) in these two decades. However, rates for some countries changed significantly. The international problem seems to be shifting from Eastern Europe to South America, where child suicide rates show a significant increase for both genders, from 1.04 to 2.32 for boys and from 1.45 to 2.30 for girls. The highest recorded suicide rates for girls between 2000 and 2009 were in Guyana (6.46), Suriname (6.11) and Ecuador (3.14), with the second highest rate for boys in Suriname

(6.36). Increased rates were also demonstrated for a number of central Asian countries, former republics of the Soviet Union. Furthermore, former republics of the Soviet Union were still recording the highest world rates for boys with 8.53 suicides per 100,000 in Kazakhstan. The Russian Federation recorded the third highest rate for boys (5.47). It is worth noting that the average suicide rate for boys in the whole of Europe declined significantly (from 2.02 in the 1990s to 1.48 in the subsequent decade); no European country reported a significant decline for girls.

Possible explanations for increased child suicides in some regions may include impacts of economic recession, and other societal changes impacting on cultures and their values and attitudes. For example, significantly higher rates have been presented in native ethnic and migrant groups. In addition, changes and improvements in mortality registration in South American countries may have contributed to higher rates; several countries changed their death recoding classifications from ICD-9 to ICD-10 in late 1990s or early 2000s. However, this potentially does not completely account for ongoing increases[3]. Child suicide is a sensitive topic and numbers are likely to be underestimated; research suggests that suicide may be more underreported among children than other age groups, possibly due to social stigma and shame, misconceptions about child ability to engage in suicidal acts, or coroner reluctance to determine a verdict of child suicide.

Implications: This international study is the first worldwide systematic analysis of child suicide rates over time. In Australia, child suicide deaths were historically included in reporting of total suicide numbers, but were not reported as a separate age group by the Australian Bureau of Statistics until 2013[4]. While the number of suicide deaths of Australian children and young people under the age of 15 years may be less than other age groups, it is significant in terms of the proportion of all deaths within this age group[4]. In Queensland between 2004 and 2012, suicide was the second leading cause of death for young people under 15 years, after transport-related fatalities[5]. It is important to note that in Australia, Aboriginal and Torres Strait Islander children have been shown to be at higher risk of suicide. A recent analysis in Queensland, using data from the Queensland Suicide Register, reported 10.15 suicides per 100,000 for Aboriginal and Torres Strait Islander children aged 10-14 years between 2000 and 2010. This was 12.63 times higher than the suicide rate for other Australian children (0.80 per 100,000) in Queensland[6]. This paper highlights the need for more attention to the child-specific prevention activities and interventions suitable for children in the 10 to 14 year age group worldwide. However, it is important to consider the impact of economic recession and other societal factors on child suicides.

Endnotes

1. Apter A, Bursztein C, Bertolote JM, Fleischmann A, Wasserman D (2009). Suicide on all continents in the young. In D Wasserman & C Wasserman (Eds.), *Oxford textbook of suicidology and suicide prevention.* New York: Oxford University Press, 621-628.
2. Mishara BL (1999). Conceptions of death and suicide in children ages 6-12 and their implications for suicide prevention. *Suicide and Life-Threatening Behavior* 29, 105-108.

3. Ferrada-Noli M, Alvarado R, Florenzano F. (2009). Suicide prevention in Chile. In D Wasserman & C Wasserman (Eds.), *Oxford textbook of suicidology and suicide prevention.* New York: Oxford University Press, 843-844.

4. Australian Bureau of Statistics (2013). *Causes of death, Australia, 2011. Appendix 1:*

5. *Suicide deaths of children and young people under the age of 15.* Cat. no. 3303.0. Canberra: ABS:

6. Soole R, Kõlves K, De Leo D (2014). Factors related to childhood suicides: Analysis of the Queensland Child Death Register. *Crisis* 35, 292-300.

7. Soole R, Kõlves K, De Leo D (2014). Suicides in Aboriginal and Torres Strait Islander children: Analysis of Queensland Suicide Register. *Australian and New Zealand Journal of Public Health.* Published online: 14 October 2014. doi: 10.1111/1753-6405.12259.

Suicide mortality in second-generation migrants, Australia, 2001-2008.

Law CK, Kõlves K, De Leo D (Australia)
Social Psychiatry and Psychiatric Epidemiology 49, 601-608, 2014

Generally, due to limited availability of official statistics on the topic, little is known about suicide mortality in second-generation migrants. A recent study from Sweden showed that these people could be at a high suicide risk. In a generalised phenomenon, this aspect would represent an important issue in suicide prevention. This paper aims to report the profile of second-generation migrants who died by suicide and the suicide risk differentials of second-generation migrants with other Australians. Official suicide data from 2001 to 2008 were linked with State/Territory registries to collect information about the birthplace of the deceased's parents to differentiate migration status (first, second or third-plus generation). The profile and suicide risk of second-generation migrants were compared with other generations by logistic and Poisson regression. Suicide in second-generation migrants accounted for 811 cases (14.6 %). These tended to be represented by younger subjects, more often never married, as compared to the other cases. Second-generation males aged 25-39 years tended to have a higher suicide risk than first-generation migrants, but the risk was lower when compared with the third-plus generation. Second-generation migrants aged 60+ tended to have a lower suicide risk than first-generation migrants. In Australia, second-generation migrants are not at a higher suicide risk as compared to first-generation migrants or locals (third-plus-generation). In males aged 25-39, a lower suicide risk was found in second-generations as compared to Australian-born third generation, which may be explained by their more advantageous socioeconomic status and the flexibility and resources rendered by having grown up in a bicultural environment. The higher suicide rates found amongst older first-generation migrants require further examination.

Comment

Main Findings: There has been little research into suicide mortality among second-generation migrants. Approximately 20% of Australian residents have at least one overseas-born parent[1]. In the current study, second-generation migrants are defined as Australian-born people living in Australia (15+ years of age), with at least one overseas-born parent. Socioeconomic and demographic characteristics of second-generation migrants from ACT and NSW who had died by suicide between 2001 and 2008 were investigated. Suicide risk among different migrant generations was also examined for comparison with previous literature[2]. Of 5,541 cases of suicide in the two specified jurisdictions, 14.6% of these were second-generation migrants. Within this population, 40.7% had both parents born overseas, 24.3% had their mother born overseas, and 35% had their father born overseas. Compared to first-generation migrants (i.e., individuals born overseas), suicides by second-generation migrants were more likely to be younger than 40 years of age, never married, and unemployed. The overall risk of suicide was not significantly different however. A significantly higher rate of suicide was only found for second-generation migrant males 25-39 years of age. When compared with third-plus-generation migrants (i.e., Australian-born people whose parents were also born in Australia), suicides by second-generation migrants were more likely to be younger than 40 years of age and never married. Again, the overall risk of suicide was not significantly different. However, a significantly lower risk was only found for second-generation migrant males 25-39 years of age.

Implications: This study provides the first analysis of suicides in second-generation migrants in Australia. The unique migrant history of Australia makes it difficult for comparisons with other countries. Second-generation migrants in Australia generally have higher education levels, higher income, and are less likely to be unemployed compared with third-generation migrants. The exposure to a bicultural environment during development may provide a greater skill set and varying attitudes, promoting greater flexibility and resilience. However, there is a need for further investigation into the suicide mortality of second-generation migrants. Particular focus should be placed on examining ethnicity and cultural background in cases of suicide among second-generation migrants to advise suicide prevention activities in culturally and linguistically diverse communities. There is support to show that first-generation migrant suicides, particularly males, are influenced by their cultures, traditions, ethnicity, and possibly genetic predispositions[3]. Acculturation appears to be an important process for individuals from various migrant generations.

Endnotes

1. Australian Bureau of Statistics (2012). *Reflecting a nation: Stories from the 2011 census, 2012-2013: Cultural diversity in Australia.* Cat. no. 2071.0. Canberra: ABS.
2. Hjern A, Allebeck P (2002). Suicide in first- and second-generation immigrants in Sweden: A comparative study. *Social Psychiatry and Psychiatric Epidemiology* 37, 423-429.
3. Ide N, Kõlves K, Cassaniti M (2012). Suicide of first-generation immigrants in Australia, 1974-2006. *Social Psychiatry and Psychiatric Epidemiology* 47, 1917-1927.

The influence of deprivation on suicide mortality in urban and rural Queensland: An ecological analysis

Law CK, Snider AM, De Leo D (Australia)

Social Psychiatry and Psychiatric Epidemiology 49, 1919-1928, 2014

Purpose: A trend of higher suicide rates in rural and remote areas as well as areas with low socioeconomic status has been shown in previous research. Little is known whether the influence of social deprivation on suicide differs between urban and rural areas. This investigation aims to examine how social deprivation influences suicide mortality and to identify which related factors of deprivation have a higher potential to reduce suicide risk in urban and rural Queensland, Australia.

Methods: Suicide data from 2004 to 2008 were obtained from the Queensland Suicide Register. Age-standardized suicide rates (15+ years) and rate ratios, with a 95 % confidence interval, for 38 Statistical Subdivisions (SSDs) in Queensland were calculated. The influence of deprivation-related variables on suicide and their rural–urban difference were modelled by log-linear regression analyses through backward elimination.

Results: Among the 38 SSDs in Queensland, eight had a higher suicide risk while eleven had a lower rate. Working-age males (15–59 years) had the most pronounced geographic variation in suicide rate. In urban areas, suicide rates were positively associated with tenant households in public housing, Aboriginal and Torres Strait Islander people, the unemployment rate and median individual income, but inversely correlated with younger age and households with no internet access. In rural areas, only tenant households in public housing and households with no internet access heightened the risk of suicide, while a negative association was found for younger and older persons, low-skilled workers or labourers, and families with low income and no cars.

Conclusions: The extent to which social deprivation contributes to suicide mortality varies considerably between rural and urban areas.

Comment

Main Findings: In Australia, numerous studies have demonstrated the presence of a notable geographical difference in age-standardised suicide mortality, in which suicide rates are generally higher in rural and remote areas, and areas with low socioeconomic status[1]. Less is known about whether the influence of deprivation on the risk of suicide would differ between urban and rural areas. Deprivation is defined in terms of a state of observable and demonstrable disadvantage relative to local community or the wider society or nation to which the individual, family or ground belongs[2]. This study aimed to fill this knowledge gap by analysing the extent to which deprivation-related factors predict suicide mortality by age and gender in urban and rural Queensland from an ecological perspective during the years 2004-2008. Suicide data was ascertained from the Queensland Suicide Register (QSR) and population data and contextual variables associated with deprivation and disadvantage were made available from the 2006 Census of Population and Housing. The state of Queensland was divided into 38 Statistical Subdivisions (SSD), as specified by the Australia Statistical Geography Classification. For the five-year period a total of 2,803 suicides aged 15 years and above were identified (78% males and 22% females; 55.8% were from urban locations and 42.5% from rural locations).

Deprivation had a prominent influence on age-standardised suicide mortality, particularly for males aged 15-59 years, in both urban and rural Queensland. Risk of suicide in urban Queensland was found to be significantly higher for those SSDs with more tenant households living in public housing, a higher share of Aboriginal and Torres Strait Islander peoples, a higher unemployment rate and higher median individual income. In contrast, those with a higher proportion of younger population aged below 30 years, and dwellings with no internet access tended to have a lower risk of suicide in urban Queensland. The analyses indicated that the influences of deprivation-related variables on the risk of suicide in rural Queensland were considerably different when compared to those in urban Queensland. Deprivation-related factors were more related to the suicide risk in urban Queensland while they seemed to produce insignificant or even inverse influences in rural Queensland. SSDs with higher proportion of dwellings with no internet access and tenant households living in public housing had a higher risk of suicide while the influence of Aboriginal and Torres Strait Islander people, unemployment and median individual income were found to be significant in rural Queensland. In addition, SSDs with more younger and older populations, low skilled workers or labourers, families with low income and no cars tended to have a lower risk of suicide in rural Queensland.

Implications: These findings strengthen the argument for targeting deprived communities through population-based efforts in suicide prevention, and also indicate the need for contextually-relevant suicide prevention strategies rather than a single and uniform intervention applied across all groups in the population. Given these findings, currently area-based indices of deprivation may be unlikely to assess the actual socioeconomic status in the context of rural Queensland. Factors that have been widely accepted as those that increase risk of suicide mortality in urban areas are not necessary to predict higher suicide rate in rural areas. As a result, to better assess the association of deprivation and suicide mortality in rural and remote areas of Australia, further attention is needed to develop a region-specific measure of socioeconomic status in future. Local authorities should respond to this broad aim by developing their own interventions and addressing their specific socioeconomic conditions.

Endnotes

1. Cheung YTD, Spittal MJ, Pirkis J, Yip PSF (2012). Spatial analysis of suicide mortality in Australia: Investigation of metropolitan-rural-remote differentials of suicide risk across states/territories. *Social Science & Medicine* 75, 1460-1468.
2. Townsend P (1978). Deprivation. *Journal of Social Policy* 16, 125-146.

Restricting access to a suicide hotspot does not shift the problem to another location. An experiment of two river bridges in Brisbane, Australia

Law C, Sveticic J, De Leo D (Australia)

Australian and New Zealand Journal of Public Health 38, 134-138, 2014

Background: Restricting access to lethal means is a well-established strategy for suicide prevention. However, the hypothesis of subsequent method substitution remains difficult to verify. In the case of jumping from high places ('hotspots'), most studies have been unable to control for a potential shift in suicide locations. This investigation aims to evaluate the short and long-term effect of safety barriers on Brisbane's Gateway Bridge and to examine whether there was substitution of suicide location.

Methods: Data on suicide by jumping – between 1990 and 2012, in Brisbane, Australia – were obtained from the Queensland Suicide Register. The effects of barrier installation at the Gateway Bridge were assessed through a natural experiment setting. Descriptive and Poisson regression analyses were used.

Results: Of the 277 suicides by jumping in Brisbane that were identified, almost half (n = 126) occurred from the Gateway or Story Bridges. After the installation of barriers on the Gateway Bridge, in 1993, the number of suicides from this site dropped 53.0% in the period 1994–1997 ($p = 0.041$) and a further reduction was found in subsequent years. Analyses confirmed that there was no evidence of displacement to a neighbouring suicide hotspot (Story Bridge) or other locations.

Conclusions: The safety barriers were effective in preventing suicide from the Gateway Bridge, and no evidence of substitution of location was found.

Comment

Main findings: Little is known about the long-term effects of installing bridge safety fences in a suicide hotspot and whether it influences epidemiological changes in other suicide locations over a long follow-up period. Brisbane is one of the few cities with two bridges (Gateway Bridge and the Story Bridge) that were identified as suicide hotspots during the 1990s[1]. Owing to the emerging number of suicides by jumping at the Gateway Bridge, safety fencing was installed in 1993[2]. As no physical barriers were installed on the Story Bridge, this provided the opportunity to examine the effectiveness of barriers in reducing risk of suicide while monitoring for a potential shifting of people attempting suicide at another suicide hotspot located close by. The three main aims of this study were: (1) to measure the immediate effectiveness of installing a safety fence to prevent suicides by jumping from the Gateway Bridge; (2) to examine whether there was a subsequent increase in suicides by jumping from the Story Bridge or other sites in Brisbane; and (3) to evaluate whether the effect of barriers at the Gateway Bridge on lowering the incidence of suicides by jumping was sustained over a longer period of time.

A total of 277 suicides by jumping from a high place were identified during the period of 1990 to 2012. Of those, 45.5% (146) occurred from bridges in Brisbane, most commonly from the Gateway Bridge (38) and the Story Bridge (88). There was a significant reduction in the number of jumping suicides at the Gateway Bridge since barrier installation. Incidence of suicide at the Gateway Bridge was only reduced by 53.0% during the first four year period following installation. However, the overall incidence of suicide reduced by 87.5% at this site across the 19 year period and this reduction did not appear to cause displacement to other locations of suicide by jumping in Brisbane during the same period. After the installation of higher barriers on the Gateway duplication bridge in 2010, individuals were completely dissuaded from considering suicide at that location (0 numbers of deaths at this location since 2010). A more detailed analysis compared all suicide by jumping rates in Brisbane over the 19 year time period following barrier installation with all suicide jumping rates in Brisbane prior to barrier installation. Results indicated there were significantly lower rates of all suicides by jumping in Brisbane between 1998 to 2001 and 2006 to 2009 when compared to the pre-installation level. However, changes in all jumping suicides were not found to be significantly different from pre-installation between 2002 to 2005 and 2010 to 2012 due to an elevated incidence at other jumping sites.

Implications: Results provided empirical support that barriers constructed at the Gateway Bridge were effective in preventing suicides by jumping with no immediate signs of displacement to another neighbouring suicide hotspot. Furthermore, the results indicated that analysing the immediate effect of barrier installation is not sufficient to reflect its true impact at a suicidal hotspot, and highlighted the importance of examining the long-term effects in future reporting. This phenomenon may suggest that some suicidal individuals would have a determined plan to die by suicide at that specific location and the presence of a barrier may not be able to prevent all of them from jumping at that location. In addition, although barrier installation at the Gateway Bridge has effectively reduced the suicide incidence at that site, with no evidence of a subsequent substitution effect, given the recent changing epidemiology of suicide, constant revision of suicide prevention strategies may be required. Despite the limitations of the study, it adds evidence that barriers are reducing suicide deaths at hotspots. In 2012, the Brisbane City Council established Story Bride Suicide Prevention Reference Group and construction work on instalment of the barriers at the Story Bridge has commenced.

Endnotes

1. Cantor CH, Hill MA. (1990). *Suicide from river bridges. Australasian Psychiatry 24*, 377-380.
2. Parkyn M, Kiemo K, Heller T, De Leo D. (2004) *Suicide from the Story Bridge: Characteristics and potential for prevention – A report to Brisbane City Council.* Brisbane: Australian Institute for Suicide Research and Prevention.

Googling self-injury: The state of health information obtained through online searches for self-injury

Lewis SP, Mahdy JC, Michal JN, Arbuthnott MA (Canada)
JAMA Paediatrics 168, 443-449, 2014

Importance: Nonsuicidal self-injury (NSSI), the deliberate destruction of one's body tissues without suicidal intent, is a significant issue for many youth. Research suggests that adolescents and emerging adults prefer the internet as a means to retrieve NSSI resources and that important others (e.g. Caregivers) may also seek this information on-line. To our knowledge no research to date has examined the quality of health information regarding NSSI on the internet.

Objectives: To examine the scope and nature of web searches for NSSI websites and to evaluate the quality of health-information websites found via these online searchers.

Design, Setting and Participants: Ninety-two NSSI-related search terms were identified using the Google AdWords Keywords program. The first page of Google search results for each term was content-analysed for website type and health-information websites were further coded for credibility. NSSI myth propagation, and quality of health information.

Main Outcomes and Measures: Frequency of NSSI web searches and indices of health information quality.

Results: Nonsuicidal self-injury-related search terms were sought more than 42 million times in the past year and health-information websites were the most common website type found (21.5%). Of these, a health and/or academic institution endorsed only 9.6%. At least one NSSI myth was propagated per website, including statements that NSSI indicates a mental disorder (493%), a history of abuse (40%), or the notion that primarily women self-injure (37%). The mean quality of health information score on the websites was 3.49 (SD = 1.40) of 7.

Conclusion and Relevance: Nonsuicidal self-injury-related search terms are frequently sought out worldwide and are likely to yield noncredible and low-quality information may propagate common NSSI myths. These data suggest health professionals need to be aware of what information is online and should refer young patients and their families to reliable online resources to enhance NSSI literacy. Efforts to facilitate people's access to credible NSSI resources vie the internet are also needed.

Comment

Main Findings: Adolescents and young adults prefer to gather information about self-harm in private via the internet. This preference may be especially true in Australia as the researchers indicated Australia was one of the highest contributors to NSSI-related Google searches. It is therefore important for researchers and health professionals to understand the type of information self-harmers are likely to find online. The present article helps to improve the understanding of the information most readily available to those using the internet to research NSSI.

The researchers used Google AdWord Keywords to determine 92 of the most common NSSI search terms. In the year prior to the review the chosen terms were Googled 42,000,000 times globally. The researchers put each term into Google and analysed the websites displayed on the first page of search results. The analysis consisted of 1) categorising the webpage, 2) rating the credibility of the information and 3) assessing whether the site perpetuated myths about NSSI.

Categorisation found that the largest portion (21.5%) of websites – excluding websites already found using previous search terms - were those designed to provide health information, while other commonly occurring websites were categorised as picture/video, interactive, blogs and news sites. When assessing quality it was noted that only a small number of the websites (9%) were endorsed by health or academic institutions; however, the authors noted non-endorsement was not synonymous with a lack of credibility. Using guidelines set by Health On the Net Foundation (an institute set up to promote reliability of online health information), NSSI health-information websites received a mean quality rating of 3.49 (SD = 1.40) of 7. Worryingly, 73.7% of these websites reinforced common myths about NSSI (M=1.18), predominantly that NSSI indicates borderline personality disorder, that NSSI results from child abuse, and that primarily women self-injure. A small number (8%) continued to maintain that self-harm is an attention seeking act.

Implications: NSSI health-information websites in general were not of high quality and most propagated self-harm misconceptions. Access to incorrect information about an already often misunderstood behaviour may prove counter-productive to patient improvement; the findings are especially worrisome as Australians are relying more and more on the internet as a source of information. Findings of this paper indicate that practitioners should be equipped with lists of quality websites that they can give to those affected by NSSI, and suggest that using search engine optimisation on credible websites would make them more accessible to users.

Interestingly, the CSIRO revealed Australian adults still prefer interpersonal contact regarding information on their health[1]. There may therefore be opportunity to encourage Australians to shift their NSSI information gathering from online to interpersonal contact with practitioners through de-stigmatisation and emphasising the behaviour as a health issue.

Endnotes

Dane SK, Mason CM, O'Brien-McInally BA (2013). *Household internet use in Australia: A study in regional communities. CSIRO Report EP1310907.* Melbourne: CSIRO.

Does resilience predict suicidality? A lifespan analysis

Liu DW, Fairweather-Schmidt AK, Roberts RM, Burns R, Anstey KJ (Australia)
Archives of Suicide Research 18, 453-464, 2014

Objective: We examined the association between resilience and suicidality across the lifespan.

Method: Participants (n=7485) from the Personality and Total Health (PATH) Through Life Project, a population sample from Canberra and Queanbeyan, Australia, were stratified into three age cohorts (20-24, 40-44, 60-64 years of age). Binary Logistic regression explored the association between resilience and suicidality.

Results: Across age cohorts, low resilience was associated with an increased risk for suicidality. However, this effect was subsequently made redundant in models that fully adjusted for other risk factors for suicidality amongst young and old adults.

Conclusions: Resilience is associated with suicidality across the lifespan, but only those in midlife continued to report increased likelihood of suicidality in fully-adjusted models.

Comment

Main findings: The concept of resilience to suicidality has attracted increasing research interest in recent years, but defining it as a construct has been problematic. Seen as comprising both environmental and genetic components, it has been operationalised in various ways. This study used the Connor-Davidson Resilience Scale, which defines resilience as ability to access internal and external sources of support while using individual qualities to enable successful development despite adversity[1]. Results demonstrated relationship of lower levels of resilience with increased suicidality across all age cohorts. Covariate constructs, such as social support, accounted for much of the effects of resilience, especially in the youngest and oldest age groups. However, the midlife group had greater vulnerability to suicidal ideation when resilience levels are low. With a large sample, and approximately equivalent gender numbers in each cohort, the study provides robust findings from an Australian sample; however, the cross-sectional design of the study prevents causal inference about the direction between suicidal ideation and resilience across life path.

Implications: This study adds to past research suggesting that strong levels of those attributes believed to comprise resilience can act as a buffer which moderates the association between risk and suicidality[2]. The finding, that those in midlife may be more vulnerable to suicidality when resilience levels are low, is in keeping with previous Australian research which has found this particularly true of men[3]. Between 2008 and 2012, men aged 35 to 44 years had the second highest suicide rate in Australia, at 26 per 100,000, followed by men aged 45 to 54 (24.4)[4]. Midlife may be a time when work, relationship and family crises are most pressing, personal accomplishments may be assessed and found wanting, and personal mortality may become more real[5]. Research seems to indicate that Australian men who are separated may be more vulnerable to experiencing shame in the context of separation, which may lead to development of suicidality[6]. Given that aspects of resilience may provide protection against vulnerability, further investigation of how this can be boosted, particularly during midlife, may assist to reduce suicide risk.

Endnotes

1. Connor KM, Davidson JRT (2003). Development of a new resilience scale: The Connor-Davidson Resilience Scale (CD-RISC). *Depression and Anxiety* 18, 76–82.

2. Johnson J, Wood, AM, Gooding P, Taylor PJ, Tarrier N (2011). Resilience to suicidality: The buffering hypothesis. *Clinical Psychology Review* 31, 563-591.

3. Johnston AK, Pirkis JE, Burgess PM (2009). Suicidal thoughts and behaviours among Australian adults: Findings from the 2007 National Survey of Mental Health and Wellbeing. *Australian and New Zealand Journal of Psychiatry* 43, 635-643.

4. Australian Bureau of Statistics (2014). *Causes of Death, Australia, 2012.* Cat. no. 3303.0. Canberra: ABS.

5. Chew KSY, McCleary R (1994). A life course theory of suicide risk. *Suicide and Life-Threatening Behavior* 24, 234-244.

6. Kõlves K, Ide N, De Leo D (2011). Marital breakdown, shame, and suicidality in men: A direct link? *Suicide and Life-Threatening Behavior* 41, 149-159.

Changes in antidepressant use by young people and suicidal behavior after FDA warnings and media coverage: Quasi-experimental study

Lu CY, Zhang F, Lakoma MD, Madden JM, Rusinak D, Penfold RB, Simon G, Ahmedani BK, Clarke G, Hunkeler EM, Waitzfelder B, Owen-Smith A, Raebel MA, Rossom R, Coleman KJ, Copeland LA, Soumerai SB (USA)

British Medical Journal 348, g3596, 2014

Objective: To investigate if the widely publicized warnings in 2003 from the US Food and Drug Administration about a possible increased risk of suicidality with antidepressant use in young people were associated with changes in antidepressant use, suicide attempts, and completed suicides among young people.

Design: Quasi-experimental study assessing changes in outcomes after the warnings, controlling for pre-existing trends.

Setting: Automated healthcare claims data (2000-10) derived from the virtual data warehouse of 11 health plans in the US Mental Health Research Network.

Participants: Study cohorts included adolescents (around 1.1 million), young adults (around 1.4 million), and adults (around 5 million).

Main Outcome Measures: Rates of antidepressant dispensings, psychotropic drug poisonings (a validated proxy for suicide attempts), and completed suicides.

Results: Trends in antidepressant use and poisonings changed abruptly after the warnings. In the second year after the warnings, relative changes in antidepressant use were -31.0% (95% confidence interval -33.0% to -29.0%) among adolescents, -24.3% (-25.4% to -23.2%) among young adults, and -14.5% (-16.0% to -12.9%) among adults. These reflected absolute reductions of 696, 1216, and 1621 dispensings per 100 000 people among adolescents, young adults, and adults, respectively. Simultaneously, there were significant, relative increases in psychotropic drug poisonings in adolescents (21.7%, 95% confidence interval 4.9% to 38.5%) and young adults (33.7%, 26.9% to 40.4%) but not among adults (5.2%, -6.5% to 16.9%). These reflected absolute increases of 2 and 4 poisonings per 100 000 people among adolescents and young adults, respectively (approximately 77 additional poisonings in our cohort of 2.5 million young people). Completed suicides did not change for any age group.

Conclusions: Safety warnings about antidepressants and widespread media coverage decreased antidepressant use, and there were simultaneous increases in suicide attempts among young people. It is essential to monitor and reduce possible unintended consequences of FDA warnings and media reporting.

Comment

Main Findings: In 2003, the USA Food and Drug Administration (FDA) issued several health warnings (i.e. boxed warnings) regarding the risk of taking antidepressants and its association with suicidal ideation[1]. There is conflicting evidence regarding the effects of antidepressants on suicide risk in young people which has generated a lot of controversy. For example, recent research to come out of the USA has indicated that children and adolescents taking antidepressants are at increased risk of suicidality[2]. However the relationship between antidepressant use and suicidal behavior is a complex one and studies using different methodologies have yielded contradictory results. Because depression is an independent risk factor for suicidality, and appropriate treatment with antidepressants is effective in reducing depressive symptoms, it was hypothesised that decreasing rates of overall antidepressant treatment after the warnings would be associated with a net increase in suicide attempts among young people.

Using an interrupted time series design, data was collected from a cohort of approximately 1.1 million adolescents (10-17 years), 1.4 million young adults (18-29 years), and five million adults (30-64 years) from 2000-2010. The results showed that after FDA warnings targeting the youth and subsequent wide spread media coverage on this issue; there were substantial reductions in antidepressant use amongst adolescents (31%) and young adults (24.3%). However, there was a simultaneous increase in psychotropic drug poisonings during the same time period for adolescents (21.7%) and young adults (33.7%). Adults had a smaller reduction in antidepressant use (14.5%) but no increase in psychotropic drug poisonings was found. There were no changes in completed suicides after the warnings.

Implications: This study was the first to provide evidence that non-fatal psychotropic self-poisonings increased rather than decreased after FDA warnings were provided and has vital policy implications. Since the increase in suicide attempts by poisoning was simultaneous with the significant reductions in antidepressant use, it might be one consequence of under-treatment of mood disorders. It is possible that warnings and extensive media attention led to unintended and unexpected population level reductions in treatment for depression and subsequent increased in suicide attempts of this nature among young people. FDA advisories and boxed warnings may have been a crude and inadequate way in which to communicate new and sometimes frightening empirical research findings to the public. Furthermore, information may be oversimplified and at times, distorted when communicated through the media.

Within the Australian context, it is highly important to understand the implications of portraying such research findings through media outlets to the general public. Communicating risk to the public and to health professionals should be taken into consideration. Active surveillance should also be considered to allow timely detection and prompt actions to reduce unintended consequences of strong warnings. This study was only able to measure psychotropic drug poisonings as an indication of suicide attempts, possibly underestimating the true impact of the warnings on suicidality. Further research on multiple attempted or completed suicide methods is warranted. In addition, a recent study has concluded only high-dosages of antidepressants are associated with increased risk amongst children and young adults and no such effect is evident in older populations. As a result, clinicians need to be aware of those at risk of suicidality after commencement of high antidepressant dosages and monitor them accordingly.

Endnotes

1. Website of U.S. Food and Drug Administration (2007). Retrieved from: http://www.fda.gov/Drugs/DrugSafety/InformationbyDrugClass/UCM096273

2. Hammad TA, Laughren T, Racoosin J (2006). Suicidality in pediatric patients treated with antidepressant drugs. *Archives of General Psychiatry* 63, 332-9.

3. Miller M, Swanson SA, Azrael D, Pate V, Stürmer T (2014). Antidepressant dose, age, and the risk of deliberate self-harm. *JAMA Internal Medicine* 48, 433-441.

How to adjust media recommendations on reporting suicidal behavior to new media developments

Maloney J, Pfuhlmann B, Arensman E, Coffey C, Gusmão R, Poštuvan V, Scheerder G, Sisak M, van der Feltz-Cornelis CM, Hegerl U, Schmidtke A (Germany, Ireland, Portugal, Slovenia, Belgium, Estonia, Netherlands)

Archives of Suicide Research 18, 156-169, 2014

This study examines the inclusion of preventive factors and new media developments in media recommendations on suicide reporting. Of the 193 member states of the United Nations screened for media recommendations, information was available for 74 countries. Similarities and differences in their contents were analyzed by cluster analysis. Results indicate that of these 74 countries, 38% have national suicide prevention programs, 38% have media recommendations, and 25% have press codes including suicide reporting. Less than 25% of the media recommendations advise against mentioning online forums, suicide notes, pacts, clusters, hotspots, details of the person, and positive consequences. No more than 15% refer to self-help groups, fictional and online reporting. We conclude that media recommendations need to be revised by adding these preventive factors and by including sections on new media reporting.

Comment

Main findings: Media portrayal of suicides carries the risk of suicide contagion, in which suicidal behaviour spreads quickly and spontaneously through a group of people. The World Health Organization and International Association for Suicide Prevention have recommended that media professionals work within guidelines developed or adopted by the suicide prevention communities in their own countries[1]. This study reviewed media recommendations regarding suicide amongst 74 United Nations (UN) member nations which had online information in English, Spanish or French regarding the existence, or non-existence, of national suicide prevention programs. Great inconsistency was found between nations, with only eight of the 74 countries reviewed (11%) having all three suicide prevention programs, press codes which include reference to suicide reporting, and media recommendations (prepared by various government and/or non-government organisations). The only preventative factor referred to in all media recommendations was advice not to describe suicide methods in detail. Only 25% of press codes identified included information about suicide reporting. Of the 34 media recommendations, 26% had not been updated since 2002, and only 15% included information about suicide portrayal on the internet. Use of new media (including internet, digital devices and other interactive user feedback) is an area of particular concern, as young people are high users of these media and are particularly susceptible to suicide imitation.

Implications: Australia currently possesses a National Suicide Prevention Strategy[2], media recommendations on suicide reporting released by Mindframe National Media Initiative[3], and updated standards on the coverage of suicide within the Australian Press Council's Standards of Practice[4]. Despite the resources available, there is sometimes confusion about whether or not media reporting of suicide is dangerous or not. While it important to encourage greater community discussion about seeking help for mental distress, reporting of actual suicidal behaviour must be considered carefully[5]. Research, including recent large-scale reviews of evidence by Australian researchers, has found an association between non-fictional (news) media portrayal of suicides and subsequent actual suicidal behaviours. While exposure to suicide related material on the internet is a growing research area, it appears that there is some support for a causal association with suicidal behaviour[6]. The negative effects of reporting, such as imitation, are attributed to glamourising and sensationalising suicide, detailed and repeated reports, prominent placement, and use of images and headlines[5].

However, media reporting can also have a positive effect if media guidelines are followed; responsible reporting following celebrity suicide has been linked to increased help-seeking[5], and reporting on people with suicidal ideation who have successfully sought help has been associated with a reduction of suicides[7]. As this international study has pointed out, many writers using 'new media' are young lay people rather than editors and journalists; determining how to best advise the virtual community may require further research. In Australia, Mindframe's resources include tips for social media users (e.g. bloggers, Tweeters, Facebookers) when communicating information about suicide, including preventative factors such as contact details for online support services and websites[3]. Compassion and respect for those bereaved by suicide should always be a vital consideration when considering media reporting.

Endnotes

1. World Health Organization & International Association for Suicide Prevention (2008). *Preventing Suicide: A Resource for Media Professionals*. Retrieved from http://www.who.int/mental_health/prevention/suicide/resource_media.pdf.

2. Webpage of Australian Government – Department of Health. Retrieved 4 November 2014 from http://www.health.gov.au/internet/main/publishing.nsf/Content/mental-nsps

3. Webpage of Mindframe National Media Initiative. Retrieved 4 November 2014 from http://www.mindframe-media.info/__data/assets/pdf_file/0014/5171/Tips-for-Social-Media-content.pdf.

4. Australian Press Council (2014). *Specific Standards on Coverage of Suicide*. Retrieved from http://www.presscouncil.org.au/uploads/52321/ufiles/SPECIFIC_STANDARDS_SUICIDE_-_July_2014.pdf.

5. Kõlves K (2012). *The facts about safe reporting of suicide*. Webpage of The Conversation. Retrieved 3 November 2014. http://theconversation.com/the-facts-about-safe-reporting-of-suicide-9501.

6. Pirkis J, Blood W. (2010). *Suicide and the news and information media: A critical review*. Retrieved from file:///C:/Users/S2969318/Downloads/Pirkis-and-Blood-2010,-Suicide-and-the-news-and-information-media.pdf.

7. Niederkrotenthaler T, Voracek M, Herberth A, Till B, Strauss M, Etzersdorfer E, Eisenwort B, Sonneck G (2010). Role of media reports in completed and prevented suicide: Werther v. Papageno effects. *British Journal of Psychiatry* 197, 234-243.

Psychotic experiences and psychological distress predict contemporaneous and future non-suicidal self-injury and suicide attempts in a sample of Australian school-based adolescents

Martin G, Thomas H, Andrews T, Hasking P, Scott JG (Australia)

Psychological Medicine 45, 429-437, 2014

Background: Recent cross-sectional studies have shown psychotic experiences (PEs) are associated with suicidal ideation and behaviours. We aimed to examine associations between psychotic experiences (including persistent PE), and contemporaneous and incident non-suicidal self-injury (NSSI) and suicide attempts.

Method: Participants were from an Australian longitudinal cohort of 1896 adolescents (12-17 years). NSSI and suicide attempts were measured using the Self-Harm Behaviour Questionnaire. Items from the Diagnostic Interview Schedule for Children were used to assess psychotic experiences, and the General Health Questionnaire-12 measured psychological distress.

Results: Adolescents both psychologically distressed and endorsing psychotic experiences had increased odds of contemporaneous and incident NSSI and attempted suicide. Psychotic experiences alone did not predict future risk. Persistent psychotic experiences were associated with increased risk of NSSI and suicide attempts.

Conclusions: Psychological distress with accompanying psychotic experiences and persistent psychotic experiences are important predictors of NSSI and suicide attempts. Screening these phenotypes in adolescents will assist in discerning those adolescents most at risk, providing opportunities for targeted suicide prevention strategies.

Comment

Main Findings: Psychotic experiences (PEs) in adolescents have been associated with an increased likelihood of poor mental health and suicidal ideation and deliberate self-harm, after controlling for the effect of psychological distress (PD)[1]. However, previous research has used cross-sectional study designs, preventing examination of the temporal relationship between PE, PD and suicidal ideation and behaviours. This longitudinal study hypothesised that PEs with, and without, PD would be associated with current and future NSSI and suicide attempts. Current NSSI and suicide attempts were measured by participants responding 'yes' at time 1 (baseline), and future NSSI and suicide attempts were measured by participants responding 'no' at time 1 but 'yes' at time 2 (one-year follow-up). The cohort consisted of 1,896 Australian adolescents aged between 12-17 years (71.6% female). To measure NSSI and suicide attempt, the Self-Harm Behaviour Questionnaire was administered. The General Health Questionnaire-12, a self-report measure, was used to examine PD and finally, the DiSC Personality Test was used to assess PEs such as delusions and hallucinations. The survey was presented to students at two separate time periods, baseline and at one-year follow-up.

At baseline, when compared with the reference group, participants who reported either PD or PEs were at an increased risk of current NSSI, and those who reported PD had increased odds of having attempted suicide. Participants with both PD and PE had the strongest association with NSSI and suicide attempts with more than one-quarter (27%) engaging in NSSI and 7% reporting having attempted suicide. When compared with the reference group, participants with PD but without PE had a three times higher risk of reporting NSSI and attempted suicide at one year follow-up. However, contrary to what was hypothesised, those reporting PE in the absence of PD were not at increased risk of future NSSI or attempted suicide. To examine the association between PE persistence and NSSI and suicide attempts independent of PD, participants were categorised into four groups: 1) those who did not report PE at baseline or follow-up (reference group); 2) those who reported PE at baseline but not follow-up (PE remit group); 3) those who did not report PE at baseline but did at follow-up (PE onset group); and 4) those who reported PE at baseline and follow-up (PE persistent group). Results showed that participants in the onset group were at increased risk of attempting suicide at follow-up whilst those in the persistent group were at increased risk of both NSSI and attempting suicide at follow-up.

Implications: This study indicated that the combination of PEs with PD in young people is a strong predictor of current and future NSSI and suicidal behaviours, identifying a symptom profile for adolescents who are at very high risk of future suicide attempts. More specifically, the co-occurrence of PD and PE in this study was 6.5%, and as a result, adolescents presenting with general PD should be carefully assessed for possible PE, even where those psychotic symptoms are attenuated. In summary, these findings highlight the importance of mental health professions needing to be aware of this at-risk group and of screening distressed help-seeking adolescents for psychotic experiences to ensure appropriate support and risk management plans can be instigated in order to reduce the likelihood of the adolescent attempting suicide. This study emphasises the importance of enhancing decision-making and access to clinical care and of providing targeted suicide prevention strategies for adolescents at high risk of suicide. Specific interventions to improve coping in these individuals are warranted.

Endnotes

1. Kelleher I, Lynch F, Harley M, Molloy C, Roddy S, Fitzpatrick C, Cannon M (2012). Psychotic symptoms in adolescence index risk for suicidal behavior: Findings from 2 population-based case-control clinical interview studies. *Archives of General Psychiatry* 69, 1277–1283.

Marital status and suicidal ideation among Australian older adults: The mediating role of sense of belonging.

McLaren S, Gomez R, Gill P, Chesler J (Australia)

International Psychogeriatrics 27, 145-154, 2014

Background: Marriage has been identified as a protective factor in relation to suicide among older adults. The current study aimed to investigate whether sense of belonging mediated the marital status-suicidal ideation relationship, and whether gender moderated the mediation model. It was hypothesized that the relationship between being widowed and lower levels of sense of belonging, and between lower levels of belonging and higher levels of suicidal ideation, would be stronger for older men than older women.

Methods: A community sample of Australian men (n = 286) and women (n = 383) aged from 65 to 98 years completed the psychological subscale of the Sense of Belonging Instrument and the suicide subscale of the General Health Questionnaire.

Results: The results supported the moderated mediation model, with gender influencing the marital status-sense of belonging relation. For men, widowhood was associated with lower levels of belongingness, whereas for women, marital status was unrelated to sense of belonging.

Conclusions: It would appear crucial to develop and implement interventions which assist

Comment

Main Findings: Marital status has been identified as a predictor of suicide among older adults, with loss of a spouse being more strongly associated with suicide among older men than women. Past research has indicated that separated males are at an increased risk of developing suicidality during the separation process compared to separated females[1]. Thwarted belongingness has been associated with loss of a spouse, and the relationship between thwarted belongingness and suicide is stronger among older men than women[2]. It was hypothesised that sense of belonging would mediate the relationship between marital status and suicidal ideation, such that being widowed would be associated with lower levels of sense of belonging, and lower levels of sense of belonging would, in turn, be associated with higher levels of suicidal ideation. Given that there is evidence that thwarted belongingness is a significant predictor of suicidal ideation in men but not women, it was hypothesised that the relationship between marital status and sense of belongingness and between sense of belongingness and suicidal ideation would be stronger for older men than older women.

A total of 676 Australian adults aged between 65 and 98 years participated in this study (286 men; 390 women). Subscales from the General Health Questionnaire[3] and the Sense of Belongingness Instrument[4] were administered to assess suicidal ideation and belongingness respectively. Demographic information was also collected. The results concluded that sense of belonging explained the relationship between marital status and suicidal ideation among older adults and that the relationship between marital status and sense of belonging was influenced by gender. For older men, being widowed was associated with lower levels of belonging. As a lower sense of belonging was found to be a risk factor for suicidal ideation, this highlights the importance of belonging for older men and the role marital status plays in levels of belonging. By contrast, for older women, there was no relationship between marital status and sense of belonging.

Implications: These findings displayed evidence that marital status is associated with sense of belonging in older men but not older women. This suggests that women may gain their sense of belonging from outside the marriage through other relationships. Furthermore, it may be that the loss of a partner and the transition into widowhood is much more consequential for men as they are more reliant on their partner to maintain their social networks and the adoption of feminine gender role tasks may be more difficult for men to take on then if the reverse occurred. These findings have intervention implications for those who work with older men.

A key challenge is how to facilitate a sense of feeling valued and important in older men who have lost their spouse. Connecting older male widowers with organisations such as a Men's Shed in Australia may assist with this, as research has indicated that the environment facilitates positive social relationships and builds a sense of belonging by providing a place for meaningful activity in the company of other men. This study was cross-sectional in design and thus, causation cannot be determined. Longitudinal research designs should be employed to assess belonging prior to and after the loss of a spouse to determine whether the loss of a spouse leads to a decrease in sense of belonging among older men, and whether belonging remains unchanged among older women who become widows.

Endnotes

1. Kõlves K, Ide N, De Leo D (2010). Suicidal ideation and behavior in the aftermath of marital separation: Gender differences. *Journal of Affective Disorders* 120, 48-53.
2. Van Orden KA, Witte TK., Cukrowicz KC, Braithwaite S, Selby EA, Joiner TE (2010). The interpersonal theory of suicide. *Psychological Review* 117, 575–600.
3. Hagerty B, Patusky K (1995). Developing a measure of sense of belonging. *Nursing Research* 44, 9-13.
4. Goldberg DP, Hillier VF (1979). A scaled version of the general health questionnaire. *Psychological Medicine* 9, 139-145.
5. Website of Men's Shed (2014). Retrieved from http://www.mensshed.org/home/.aspx.

Antidepressant dose, age, and the risk of deliberate self-harm

Miller M, Swanson SA, Azrael D, Pate V, Stürmer T (USA)

JAMA Internal Medicine 48, 433-441, 2014

Importance: A comprehensive meta-analysis of randomized trial data suggests that suicidal behavior is twice as likely when children and young adults are randomized to antidepressants compared with when they are randomized to placebo. Drug-related risk was not elevated for adults older than 24 years. To our knowledge, no study to date has examined whether the risk of suicidal behavior is related to antidepressant dose, and if so, whether risk depends on a patient's age.

Objective: To assess the risk of deliberate self-harm by antidepressant dose, by age group.

Design, setting, and participants: This was a propensity score-matched cohort study using population-based health care utilization data from 162 625 US residents with depression ages 10 to 64 years who initiated antidepressant therapy with selective serotonin reuptake inhibitors at modal or at higher than modal doses from January 1, 1998, through December 31, 2010.

Main outcomes and measures: International Classification of Diseases, Ninth Revision (ICD-9) external cause of injury codes E950.x-E958.x (deliberate self-harm).

Results: The rate of deliberate self-harm among children and adults 24 years of age or younger who initiated high-dose therapy was approximately twice as high as among matched patients initiating modal-dose therapy (hazard ratio [HR], 2.2 [95% CI, 1.6-3.0]), corresponding to approximately 1 additional event for every 150 such patients treated with high-dose (instead of modal-dose) therapy. For adults 25 to 64 years of age, the absolute risk of suicidal behavior was far lower and the effective risk difference null (HR, 1.2 [95% CI, 0.8-1.9]).

Conclusions and relevance: Children and young adults initiating therapy with antidepressants at high-therapeutic (rather than modal-therapeutic) doses seem to be at heightened risk of deliberate self-harm. Considered in light of recent meta-analyses concluding that the efficacy of antidepressant therapy for youth seems to be modest, and separate evidence that antidepressant dose is generally unrelated to therapeutic efficacy, our findings offer clinicians an additional incentive to avoid initiating pharmacotherapy at high-therapeutic doses and to closely monitor patients starting antidepressants, especially youth, for several months.

Comment

Main Findings: There is evidence to suggest that those who receive antidepressants, particularly high dosages, are at an elevated risk of suicidal thoughts and behaviours[1]. However, there is no research conducted on exploring whether the risk of suicidal behaviour is related to antidepressant dose. This study assessed this question among a cohort of initiators of antidepressant therapy and addressed whether dose related risk is modified by a patients' age. There were 162,625 patients involved in this study ranging from 10 to 64 years of age with a depression diagnosis who initiated therapy with selective serotonin reuptake inhibitors (SSRIs) from January 1998 through to December 2010. Patients were assigned to one or three dose categories (modal dose, higher than modal, lower than modal). For statistical analysis, patients were divided into two age groups (ages 10-24 years vs. 25-64 years). Using propensity-matched analysis, based on the intensity of their depression symptoms, previous self-harm and other factors, the results indicated that after one year, deliberate self-harm for children and young adults was approximately double among patients initiating high-dose therapy compared with those initiating modal-dose therapy. This was particularly evident within the first three months of treatment. However, there was no such effect found for the older cohorts. Overall, 142 out of 21,305 young people self-harmed throughout the study period. The risk of deliberate self-harm was 1.4% at typical doses and a 3.1% at higher doses.

Implications: Although the mechanisms whereby higher doses might lead to higher suicidal risk remain unclear, one possible explanation is that antidepressants have an 'energising' effect that allows young people to act on their suicidal impulses[2]. Regardless, these findings offer clinicians an additional incentive to avoid initiating pharmacotherapy at high-therapeutic doses and to monitor all patients starting antidepressants, especially youth, for several months and regardless of their history of deliberate self-harm. Furthermore, given that most suicidal behaviour in the study occurred within the first three months of treatment, health professionals should more closely monitor their patients for behavioural changes during that time. Taken altogether, this study provides support for guidelines that promote the initiation of antidepressants at low doses. This means balancing the risks and benefits of antidepressants, along with carefully choosing the dose and type of drug.

Endnotes

1. Stone M, Laughren T, Jones ML, Levenson M, Holland PC, Hughes A, Hammad TA, Temple R, Rochester G (2009). Risk of suicidality in clinical trials of antidepressants in adults: Analysis of proprietary data submitted to US Food and Drug Administration. *British Medical Journal* 339, b2880.
2. Friedman RA, Leon AC (2007). Expanding the black box - depression, antidepressants, and the risk of suicide. *New England Journal of Medicine* 356, 2343-2346.

Genetic and familial environmental effects on suicide attempts: A study of Danish adoptees and their biological and adoptive siblings

Petersen L, Sorensen TIA, Andersen PK, Mortensen PB, Hawton K (Denmark, UK)

Journal of Affective Disorders 155, 273-277, 2014

Objectives: Genetic factors have been found to influence the risk of suicide. It is less clear if this also applies to attempted suicide. We have investigated genetic and familial environmental factors by studying the occurrence of suicide attempts in biological and adoptive siblings of adoptees who attempted suicide compared to siblings of adoptees with no suicide attempts.

Method: We used a random sample of 1933 adoptees from the Danish Adoption Register, a register of non-familial adoptions of Danish children, i.e. the adoptive parents are biologically unrelated to the adoptee. Analyses were conducted on incidence rates of attempted suicide in biological and adoptive siblings given occurrence of attempted suicide in the adoptees while also taking into account psychiatric disorders. Information about suicidal attempt and history of psychiatric disorder was based on hospital admissions.

Results: The rate of attempted suicide in full siblings of adoptees who attempted suicide before age 60 years was higher than in full siblings of adoptees who had not attempted suicide (incidence rate ratios (IRR)=3A5; 95% confidence interval [CI]=0.94-12.7). After adjustment for history of psychiatric admission of siblings the increased rate was statistically significant (IRR=3.88; 95% CI-1.42-10.6).

Limitations: Information on attempted suicide and psychiatric history was limited to that which involved hospitalisation.

Conclusions: Genetic factors influence risk of suicide attempts.

Comment

Main findings: The findings of this study are in keeping with considerable research in the past identifying genetic factors as increasing risk of suicide[1]. This paper investigated the role of genetic factors in suicide attempts by comparing two cohorts of siblings. One cohort included siblings of adoptees who had attempted suicide, and the other included siblings of adoptees who had not attempted suicide. Within each cohort, siblings were differentiated by whether they were adoptive siblings (biologically unrelated to the adoptee, but raised with the adoptee therefore sharing environmental influence) or biological siblings (genetically related to the adoptee, but not raised with them). The study excluded siblings of adoptees who had been adopted by biological relatives. Cox regression models were used to provide estimates of the rate of attempted suicide among the two cohorts. Results showed an increased rate of attempted suicide among full biological siblings of adoptees who had attempted suicide compared with full biological siblings of adoptees not attempting suicide, but the result was not statistically significant. Data for biological half siblings did not provide a clear outcome, and the rate ratio could not be estimated for adoptive siblings, since no attempted suicides were recorded for adoptive siblings of adoptees who had attempted suicide. Adjustment for psychiatric admission changed the associations slightly, and the increased rate of attempted suicide in full biological siblings became significant. Information about the suicide attempts in the study may be less reliable than information about suicide deaths due to limitations in hospital registrations, including lack of information about suicidal intent. Severe psychiatric disorders are strongly associated with risk of suicide[2], and there has been some debate as to whether suicide within families increases suicide risk independently of mental illness[3]. This research suggests that this can be the case, although it is acknowledged that history of psychiatric hospital admission did not necessarily represent the full number of siblings who experienced mental illness.

Implications: Heritability of 'serious' suicide attempts has been estimated at 55%, based on a study of Australian twins; monozygotic twins whose co-twin had attempted suicide had a much higher risk of similar behaviour[1]. Studies of twins raised together cannot distinguish between genetic and environmental influences; unfortunately, there is little available information about suicide behaviours of twins reared apart, and adoptee studies are relied upon to make the distinction. While this study supports previous evidence showing that genetic factors play a role in both suicide and suicide attempts, the means of transmission are still not completely understood. As well as possibility of vulnerability to psychiatric illness, transmission may include factors subject to genetic influence such as a personality trait of impulsive aggression[4]. A number of studies have focused on identifying specific genes linked to suicide risk; for example, a current study has reported that the gene SKA2 may indicate whether a person is vulnerable to the impact of stress and anxiety, and therefore at risk of suicidal thoughts or attempts[5]. However, it is likely that no single gene, hormone or other factor alone is responsible for genetic risk. Research indicates that biological processes contributing to suicide are likely to work together, such as co-regulated gene groups in several brain areas. Both psychological and biological factors affect moods, and environmental factors can exert their effects through both of these influences[6]. Regardless of how genetic factors are transmitted, it is becoming clear that, where possible, suicide risk assessment should take heritability into account, even when the environmental family influences are not considered to increase risk to a high level[4].

Endnotes

1. Statham DJ, Heath AC, Madden PA, Bucholz KK, Bier Ut L, Dinwiddie SH, Slutske SH, Dunne MP, Martin NG (1998). Suicidal behaviour: An epidemiological and genetic study. *Psychological Medicine* 28, 839-855.
2. Nordentoft M, Mortensen PB, Pedersen CB (2011). Absolute risk of suicide after first hospital contact in mental disorder. *Archives of General Psychiatry* 68, 1058-1064.
3. Qin P, Agerbo E, Mortensen PB (2002). Suicide risk in relation to family history of completed

suicide and psychiatric disorders: A nested case-control study based on longitudinal registers. *Lancet* 360, 1126-1130.

4. Brent DA, Mann JJ (2005). Family genetic studies, suicide, and suicidal behavior. *American Journal of Medical Genetics* 133, 13-24.

5. Guintivano J, Brown T, Newcomer A, Jones M, Cox O, Maher BS, Eaton WW, Payne JL, Wilcox HC, Kaminsky ZA (2014). Identification and replication of a combined epigenetic and genetic biomarker predicting suicide and suicidal behaviors. *American Journal of Psychiatry*. Published online: 19 May 2014. doi: 10.1176/appi.ajp.2014.14010008.

6. Kõlves K, Kumpula E-K, De Leo D (2013). *Suicidal behaviours in men: Determinants and prevention*. Brisbane: Australian Institute for Suicide Research and Prevention.

Stigmatising attitudes towards people with mental disorders: A comparison of Australian health professionals with the general community

Reavley NJ, Mackinnon AJ, Morgan AJ, Jorm AF (Australia)

Australian and New Zealand Journal of Psychiatry 48, 433-441, 2014

Objective: The aim of this paper was to explore attitudes towards people with mental disorders among Australian health professionals (psychiatrists, psychologists and general practitioners (GPs)) and to compare their attitudes with members of the general community.

Methods: The study involved a postal survey of 518 GPs, 506 psychiatrists and 498 clinical psychologists and a telephone survey of 6019 members of the general community. Participants were given a case vignette describing a person with either depression, depression with suicidal thoughts, early schizophrenia, chronic schizophrenia, post-traumatic stress disorder (PTSD) or social phobia and two questionnaires to assess stigmatising attitudes (the Depression Stigma Scale and the Social Distance Scale). Exploratory structural equation modelling was used to elucidate the structure of stigma as measured by the two scales, to establish dimensions of stigma and to compare patterns of association according to gender, age, vignette and professional grouping.

Results: The measurement characteristics of stigmatising attitudes in health professionals were found to be comparable to those in members of the general community in social distance and also in personal and perceived attitude stigma, with each forming distinct dimensions and each comprising 'Weak-not-sick' and 'Dangerous/unpredictable' components. Among health professionals, female gender, age and being a GP were associated with higher scores on the personal stigma scales. Mental health professionals had lower scores on the personal 'Weak-not-sick' and 'Dangerous/unpredictable' scales than members of the general community, while there were no significant differences in the desire for social distance between health professionals and the general community.

Conclusions: While mental health professionals have less stigmatising attitudes than the general public, the greater beliefs in dangerousness and personal weakness by GPs should be addressed.

Comment

Main Findings: There is a growing need for mental health professionals to be aware of their own attitudes to those with mental disorders and the adverse consequences that stigmatising attitudes and discriminatory behaviours might have for patients[1]. The aim of the current study was to explore the attitudes of psychiatrists, clinical psychologists and general practitioners (GPs) towards people with mental disorders. A further aim of this study was to compare levels of the various dimensions of stigma between these professional groups and also to members of the general community. A total of 6,019 members of the general community and 1,536 Australian health professionals (518 GPs, 506 psychiatrists and 498 psychologists) responded to a questionnaire based on a vignette of a person with a mental disorder. Each participant randomly received one of six vignettes: depression, depression with suicidal thoughts, early schizophrenia, chronic schizophrenia, social phobia and PTSD. Respondents were asked what they thought was wrong with the person and about the likely helpfulness of a wide range of interventions, likely outcomes for the person with and without professional help, and stigmatising attitudes towards the person. Stigmatising attitudes were assessed with two sets of statements: one assessing the respondent's personal attitudes towards the person described in the vignette (personal stigma) and the other assessing the respondent's beliefs about other people's attitudes towards the person in the vignette (perceived stigma). Willingness to have contact with the person described in the vignette was also measured (desire for social distance).

Among health professionals, scales reflecting these dimensions had different patterns of association with age, gender, vignette and professional group, with stigmatising attitudes typically higher for the schizophrenia vignettes, in males and increasing with age. GPs typically had the highest stigmatising attitudes and psychologists had the lowest. Preference to avoid people with mental disorders in health professionals was associated with both the belief that mental illness is a reflection of a personal weakness, as well as the belief that it makes the person dangerous or unpredictable. Psychologists were less likely to hold stigmatising attitudes or desire social distance, and GPs were generally more likely to do so, possibly due to workload pressures or a lack of awareness and training about mental health. Health professionals had less personally stigmatising attitudes than members of the general public, where there were no significant differences in the desire for social distance between the general community survey participants and the professional groups. While GPs and psychiatrists were found to be less personally stigmatising than the general population, they were likely to believe that other people would stigmatise.

Implications: These results indicate that there is a need to better understand and address the attitudes of GPs, particularly those relating to personal beliefs about dangerousness and mental disorders as personal weakness. This might be achieved through anti-stigma interventions involving education and contact with a person with a mental illness. SANE Australia is a national charity that has a strong focus on stigma-reduction through its award-winning programs such as 'StigmaWatch' and 'Say no to Stigma'[2]. Their campaigns have long-term strategies aiming to reduce the stigma and discrimination associated with mental illness, with a particular focus on psychotic illnesses. Although their anti-stigma campaigns target a vast array of the Australian population through the internet and media announcements, suicide prevention strategies need to target health professionals specifically, by providing appropriate training based on evidence of good practice in order to reduce their stigmatising attitudes. In summary, a national strategy to tackle stigma and discrimination associated with mental illness is vital, and should be a non-negotiable component of mental health policies and plans.

Endnotes

1. Corrigan PW, Morris SB, Michaels PJ, Rafacz JD, Rüsch N (2012). Challenging the public stigma of mental illness: A meta-analysis of outcome studies. *Psychiatric Services* 63, 963-973.
2. Website of SANE Australia (2014). Retrieved from http://www.sane.org/.

Suicides among lesbian, gay, bisexual, and transgender populations in Australia: An analysis of the Queensland Suicide Register

Skerrett DM, Kõlves K, De Leo D (Australia)

Journal of Asia-Pacific Psychiatry 6, 440-446, 2014

Introduction: Sexual orientation is seldom recorded at death in Australia, and to date there have been no studies on the relationship between those that have died by suicide and sexuality or minority gender identity in Australia. The aim of the present study is to determine whether or not lesbian, gay, bisexual, transgender (LGBT), and intersex individuals who die by suicide constitute a unique subpopulation of those who die by suicide, when compared with non-lesbian, gay, bisexual, transgender, and intersex suicide deaths.

Methods: The Queensland Suicide Register holds records of all suicides in Queensland since 1990. All cases from 2000 to 2009 (inclusive; a total of 5,966 cases) were checked for potential indicators of individuals' sexual orientation and gender identification. A total of 35 lesbian (n = 10), gay (n = 22), bisexual (n = 2), and transgender (n = 1) suicide cases were identified. Three comparison cases of non-LGBT suicides for each LGBT suicide were then located, matched by age and gender. Conditional logistic regression was used to calculate odds ratios with 95% confidence intervals.

Results: It was significantly more likely that depression was mentioned in the cases of LGBT suicides than in non-LGBT cases. While 12.4% of the comparison group had been diagnosed with psychotic disorders, there were no such diagnoses among LGBT individuals. LGBT individuals experienced relationship problems more often, with relationship conflict also being more frequent than in non-LGBT cases.

Discussion: Despite its limitations, this study - the first of its kind in Australia - seems to indicate that LGBT people would require targeted approaches in mental and general health services.

Comment

Main findings: Owing to the lack of information gathered on sexual orientation or gender identification for suicide cases, suicide in lesbian, gay, bisexual, transgender, and intersex (LGBTI) individuals is underreported in Australia. This article is the first of its kind in Australia, aiming to determine whether or not LGBTI individuals constitute a unique subpopulation of those who die by suicide, when compared with non-LGBTI suicide deaths. At present, the Queensland Suicide register (QSR) does not systematically collect information on sexuality or transgendered status. As a result, all QSR records from 2000 to 2009 were reviewed to detect potential indicators of individuals' sexual orientation and gender identification. Thirty-five cases were identified as lesbian (10), gay (22), bisexual (two) and transgender (one). Three cases of non-LGBT suicides, matched by age and gender were compared with each LGBT suicide.

While LGBT suicide prevalence was unable to be determined owing to the unsystematic way in which data regarding sexuality or gender identity in Australia is gathered, factors that were specific to LGBT suicide cases when compared with non-LGBT suicides were identified. The data indicated that both LGBT and non-LGBT suicide cases resided in metropolitan areas (57.1% and 59% respectively). No differences were uncovered between the two comparison groups regarding suicide method (hanging, motor vehicle exhaust gas, firearm, and poisoning). LGBT individuals more often were found by their partner, left a suicide note and had three times greater odds of treatment by an ambulance at the scene. A greater proportion of LGBT individuals had an infectious disease (11.4% compared with 2.9% in the comparison group), mostly HIV/AIDS. The results also suggested that the LGBT suicide cases had experienced a greater level of emotional distress and conflict than non-LGBT suicides, and presented with a significantly higher prevalence of depression (70.6% and 52.4% respectively) and relationship problems (65.7% and 33.3% respectively).

Implications: This study was limited by the potential under-identification of LGBT suicide cases in the QSR and therefore restricted the number of suicide cases available for analysis. Furthermore, the information may have been compromised as it was collected primarily by police officers through interviews with a next of kin who was most probably grieving at that time. Consequently due to the nature of this study, the factors that were identified cannot be claimed to have a causal relationship with the suicidal act, and caution is encouraged in interpreting the results.

Despite these limitations, this article has been able to identify LGBT suicides in Queensland as a distinct subgroup. Considering the greater presence of depression, HIV/AIDS and interpersonal conflict for LGBT individuals, these findings suggest the need for targeted approaches in mental and general health services, schools, and public health and stigma reduction campaigns. The greater level of emotionality in LGBT suicides indicates a need for preventative activities that address the high degree of interpersonal conflict and distress experienced by these people. Self-acceptance and stigma reduction are also important foci to target, particularly as LGBT individuals who died by suicide experienced greater conflict over sexuality. The higher prevalence of HIV/AIDS in LGBT individuals highlights the importance of ongoing government initiatives and support for non-government organisations working to prevent HIV infection.

Factors related to childhood suicides:
Analysis of the Queensland Child Death Register

Soole R, Kõlves K, De Leo D (Australia)

Crisis 35, 292-300, 2014

Background: Suicide among children under the age of 15 years is a leading cause of death.

Aims: The aim of the current study is to identify demographic, psychosocial, and psychiatric factors associated with child suicides. Method: Using external causes of deaths recorded in the Queensland Child Death Register, a case-control study design was applied. Cases were suicides of children (10–14 years) and adolescents (15–17 years); controls were other external causes of death in the same age band.

Results: Between 2004 and 2012, 149 suicides were recorded: 34 of children aged 10–14 years and 115 of adolescents aged 15–17 years. The gender asymmetry was less evident in child suicides and suicides were significantly more prevalent in indigenous children. Children residing in remote areas were significantly more likely to die by suicide than other external causes compared with children in metropolitan areas. Types of precipitating events differed between children and adolescents, with children more likely to experience family problems. Disorders usually diagnosed during infancy, childhood, and adolescence (e.g., ADHD) were significantly more common among children compared with adolescents who died by suicide.

Conclusion: Psychosocial and environmental aspects of children, in addition to mental health and behavioral difficulties, are important in the understanding of suicide in this age group and in the development of targeted suicide prevention.

Comment

Main Findings: Among children younger than 15 years, suicide is a leading cause of death worldwide[1]. Few studies have specifically focused on children younger than 15 years and as a result, it is currently unclear whether existing knowledge about suicide-related factors for adolescence and adults is relevant to children. This current study aimed to firstly, assess demographic factors associated with child (10-14 years) and adolescent suicide (15-17 years) when compared with children and adolescents who died by other external causes of death. Demographic, psychosocial, and psychiatric factors between child and adolescent suicide were then compared. External causes of death of children and young people ages 10-17 years occurring during the period of 2004-2012 in Queensland were derived from the Queensland Child Death Register (CDR). Suicides in children and adolescents were compared with the control group of other external causes of death in the same age bands. A total of 469 deaths by external causes were recorded for children and adolescence.

Suicide accounted for almost one-third of external causes of death for children and adolescents. Number of suicides increased with age and occurred more frequently within the adolescent group. Boys died by suicide more often than girls both in children (61.8%) and adolescents (64.3%). Aboriginal and Torres Strait Islander children made up 47% of all suicides and only 6% of external causes of death. Aboriginal and Torres Strait Islander adolescents made up 25% of suicides and 10% of external causes of death. More than 90% of children used hanging compared with 79% of adolescents. Half of the children who died by suicide had mental health and behavioural problems; more specifically, disorders usually diagnosed in infancy, childhood or adolescence, such as ADHD, were the most prevalent psychiatric disorders. Mood disorders were significantly more common in adolescents. Any type of previous suicidality was found in almost half of children and 60% of adolescents. Presence of physical, sexual, emotional abuse and/or neglect was evident in over a third of children and adolescents who died by suicide. Precipitating events within six months prior to suicide were identified in almost 80% of children and 87% of adolescents.

Implications: The cut-off age between children and adolescents was debatable in this study. Biological age is often used to portray a child's transition into adolescence marked with the onset of puberty. While there is an approximate trajectory for these development stages, there is large variation in the onset of puberty through genetic, environmental, and social influences. As such, defining childhood using an age-related schema without consideration of social and other forces is considered problematic. Despite the potential difficulties in defining childhood and adolescence in this age-related context, doing so allows the creation of consistent appropriate boundaries to separate children from adults[2].

Notwithstanding this limitation, the findings of this study highlight the importance of considering the differences between children and adolescents and show the multifaceted nature of suicide, demonstrating the importance of considering socioenvironmental elements in the prevention of child suicide. As previous suicidality was found in many children and adolescents, this emphasises the danger of underestimating the intensity of children's emotions and seriousness of suicidal expression or behavior, regardless of the child's cognitive understanding of the lethality of their actions. The findings from this study have practical implications by providing a better understanding of the factors associated with child suicide so that Australian services such as Kid's Help Line[3] and KidsMatter[4] can utilise this information to inform child suicide prevention strategies.

Endnotes

1. Apter A, Bursztein C, Bertolote JM, Fleischmann A, Wasserman D (2009). Suicide on all the continents in the young. *Oxford textbook of suicidology and suicide prevention.* New York: Oxford University Press, 621-627.
2. James A, James A (2008). *Key concepts in childhood studies.* Wiltshire, UK: Cromwell Press.
3. Website of Kids Help (2014). Retrieved from http://www.kidshelp.com.au/.
4. Website of Kids Matter (2014). Retrieved from http://www.kidsmatter.edu.au/.

Suicide in adults released from prison in Queensland, Australia: A cohort study.

Spittal MJ, Forsyth S, Pirkis J, Alati R, Kinner SA (Australia)

Journal of Epidemiology and Community Health 68, 993-998, 2014

Background: Previous research has demonstrated elevated mortality following release from prison. We contrasted the risk of opioid overdose death with the risk of suicide in a cohort of adults released from prison in Queensland, Australia over a 14-year-period. We examine risk factors for suicide in the cohort, and make comparisons with the general population.

Method: We constructed a retrospective cohort of all adults released from prison between 1994 and 2007 and linked this to the National Death Index for deaths up to 31 December 2007.

Results: We identified 41 970 individuals released from prison. Of the 2158 deaths in the community, 371 were suicides (crude mortality rate (CMR) 13.7/10 000 person-years) and 396 were due to drug-related causes (CMR 14.6/10 000 person-years). We observed a spike in drug-related deaths in the first 2 weeks after release from prison but no such pattern was observed for suicide. Being married (HR 0.40) and number of prior imprisonments (HR 3.1 for ≥5 prior incarcerations compared with none) independently predicted suicide. Age, sex, Indigenous status, length of incarceration and offence history were not associated with suicide. The standardised mortality ratios indicated that released women were 14.2 times and released men 4.8 times more likely to die from suicide than would be expected in the population.

Conclusions: This study demonstrates that the rate of suicide in adults released from prison is similar to the rate of drug-related deaths. Strategies that provide support to vulnerable people after release may reduce suicide in this population.

Comment

Main Findings: There is growing evidence that adults released from prison are at an elevated risk of mortality compared with the general population[1]. This study compared observed mortality rates for prisoners released over a 14-year period with population-level data from Queensland. The authors aimed to firstly, compare the mortality rates for drug-related deaths and suicides over the entire study period and in the first six months after release from prison. The second aim was to identify risk and protective factors for suicide and finally, compare the suicide rate for adults released from prison with that of the general population, matched by age and sex. A total of 41,970 adults released from prison in Queensland from 1 January 1994 to 31 December 2007 were identified. Suicide and population counts for the Queensland population over the same period were also obtained. Of the 41,970 prisoners released, 2,158 deaths occurred in the community, 371 and 396 being suicides and drug related deaths respectively. Drug related death rates were highest in the first two weeks after release than subsequent 24 weeks. By contrast, rates of suicide during the first two weeks after release were similar to subsequent 24 weeks. Together, rates of drug related deaths and suicides were significantly higher in the first six months following release than subsequent time periods. Marital status and number of imprisonments independently predicted suicides. Prisoners who were married had a 40% lower risk of suicide as marriage is likely to be a protective factor against suicide, providing stable accommodation and emotional support for ex-prisoners. Risk of suicide increased as the number of imprisonments increased; a person with five or more imprisonments was 3.1 times at more risk of suicide than an individual who was imprisoned only once. Finally, this study found that when comparing the cohort with the general population, people released from prison were at a markedly higher risk of suicide. Young people, especially young women, particularly appeared to be at a higher risk.

Implications: In order for interventions to be successful at reducing suicide, more information is needed to identify high-risk periods after release from prison for suicide and modifiable risk and protective factors. This study indicated that while the focus on avoiding opioid-related deaths after release from prison is clearly warranted, attention should also be given to preventing suicide after release from prison. Though the knowledge on ways to minimise risk of suicide for people released from prison is limited, there are system-level strategies that show promise, and further work is needed to build the evidence for these in ex-prisoner populations. A review on current literature regarding suicide prevention strategies for prisoners showed that multi-factored suicide prevention programs focusing specifically on reducing unique risk factors for suicide in prison have the potential to lower incidence of suicide[2]. Programs which are implemented as prisoners arrive and maintained until they leave the facility are more likely to succeed, including screening and assessment of inmates on intake, improved staff training, post-intake observation for suicide risk, monitoring and psychological treatment of suicidal inmates, limited use of isolation, increased social support, and adequate and safe housing facilities for at-risk individuals. Recent research has indicated that far less attention has been paid to the post-release period[3]. A recent editorial highlighted the poor provision of health care for mentally ill prisoners and called on policymakers and politicians to improve and expand prison mental health services, court diversion programs, and community forensic mental health services, as well as to provide access to stable housing and appropriate vocational rehabilitation services after release, as part of extended mental health services in Australia[4]. One possible recommendation is giving short-term support until other services become available by making 24-hour teams accessible to provide single point access to people in crisis after having been released from prison[5].

Endnotes

1. Binswanger IA, Stern MF, Deyo RA, et al. (2007). Release from prison - a high risk of death for former inmates. *New England Journal of Medicine* 356, 157–165.

2. Baker E, Kõlves K, De Leo D (2014). Management of suicidal and self-harming behaviours in prisons: Systematic literature review of evidence-based activities. *Archives of Suicide Research* 18, 227-240.

3. Kariminia A, Law MG, Butler TG, Levy MH, Corben SP, Kaldor JM, Grant L (2007). Suicide risk among recently released prisoners in New South Wales, Australia. *Medical Journal of Australia* 187, 387-390.

4. White P, Whiteford H (2006). Prisons: Mental health institutions of the 21st century. *Medical Journal of Australia* 185, 302-303.

5. Jenkins R, Bhugra D, Meltzer H, Singleton N, Bebbington P, Brugha T, Coid J, Farrell M, Lewis G, Paton J (2005). Psychiatric and social aspects of suicidal behaviour in prisons. *Psychological Medicine*, 35, 257-269.

Direct effect of sunshine on suicide

Vyssoki B, Kapusta ND, Praschak-Rieder N, Dorffner G, Willeit M
JAMA Psychiatry 71, 1231-137, 2014

Importance: It has been observed that suicidal behavior is influenced by sunshine and follows a seasonal pattern. However, seasons bring about changes in several other meteorological factors and a seasonal rhythm in social behavior may also contribute to fluctuations in suicide rates.

Objective: To investigate the effects of sunshine on suicide incidence that are independent of seasonal variation.

Design, Setting, and Participants: Retrospective analysis of data on all officially confirmed suicides in Austria between January 1, 1970, and May 6, 2010 (n = 69 462). Data on the average duration of sunshine per day (in hours) were calculated from 86 representative meteorological stations. Daily number of suicides and daily duration of sunshine were differentiated to remove variation in sunshine and variation in suicide incidence introduced by season. Thereafter, several models based on Pearson correlation coefficients were calculated.

Main Outcomes and Measures: Correlation of daily number of suicides and daily duration of sunshine after mathematically removing the effects of season.

Results: Sunshine hours and number of suicides on every day from January 1, 1970, to May 6, 2010, were highly correlated ($r = 0.4870$; $P < 10-9$). After differencing for the effects of season, a mathematical procedure that removes most of the variance from the data, a positive correlation between number of suicides and hours of daily sunshine remained for the day of suicide and up to 10 days prior to suicide ($r_{maximum} = 0.0370$; $P < 10-5$). There was a negative correlation between the number of suicides and daily hours of sunshine for the 14 to 60 days prior to the suicide event ($r_{minimum} = -0.0383$; $P < 10-5$). These effects were found in the entire sample and in violent suicides.

Conclusions and Relevance: Duration of daily sunshine was significantly correlated with suicide frequency independent of season, but effect sizes were low. Our data support the hypothesis that sunshine on the day of suicide and up to 10 days prior to suicide may facilitate suicide. More daily sunshine 14 to 60 days previously is associated with low rates of suicide. Our study also suggests that sunshine during this period may protect against suicide.

Comment

Main Findings: Light has been shown to interact with brain serotonin systems and possibly influences serotonin-related behaviours[1,2]. Some of these behaviours such as mood, impulsiveness, and aggression, are known to play a key role in suicidal behaviour[3, 4]. This study examined the relationship between suicide numbers in Austria and duration of sunshine over a 40 year time period. As seasons affect a number of interrelated climatic variables as well as social behaviours, seasonal variation was mathematically removed. Suicide data was obtained from Statistics

Austria from January 1 1970 to May 6 2010. Suicide methods were classified by the most common method of distinction as violent (hanging, drowning, shooting, jumping) or nonviolent (poisoning). A total of 69,462 suicides were registered during this period. Data regarding average duration of sunshine per day for the same period of 40 years was calculated from 86 representative meteorological stations in Austria. The aim of the study was to further substantiate the hypothesis that sunshine has a direct role in the variation in suicide incidence. Authors expected a positive correlation between the number of sunshine hours and the number of suicides on a daily basis, beyond what can be explained through the previously known seasonality in both sunshine patterns and suicides during the year. Two main results emerged. Firstly, sunshine on the day of suicide and up to 10 days prior to suicide seemed to facilitate suicide, as a positive correlation was found between duration of sunshine and suicide numbers in this period. Secondly, sunshine may also have a protective effect against suicide as a negative correlation was found between suicide numbers and daily hours of sunshine for the 14 to 60 days prior to the suicide incident. Once data was separated and analysed according to suicide method, these two effects were only significant for violent suicides.

Implications: Duration of sunshine explained a substantial proportion of the daily variation in suicide numbers in Austria whilst mathematically removing the effects of season. Previous research has indicated a close relation between suicidal behaviour and mood disorders, which are known to be associated with serotonin dysfunction and are highly sensitive to seasonal changes, predominantly to sunshine[5, 6]. In the long term, sunshine, similarly to antidepressants, improves mood and thereby may contribute to decreased suicide[7]. This study suggests a possible interaction between the serotonergic system, which has been associated with suicidal behaviours, and duration of sunshine[3,4]. In sum, these findings highlight the importance of monitoring the bimodal effect sunshine has on suicidal behaviour as an increase in suicide was found over shorter periods of sunshine exposure, while after longer periods, more sunshine was associated with decreased suicide. Further research whether people with severe episodes of depression are more susceptible to the suicide-triggering effects of sunshine is recommended. Replicating this study in countries with different climates, such as Australia, would be valuable to ascertain whether the effect of sunshine duration on suicide numbers remains consistent.

Endnotes

1. Kennaway DJ, Moyer RW (1998). Serotonin 5-HT2c agonists mimic the effect of light pulses on circadian rhythms. *Brain Research* 806, 257-270.

2. Lambert GW, Reid C, Kaye DM, Jennings GL, Esler MD (2002). Effect of sunlight and season on serotonin turnover in the brain. *Lancet* 360, 1840-1842.

3. Mann JJ, Brent DA, Arango V (2001). The neurobiology and genetics of suicide and attempted suicide: A focus on the serotonergic system. *Neuropsychopharmacology* 24, 467-477.

4. Arango V, Huang YY, Underwood MD, Mann JJ (2003). Genetics of the serotonergic system in suicidal behavior. *Journal of Psychiatric Research* 37, 375-386.

5. Praschak-Rieder N, Willeit M, Wilson AA, Houle S, Meyer JH (2008). Seasonal variation in human brain serotonin transporter binding. *Archives of General Psychiatry* 65, 1072-1078.
6. Barton DA, Esler MD, Dawood T, Lambert EA, Haikerwal D, Brenchley C, Socratous F, Hastings J, Guo L, Wiesner G, Kaye DM, Bayles R, Schlaich MP, Lambert GW. (2008). Elevated brain serotonin turnover in patients with depression: Effect of genotype and therapy. *Archives of General Psychiatry* 65, 38-46.
7. Vyssoki B, Praschak-Rieder N, Sonneck G, Bluml V, Willeit M, Kasper S, Kapusta ND (2012). Effects of sunshine on suicide rates. *Comprehensive Psychiatry* 53, 535-539.

Do depression treatments reduce suicidal ideation? The effects of CBT, IPT, pharmacotherapy, and placebo on suicidality

Weitz E, Hollon SD, Kerkhof A, Cuijpers P (Netherlands, USA, Germany)

Journal of Affective Disorders 167, 98-103, 2014

Background: Many well-researched treatments for depression exist. However, there is not yet enough evidence on whether these therapies, designed for the treatment of depression, are also effective for reducing suicidal ideation. This research provides valuable information for researchers, clinicians, and suicide prevention policy makers.

Method: Analysis was conducted on the Treatment for Depression Research Collaborative (TDCRP) sample, which included CBT, IPT, medication, and placebo treatment groups. Participants were included in the analysis if they reported suicidal ideation on the HRSD or BDI (score of ≥1).

Results: Multivariate linear regression indicated that both IPT (b=.41, p<.05) and medication (b =.47, p<.05) yielded a significant reduction in suicide symptoms compared to placebo on the HRSD. Multivariate linear regression indicated that after adjustment for change in depression these treatment effects were no longer significant. Moderate Cohen's d effect sizes from baseline to post-test differences in suicide score by treatment group are reported.

Limitations: These analyses were completed on a single suicide item from each of the measures. Moreover, the TDCRP excluded participants with moderate to severe suicidal ideation.

Conclusion: This study demonstrates the specific effectiveness of IPT and medications in reducing suicidal ideation (relative to placebo), albeit largely as a consequence of their more general effects on depression. This adds to the growing body of evidence that depression treatments, specifically IPT and medication, can also reduce suicidal ideation and serves to further our understanding of the complex relationship between depression and suicide.

Comment

Main findings: The nature of the relationship between suicide and depression appears to be complex. Clinicians generally use depression treatments for patients with suicidal ideation, but it is not clear whether this is the best course of action. Participants (with a mean age of 35 years) were included in this study if they met criteria for a current major depressive episode and scored one or above on the single suicide item of either the Hamilton Rating Scale for Depression (HRSD) or the Beck Depression Inventory (BDI), but were excluded if they had moderate to severe suicidal ideation or current active potential for suicide. Sixteen weeks of randomly assigned treatment was conducted using either cognitive behaviour therapy (CBT), interpersonal therapy (IPT), imipramine (plus clinical management) or placebo (plus clinical management). Analysis of results found that both IPT and medication resulted in a significant reduction in suicide symptoms compared to the placebo group when measured on the HRSD; no effect was seen between the CBT and placebo groups on the HRSD. No effect was seen between any treatment group and placebo on the BDI, which may be due to attributes of this scale. The findings offer some preliminary evidence to support existing treatment guidelines for depression and suicide. The researchers also reported a highly significant relationship between changes in depression scores and in suicidal ideation scores over the course of treatment; they believe the fact that effect of treatment on suicidality diminished when changes in depression were controlled for suggests that depression may drive changes in suicidal ideation.

Implications: In Australia, CBT and IPT are considered as therapies with the strongest evidence base to support treatment of depression in adults[1]. This paper has possibly provided support for use of IPT, and medication, amongst those people with MDD who are also experiencing mild suicidal ideation. While adding to the available information regarding the interplay between diagnosed depression and suicidal ideation, the relationship between depression, suicide ideation and suicide behaviours is not so straightforward. Depression and suicide are regarded as quite separate constructs. Although suicidal ideation can appear to be a symptom of depression, a majority of patients with major depressive disorder (MDD) do not exhibit suicidal ideation. Conversely, people experiencing suicidal ideation or engaged in suicidal behaviour are not necessarily depressed. A review of more than 15,000 cases of suicide associated with a mental disorder found that depression was associated with only 30.2% of cases[2]. Further, a review of international suicide cases found that whether or not diagnosis of any type of mental disorder had been previously applied to people who died by suicide was related to cultural expression of distress and treatment approaches[3]. While preventing and monitoring mood disorders is an important component of suicide prevention, clearly many other factors are involved including social connectedness, good physical health, personal autonomy, optimism and openness[4].

Endnotes

1. Australian Psychological Society (2010). Evidence-based psychological interventions in the treatment of mental disorders: A literature review (3rd ed). Retrieved from https://www.psychology.org.au/Assets/Files/Evidence-Based-Psychological-Interventions.pdf

2. Bertolote JM, Fleischmann A, De Leo D, Wasserman D (2004). Psychiatric diagnoses and suicide: Revisiting the evidence. *Crisis* 25, 147-155.

3. Milner A, Sveticic J, De Leo D (2012). Suicide in the absence of mental disorder? A review of psychological autopsy studies across countries. *International Journal of Social Psychiatry* 59, 545–554.

4. De Leo D, Kõlves K (2012). Suicidality in old age not always mediated by depression. *Annals of Family Medicine*. Published online: 17 July 2012 (letter).

Anhedonia predicts suicidal ideation in a large psychiatric inpatient sample

Winer S, Nadorff MR, Ellis TE, Allen JG, Allen JG, Herrera S, Salen T (USA)

Psychiatry Research 218, 124-128, 2014

This study examined the relationship among symptoms of anhedonia and suicidal ideation at baseline, at termination, and over time in 1529 adult psychiatric inpatients. Anhedonia was associated with suicidality cross-sectionally at baseline and at termination. In addition, change in anhedonia from baseline to termination predicted change in suicidality from baseline to termination, as well as level of suicidality at termination; moreover, anhedonia remained a robust predictor of suicidal ideation independent of cognitive/affective symptoms of depression. Symptom-level analyses also revealed that, even after accounting for the physical aspect of anhedonia (e.g., loss of energy), loss of interest and loss of pleasure were independently associated with higher levels of suicidal ideation at baseline, overtime, and at discharge. Loss of interest was most highly predictive of suicidal ideation, providing support for recent differential conceptualizations of anhedonia. Taken together, these findings indicate that the manner in which anhedonia is conceptualized is important in predicting suicidal ideation, and that anhedonia symptoms warrant particular clinical attention in the treatment of suicidal patients.

Comment

Main findings: Assessing suicidal ideation is an important task in working to manage suicide risk. Anhedonia, defined as the loss of interest or pleasure during the same two-week period that represents a change from previous functioning diagnoses, has found to be associated with suicidality, independently of other depressive symptoms[1]. In line with previous work to investigate changes in the state of anhedonia, this study used the anhedonia subscale of the Beck Depression Inventory-II (BDI)[2] comprised of items specifically related to recent changes and to loss of interest in people. The finding that the subscale was a robust predictor of suicidality over time suggests that anhedonia may be of importance in assessing and treating suicidal patients. The 'loss of interest' item was most highly predictive of suicidal ideation, suggesting that recent changes in the social aspect of anhedonia are potentially associated with a lack of belongingness.

Implications: The assessment of suicide risk is extremely challenging; to date, there is no recognised tool able to reliably predict suicide. Any form of current or past history of suicide ideation must be taken seriously, as both are known to increase the risk of future suicide. Suicidal ideation is prevalent in the community; a survey of more than 11,000 Australian adults found that 21.1% of respondents had at some time believed that life was not worth living, with 10.4% having seriously considered suicide[3]. However, those experiencing suicidal ideation may not be forthcoming in revealing such thoughts to clinicians, possibly because of the stigma attached to suicide[4]. Possible determinants of suicidal ideation amongst

Australians have been found to include factors such as health and financial problems, lack of fruit consumption, lack of physical activity, and being separated, divorced or never married[5]. Interpersonal connectedness with others is a significant protective factor for those who are potentially at risk of suicide[4]; research into anhedonia as an independent predictor of suicidal ideation warrants further investigation, and may particularly help to identify those at risk of beginning a harmful pattern of social isolation eventuating in suicidality.

Endnotes

1. American Psychiatric Association (2000). *Diagnostic and Statistical Manual of Mental Disorders*, 4th ed. (Text Revised Ed.) Washington: American Psychiatric Association.
2. Beck AT, Steer RA (1987). *Manual for revised Beck Depression Inventory*. San Antonio: Psychological Corporation.
3. De Leo D, Cerin E, Spathonis K, Burgis S (2005). Lifetime risk of suicide ideation and attempts in an Australian community: Prevalence, suicidal process, and help-seeking behaviour. *Journal of Affective Disorders* 86, 215-224.
4. De Gioannis A, De Leo (2012). Managing suicidal patients in clinical practice. *Open Journal of Psychiatry* 2, 49-60.
5. Taylor A, Dal Grande E, Gill T, Fisher L, Goldney R (2007). Detecting determinants of suicidal ideation: South Australian surveillance system results. *International Journal of Public Health* 52, 142-152.

Recommended Readings

Family centered brief intensive treatment: A pilot study of an outpatient treatment for acute suicidal ideation

Anastasia TT, Humphries-Wadsworth T, Pepper CM, Pearson TM (USA)
Suicide and Life-Threataning Behavior. Published online: 28 August 2014. doi: 10.1111/sltb.12114, 2014

Family Centered Brief Intensive Treatment (FC BIT), a hospital diversion treatment program for individuals with acute suicidal ideation, was developed to treat suicidal clients and their families. Individuals who met criteria for hospitalization were treated as outpatients using FC BIT (n = 19) or an intensive outpatient treatment without the family component (IOP; n = 24). Clients receiving FC BIT identified family members or supportive others to participate in therapy. FC BIT clients had significantly greater improvement at the end of treatment compared to IOP clients on measures of depression, hopelessness, and suicidality. Further research is needed to test the efficacy of FC BIT.

The SAFETY program: A treatment-development trial of a cognitive-behavioral family treatment for adolescent suicide attempters

Asarnow JR, Berk M, Hughes JL, Anderson NL (USA)
Journal of Clinical Child and Adolescent Psychology. Published online: 25 September 2014. doi: 10.1080/15374416.2014.940624, 2014

The purpose of this article is to describe feasibility, safety, and outcome results from a treatment development trial of the SAFETY Program, a brief intervention designed for integration with emergency services for suicide-attempting youths. Suicide-attempting youths, ages 11 to 18, were enrolled in a 12-week trial of the SAFETY Program, a cognitive-behavioral family intervention designed to increase safety and reduce suicide attempt (SA) risk (N = 35). Rooted in a social-ecological cognitive-behavioral model, treatment sessions included individual youth and parent session-components, with different therapists assigned to youths and parents, and family session-components to practice skills identified as critical in the pathway for preventing repeat SAs in individual youths. Outcomes were evaluated at baseline, 3-month, and 6-month follow-ups. At the 3-month posttreatment assessment, there were statistically significant improvements on measures of suicidal behavior, hopelessness, youth and parent depression, and youth social adjustment. There was one reported SA by 3 months and another by 6 months, yielding cumulative attempt rates of 3% and 6% at 3 and 6 months, respectively. Treatment satisfaction was high. Suicide-attempting youths are at high risk for repeat attempts and continuing mental health problems. Results support the value of a randomized controlled trial to further evaluate the SAFETY intervention. Extension of treatment effects to parent depression and youth social adjustment are consistent with our strong family focus and social-ecological model of behavior change.

Improvement in suicidal ideation after ketamine infusion: Relationship to reductions in depression and anxiety

Ballard ED, Ionescu DF, Vande Voort JL, Niciu MJ, Richards EM, Luckenbaugh DA, Brutsché NE, Ameli R, Furey ML, Zarate Jr CA (USA)

Journal of Psychiatric Research 58, 161–166, 2014

Objective: Suicide is a psychiatric emergency. Currently, there are no approved pharmacologic treatments for suicidal ideation. Ketamine is an N-methyl-D-aspartate (NMDA) receptor antagonist that rapidly reduces suicidal ideation as well as depression and anxiety, but the dynamic between these symptoms is not known. The aim of this analysis was to evaluate whether ketamine has an impact on suicidal thoughts, independent of depressive and anxiety symptoms.

Methods: 133 patients with treatment-resistant depression (major depressive disorder or bipolar I/II disorder) received a single subanesthetic infusion of ketamine (0.5 mg/kg over 40 min). Post-hoc correlations and linear mixed models evaluated the relationship between suicidal ideation and depression and anxiety symptoms using the Hamilton Depression Rating Scale (HAMD), Scale for Suicidal Ideation (SSI), Beck Depression Inventory (BDI), and Hamilton Anxiety Rating Scale (HAMA) focusing on 230 min post-infusion.

Results: At 230 min post-infusion, correlations between changes in suicidal ideation and depression ranged from 0.23 to 0.44 ($p < .05$), accounting for up to 19% in the variance of ideation change. Correlations with anxiety ranged from 0.23 to 0.40 ($p < .05$), accounting for similar levels of variance. Ketamine infusion was associated with significant reductions in suicidal ideation compared to placebo, when controlling for the effects of ketamine on depression ($F_{1,587} = 10.31$, $p = .001$) and anxiety ($F_{1,567} = 8.54$, $p = .004$).

Conclusions: Improvements in suicidal ideation after ketamine infusion are related to, but not completely driven by, improvements in depression and anxiety. Investigation of the specific effects of ketamine on suicidal thoughts is warranted.

Adverse conditions at the workplace are associated with increased suicide risk

Baumert J, Schneider B, Lukaschek K, Emeny RT, Meisinger C, Erazo N, Dragano N, Ladwig KH (Germany)

Journal of Psychiatric Research 57, 90–95, 2014.

Object: The present study addressed potential harms of a negative working environment for employed subjects. The main aim was to evaluate if adverse working conditions and job strain are related to an increase in suicide mortality.

Methods: The study population consisted of 6817 participants drawn from the MONICA/KORA Augsburg, Germany, surveys conducted in 1984-1995, being employed at baseline examination and followed up on average for 12.6 years. Adverse working conditions were assessed by an instrument of 16 items about chronobiological, physical and psychosocial conditions at the workplace, job strain was assessed as defined by Karasek. Suicide risks were estimated by Cox regression adjusted for suicide-related risk factors.

Results: A number of 28 suicide cases were observed within follow-up. High levels of adversity in chronobiological/physical working conditions significantly increased the risk for suicide mortality (HR 3.28, 95% CI 1.43-7.54) compared to low/intermediate levels in a model adjusted for age, sex and survey (p value 0.005). Additional adjustment for living alone, low educational level, smoking, high alcohol consumption, obesity and depressed mood attenuated this effect (HR 2.73) but significance remained (p value 0.022). Adverse psychosocial working conditions and job strain, in contrast, had no impact on subsequent suicide mortality risk (p values > 0.200).

Conclusions: A negative working environment concerning chronobiological or physical conditions at the workplace had an unfavourable impact on suicide mortality risk, even after controlling for relevant suicide-related risk factors. Employer interventions aimed to improve workplace conditions might be considered as a suitable means to prevent suicides among employees

Harmful or helpful? The role of the internet in self-harming and suicidal behaviour in young people

Bell J (Australia)
Mental Health Review Journal 19, 61-71, 2014

Purpose: The internet plays an important role in the lives of self-harming and suicidal young people yet little is known about how internet use influences this behaviour. The purpose of this paper is to examine the evidence base with a view to determining directions for future research and practice.

Design/methodology/approach: Literature relating to self-harming and suicidal behaviour, young people, and the internet is reviewed with a focus on content and methodology.

Findings: The internet provides access to: "how-to" descriptions of suicide; unregulated/illegal online pharmacies; forums to spread this information; access to others seeking to end their own lives. Such sites are believed to elevate risk amongst vulnerable individuals. Conversely, the internet provides access to intervention and prevention activity, online support groups, advice, and personal chat. These can be a key resource in helping young people. There is a lack of consensus on what constitutes harmful and helpful online exchange, often evidenced in disparity between the perceptions of professionals and users.

Research limitations/implications: Research is needed to map out a more accurate picture of suicide and self-harm resources on the internet and to establish a consensus about what constitutes harmful and helpful exchange. This needs to be based on: a comprehensive and informed range of search terms; a clear distinction between types of resource; a clear and consistent rationale for distinguishing and categorizing sites; a systematic replicable methodology for plotting the scope, content, accessibility, and popularity of web resources at a given point in time; the views of young people who use these sites, as well as practitioners and professionals.

Practical implications: Practitioners need to: regularly assess the quantity, quality, and nature of selfharm/suicide focused internet use amongst service users; be aware of which sites are most appropriate for particular individuals; promote sites directed at young people that enhance effective coping. Professional mental health organizations need to find ways of ensuring that: they are consistently well represented amongst search results online; sites are readily accessible; more practitioners are trained in text-based communications.

Originality/value: This paper offers a framework and rationale for future research and for those involved in service provision, policy, and practice.

A contact-based intervention for people recently discharged from inpatient psychiatric care: A pilot study

Bennewith O, Evans J, Donovan J, Paramasivan S, Owen-Smith A, Hollingworth W, Davies R, O'Connor S, Hawton K, Kapur N, Gunnell D (UK)

Archives of Suicide Research 18, 131-143, 2014

People recently discharged from inpatient psychiatric care are at high risk of suicide and self-harm, with 6% of all suicides in England occurring in the 3 months after discharge. There is some evidence from a randomised trial carried out in the United States in the 1960s-70 s that supportive letters sent by psychiatrists to high-risk patients in the period following hospital discharge resulted in a reduction in suicide. The aim of the current pilot study was to assess the feasibility of conducting a similar trial, but in a broader group of psychiatric discharges, in the context of present day UK clinical practice. The intervention was piloted on three psychiatric inpatient wards in South West England. On two wards a series of eight letters were sent to patients over the 12 months after discharge and 6 letters were sent from the third ward over a 6 month period. 102 patients discharged from the wards received at least one letter, but only 45 (44.1%) received the full series of letters. The main reasons for drop-out were patient opt-out (n = 24) or readmission (n = 26). In the context of a policy of intensive follow-up post-discharge, qualitative interviews with service users showed that most already felt adequately supported and the intervention added little to this. Those interviewed felt that it was possible that the intervention might benefit people new to or with little follow-up from mental health services but that fewer letters should be mailed.

A review of multidisciplinary clinical practice guidelines in suicide prevention: Toward an emerging standard in suicide risk assessment and management, training and practice

Bernert RA, Hom MA, Roberts LW (USA)

Academic Psychiatry 38, 585-592, 2014

Objective: The current paper aims to: (1) examine clinical practice guidelines in suicide prevention across fields, organizations, and clinical specialties and (2) inform emerging standards in clinical practice, research, and training.

Methods: The authors conducted a systematic literature review to identify clinical practice guidelines and resource documents in suicide prevention and risk management. The authors used PubMed, Google Scholar, and Google Search, and keywords included: clinical practice guideline, practice guideline, practice parameters, suicide, suicidality, suicidal behaviors, assessment, and management. To assess for commonalities, the authors reviewed guidelines and resource documents across 13 key content categories and assessed whether each document suggested validated assessment measures.

Results: The search generated 101 source documents, which included N = 10 clinical practice guidelines and N = 12 additional resource documents (e.g., non-formalized guidelines, tool-kits). All guidelines (100 %) provided detailed recommendations for the use of evidence-based risk factors and protective factors, 80 % provided brief (but not detailed) recommendations for the assessment of suicidal intent, and 70 % recommended risk management strategies. By comparison, only 30 % discussed standardization of risk-level categorizations and other content areas considered central to best practices in suicide prevention (e.g., restricting access to means, ethical considerations, confidentiality/legal issues, training, and postvention practices). Resource documents were largely consistent with these findings.

Conclusions: Current guidelines address similar aspects of suicide risk assessment and management, but significant discrepancies exist. A lack of consensus was evident in recommendations across core competencies, which may be improved by increased standardization in practice and training. Additional resources appear useful for supplemental use.

Association of poor subjective sleep quality with risk for death by suicide during a 10-year period: A longitudinal, population-based study of late life

Bernert RA, Turvey CL, Conwell Y, Joiner TE (USA)

JAMA Psychiatry 71, 1129-1137, 2014

Importance: Older adults have high rates of sleep disturbance, die by suicide at disproportionately higher rates compared with other age groups, and tend to visit their physician in the weeks preceding suicide death. To our knowledge, to date, no study has examined disturbed sleep as an independent risk factor for late-life suicide.

Objective: To examine the relative independent risk for suicide associated with poor subjective sleep quality in a population-based study of older adults during a 10-year observation period.

Design, Setting, and Participants: A longitudinal case-control cohort study of late-life suicide among a multisite, population-based community sample of older adults participating in the Established Populations for Epidemiologic Studies of the Elderly. Of 14 456 community older adults sampled, 400 control subjects were matched (on age, sex, and study site) to 20 suicide decedents.

Main Outcomes and Measures: Primary measures included the Sleep Quality Index, the Center for Epidemiologic Studies-Depression Scale, and vital statistics.

Results: Hierarchical logistic regressions revealed that poor sleep quality at baseline was significantly associated with increased risk for suicide (odds ratio [OR], 1.39; 95% CI, 1.14-1.69; $P < .001$) by 10 follow-up years. In addition, 2 sleep items were individually associated with elevated risk for suicide at 10-year follow-up: difficulty falling asleep (OR, 2.24; 95% CI, 1.27-3.93; $P < .01$) and nonrestorative sleep (OR, 2.17; 95% CI, 1.28-3.67; $P < .01$). Controlling for depressive symptoms, baseline self-reported sleep quality was associated with increased risk for death by suicide (OR, 1.30; 95% CI, 1.04-1.63; $P < .05$).

Conclusions and Relevance: Our results indicate that poor subjective sleep quality is associated with increased risk for death by suicide 10 years later, even after adjustment for depressive symptoms. Disturbed sleep appears to confer considerable risk, independent of depressed mood, for the most severe suicidal behaviors and may warrant inclusion in suicide risk assessment frameworks to enhance detection of risk and intervention opportunity in late life.

Method of suicide attempt and reaction to survival as predictors of repeat suicide attempts: A longitudinal analysis

Bhaskaran J, Wang Y, Roos L, Sareen J, Skakum K, Bolton JM (Canada)
Journal of Clinical Psychiatry 75, e802-808, 2014

Objective: To evaluate whether reaction to survival of a suicide attempt and method of the index attempt predicted repeat suicide attempts within 6 months.
Method: Data came from the Suicide Assessment Form in Emergency Psychiatry (SAFE) Database Project, which contains information on all presentations to emergency psychiatric services at the 2 tertiary hospitals in Manitoba, Winnipeg, Canada (N = 7,007). During a 4-year period (2009-2012), 922 individuals presented with suicide attempts. Logistic regressions were used to examine whether a person's reaction to attempt survival and the method of attempt predicted repeat suicide attempt within 6 months.
Results: Of the 922 participants, 82 (8.8%) presented with another suicide attempt within 6 months. Ambivalence about attempt survival (adjusted odds ratio [OR] = 2.84; 95% CI, 1.45-5.54; P <.01) and wishing to be dead (adjusted OR = 2.68; 95% CI, 1.17-6.17; P <.05) predicted future attempts even when adjusted for age, sex, depression, substance abuse, and method of the initial attempt. Method of the index attempt did not predict future suicide attempts in adjusted models (adjusted OR = 0.66; 95% CI, 0.35-1.25; P >.05).
Conclusions: Assessment of the patient's reaction to survival, regardless of method of attempt, is important to identify risk of repeat attempts.

Risk of suicide and suicide attempts associated with physical disorders: A population-based, balancing score-matched analysis

Bolton JM, Walld R, Chateau D, Finlayson G, Sareen J (Canada)
Psychological Medicine. Published online: 17 July 2014. doi: 10.1017/S0033291714001639, 2014

Background: The association between physical disorders and suicide remains unclear. The aim of this study was to examine the relationship between physical disorders and suicide after accounting for the effects of mental disorders.
Method: Individuals who died by suicide (n = 2100) between 1996 and 2009 were matched 3:1 by balancing score to general population controls (n = 6300). Multivariate conditional logistic regression compared the two groups across physician-diagnosed physical disorders [asthma, chronic obstructive pulmonary disease (COPD), ischemic heart disease, hypertension, diabetes, cancer, multiple sclerosis and inflammatory bowel disease], adjusting for mental disorders and co-morbidity. Secondary analyses examined the risk of suicide according to time since first diagnosis of each physical disorder (1-90, 91-364, ≥ 365 days). Similar analyses also compared individuals with suicide attempts (n = 8641) to matched controls (n = 25 923).
Results: Cancer was associated with increased risk of suicide [adjusted odds ratio (AOR) 1.40, 95% confidence interval (CI) 1.03-1.91, p < 0.05] even after adjusting for all mental disorders. The risk of suicide with cancer was particularly high

in the first 90 days after initial diagnosis (AOR 4.10, 95% CI 1.71-9.82, p < 0.01) and decreased to non-significance after 1 year. Women with respiratory diseases had elevated risk of suicide whereas men did not. COPD, hypertension and diabetes were each associated with increased odds of suicide attempts in adjusted models (AORs ranged from 1.20 to 1.73).

Conclusions: People diagnosed with cancer are at increased risk of suicide, especially in the 3 months following initial diagnosis. Increased support and psychiatric involvement should be considered for the first year after cancer diagnosis.

Suicide contagion: A systematic review of definitions and research utility

Cheng Q, Li H, Silenzio V, Caine ED (USA)

PLoS ONE. Published online: 26 September 2014. doi: 10.1371/journal.pone.0108724, 2014

Objectives: Despite the common use of contagion to analogize the spread of suicide, there is a lack of rigorous assessment of the underlying concept or theory supporting the use of this term. The present study aims to examine the varied definitions and potential utility of the term contagion in suicide-related research.

Methods: 100 initial records and 240 reference records in English were identified as relevant with our research objectives, through systematic literature screening. We then conducted narrative syntheses of various definitions and assessed their potential value for generating new research.

Results: 20.3% of the 340 records used contagion as equivalent to clustering (contagion-as-cluster); 68.5% used it to refer to various, often related mechanisms underlying the clustering phenomenon (contagion-as-mechanism); and 11.2% without clear definition. Under the category of contagion-as-mechanism, four mechanisms have been proposed to explain how suicide clusters occurred: transmission (contagion-as-transmission), imitation (contagion-as-imitation), contextual influence (contagion-as-context), and affiliation (contagion-as-affiliation). Contagion-as-cluster both confounds and constrains inquiry into suicide clustering by blending proposed mechanism with the phenomenon to be studied. Contagion-as-transmission is, in essence, a double or internally redundant metaphor. Contagion-as-affiliation and contagion-as-context involve mechanisms that are common mechanisms that often occur independently of apparent contagion, or may serve as a facilitating background. When used indiscriminately, these terms may create research blind spots. Contagion-as-imitation combines perspectives from psychology, sociology, and public health research and provides the greatest heuristic utility for examining whether and how suicide and suicidal behaviors may spread among persons at both individual and population levels.

Conclusion: Clarifying the concept of "suicide contagion" is an essential step for more thoroughly investigating its mechanisms. Developing a clearer understanding of the apparent spread of suicide-promoting influences can, in turn, offer insights necessary to build the scientific foundation for prevention and intervention strategies that can be applied at both individual and community levels.

Reducing the burden of suicide in the U.S. The aspirational research goals of the national action alliance for suicide prevention research prioritization task force

Claassen CA, Pearson JL, Khodyakov D, Satow PM, Gebbia R, Berman AL, Reidenberg DJ, Feldman S, Molock S, Carras MC, Lento RM, Sherrill J, Pringle B, Dalal S, Insel TR (USA)

American Journal of Preventive Medicine 47, 309-314, 2014

Background: The National Action Alliance for Suicide Prevention Research Prioritization Task Force (RPTF) has created a prioritized national research agenda with the potential to rapidly and substantially reduce the suicide burden in the U.S. if fully funded and implemented.

Purpose: Viable, sustainable scientific research agendas addressing challenging public health issues such as suicide often need to incorporate perspectives from multiple stakeholder groups (e.g., researchers, policymakers, and other end-users of new knowledge) during an agenda-setting process. The Stakeholder Survey was a web-based survey conducted and analyzed in 2011-2012 to inform the goal-setting step in the RPTF agenda development process. The survey process, and the final list of "aspirational" research goals it produced, are presented here.

Methods: Using a modified Delphi process, diverse constituent groups generated and evaluated candidate research goals addressing pressing suicide prevention research needs.

Results: A total of 716 respondents representing 49 U.S. states and 18 foreign countries provided input that ultimately produced 12 overarching, research-informed aspirational goals aimed at reducing the U.S. suicide burden. Highest-rated goals addressed prevention of subsequent suicidal behavior after an initial attempt, strategies to retain patients in care, improved healthcare provider training, and generating care models that would ensure accessible treatment.

Conclusions: The Stakeholder Survey yielded widely valued research targets. Findings were diverse in focus, type, and current phase of research development but tended to prioritize practical solutions over theoretical advancement. Other complex public health problems requiring input from a broad-based constituency might benefit from web-based tools that facilitate such community input.

Mortality risks among persons reporting same-sex sexual partners: Evidence from the 2008 general social survey-national death index data set

Cochran SD, Mays VM (USA)

American Journal of Public Health. Published online: 17 July 2014. doi: 10.2105/AJPH.2014.301974, 2014

Objectives: We investigated the possibility that men who have sex with men (MSM) and women who have sex with women (WSW) may be at higher risk for early mortality associated with suicide and other sexual orientation-associated health risks.

Methods: We used data from the 1988-2002 General Social Surveys, with respondents followed up for mortality status as of December 31, 2008. The surveys included 17 886 persons aged 18 years or older, who reported at least 1 lifetime sexual partner. Of these, 853 reported any same-sex partners; 17 033 reported only different-sex partners. Using gender-stratified analyses, we compared these 2 groups for all-cause mortality and HIV-, suicide-, and breast cancer-related mortality.

Results: The WSW evidenced greater risk for suicide mortality than presumptively heterosexual women, but there was no evidence of similar sexual orientation-associated risk among men. All-cause mortality did not appear to differ by sexual orientation among either women or men. HIV-related deaths were not elevated among MSM or breast cancer deaths among WSW.

Conclusions: The elevated suicide mortality risk observed among WSW partially confirms public health concerns that sexual minorities experience greater burden from suicide-related mortality.

Sources of psychological pain and suicidal thoughts among homeless adults

Coohey C, Easton SD, Kong J, Bockenstedt JKW (USA)

Suicide and Life-Threatening Behavior. Published online: 25 September 2014. doi: 10.1111/sltb.12126, 2014

Homeless adults experience problems in multiple areas of their lives. It was hypothesized that adults who were troubled by problems in more areas of their lives would be more likely to report suicidal thoughts. The sample included 457 homeless men and women who resided in three emergency shelters. The number of sources of psychological pain, past suicide attempts, and being a man predicted current suicidal thoughts, but being diagnosed with a depressive disorder did not. Shelter workers should ask adults whether they have attempted suicide in the past and how troubled they are by each area of their lives.

Suicide and the 2008 economic recession: Who is most at risk? Trends in suicide rates in England and Wales 2001-2011

Coope C, Gunnell D, Hollingworth W, Hawton K, Kapur N, Fearn V, Wells C, Metcalfe C (UK)
Social Science & Medicine 117, 76-85, 2014

The negative impacts of previous economic recessions on suicide rates have largely been attributed to rapid rises in unemployment in the context of inadequate social and work protection programmes. We have investigated trends in indicators of the 2008 economic recession and trends in suicide rates in England and Wales in men and women of working age (16-64 years old) for the period 2001-2011, before, during and after the economic recession, our aim was to identify demographic groups whose suicide rates were most affected. We found no clear evidence of an association between trends in female suicide rates and indicators of economic recession. Evidence of a halt in the previous downward trend in suicide rates occurred for men aged 16-34 years in 2006 (95% CI Quarter 3 (Q3) 2004, Q3 2007 for 16-24 year olds & Q1 2005, Q4 2006 for 25-34 year olds), whilst suicide rates in 35-44 year old men reversed from a downward to upward trend in early 2010 (95% CI Q4 2008, Q2 2011). For the younger men (16-34 years) this change preceded the sharp increases in redundancy and unemployment rates of early 2008 and lagged behind rising trends in house repossessions and bankruptcy that began around 2003. An exception were the 35-44 year old men for whom a change in suicide rate trends from downwards to upwards coincided with peaks in redundancies, unemployment and rises in long-term unemployment. Suicide rates across the decade rose monotonically in men aged 45-64 years. Male suicide in the most-to-medium deprived areas showed evidence of decreasing rates across the decade, whilst in the least-deprived areas suicide rates were fairly static but remained much lower than those in the most-deprived areas. There were small post-recession increases in the proportion of suicides in men in higher management/professional, small employer/self-employed occupations and fulltime education. A halt in the downward trend in suicide rates amongst men aged 16-34 years, may have begun before the 2008 economic recession whilst for men aged 35-44 years old increased suicide rates mirrored recession related unemployment. This evidence suggests indicators of economic strain other than unemployment and redundancies, such as personal debt and house repossessions may contribute to increased suicide rates in younger-age men whilst for men aged 35-44 years old job loss and long-term unemployment is a key risk factor.

Effectiveness of community facilitator training in improving knowledge, attitudes, and confidence in relation to depression and suicidal behavior: Results of the OSPI-Europe intervention in four European countries

Coppens E, Van Audenhove C, Iddi S, Arensman E, Gottlebe K, Koburger N, Coffey C, Gusmão R, Quintão S, Costa S, Székely A, Hegerl U (Belgium, Ireland, Germany, Portugal, Hungary)
Journal of Affective Disorders 165, 142-150, 2014

Background: Community facilitators (CFs), such as teachers, nurses and social workers, are well placed as gatekeepers for depression and suicidal behavior, but not properly prepared to provide preventive and supportive services. The current study aimed: (1) to improve CFs' attitudes toward depression, knowledge on suicide, and confidence to detect suicidal behavior in four European countries and (2) to identify specific training needs across regions and CF groups.

Methods: A standardized training program was provided to 1276 CFs in Germany, Hungary, Ireland, and Portugal. Attitudes toward depression, knowledge about suicide, and confidence in identifying suicidal persons were assessed before training, after training, and at three to six months follow-up. Additionally, several participants' characteristics were registered.

Results: At baseline, CFs showed relatively favorable attitudes toward depression, but limited knowledge on suicide, and little confidence to identify suicidal behavior. Basic skills strongly differed across CF groups and countries. For example, in Germany, carers for the elderly, nurses, teachers, and managers were most in need of training, while in Portugal pharmacists and the clergy appeared to be important target groups. Most importantly, the training program improved the competencies of CF groups across countries and these improvements were sustained after three to six months. CFs with low basic skills benefited most of the training.

Limitations: The observed training effects could be influenced by other external factors as our results are based upon a pre-post comparison with no control group.

Conclusions: Gatekeeper trainings in community settings are successful in improving knowledge, reshaping attitudes, and boosting the confidence of gatekeepers. The most effective strategy to achieve the preferred objectives is to target those CF groups that are most in need of training and to tailor the content of the training program to the individual needs of the target group.

Awareness, attitudes, and use of crisis hotlines among youth at-risk for suicide

Crosby Budinger M, Cwik MF, Riddle MA (USA)

Suicide and Life-Threatening Behavior. Published online: 5 August 2014. doi: 10.1111/sltb.12112, 2014

Crisis hotlines have been central to suicide prevention efforts; however, utilization among youth remains low. A sample of at-risk youth was surveyed about their awareness, utilization, and attitudes toward local and national crisis hotlines. Youth reported low rates of awareness and utilization, yet expressed a strong interest in phone hotlines (41% vs. 59% for new media categories combined). Youth reported stigma, but that help-seeking could be positively influenced by peers and adults in their support system. Implications include making crisis services available across several mediums and the importance of engaging trusted others in youth suicide awareness campaigns and prevention efforts.

Does asking about suicide and related behaviours induce suicidal ideation? What is the evidence?

Dazzi T, Gribble R, Wessely S, Fear NT (UK)

Psychological Medicine 44, 3361-3363, 2014

There is a commonly held perception in psychology that enquiring about suicidality, either in research or clinical settings, can increase suicidal tendencies. While the potential vulnerability of participants involved in psychological research must be addressed, apprehensions about conducting studies of suicidality create a Catch-22 situation for researchers. Ethics committees require evidence that proposed studies will not cause distress or suicidal ideation, yet a lack of published research can mean allaying these fears is difficult. Concerns also exist in psychiatric settings where risk assessments are important for ensuring patient safety. But are these concerns based on evidence? We conducted a review of the published literature examining whether enquiring about suicide induces suicidal ideation in adults and adolescents, and general and at-risk populations. None found a statistically significant increase in suicidal ideation among participants asked about suicidal thoughts. Our findings suggest acknowledging and talking about suicide may in fact reduce, rather than increase suicidal ideation, and may lead to improvements in mental health in treatment-seeking populations. Recurring ethical concerns about asking about suicidality could be relaxed to encourage and improve research into suicidal ideation and related behaviours without negatively affecting the well-being of participants.

Suicide ideation and attempts and bullying in children and adolescents

Dickerson Mayes S, Baweja R, Calhoun SL, Syed E, Mahr F, Siddiqui F (USA)

Crisis 35, 301-309, 2014

Background: Studies of the relationship between bullying and suicide behavior yield mixed results.

Aims: This is the first study comparing frequencies of suicide behavior in four bullying groups (bully, victim, bully/victim, and neither) in two large psychiatric and community samples of young children and adolescents.

Method: Maternal ratings of bullying and suicide ideation and attempts were analyzed for 1,291 children with psychiatric disorders and 658 children in the general population 6-18 years old.

Results: For both the psychiatric and community samples, suicide ideation and attempt scores for bully/victims were significantly higher than for victims only and for neither bullies nor victims. Differences between victims only and neither victims nor bullies were nonsignificant. Controlling for sadness and conduct problems, suicide behavior did not differ between the four bullying groups. All children with suicide attempts had a comorbid psychiatric disorder, as did all but two children with suicide ideation.

Conclusion: Although the contribution of bullying per se to suicide behavior independent of sadness and conduct problems is small, bullying has obvious negative psychological consequences that make intervention imperative. Interventions need to focus on the psychopathology associated with being a victim and/or perpetrator of bullying in order to reduce suicide behavior.

Associations between bullying and engaging in aggressive and suicidal behaviors among sexual minority youth: The moderating role of connectedness

Duong J, Bradshaw C (USA)

Journal of School Health 84, 636-645, 2014

Purpose: To report the prevalence of students according to four gender groups (i.e., those who reported being non-transgender, transgender, or not sure about their gender, and those who did not understand the transgender question), and to describe their health and well-being.

Methods: Logistic regressions were used to examine the associations between gender groups and selected outcomes in a nationally representative high school health and well-being survey, undertaken in 2012.

Results: Of the students (n = 8,166), 94.7% reported being non-transgender, 1.2% reported being transgender, 2.5% reported being not sure about their gender, and 1.7% did not understand the question. Students who reported being transgender or not sure about their gender or did not understand the question had compromised health and well-being relative to their non-transgender peers; in particular, for transgender students perceiving that a parent cared about them (odds ratio [OR], .3; 95% confidence interval [CI], .2-.4), depressive symptoms (OR, 5.7; 95% CI, 3.6-9.2), suicide attempts (OR, 5.0; 95% CI, 2.9-8.8), and school bullying (OR, 4.5; 95% CI, 2.4-8.2).

Conclusions: This is the first nationally representative survey to report the health and well-being of students who report being transgender. We found that transgender students and those reporting not being sure are a numerically small but important group. Transgender students are diverse and are represented across demographic variables, including their sexual attractions. Transgender youth face considerable health and well-being disparities. It is important to address the challenging environments these students face and to increase access to responsive services for transgender youth

Violent crime, suicide, and premature mortality in patients with schizophrenia and related disorders: A 38-year total population study in Sweden

Fazel S, Wolf A, Palm C, Lichtenstein P (UK, Sweden)
Lancet Psychiatry 1, 44-54, 2014

Background: People with schizophrenia and related disorders are at an increased risk of adverse outcomes, including conviction of a violent offence, suicide, and premature mortality. However, the rates of, and risk factors for, these outcomes need clarification as a basis for population-based and targeted interventions. We aimed to determine rates and risk factors for these outcomes, and investigate to what extent they are shared across outcomes and are specific to schizophrenia and related disorders.

Methods: We undertook a total population cohort study in Sweden of 24 297 patients with schizophrenia and related disorders between January, 1972 and December, 2009. Patients were matched by age and sex to people from the general population (n=485 940) and also to unaffected sibling controls (n=26 357). First, we investigated rates of conviction of a violent offence, suicide, and premature mortality, with follow-up until conviction of a violent offence, emigration, death, or end of follow-up (Dec 31, 2009), whichever occurred first. Second, we analysed associations between these adverse outcomes and sociodemographic, individual, familial, and distal risk factors, for men and women separately, with Cox proportional hazards models. Finally, we assessed time trends in adverse outcomes between 1972 and 2009, for which we compared patients with unaffected siblings, and analysed associations with changes in the number of nights spent in inpatient beds in psychiatric facilities nationwide.

Findings: Within 5 years of their initial diagnosis, 13.9% of men and 4.7% of women with schizophrenia and related disorders had a major adverse outcome (10.7% of men and 2.7% of women were convicted of a violent offence, and 3.3% of men and 2.0% of women died prematurely of any cause). During the study, the adjusted odds ratio of any adverse outcomes for patients compared with general population controls was 7.5 (95% CI 7.2-7.9) in men and 11.1 (10.2-12.1) in women. Three risk factors that were present before diagnosis were predictive of any adverse outcome: drug use disorders, criminality, and self-harm, which were also risk factors for these outcomes in unaffected siblings and in the general population. Over the period 1973-2009, the odds of these outcomes increased in patients with schizophrenia and related disorders compared with unaffected siblings.

Interpretation: Schizophrenia and related disorders are associated with substantially increased rates of violent crime, suicide, and premature mortality. Risk factors for these three outcomes included both those specific to individuals with schizophrenia and related disorders, and those shared with the general population. Therefore, a combination of population-based and targeted strategies might be necessary to reduce the substantial rates of adverse outcomes in patients with schizophrenia and related disorders.

Ketamine administration in depressive disorders: A systematic review and meta-analysis

Fond G, Loundou A, Rabu C, Macgregor A, Lancon C, Brittner M, Micoulaud-Franchi JA, Richieri R, Courtet P, Abbar M, Roger M, Leboyer M, Boyer L (France)
Psychopharmacology 231, 3663-3676, 2014

Introduction: Ketamine's efficacy in depressive disorders has been established in several controlled trials. The aim of the present study was to determine whether or not ketamine administration significantly improves depressive symptomatology in depression and more specifically in major depressive disorder (MDD), bipolar depression, resistant depression (non-ECT studies), and as an anesthetic agent in electroconvulsive therapy (ECT) for resistant depression (ECT studies). Secondary outcomes were the duration of ketamine's effect, the efficacy on suicidal ideations, the existence of a dose effect, and the safety/tolerance of the treatment.

Methods: Studies were included if they met the following criteria (without any language or date restriction): design: randomized controlled trials, intervention: ketamine administration, participants: diagnosis of depression, and evaluation of severity based on a validated scale. We calculated standardized mean differences (SMDs) with 95 % confidence intervals (CIs) for each study. We used fixed and random effects models. Heterogeneity was assessed using the I2 statistic.

Results: We included nine non-ECT studies in our quantitative analysis (192 patients with major depressive disorder and 34 patients with bipolar depression). Overall, depression scores were significantly decreased in the ketamine groups compared to those in the control groups (SMD = -0.99; 95 % CI -1.23, -0.75; p < 0.01). Ketamine's efficacy was confirmed in MDD (resistant to previous pharmacological treatments or not) (SMD = -0.91; 95 % CI -1.19,-0.64; p < 0.01), in bipolar depression (SMD = -1.34; 95 % CI -1.94, -0.75), and in drug-free patients as well as patients under medication. Four ECT trials (118 patients) were included in our quantitative analysis. One hundred and three patients were diagnosed with major depressive disorder and 15 with bipolar depression. Overall, depression scores were significantly improved in the 58 patients receiving ketamine in ECT anesthesia induction compared to the 60 patients (SMD = -0.56; 95 % CI -1.10, -0.02; p = 0.04; I2 = 52.4 %). The duration of ketamine's effects was assessed in only two non-ECT studies and seemed to persist for 2-3 days; this result needs to be confirmed. Three of four studies found significant decrease of suicidal thoughts and one found no difference between groups, but suicidal ideations were only studied by the suicide item of the depressive scales. It was not possible to determine a dose effect; 0.5 mg/kg was used in the majority of the studies. Some cardiovascular events were described (mostly transient blood pressure elevation that may require treatment), and ketamine's use should remain cautious in patients with a cardiovascular history.

Conclusion: The present meta-analysis confirms ketamine's efficacy in depressive disorders in non-ECT studies, as well as in ECT studies. The results of this first meta-analysis are encouraging, and further studies are warranted to detail efficacy in bipolar disorders and other specific depressed populations. Middle- and long-term efficacy and safety have yet to be explored. Extrapolation should be cautious: Patients included had no history of psychotic episodes and no history of alcohol or substance use disorders, which is not representative of all the depressed patients that may benefit from this therapy

Increase in suicides associated with home eviction and foreclosure during the us housing crisis: Findings from 16 national violent death reporting system states, 2005-2010

Fowler KA, Gladden RM, Vagi KJ, Barnes J, Frazier L (USA)

American Journal of Public Health. Published online: 17 July 2014. doi: doi:10.2105/AJPH.2014.301945, 2014

Objectives: We aimed to determine the frequency, characteristics, and precipitating circumstances of eviction- and foreclosure-related suicides during the US housing crisis, which resulted in historically high foreclosures and increased evictions beginning in 2006.

Methods: We examined all eviction- and foreclosure-related suicides in the years 2005 to 2010 in 16 states in the National Violent Death Reporting System, a surveillance system for all violent deaths within participating states that abstracts information across multiple investigative sources (e.g., law enforcement, coroners, medical examiners).

Results: We identified 929 eviction- or foreclosure-related suicides. Eviction- and foreclosure-related suicides doubled from 2005 to 2010 (n = 88 in 2005; n = 176 in 2010), mostly because of foreclosure-related suicides, which increased 253% from 2005 (n = 30) to 2010 (n = 106). Most suicides occurred before the actual housing loss (79%), and 37% of decedents experienced acute eviction or foreclosure crises within 2 weeks of the suicide.

Conclusions: Housing loss is a significant crisis that can precipitate suicide. Prevention strategies include support for those projected to lose homes, intervention before move-out date, training financial professionals to recognize warning signs, and strengthening population-wide suicide prevention measures during economic crises.

A two-site pilot randomized 3 day trial of high dose left prefrontal repetitive transcranial magnetic stimulation (RTMS) for suicidal inpatients

George MS, Raman R, Benedek DM, Pelic CG, Grammer GG, Stokes KT, Schmidt M, Spiegel C, DeAlmeida N, Beaver KL, Borckardt JJ, Sun X, Jain S, Stein MB (USA)

Brain Stimulation 7, 421-431, 2014

Background: Suicide attempts and completed suicides are common, yet there are no proven acute medication or device treatments for treating a suicidal crisis. Repeated daily left prefrontal repetitive transcranial magnetic stimulation (rTMS) for 4-6 weeks is a new FDA-approved treatment for acute depression. Some open-label rTMS studies have found rapid reductions in suicidality.

Design: This study tests whether a high dose of rTMS to suicidal inpatients is feasible and safe, and also whether this higher dosing might rapidly improve suicidal thinking. This prospective, 2-site, randomized, active sham-controlled (1:1 randomization) design incorporated 9 sessions of rTMS over 3 days as adjunctive to usual inpatient suicidality treatment. The setting was two inpatient military hospital wards (one VA, the other DOD).

Patients: Research staff screened approximately 377 inpatients, yielding 41 adults admitted for suicidal crisis. Because of the funding source, all patients also had either post-traumatic stress disorder, mild traumatic brain injury, or both.

TMS methods: Repetitive TMS (rTMS) was delivered to the left prefrontal cortex with a figure-eight solid core coil at 120% motor threshold, 10 Hertz (Hz), 5 second (s) train duration, 10 s intertrain interval for 30 minutes (6000 pulses) 3 times daily for 3 days (total 9 sessions; 54,000 stimuli). Sham rTMS used a similar coil that contained a metal insert blocking the magnetic field and utilized electrodes on the scalp, which delivered a matched somatosensory sensation.

Main outcome measure: Primary outcomes were the daily change in severity of suicidal thinking as measured by the Beck Scale of Suicidal Ideation (SSI) administered at baseline and then daily, as well as subjective visual analog scale measures before and after each TMS session. Mixed model repeated measures (MMRM) analysis was performed on modified intent to treat (mITT) and completer populations.

Results: This intense schedule of rTMS with suicidal inpatients was feasible and safe. Minimal side effects occurred, none differing by arm, and the 3-day retention rate was 88%. No one died of suicide within the 6 month followup. From the mITT analyses, SSI scores declined rapidly over the 3 days for both groups (sham change -15.3 points, active change -15.4 points), with a trend for more rapid decline on the first day with active rTMS (sham change -6.4 points, active -10.7 points, P = 0.12). This decline was more pronounced in the completers subgroup [sham change -5.9 (95% CI: -10.1, -1.7), active -13 points (95% CI: -18.7, -7.4); P = 0.054]. Subjective ratings of 'being bothered by thoughts of suicide' declined non-significantly more with active rTMS than with sham at the end of 9 sessions of treatment in the mITT analysis [sham change -31.9 (95% CI: -41.7, -22.0), active change -42.5 (95% CI: -53.8, -31.2); P = 0.17]. There was a significant decrease in the completers sample [sham change -24.9 (95% CI: -34.4, -15.3), active change -43.8 (95% CI: -57.2, -30.3); P = 0.028].

Conclusions: Delivering high doses of left prefrontal rTMS over three days (54,000 stimuli) to suicidal inpatients is possible and safe, with few side effects and no worsening of suicidal thinking. The suggestions of a rapid anti-suicide effect (day 1 SSI data, Visual Analogue Scale data over the 3 days) need to be tested for replication in a larger sample.

Parental suicide attempt and offspring self-harm and suicidal thoughts: Results from the Avon longitudinal study of parents and children (ALSPAC) birth cohort

Geulayov G, Metcalfe C, Heron J, Kidger J, Gunnell D (UK)
Journal of the American Academy of Child and Adolescent Psychiatry 53, 509-517, 2014

Objective: Parental suicidal behavior is associated with offspring's risk of suicidal behavior. However, much of the available evidence is from population registers or clinical samples. We investigated the associations of self-reported parental suicide attempt (SA) with offspring self-harm and suicidal thoughts in the Avon Longitudinal Study of Parents and Children (ALSPAC), a prospective birth cohort.

Method: Parental SA was self-reported on 10 occasions from pregnancy until their child was 11 years of age. Offspring self-reported lifetime self-harm, with and without suicidal intent, suicidal thoughts, and suicide plans, at age 16 to 17 years. Multivariable regression models quantified the association between parental SA and offspring outcomes controlling for confounders.

Results: Data were available for 4,396 mother-child and 2,541 father-child pairs. Adjusting for confounders including parental depression, maternal SA was associated with a 3-fold increased risk of self-harm with suicidal intent in their children (adjusted odds ratio [aOR] = 2.94, 95% confidence interval [CI] = 1.43-6.07) but not with self-harm without suicidal intent (aOR = 0.83, 95% CI = 0.35-1.99). Children whose mother attempted suicide were more likely to report suicidal thoughts and plans (aOR = 5.04, 95% CI = 2.24-11.36; aOR = 2.17, 95% CI = 1.07-4.38, respectively). Findings in relation to paternal SA were somewhat weaker and not significant.

Conclusions: Maternal SA increased their offspring's risk of self-harm with suicidal intent and of suicidal thoughts, but was unrelated to self-harm without intent; findings for paternal suicide attempt were weaker and not significant. Maternal SA, which may not come to the attention of health care professionals, represents a major risk for psychiatric morbidity in their offspring.

Dialectical behaviour therapy-informed skills training for deliberate self-harm: A controlled trial with 3-month follow-up data

Gibson J, Booth R, Davenport J, Keogh K, Owens T (Ireland)

Behaviour Research and Therapy 60, 8-14, 2014

Dialectical Behaviour Therapy (DBT) has been shown to be an effective treatment for deliberate self-harm (DSH) and emerging evidence suggests DBT skills training alone may be a useful adaptation of the treatment. DBT skills are presumed to reduce maladaptive efforts to regulate emotional distress, such as DSH, by teaching adaptive methods of emotion regulation. However, the impact of DBT skills training on DSH and emotion regulation remains unclear. This study examined the Living Through Distress (LTD) programme, a DBT-informed skills group provided in an inpatient setting. Eighty-two adults presenting with DSH or Borderline Personality Disorder (BPD) were offered places in LTD, in addition to their usual care. A further 21 clients on the waiting list for LTD were recruited as a treatment-as-usual (TAU) group. DSH, anxiety, depression, and emotion regulation were assessed at baseline and either post-intervention or 6 week follow-up. Greater reductions in the frequency of DSH and improvements in some aspects of emotion regulation were associated with completion of LTD, as compared with TAU. Improvements in DSH were maintained at 3 month follow-up. This suggests providing a brief intensive DBT-informed skills group may be a useful intervention for DSH.

Violent and serious suicide attempters: One step closer to suicide?

Giner L, Jaussent I, Olie E, Beziat S, Guillaume S, Baca-Garcia E, Lopez-Castroman J, Courtet P (Spain)

The Journal of Clinical Psychiatry 75, e191-e197, 2014

Background: The use of violence in a suicide attempt and its medical consequences can be used to characterize specific subpopulations of suicide attempters that could be at higher risk of ever completing suicide.

Method: A population of 1,148 suicide attempters was consecutively recruited from 2001 to 2010. Violent suicide attempts were classified using Asberg's criteria. An overdose requiring hospitalization in an intensive care unit was considered a serious suicide attempt. In this exploratory study, we retrospectively compared 183 subjects who made a serious suicide attempt, 226 that made a violent suicide attempt, and 739 without any history of serious or violent suicide attempts with regard to demographic, clinical, and psychological characteristics and features of the suicide attempts using univariate and multivariate analyses.

Results: In comparison with subjects whose attempts were neither violent nor serious, violent attempters and serious attempters were more likely to make repeated suicide attempts (OR = 3.27 [95% CI, 1.39-7.70] and OR = 2.66 [95%

CI, 1.29-5.50], respectively), with higher medical lethality (OR = 6.66 [95% CI, 4.74-9.38] and OR = 3.91 [95% CI, 2.89-5.29], respectively). Additionally, violent attempts were associated with male gender (OR = 6.79; 95% CI, 3.59-12.82) and family history of suicidal behavior (particularly if serious or violent: OR = 6.96; 95% CI, 2.82-17.20), and serious attempters were more likely to be older (OR = 1.49, 95% CI, 1.12-1.99).

Conclusions: One of every 3 attempters in our sample had made violent or serious suicide attempts in their lifetime. Violent attempters and serious attempters presented differential characteristics, closer to those of suicide completers, compared to the rest of the sample.

Suicidal patients are deficient in vitamin D, associated with a pro-inflammatory status in the blood

Grudet C, Malm J, Westrin A, Brundin L (Sweden, USA)
Psychoneuroendocrinology 50, 210-219, 2014

Background: Low levels of vitamin D may play a role in psychiatric disorders, as cross-sectional studies show an association between vitamin D deficiency and depression, schizophrenia and psychotic symptoms. The underlying mechanisms are not well understood, although vitamin D is known to influence the immune system to promote a T helper (Th)-2 phenotype. At the same time, increased inflammation might be of importance in the pathophysiology of depression and suicide. We therefore hypothesized that suicidal patients would be deficient in vitamin D, which could be responsible for the inflammatory changes observed in these patients.

Methods: We compared vitamin D levels in suicide attempters (n=59), non-suicidal depressed patients (n=17) and healthy controls (n=14). Subjects were diagnosed according to the Diagnostic and Statistical Manual of Mental Disorders, 4th edition, and went through a structured interview by a specialist in psychiatry. 25(OH)D2 and 25(OH)D3 were measured in plasma using liquid-chromatography-mass-spectrometry (LC-MS). We further explored vitamin D's association with plasma IL-1beta, IL-6 and TNF-alpha.

Results: Suicide attempters had significantly lower mean levels of vitamin D than depressed non-suicidal patients and healthy controls. 58 percent of the suicide attempters were vitamin D deficient according to clinical standard. Moreover, there was a significant negative association between vitamin D and pro-inflammatory cytokines in the psychiatric patients. Low vitamin D levels were associated with higher levels of the inflammatory cytokines IL-6 and IL-1beta in the blood.

Conclusion: The suicide attempters in our study were deficient in vitamin D. Our data also suggest that vitamin D deficiency could be a contributing factor to the elevated pro-inflammatory cytokines previously reported in suicidal patients. We propose that routine clinical testing of vitamin D levels could be beneficial in patients with suicidal symptoms, with subsequent supplementation in patients found to be deficient.

Suicide by gases in England and Wales 2001-2011: Evidence of the emergence of new methods of suicide

Gunnell D, Coope C, Fearn V, Wells C, Chang SS, Hawton K, Kapur N (UK, China)

Journal of Affective Disorders 170, 190-195, 2014

Background: Increases in suicide deaths by gassing, particularly carbon monoxide poisoning from burning barbecue charcoal, have occurred in many parts of East Asia and resulted in rises in overall suicide rates in some countries. Recent trends in gas poisoning suicides outside Asia have received little attention.

Methods: We analysed suicides by gassing in England and Wales (2001-2011) using national suicide mortality data enhanced by free text searching of information sent by coroners to the Office for National Statistics (ONS). We conducted specific searches for suicides involving barbecue charcoal gas, helium, and hydrogen sulphide. We analysed coroners records of eight people who used helium as a method of suicide, identified from systematic searches of the records of four coroners.

Results: Gassing accounted for 5.2% of suicide deaths in England and Wales during 2001-2011. The number of gas suicides declined from 368 in 2001 to 174 by 2011 (a 53% reduction). The fall was due to a decline in deaths involving car exhaust and other sources of carbon monoxide. There was a rapid rise in deaths due to helium inhalation over the period, from five deaths in the two year period 2001-2002 to 89 in 2010-2011 (a 17-fold increase). There were small rises in deaths involving hydrogen sulphide (0 cases in 2001-2002 versus 14 cases in 2010-2011) and barbecue charcoal gas (1 case in 2001-2002 versus 11 cases in 2010-2011). Compared to individuals using other methods, those suicides adopting new types of gas for suicide were generally younger and from more affluent socioeconomic groups. The coroners records of four of the eight individuals dying by helium inhalation whose records were reviewed showed evidence of Internet involvement in their choice of method.

Limitations: We were not able to identify the source of carbon monoxide (car exhaust or barbecue charcoal) for over 50% of cases.

Conclusion: Increases in helium inhalation as a method of suicide have partially offset recent decreases in suicide by the use of car exhaust. Public health measures are urgently needed to prevent a potential epidemic rise in the use of helium similar to the recent rises in charcoal burning suicides in East Asia.

Improving national data systems for surveillance of suicide-related events

Ikeda R, Hedegaard H, Bossarte R, Crosby AE, Hanzlick R, Roesler J, Seider R, Smith P, Warner M (USA)

Journal of Preventive Medicine 47, S122-S129, 2014

Background: Describing the characteristics and patterns of suicidal behavior is an essential component in developing successful prevention efforts. The Data and Surveillance Task Force (DSTF) of the National Action Alliance for Suicide Prevention was charged with making recommendations for improving national data systems for public health surveillance of suicide-related problems, including suicidal thoughts, suicide attempts, and deaths due to suicide.

Purpose: Data from the national systems can be used to draw attention to the magnitude of the problem and are useful for establishing national health priorities. National data can also be used to examine differences in rates across groups (e.g., sex, racial/ethnic, and age groups) and geographic regions, and are useful in identifying patterns in the mechanism of suicide, including those that rarely occur.

Methods: Using evaluation criteria from the CDC, WHO, and the U.S.A.-based Safe States Alliance, the DSTF reviewed 28 national data systems for feasibility of use in the surveillance of suicidal behavior, including deaths, nonfatal attempts, and suicidal thoughts. The review criteria included attributes such as the aspects of the suicide-related spectrum (e.g., thoughts, attempts, deaths) covered by the system; how the data are collected (e.g., census, sample, survey, administrative data files, self-report, reporting by care providers); and the strengths and limitations of the survey or data system.

Results: The DSTF identified common strengths and challenges among the data systems based on the underlying data source (e.g., death records, healthcare provider records, population-based surveys, health insurance claims). From these findings, the DSTF proposed several recommendations for improving existing data systems, such as using standard language and definitions, adding new variables to existing surveys, expanding the geographic scope of surveys to include areas where data are not currently collected, oversampling of underrepresented groups, and improving the completeness and quality of information on death certificates.

Conclusions: Some of the DSTF recommendations are potentially achievable in the short term (<1-3 years) within existing data systems, whereas others involve more extensive changes and will require longer-term efforts (4-10 years). Implementing these recommendations would assist in the development of a national coordinated program of fatal and nonfatal suicide surveillance to facilitate evidence-based action to reduce the incidence of suicide and suicidal behavior in all populations.

Post-discharge suicides of inpatients with bipolar disorder in Finland

Isometsä E, Sund R, Pirkola S (Finland)

Bipolar Disorders. Published online: 24 July 2014. doi: 10.1111/bdi.12237, 2014

Objectives: Suicide risk in psychiatric inpatients is known to be remarkably high after discharge. However, temporal patterns and risk factors among patients with bipolar disorder remain obscure. We investigated post-discharge temporal patterns of hazard and risk factors by type of illness phase among patients with bipolar disorder.

Methods: Based on national registers, all discharges of patients with bipolar disorder from a psychiatric ward in Finland in 1987-2003 (n = 52,747) were identified, and each patient was followed up to post-index discharge or to suicide (n = 466). For discharges occurring in 1995-2003 (n = 35,946), factors modifying hazard of suicide during the first 120 days (n = 129) were investigated.

Results: The temporal pattern of suicide risk depended on the type of illness phase, being highest but steeply declining after discharge with depression; less high and declining in mixed states; lower and relatively stable after mania. In Cox models, for post-discharge suicides (n = 65) after hospitalizations for bipolar depression (n = 9,635), the hazard ratio was 8.05 (p = 0.001) after hospitalization with a suicide attempt and 3.63 (p < 0.001) for male patients, but 0.186 (p = 0.001) for patients taking lithium. Suicides after mania (n = 28) or mixed episodes (n = 20) were predicted by male sex and preceding suicide attempts, respectively.

Conclusions: Among inpatients with bipolar disorder, suicide risk is high and related strongly to the time elapsed from discharge after hospitalizations for depressive episodes, and less strongly after hospitalizations for mixed episodes. Intra-episodic suicide attempts and male sex powerfully predict suicide risk. Lower suicide rate after hospitalizations for depression among patients prescribed lithium is consistent with a preventive effect.

Suicide prevention via the internet: A descriptive review

Jacob N, Scourfield J, Evans R (UK)

Crisis 35, 261-267, 2014

Background: While concerns abound regarding the impact of the internet on suicidal behaviors, its role as a medium for suicide prevention remains underexplored.

Aims: The study examines what is currently known about the operation and effectiveness of internet programs for suicide and self-harm prevention that are run by professionals.

Method: Systematic searches of scholarly databases and suicide-related academic journals yielded 15 studies that presented online prevention strategies.

Results: No professional programs with a sole focus on nonsuicidal self-harm were identified, thus all studies reviewed focused on suicide prevention. Studies were predominantly descriptive and summarized the nature of the strategy and the target audience. There was no formal evaluation of program effectiveness in preventing suicide. Studies either presented strategies that supported individuals at risk of suicide (n = 8), supported professionals working with those at risk (n = 6), or attempted to improve website quality (n = 1).

Conclusion: Although the internet increasingly serves as an important medium for suicidal individuals, and there is concern about websites that both promote and encourage suicidal activity, there is lack of published evidence about online prevention strategies. More attention is needed in the development and evaluation of such preventative approaches.

Cross-sectional study of attitudes about suicide among psychiatrists in Shanghai

Jiao Y, Phillips MR, Sheng Y, Wu G, Li X, Xiong W, Wang L (Norway, China, USA)
BMC Psychiatry 14, 87, 2014

Background: Attitudes and knowledge about suicide may influence psychiatrists' management of suicidal patients but there has been little research about this issue in China.

Methods: We used the Scale of Public Attitudes about Suicide (SPAS) - a 47-item scale developed and validated in China - to assess knowledge about suicide and seven specific attitudes about suicide in a sample of 187 psychiatrists from six psychiatric hospitals in Shanghai. The results were compared to those of 548 urban community members (assessed in a previous study).

Results: Compared to urban community members, psychiatrists were more likely to believe that suicide can be prevented and that suicide is an important social problem but they had more stigmatizing beliefs about suicidal individuals and felt less empathy for them. The belief that suicide can be prevented was more common among female psychiatrists than male psychiatrists but male psychiatrists felt more empathy for suicidal individuals. Only 37% of the psychiatrists correctly agreed that talking about suicide-related issues with an individual would not precipitate suicidal behavior and only 41% correctly agreed that those who state that they intend to kill themselves may actually do so.

Conclusions: Many psychiatrists in Shanghai harbor negative attitudes about suicidal individuals and are concerned that directly addressing the issue with patients will increase the risk of suicide. Demographic factors, educational status and work experience are associated with psychiatrists' attitudes about suicide and, thus, need to be considered when training psychiatrists about suicide prevention.

Suicide in Sri-Lanka 1975-2012: Age, period and cohort analysis of police and hospital data

Knipe DW, Metcalfe C, Fernando R, Pearson M, Konradsen F, Eddleston M, Gunnell D (UK, Sri Lanka, Denmark)

BioMedCentral Public Health 14, 839, 2014

Background: Sri Lanka has experienced major changes in its suicide rates since the 1970s, and in 1995 it had one of the highest rates in the world. Subsequent reductions in Sri Lanka's suicide rates have been attributed to the introduction of restrictions on the availability of highly toxic pesticides. We investigate these changes in suicide rates in relation to age, gender, method specific trends and birth-cohort and period effects, with the aim of informing preventative strategies.

Methods: Secular trends of suicide in relation to age, sex, method, birth-cohort and period effects were investigated graphically using police data (1975-2012). Poisoning case-fatality was investigated using national hospital admission data (2004-2010).

Results: There were marked changes to the age-, gender- and method-specific incidence of suicide over the study period. Year on year declines in rates began in 17-25 year olds in the early 1980s. Reduction in older age groups followed and falls in all age groups occurred after all class I (the most toxic) pesticides were banned. Distinct changes in the age/gender pattern of suicide are observed: in the 1980s suicide rates were highest in 21-35 year old men; by the 2000s, this pattern had reversed with a stepwise increase in male rates with increasing age. Throughout the study period female rates were highest in 17-25 year olds. There has been a rise in suicide by hanging, though this rise is relatively small in relation to the marked decline in self-poisoning deaths. The patterns of suicides are more consistent with a period rather than birth-cohort effect.

Conclusions: The epidemiology of suicide in Sri Lanka has changed noticeably in the last 30 years. The introduction of pesticide regulations in Sri Lanka coincides with a reduction in suicide rates, with evidence of limited method substitution.

Suicide in children and young adolescents: A 25-year database on suicides from northern Finland

Lahti A, Harju A, Hakko H, Riala K, Räsänen P (Finland)
Journal of Psychiatric Research 58, 123-128, 2014

Despite the large amount of research on adolescent suicidality, there are few detailed studies illustrating the characteristics of child and adolescent completed suicide. Our study presents the characteristics of child and adolescent suicides occurring over a period of 25 years within a large geographical area in Northern Finland, with a special focus on gender differences. The study sample included all 58 suicides among children and adolescents (<18 years) occurring in the province of Oulu in Finland between 1988 and 2012. The data is based on documents pertaining to establish the cause of death from forensic autopsy investigations. A register linkage to the data from the Finnish Hospital Discharge Register (FHDR) was also made. 79% of the suicide victims were male. Violent suicide methods predominated in both genders (males 98%, females 83%). While symptoms of mental illness were common, only a minority (15% of males and 17% of females) had a previous history of psychiatric hospitalization. 17% of females but none of the males had been hospitalized previously due to self-poisoning. A greater proportion of females than males had a history of self-cutting (33% vs. 7%) and previous suicide attempts (25% vs. 4%). 48% of males and 58% of females were under the influence of alcohol at the time of their suicide, and alcohol intoxication was related to suicides during the night. One fifth of the adolescents screened positive for substances other than alcohol. The results of this study indicate that there are similarities but also some differences in the characteristics of male and female suicides in adolescents.

Risk of suicidal behavior with antidepressants in bipolar and unipolar disorders

Leon AC, Fiedorowicz JG, Solomon DA, Li C, Coryell WH, Endicott J, Fawcett J, Keller MB (USA)
Journal of Clinical Psychiatry 75, 720-727, 2014

Objective: To examine the risk of suicidal behavior (suicide attempts and deaths) associated with antidepressants in participants with bipolar I, bipolar II, and unipolar major depressive disorders.

Design: A 27-year longitudinal (1981-2008) observational study of mood disorders (Research Diagnostic Criteria diagnoses based on Schedule for Affective Disorders and Schizophrenia and review of medical records) was used to evaluate antidepressants and risk for suicidal behavior. Mixed-effects logistic regression models examined propensity for antidepressant exposure. Mixed-effects survival models that were matched on the propensity score examined exposure status as a risk factor for time until suicidal behavior.

Setting: Five US academic medical centers.

Results: Analyses of 206 participants with bipolar I disorder revealed 2,010 exposure intervals (980 exposed to antidepressants; 1,030 unexposed); 139 participants with bipolar II disorder had 1,407 exposure intervals (694 exposed; 713 unexposed); and 361 participants with unipolar depressive disorder had 2,745 exposure intervals (1,328 exposed; 1,417 unexposed). Propensity score analyses confirmed that more severely ill participants were more likely to initiate antidepressant treatment. In mixed-effects survival analyses, those with bipolar I disorder had a significant reduction in risk of suicidal behavior by 54% (HR = 0.46; 95% CI, 0.31-0.69; t = -3.74; P <.001) during periods of antidepressant exposure compared to propensity-matched unexposed intervals. Similarly, the risk was reduced by 35% (HR = 0.65; 95% CI, 0.43-0.99; t = -2.01; P =.045) in bipolar II disorder. By contrast, there was no evidence of an increased or decreased risk with antidepressant exposure in unipolar disorder.

Conclusions: Based on observational data adjusted for propensity to receive antidepressants, antidepressants may protect patients with bipolar disorders but not unipolar depressive disorder from suicidal behavior.

Assessing suicide attempts and depression among Chinese speakers over the internet

Liu NH, Contreras O, Muñoz RF, Leykin Y (USA)
Crisis 35, 322-329, 2014

Background: In populations where mental health resources are scarce or unavailable, or where stigma prevents help-seeking, the Internet may be a way to identify and reach at-risk persons using self-report validated screening tools as well as to characterize individuals seeking health information online.

Aims: We examined the feasibility of delivering an Internet-based Chinese-language depression and suicide screener and described its users.

Method: An Internet-based depression and suicide screener was created and advertised primarily through Google AdWords. Participants completed a suicide and depression screening measure and received individualized feedback, which, if necessary, included the suggestion to seek additional mental health resources.

Results: In 7 months, 11,631 individuals visited the site; 4,709 provided valid information. Nearly half reported a current major depressive episode (MDE) and 18.3% a recent suicide attempt; however, over 75% reported never having sought help, including 77.7% of those with MDEs and 75.9% of those reporting a suicide attempt. As participants found the site by searching for depression information online, results may not generalize to the entire Chinese-speaking population.

Conclusion: Online screening can feasibly identify and reach many at-risk Chinese-speaking persons. It may provide resources to those with limited access to services or to those reluctant to seek such services.

Population health outcome models in suicide prevention policy

Lynch FL (USA)
Preventive Medicine 47, S137-S143, 2014

Background: Suicide is a leading cause of death in the U.S. and results in immense suffering and significant cost. Effective suicide prevention interventions could reduce this burden, but policy makers need estimates of health outcomes achieved by alternative interventions to focus implementation efforts.

Purpose: To illustrate the utility of health outcome models to help in achieving goals defined by the National Action Alliance for Suicide Prevention's Research Prioritization Task Force. The approach is illustrated specifically with psychotherapeutic interventions to prevent suicide reattempt in emergency department settings.

Methods: A health outcome model using decision analysis with secondary data was applied to estimate suicide attempts and deaths averted from evidence-based interventions.

Results: Under optimal conditions, the model estimated that over 1 year, implementing evidence-based psychotherapeutic interventions in emergency departments could decrease the number of suicide attempts by 18,737, and if offered over 5 years, it could avert 109,306 attempts. Over 1 year, the model estimated 2,498 fewer deaths from suicide, and over 5 years, about 13,928 fewer suicide deaths.

Conclusions: Health outcome models could aid in suicide prevention policy by helping focus implementation efforts. Further research developing more sophisticated models of the impact of suicide prevention interventions that include a more complex understanding of suicidal behavior, longer time frames, and inclusion of additional outcomes that capture the full benefits and costs of interventions would be helpful next steps.

Differences in risk factors for self-harm with and without suicidal intent: Findings from the ALSPAC cohort

Mars B, Heron J, Crane C, Hawton K, Kidger J, Lewis G, MacLeod J, Tilling K, Gunnell D (UK)
Journal of Affective Disorders 168, 407-414, 2014

Background: There is a lack of consensus about whether self-harm with suicidal intent differs in aetiology and prognosis from non-suicidal self-harm, and whether they should be considered as different diagnostic categories.

Method: Participants were 4799 members of the Avon Longitudinal Study of Parents and Children (ALSPAC), a UK population-based birth cohort who completed a postal questionnaire on self-harm with and without suicidal intent at age 16 years. Multinomial logistic regression analyses were used to examine differences in the risk factor profiles of individuals who self-harmed with and without suicidal intent.

Results: Many risk factors were common to both behaviours, but associations were generally stronger in relation to suicidal self-harm. This was particularly true for mental health problems; compared to those with non-suicidal self-harm, those who had harmed with suicidal intent had an increased risk of depression (OR 3.50[95% CI 1.64, 7.43]) and anxiety disorder (OR 3.50[95% CI 1.72, 7.13]). Higher IQ and maternal education were risk factors for non-suicidal self-harm but not suicidal self-harm. Risk factors that appeared specific to suicidal self-harm included lower IQ and socioeconomic position, physical cruelty to children in the household and parental self-harm.

Limitations: i) There was some loss to follow-up, ii) difficulty in measuring suicidal intent, iii) we cannot rule out the possibility of reverse causation for some exposure variables, iv) we were unable to identify the subgroup that had only ever harmed with suicidal intent.

Conclusion: Self-harm with and without suicidal intent are overlapping behaviours but with some distinct characteristics, indicating the importance of fully exploring vulnerability factors, motivations, and intentions in adolescents who self harm.

Depressed parents' attachment: Effects on offspring suicidal behavior in a longitudinal family study

MacGregor EK, Grunebaum MF, Galfalvy HC, Melhem N, Burke AK, Brent DA, Oquendo MA, Mann JJ (USA)

Journal of Clinical Psychiatry 75, 879-885, 2014

Objective: To investigate relationships of depressed parents' attachment style to offspring suicidal behavior.

Method: 244 parents diagnosed with a DSM-IV depressive episode completed the Adult Attachment Questionnaire at study entry. Baseline and yearly follow-up interviews of their 488 offspring tracked suicidal behavior and psychopathology. Survival analysis and marginal regression models with correlated errors for siblings investigated the relationship between parent insecure attachment traits and offspring characteristics. Data analyzed were collected 1992-2008 during a longitudinal family study completed January 31, 2014.

Results: Parental avoidant attachment predicted offspring suicide attempts at a trend level (P =.083). Parental anxious attachment did not predict offspring attempts (P =.961). In secondary analyses, anxious attachment in parents was associated with offspring impulsivity (P =.034) and, in offspring suicide attempters, was associated with greater intent (P =.045) and lethality of attempts (P =.003). Avoidant attachment in parents was associated with offspring impulsivity (P =.025) and major depressive disorder (P =.012). Parental avoidant attachment predicted a greater number of suicide attempts (P =.048) and greater intent in offspring attempters (P =.003). Results were comparable after adjusting for parent diagnosis of borderline personality disorder.

Conclusions: Insecure avoidant, but not anxious, attachment in depressed parents may predict offspring suicide attempt. Insecure parental attachment traits were associated with impulsivity and major depressive disorder in all offspring and with more severe suicidal behavior in offspring attempters. Insecure parental attachment merits further study as a potential target to reduce risk of offspring psychopathology and more severe suicidal behavior.

Does the installation of blue lights on train platforms shift suicide to another station?: Evidence from Japan

Matsubayashi T, Sawada Y, Ueda M (Japan, USA)
Journal of Affective Disorders 169, 57-60, 2014

Background: This study examines the extent to which the indiscriminate media coverage of the famous young actress Lee Eun-ju's suicide in 2005 affected suicides overall and in specific subgroups (by age, gender, and suicide method) in a suicide-prone society, South Korea.

Methods: South Korea's 2003-2005 suicide data (n=34,237) were obtained from death certificate records of the National Statistical Office (NSO). Data was analyzed with Poisson time series auto-regression models.

Results: After adjusting for confounding factors (such as seasonal variation, calendar year, temperature, humidity, and unemployment rate), there was a significant increase in suicide (RR=1.40, 95%, CI=1.30-1.51, no. of excess mortalities=331; 95% CI=267-391) during the 4 weeks after Lee's suicide. This increase was more prominent in subgroups with similar characteristics to the celebrity. In particular, the relative risk of suicide during this period was the largest (5.24; 95% CI=3.31-8.29) in young women who used the same suicide method as the celebrity. Moreover, the incidence of these copycat suicides during the same time significantly increased in both genders and in all age subgroups among those who committed suicide using the same method as the celebrity (hanging).

Limitations: It is difficult to prove conclusively that the real motivation of the suicides was Lee's death.

Conclusions: The findings from this study imply that, if the media indiscreetly reports the suicide of a celebrity in a suicide-prone society, the copycat effect can be far-reaching and very strong, particularly for vulnerable people.

Dialectical behavior therapy for adolescents with repeated suicidal and self-harming behavior: A randomized trial

Mehlum L, Tormoen AJ, Ramberg M, Haga E, Diep LM, Laberg S, Larsson BS, Stanley BH, Miller AL, Sund AM, Groholt B (Norway, USA)

Journal of the American Academy of Child and Adolescent Psychiatry 53, 1082–1091, 2014

Objective: We examined whether a shortened form of dialectical behavior therapy, dialectical behavior therapy for adolescents (DBT-A) is more effective than enhanced usual care (EUC) to reduce self-harm in adolescents.

Method: This was a randomized study of 77 adolescents with recent and repetitive self-harm treated at community child and adolescent psychiatric outpatient clinics who were randomly allocated to either DBT-A or EUC. Assessments of self-harm, suicidal ideation, depression, hopelessness, and symptoms of borderline personality disorder were made at baseline and after 9, 15, and 19 weeks (end of trial period), and frequency of hospitalizations and emergency department visits over the trial period were recorded.

Results: Treatment retention was generally good in both treatment conditions, and the use of emergency services was low. DBT-A was superior to EUC in reducing self-harm, suicidal ideation, and depressive symptoms. Effect sizes were large for treatment outcomes in patients who received DBT-A, whereas effect sizes were small for outcomes in patients receiving EUC. Total number of treatment contacts was found to be a partial mediator of the association between treatment and changes in the severity of suicidal ideation, whereas no mediation effects were found on the other outcomes or for total treatment time.

Conclusion: DBT-A may be an effective intervention to reduce self-harm, suicidal ideation, and depression in adolescents with repetitive self-harming behavior. Clinical trial registration information-Treatment for Adolescents With Deliberate Self Harm; http://ClinicalTrials.gov/; NCT00675129.

School bullying, cyberbullying, or both: Correlates of teen suicidality in the 2011 CDC youth risk behavior survey

Messias E, Kindrick K, Castro J (USA)

Comprehensive Psychiatry 55, 1063-1068, 2014

While school bullying has been shown to be associated with depression and suicidality among teens, the relationship between these outcomes and cyberbullying has not been studied in nationally representative samples. Data came from the 2011 CDC Youth Risk Behavior Survey (YRBS), a nationally representative sample of high-school students (N = 15,425). We calculated weighted estimates representative of all students in grades 9-12 attending school in the US. Logistic regression was used to calculate adjusted odds ratios. Overall, girls are more likely to be report being bullied (31.3% vs. 22.9%), in particularly to be cyberbullied (22.0% vs. 10.8%), while boys are only more likely to report exclusive school bullying (12.2% vs. 9.2%). Reports of 2-week sadness and all suicidality items were highest among teens reporting both forms of bullying, followed by those reporting cyber-bullying only, followed by those reporting school bullying only. For example, among those reporting not being bullied 4.6% reported having made a suicide attempt, compared to 9.5% of those reporting school bullying only (adjusted odd ratio (AOR) 2.3, 95% C.I. 1.8-2.9), 14.7% of those reporting cyberbullying only (AOR 3.5 (2.6-4.7)), and 21.1% of those reporting victimization of both types of bullying (AOR 5.6 (4.4-7)). Bullying victimization, in school, cyber, or both, is associated with higher risk of sadness and suicidality among teens. Interventions to prevent school bullying as well as cyberbullying are needed. When caring for teens reporting being bullied.

Characteristics of suicidal ideation that predict the transition to future suicide attempts in adolescents

Miranda R, Ortin A, Scott M, Shaffer D (USA, Spain)
Journal of Child Psychology and Psychiatry 55, 1288–1296, 2014

Background: The present study sought to examine characteristics of suicidal ideation (SI) that predict a future suicide attempt (SA), beyond psychiatric diagnosis and previous SA history.

Methods: Participants were 506 adolescents (307 female) who completed the Columbia Suicide Screen (CSS) and selected modules from the Diagnostic Interview Schedule for Children (C-DISC 2.3) as part of a two-stage high school screening and who were followed up 4-6 years later to assess for a SA since baseline. At baseline, participants who endorsed SI on the CSS responded to four questions regarding currency, frequency, seriousness, and duration of their SI. A subsample of 122 adolescents who endorsed SI at baseline also completed a detailed interview about their most recent SI.

Results: Thinking about suicide often (OR = 3.5, 95% CI = 1.7-7.2), seriously (OR = 3.1, 95% CI = 1.4-6.7), and for a long time (OR = 2.3, 95% CI = 1.1-5.2) were associated with a future SA, adjusting for sex, the presence of a mood, anxiety, and substance use diagnosis, and baseline SA history. However, only SI frequency was significantly associated with higher odds of a future SA (OR = 3.6, 95% CI = 1.4-9.1) when also adjusting for currency, seriousness, and duration. Among ideators interviewed further about their most recent SI, ideating 1 hr or more (vs. less than 1 hr) was associated with a future SA (OR = 3.6, 95% CI = 1.0-12.7), adjusting for sex, depressive symptoms, previous SA history, and other baseline SI characteristics, and it was also associated with making a future SA earlier.

Conclusions: Assessments of SI in adolescents should take special care to inquire about frequency of their SI, along with length of their most recent SI.

Yearning to be heard

Montross Thomas LP, Palinkas LA, Meier EA, Iglewicz A, Kirkland T, Zisook S (USA)

Crisis 35, 161-167, 2014

Background: Patients with serious mental illness can be at higher risk for suicide. Most research has focused on determining the risk factors for suicide-related events using quantitative methodologies and psychological autopsies. However, fewer studies have examined patients' perspectives regarding the experience of suicidal events.

Aims: To better understand suicide experiences from the perspective of patients diagnosed with serious mental illness.

Method: This study purposively sampled and qualitatively interviewed 23 patients within the Veterans Affairs Hospital who were diagnosed with serious mental illness and who had attempted suicide. Using a phenomenological design, hermeneutic interviews included questions about the precursors, characteristics, and treatment of the suicide events, as well as patients' recommendations for care.

Results: Loneliness, isolation, depression, and hopelessness were commonly described as emotional precursors to the suicide events for all patients, while command hallucinations were reported among patients with schizophrenia-spectrum disorders. When evaluating whether treatments were effective, patients focused primarily on the level of empathy and compassion shown by their providers.

Conclusion: The most common recommendation for the improvement of care was to increase clinicians' empathy, compassion, and listening skills. Additionally, efforts to bolster social supports were highlighted as a means to diminish suicide events.

National strategy for suicide prevention in Japan: The impact of a national fund on the progress of developing systems for suicide prevention and implementing initiatives among local authorities

Nakanishi M, Yamauchi T, Takeshima T (Japan)

Psychiatry and Clinical Neurosciences. Published online: 10 July 2014. doi: 10.1111/pcn.12222, 2014

Aim: In Japan, the Cabinet Office released the "General Principles of Suicide Prevention Policy" in 2007 and suggested nine initiatives. In 2009, a national fund was launched to help prefectures (the administrative divisions of Japan) and local authorities implement five categories of suicide prevention programs. This paper examines the impact of the national fund on the establishment of the systems for suicide prevention and the implementation of these initiatives among local authorities.

Methods: The present study included 1385 local authorities (79.5%) from all 47 prefectures that responded to the cross-sectional questionnaire survey.

Results: Improved suicide prevention systems and the implementation of nine initiatives in April 2013 were observed among 265 local authorities (19.1%) that implemented "Training of community service providers" and "Public awareness campaigns"; 178 local authorities (12.9%) that implemented "Face-to-face counseling", "Training of community service providers" and "Public awareness campaigns"; and 324 local authorities (23.4%) that implemented "Trauma-informed policies and practices". There was no significant difference in suicide prevention systems and the implementation of nine initiatives between 203 local authorities (14.7%) that implemented only "Public awareness campaigns" and 231 local authorities (16.7%) that did not implement any suicide prevention programs.

Conclusion: The results of our study suggest that the national fund promoted the establishment of community systems for suicide prevention and helped implement initiatives among local authorities. The national suicide prevention strategy in Japan should explore a standard package of programs to guide community suicide prevention efforts with a sustained workforce among local authorities.

A comparison of suicides and undetermined deaths by poisoning among women: An analysis of the national violent death reporting system

Nathalie H, Bentson M, Mark K (USA)

Archives of Suicide Research. Published online: 10 July 2014. doi:10.1080/13811118.2014.915275, 2014

Background: The study compared the prevalence of common suicide risk factors between poisoning deaths classified as injuries of undetermined intent or suicides among women.

Methods: Data derived from the 2003-10 National Violent Death Reporting System. Multiple logistic regression assessed the factors associated with 799 undetermined deaths (relative to 3,233 suicides).

Results: Female decedents with lower education, a substance problem, and a health problem were more likely to be classified as undetermined death. Older women, those with an intimate partner problem, financial problem, depressed mood, mental health problem, attempted suicide, and disclosed intent to die were less likely to be classified as undetermined death.

Conclusions: The present study raises the possibility that many (perhaps most) undetermined female poisoning deaths are suicides.

Increasing help-seeking and referrals for individuals at risk for suicide by decreasing stigma: The role of mass media

Niederkrotenthaler T, Reidenberg DJ, Till B, Gould MS (Austria, USA)

American Journal of Preventative Medicine 47, S235-S243, 2014

Increasing help-seeking and referrals for at-risk individuals by decreasing stigma has been defined as Aspirational Goal 10 in the National Action Alliance for Suicide Prevention's Research Prioritization Task Force's 2014 prioritized research agenda. This article reviews the research evidence on the impact of mass media awareness campaigns on reducing stigma and increasing help-seeking. The review will focus on both beneficial and iatrogenic effects of suicide preventive interventions using media campaigns to target the broad public. A further focus is on collaboration between public health professionals and news media in order to reduce the risk of copycat behavior and enhance help-seeking behavior. Examples of multilevel approaches that include both mass media interventions and individual-level approaches to reduce stigma and increase referrals are provided as well. Multilevel suicide prevention programs that combine various approaches seem to provide the most promising results, but much more needs to be learned about the best possible composition of these programs. Major research and practice challenges include the identification of optimal ways to reach vulnerable populations who likely do not benefit from current awareness strategies. Caution is needed in all efforts that aim to reduce the stigma of suicidal ideation, mental illness, and mental health treatment in order to avoid iatrogenic effects. The article concludes with specific suggestions for research questions to help move this line of suicide research and practice forward.

Future risk of labour market marginalization in young suicide attempters-a population-based prospective cohort study

Niederkrotenthaler T, Tinghög P, Alexanderson K, Dahlin M, Wang M, Beckman K, Gould M, Mittendorfer-Rutz E (Austria, Sweden, USA)

International Journal of Epidemiology 43, 1520-1530, 2014

Background: Research on future labour market marginalization following suicide attempt at young age is scarce. We investigated the effects of suicide attempts on three labour market outcomes: unemployment, sickness absence and disability pension.

Methods: We conducted a prospective cohort study based on register linkage of 1 613 816 individuals who in 1994 were 16-30 years old and lived in Sweden. Suicide attempters treated in inpatient care during the 3 years preceding study entry, i.e. 1992-94 (N = 5649) were compared with the general population of the same age without suicide attempt between 1973 and 2010 (n = 1 608 167). Hazard ratios (HRs) for long-term unemployment (>180 days), sickness absence (>90 days) and disability pension in 1995-2010 were calculated by Cox regression models, adjusted for a number of parental and individual risk markers, and stratified for previous psychiatric inpatient care not due to suicide attempt.

Results: The risks for unemployment [HR 1.58; 95% confidence interval (CI) 1.52-1.64), sickness absence (HR 2.16; 2.08-2.24) and disability pension (HR 4.57; 4.34-4.81) were considerably increased among suicide attempters. There was a dose-response relationship between number of suicide attempts and the risk of disability pension, for individuals both with or without previous psychiatric hospitalizations not due to suicide attempts. No such relationship was present with regard to unemployment.

Conclusions: This study highlights the strong association of suicide attempts with future marginalization from the labour market, particularly for outcomes that are based on a medical assessment. Studies that focus only on unemployment may largely underestimate the true detrimental impact of suicide attempt on labour market marginalization.

Intrapersonal positive future thinking predicts repeat suicide attempts in hospital-treated suicide attempters

O'Connor RC, Smyth R, Williams JMG (Scotland)

Journal of Consulting and Clinical Psychology. Published online: 1 September 2014. doi: 10.1037/a0037846, 2014

Objective: Although there is clear evidence that low levels of positive future thinking (anticipation of positive experiences in the future) and hopelessness are associated with suicide risk, the relationship between the content of positive future thinking and suicidal behavior has yet to be investigated. This is the first study to determine whether the positive future thinking-suicide attempt relationship varies as a function of the content of the thoughts and whether positive future thinking predicts suicide attempts over time.

Method: A total of 388 patients hospitalized following a suicide attempt completed a range of clinical and psychological measures (depression, hopelessness, suicidal ideation, suicidal intent and positive future thinking). Fifteen months later, a nationally linked database was used to determine who had been hospitalized again after a suicide attempt.

Results: During follow-up, 25.6% of linked participants were readmitted to hospital following a suicide attempt. In univariate logistic regression analyses, previous suicide attempts, suicidal ideation, hopelessness, and depression-as well as low levels of achievement, low levels of financial positive future thoughts, and high levels of intrapersonal (thoughts about the individual and no one else) positive future thoughts predicted repeat suicide attempts. However, only previous suicide attempts, suicidal ideation, and high levels of intrapersonal positive future thinking were significant predictors in multivariate analyses.

Discussion: Positive future thinking has predictive utility over time; however, the content of the thinking affects the direction and strength of the positive future thinking-suicidal behavior relationship. Future research is required to understand the mechanisms that link high levels of intrapersonal positive future thinking to suicide risk and how intrapersonal thinking should be targeted in treatment interventions.

Viewing the body after bereavement due to suicide: A population-based survey in Sweden

Omerov P, Steineck G, Nyberg T, Runeson B, Nyberg U (Sweden)

PLoS ONE. Published online: 7 July 2014. doi: 10.1371/journal.pone.0101799, 2014

Background: Research on the assumed, positive and negative, psychological effects of viewing the body after a suicide loss is sparse. We hypothesized that suicide-bereaved parents that viewed their child's body in a formal setting seldom regretted the experience, and that viewing the body was associated with lower levels of psychological morbidity two to five years after the loss.

Methods and findings: We identified 915 suicide-bereaved parents by linkage of nationwide population-based registries and collected data by a questionnaire. The outcome measures included the Patient Health Questionnaire (PHQ-9). In total, 666 (73%) parents participated. Of the 460 parents (69%) that viewed the body, 96% answered that they did not regret the experience. The viewing was associated with a higher risk of reliving the child's death through nightmares (RR 1.61, 95% CI 1.13 to 2.32) and intrusive memories (RR 1.20, 95% CI 1.04 to 1.38), but not with anxiety (RR 1.02, 95% CI 0.74 to 1.40) and depression (RR 1.25, 95% CI 0.85 to 1.83). One limitation of our study is that we lack data on the informants' personality and coping strategies.

Conclusions: In this Swedish population-based survey of suicide-bereaved parents, we found that by and large everyone that had viewed their deceased child in a formal setting did not report regretting the viewing when asked two to five years after the loss. Our findings suggest that most bereaved parents are capable of deciding if they want to view the body or not. Officials may assist by giving careful information about the child's appearance and other details concerning the viewing, thus facilitating mental preparation for the bereaved person. This is the first large-scale study on the effects of viewing the body after a suicide and additional studies are needed before clinical recommendations can be made.

"When you're in the hospital, you're in a sort of bubble."

Owen-Smith A, Bennewith O, Donovan J, Evans J, Hawton K, Kapur N, O'Connor S, Gunnell D (UK)

Crisis 35, 154-160, 2014

Background: Individuals are at a greatly increased risk of suicide and self-harm in the months following discharge from psychiatric hospital, yet little is known about the reasons for this.

Aims: To investigate the lived experience of psychiatric discharge and explore service users' experiences following discharge.

Method: In-depth interviews were undertaken with recently discharged service users (n = 10) in the UK to explore attitudes to discharge and experiences since leaving hospital.

Results: Informants had mixed attitudes to discharge, and those who had not felt adequately involved in discharge decisions, or disagreed with them, had experienced urges to self-harm since being discharged. Accounts revealed a number of factors that made the postdischarge period difficult; these included both the reemergence of stressors that existed prior to hospitalization and a number of stressors that were prompted or exacerbated by hospitalization.

Conclusion: Although inferences that can be drawn from the study are limited by the small sample size, the results draw attention to a number of factors that could be investigated further to help explain the high risk of suicide and self-harm following psychiatric discharge. Findings emphasize the importance of adequate preparation for discharge and the maintenance of ongoing relationships with known service providers where possible.

Utility of local suicide data for informing local and national suicide prevention strategies

Owens C, Roberts S, Taylor J (UK)
Public Health 128, 424-429, 2014

Objectives: The practice of 'suicide audit' refers to the systematic collection of local data on suicides in order to learn lessons and inform suicide prevention plans. Little is known about the utility of this activity. The aim of this study was to ascertain from Directors of Public Health in England how they were conducting suicide audit and what resources they were investing in it; how the findings were being used, and how the process might be improved.

Study design: E-mail survey.

Methods: A questionnaire was sent to all 153 Primary Care Trusts (PCTs) in England prior to their dissolution in 2013. Simple descriptive statistics were performed in an Excel database.

Results: Responses were received from 49% of PCTs, of which 83% were conducting a regular audit of deaths by suicide. Many had worked hard to overcome procedural obstacles and were investing huge amounts of time and effort in collecting data, but it is not clear that the findings were being translated effectively into action. With few exceptions, PCTs were unable to demonstrate that the findings of local audits had influenced their suicide prevention plans.

Conclusions: In the light of fresh calls for the practice of suicide audit to be made mandatory in England, these results are worrying. The study suggests that there is a pressing need for practical guidance on how the findings of local suicide audits can be put to use, and proposes a framework within which such guidance could be developed.

History of suicide attempts in adults with Asperger syndrome

Paquette-Smith M, Weiss J, Lunsky Y (Canada)

Crisis 35, 273-277, 2014

Background: Individuals with Asperger syndrome (AS) may be at higher risk for attempting suicide compared to the general population.

Aims: This study examines the issue of suicidality in adults with AS.

Method: An online survey was completed by 50 adults from across Ontario. The sample was dichotomized into individuals who had attempted suicide (n = 18) and those who had not (n = 32). We examined the relationship between predictor variables and previous attempts, and compared the services that both groups are currently receiving.

Results: Over 35% of individuals with AS reported that they had attempted suicide in the past. Individuals who attempted suicide were more likely to have a history of depression and self-reported more severe autism symptomatology. Those with and without a suicidal history did not differ in terms of the services they were currently receiving. This study looks at predictors retrospectively and cannot ascertain how long ago the attempt was made. Although efforts were made to obtain a representative sample, there is the possibility that the individuals surveyed may be more or less distressed than the general population with AS.

Conclusion: The suicide attempt rate in our sample is much higher than the 4.6% lifetime prevalence seen in the general population. These findings highlight a need for more specialized services to help prevent future attempts and to support this vulnerable group.

Age-related differences in the influence of major mental disorders on suicidality: A Korean nationwide community sample

Park JE, Lee JY, Jeon HJ, Han KH, Sohn JH, Sung SJ, Cho MJ (South Korea)

Journal of Affective Disorders 162, 96-101, 2014

Background: We compared the influence of major mental disorders on suicidality according to age, adjusting for suicide-related correlates.

Methods: This study was based on the Korean national epidemiological survey of mental disorders including community-dwelling adults between 18 and 74 years of age (n=6022). Subjects were classified into three age groups; young (18-39), middle-aged (40-59), and late adulthood (60-74). Face-to-face interviews were conducted using the Korean version of the Composite International Diagnostic Interview. According to age groups, the influence of major depressive disorder (MDD), anxiety disorder, and alcohol use disorder on risk for suicidality were investigated by multiple logistic regression models adjusting for sex, years of education, marital status, income, employment, presence of chronic medical illness, and lifetime history of suicide attempt.

Results: After including MDD as a covariate, anxiety disorder remained a risk factor only in the middle-aged group (adjusted OR: 2.83, 95% CI: 1.54-5.22), and alcohol use disorder was a risk factor for suicidality only in the young group (adjusted OR: 2.81, 95% CI: 1.06-7.43). Conversely, MDD was the only mental disorder that significantly increased suicidality in all age groups.

Limitations: This was a cross-sectional study and did not include subjects over 75 years of age.

Conclusion: This study showed that the contribution of psychiatric disorders to risk for suicidality varied according to age group. Therefore, strategies for suicide prevention should be specifically designed for different age groups.

Suicide in happy places revisited: The geographical unit of analysis matters

Park N, Peterson C (USA)
Applied Psychology: Health and Well-Being 6, 318–323, 2014

Background: A recent study reported that the highest suicide rates in the US occurred in the happiest states. This is a counter-intuitive finding. The present research investigated whether the same result occurred when the unit of analysis was city. The association between happiness (of most) and suicide (by some) might differ in cities versus states because those in a city provide a more immediate influence.

Method: Suicide rates were examined in 44 large US cities as a function of the average happiness reported by residents.

Results: According to our results, happier cities had lower suicide rates (Spearman's rho = -.37, p < .014), implying that cities may be a more meaningful unit of analysis than states for studies of suicide risk.

Conclusion: The appropriate geographical unit of analysis needs to be considered seriously in psychological studies.

Relationship between acculturation, discrimination, and suicidal ideation and attempts among US Hispanics in the national epidemiologic survey of alcohol and related conditions

Perez-Rodriguez MM, Baca-Garcia E, Oquendo MA, Wang S, Wall MM, Liu SM, Blanco C (USA)
Journal of Clinical Psychiatry 75, 399-407, 2014

Objective: Acculturation is the process by which immigrants acquire the culture of the dominant society. Little is known about the relationship between acculturation and suicidal ideation and attempts among US Hispanics. Our aim was to examine the impact of 5 acculturation measures (age at migration, time in the United States, social network composition, language, race/ethnic orientation) on suicidal ideation and attempts in the largest available nationally representative sample of US Hispanics.

Method: Study participants were US Hispanics (N 6,359) from Wave 2 of the 2004 2005 National Epidemiologic Survey of Alcohol and Related Conditions (N 34,653). We used linear x2 tests and logistic regression models to analyze the association between acculturation and risk of suicidal ideation and attempts.

Results: Factors associated with a linear increase in lifetime risk for suicidal ideation and attempts were (1) younger age at migration (linear X2i 57.15; P <.0001), (2) longer time in the United States (linear X2i 36.09; P <.0001), (3) higher degree of English- language orientation (linear X2i 74.08; P <.0001), (4) lower Hispanic composition of social network (linear X2i 36.34;P<.0001),and (5) lower Hispanic racial/ethnic identification (linear X2i 47.77; P <.0001). Higher levels of perceived discrimination were associated with higher lifetime riskfor suicidal ideation (13 0.051;P<.001) and attempts (13 0.020; P .003).

Conclusions: There was a linear association between multiple dimensions of acculturation and lifetime suicidal ideation and attempts. Discrimination was also associated with lifetime risk for suicidal ideation and attempts. Our results highlight protective aspects of the traditional Hispanic culture, such as high social support, coping strategies, and moral objections to suicide, which are modifiable factors and potential targets for public health interventions aimed at decreasing suicide risk. Culturally sensitive mental health resources need to be made more available to decrease discrimination and stigma.

Effects of ketamine on explicit and implicit suicidal cognition: A randomized controlled trial in treatment-resistant depression

Price RB, Iosifescu DV, Murrough JW, Chang LC, Al Jurdi RK, Iqbal SZ, Soleimani L, Charney DS, Foulkes AL, Mathew SJ (USA)

Depression and Anxiety 31, 335-343, 2014

Background: Preliminary evidence suggests intravenous ketamine has rapid effects on suicidal cognition, making it an attractive candidate for depressed patients at imminent risk of suicide. In the first randomized controlled trial of ketamine using an anesthetic control condition, we tested ketamine's acute effects on explicit suicidal cognition and a performance-based index of implicit suicidal cognition (Implicit Association Test; IAT) previously linked to suicidal behavior.

Method: Symptomatic patients with treatment-resistant unipolar major depression (inadequate response to >/=3 antidepressants) were assessed using a composite index of explicit suicidal ideation (Beck Scale for Suicidal Ideation, Montgomery-Asberg Rating Scale suicide item, Quick Inventory of Depressive Symptoms suicide item) and the IAT to assess suicidality implicitly. Measures were taken at baseline and 24 hr following a single subanesthetic dose of ketamine (n = 36) or midazolam (n = 21), a psychoactive placebo agent selected for its similar, rapid anesthetic effects. Twenty four hours postinfusion, explicit suicidal cognition was significantly reduced in the ketamine but not the midazolam group.

Results: Fifty three percent of ketamine-treated patients scored zero on all three explicit suicide measures at 24 hr, compared with 24% of the midazolam group (chi2 = 4.6; P = .03). Implicit associations between self- and escape-related words were reduced following ketamine (P = .01; d = .58) but not midazolam (P = .68; d = .09). Ketamine-specific decreases in explicit suicidal cognition were largest in patients with elevated suicidal cognition at baseline, and were mediated by decreases in nonsuicide-related depressive symptoms.

Conclusions: Intravenous ketamine produces rapid reductions in suicidal cognition over and above active placebo. Further study is warranted to test ketamine's antisuicidal effects in higher-risk samples.

Scales for predicting risk following self-harm: An observational study in 32 hospitals in England

Quinlivan L, Cooper J, Steeg S, Davies L, Hawton K, Gunnell D, Kapur N (UK)
British Medical Journal Open 4, e004732, 2014

Objective: To investigate the extent to which risk scales were used for the assessment of self-harm by emergency department clinicians and mental health staff, and to examine the association between the use of a risk scale and measures of service quality and repeat self-harm within 6 months.

Design: Observational study.

Setting: A stratified random sample of 32 hospitals in England.

Participants: 6442 individuals presenting with self-harm to 32 hospital services during a 3-month period between 2010 and 2011.

Outcomes: 21-item measure of service quality, repeat self-harm within 6 months.

Results: A variety of different risk assessment tools were in use. Unvalidated locally developed proformas were the most commonly used instruments (reported in n=22 (68.8%) mental health services). Risk assessment scales were used in one-third of services, with the SAD PERSONS being the single most commonly used scale. There were no differences in service quality score between hospitals which did and did not use scales as a component of risk assessment (median service quality score (IQR): 14.5 (12.8, 16.4) vs 14.5 (11.4, 16.0), U=121.0, p=0.90), but hospitals which used scales had a lower median rate of repeat self-harm within 6 months (median repeat rate (IQR): 18.5% vs 22.7%, p=0.008, IRR (95% CI) 1.18 (1.00 to 1.37). When adjusted for differences in casemix, this association was attenuated (IRR=1.13, 95% CI (0.98 to 1.3)).

Conclusions: There is little consensus over the best instruments for risk assessment following self-harm. Further research to evaluate the impact of scales following an episode of self-harm is warranted using prospective designs. Until then, it is likely that the indiscriminant use of risk scales in clinical services will continue.

Economic suicides in the great recession in Europe and North America

Reeves A, McKee M, Stuckler D (UK)
British Journal of Psychiatry. Published online: 12 June 2014. doi: 10.1192/bjp.bp.114.144766, 2014

There has been a substantial rise in 'economic suicides' in the Great Recessions afflicting Europe and North America. We estimate that the Great Recession is associated with at least 10 000 additional economic suicides between 2008 and 2010. A critical question for policy and psychiatric practice is whether these suicide rises are inevitable. Marked cross-national variations in suicides in the recession offer one clue that they are potentially avoidable. Job loss, debt and foreclosure increase risks of suicidal thinking. A range of interventions, from upstream return-to-work programmes through to antidepressant prescriptions may help mitigate suicide risk during economic downturn

Suicide prevention in Australian Aboriginal communities: A review of past and present programs

Ridani R, Shand FL, Christensen H, McKay K, Tighe J, Burns J, Hunter E (Australia)
Suicide and Life-Threatening-Behavior. Published online: 16 September 2014 doi: 10.1111/sltb.12121, 2014

A review of Aboriginal suicide prevention programs were conducted to highlight promising projects and strategies. A content analysis of gray literature was conducted to identify interventions reported to have an impact in reducing suicidal rates and behaviors. Most programs targeted the whole community and were delivered through workshops, cultural activities, or creative outlets. Curriculums included suicide risk and protective factors, warning signs, and mental health. Many programs were poorly documented and evaluations did not include suicidal outcomes. Most evaluations considered process variables. Results from available outcome evaluations suggest that employing a whole of community approach and focusing on connectedness, belongingness and cultural heritage may be of benefit. Despite the challenges, there is a clear need to evaluate outcomes if prevention is to be progressed.

The return on investment of postdischarge follow-up calls for suicidal ideation or deliberate self-harm

Richardson JS, Mark TL, McKeon R (USA)
Psychiatric Services 65, 1012-1019, 2014

Objective: Transitions of care are critical for individuals at risk of suicide. This study determined the return on investment (ROI) for providing postdischarge follow-up calls to patients at risk of suicide who are discharged from a hospital or an emergency department.

Methods: Claims data were from the 2006-2011 Truven Health MarketScan Commercial Claims and Encounters Database and Multi-State Medicaid Database. Cost estimates were from eight call centers that provide postdischarge follow-up calls. The ROI was estimated for the 30 days after discharge and was calculated from a payer's perspective (return gained for every $1 invested). One-way and probabilistic sensitivity analyses were used to examine the influence of variations of ROI model inputs.

Results: Under base case assumptions, the estimated ROI was $1.76 for commercial insurance and $2.43 for Medicaid for patients discharged from a hospital and $1.70 for commercial insurance and $2.05 for Medicaid for those discharged from an emergency department. Variation in the effect size of postdischarge contacts on reducing readmission had the largest effect on the ROI, producing a range from $0 to $4.11. The ROI would be greater than $1 for both payers and across both discharge settings as long as postdischarge contact could reduce readmission by at least 13.3%. Sensitivity analyses indicated a 77% probability (commercial) and an 88% probability (Medicaid) that the ROI would be greater than $1 among hospital discharges; the probabilities among emergency department discharges were 74% (commercial) and 82% (Medicaid).

Conclusions: The study supports the business case for payers, particularly Medicaid, to invest in postdischarge follow-up calls.

Influencing public awareness to prevent male suicide

Robinson M, Braybrook D, Robertson S (Australia)
Journal of Public Mental Health 13, 40-50, 2014

Purpose: The purpose of this paper is to report findings from a formative evaluation of a suicide prevention public awareness campaign — Choose Life, North Lanarkshire. The focus is on preventing male suicide. The paper explores how the public campaign supports a co-ordinated and community-based direction for suicide prevention work, and examines how good practice can be identified, spread, and sustained.

Design/methodology/approach: The paper draws on data collected from March to November 2011, using mixed primary research methods, including a quota survey, discussion groups with the general public, and stakeholder interviews.

Findings: The campaign effectively raised the suicide awareness of a substantial proportion of those targeted, but with regional variations. It also affected the attitudes and behaviour of those who were highly aware. However, men and women engaged somewhat differently with the campaign. The sports and leisure settings approach was effective in reaching younger men.

Practical implications: The paper discusses emerging considerations for suicide prevention, focusing on gender and approaches and materials for engaging with the public as "influencers". There are challenges to target audiences more specifically, provide a clear call to action, and engage the public in a sustained way.

Originality/value: This paper reflects on insights from a complex programme, exceptional in its focus on targeted sections of the public, especially young males. The paper indicates the importance for research and practice of intersecting dimensions of male identity, stigma and mental health, and other risk and protective factors which can inform campaigns highlighting talk about suicide among men.

Restricting youth suicide: Behavioral health patients in an urban pediatric emergency department

Rogers SC, DiVietro S, Borrup K, Brinkley A, Kaminer Y, Lapidus G (USA)

Journal of Trauma and Acute Care Surgery 77, S23-S28, 2014

Background: Suicide is the third leading cause of death among individuals age 10 years to 19 years in the United States. Adolescents with suicidal behaviors are often cared for in emergency departments (EDs)/trauma centers and are at an increased risk for subsequent suicide. Many institutions do not have standard procedures to prevent future self-harm. Lethal means restriction (LMR) counseling is an evidence-based suicide prevention strategy that informs families to restrict access to potentially fatal items and has demonstrated efficacy in preventing suicide. The objectives of this study were to examine suicidal behavior among behavioral health patients in a pediatric ED and to assess the use of LMR by hospital staff.

Methods: A sample of 298 pediatric patients was randomly selected from the population of behavioral health patients treated at the ED from January 1 through December 31, 2012 (n = 2,294). Descriptive data include demographics (age, sex, race/ethnicity, etc,), chief complaint, current and past psychiatric history, primary diagnosis, disposition, alcohol/drug abuse, and documentation of any LMR counseling provided in the ED.

Results: Of the 298 patients, 52% were female, 47% were white, and 76% were in the custody of their parents. Behavior/out of control was the most common chief complaint (43%). The most common diagnoses were mood disorder (25%) and depression (20%). Thirty-four percent of the patients had suicidal ideation, 22% had a suicide plan, 32% had documented suicidal behavior, and 25% of the patients reported having access to lethal means. However, only 4% of the total patient population received any LMR counseling, and only 15% of those with access to lethal means had received LMR counseling.

Conclusion: Providing a safe environment for adolescents at risk for suicidal behaviors should be a priority for all families/caretakers and should be encouraged by health care providers. The ED is a key point of entry into services for suicidal youth and presents an opportunity to implement effective secondary prevention strategies. The low rate of LMR counseling found in this study suggests a need for improved LMR counseling for all at-risk youth.

Level of Evidence: Epidemiologic study, level III.

Assessment and management of suicide risk in primary care

Saini P, While D, Chantler K, Windfuhr K, Kapur N (UK)
Crisis. Published online: 18 September 2014. doi: 10.1027/0227-5910/a000277, 2014

Background: Risk assessment and management of suicidal patients is emphasized as a key component of care in specialist mental health services, but these issues are relatively unexplored in primary care services.

Aims: To examine risk assessment and management in primary and secondary care in a clinical sample of individuals who were in contact with mental health services and died by suicide.

Method: Data collection from clinical proformas, case records, and semistructured face-to-face interviews with general practitioners.

Results: Primary and secondary care data were available for 198 of the 336 cases (59%). The overall agreement in the rating of risk between services was poor (overall $=.127$, p $=.10$). Depression, care setting (after discharge), suicidal ideation at last contact, and a history of self-harm were associated with a rating of higher risk. Suicide prevention policies were available in 25% of primary care practices, and 33% of staff received training in suicide risk assessments.

Conclusion: Risk is difficult to predict, but the variation in risk assessment between professional groups may reflect poor communication. Further research is required to understand this. There appears to be a relative lack of suicide risk assessment training in primary care.

Review of point-of-reception mental health screening outcomes in an Australian prison

Schilders MR, Ogloff JRP (Australia)

Journal of Forensic Psychiatry and Psychology 25, 480–494, 2014

The objective of this study was to evaluate associations between self-injury training and attitudes across different health care professions. In the study, 342 psychologists, social workers, psychiatric, and medical nurses were recruited from 12 hospitals in Belgium. Participants completed a confidential questionnaire assessing attitudes, perceived knowledge/competence in self-injury, and prior self-injury training. Professionals with training reported more positive empathy, less negative attitudes, and greater perceived knowledge/competence, which was related to positive attitudes. Mental health providers had more positive attitudes than medical professionals. Conclusions: Attitudes towards self-injuring patients are multifaceted and vary across health professions. Training on self-injury should be incorporated into the educational curriculum of all health care professions.

Developmental model of suicide trajectories

Seguin M, Beauchamp G, Robert M, Dimambro M, Turecki G (Canada)

British Journal of Psychiatry. Published online: 8 May 2014. doi: 10.1192/bjp.bp.113.139949, 2014

Background: Most developmental studies on suicide do not take into account individual variations in suicide trajectories.
Aims: Using a life course approach, this study explores developmental models of suicide trajectories.
Methods: Two hundred and fourteen suicides were assessed with mixed methods. Statistical analysis using combined discrete-time survival (DTS) and growth mixture modelling (GMM) generated various trajectories, and path analysis (Mplus) identified exogenous and mediating variables associated with these trajectories.
Results: Two groups share common risk factors, and independently of these major risk factors, they have different developmental trajectories: the first group experienced a high burden of adversity and died by suicide in their early 20s; and the second group experienced a somewhat moderate or low burden of adversity before they took their own life. Structural equation modelling identified variables specific to the early suicide trajectory: conduct and behavioural difficulties, social isolation/conflicts mediated by school-related difficulties, the end of a love relationship, and previous suicide attempts.
Conclusions: Psychosocial adversity between 10 and 20 years of age may warrant key periods of intervention.

Training for suicide risk assessment and suicide risk formulation

Silverman MM, Berman AL (USA)

Academic Psychiatry 38, 526-537, 2014

Suicide and suicidal behaviors are highly associated with psychiatric disorders. Psychiatrists have significant opportunities to identify at-risk individuals and offer treatment to reduce that risk. Although a suicide risk assessment (SRA) is a core competency requirement, many lack the requisite training and skills to appropriately assess for suicide risk. Moreover, the standard of care requires psychiatrists to foresee the possibility that a patient might engage in suicidal behavior, hence to conduct a suicide risk formulation (SRF) sufficient to guide triage and treatment planning. An SRA gathers data about observable and reported symptoms, behaviors, and historical factors that are associated with suicide risk and protection, ascertained by way of psychiatric interview; collateral information from family, friends, and medical records; and psychometric scales and/or screening tools. Based on data collected via an SRA, an SRF is a process whereby the psychiatrist forms a judgment about a patient's foreseeable risk of suicidal behavior in order to inform triage decisions, safety and treatment plans, and interventions to reduce risk. This paper addresses the need for a revised training model in SRA and SRF, and proposes a model of training that incorporates the acquisition of skills, relying heavily on case application exercises.

Frequent callers to crisis helplines: Who are they and why do they call?

Spittal MJ, Fedyszyn I, Middleton A, Bassilios B, Gunn J, Woodward A, Pirkis J (Australia)

Australia and New Zealand Journal of Psychiatry. Published online: 27 June 2014. doi: 10.1177/0004867414541154, 2014

Objective: Frequent callers present a challenge for crisis helplines, which strive to achieve optimal outcomes for all callers within finite resources. This study aimed to describe frequent callers to Lifeline (the largest crisis helpline in Australia) and compare them with non-frequent callers, with a view to furthering knowledge about models of service delivery that might meet the needs of frequent callers.

Method: Lifeline provided an anonymous dataset on calls made between December 2011 and May 2013. We assumed calls from the same (encrypted) phone number were made by the same person, and aggregated call level data up to the person level. Individuals who made 0.667 calls per day in any period from 1 week to the full 549 days for which we had data (i.e. 4.7 calls in 7 days, 20 calls in 30 days, 40 calls in 60 days, etc.) were regarded as frequent callers.

Results: Our analysis dataset included 411,725 calls made by 98,174 individuals, 2594 (2.6%) of whom met our definition of frequent callers. We identified a number of predictors of being a frequent caller, including being male or transgender, and never having been married. The odds increased with age until 55-64 years, and then declined. Suicidality, self-harm, mental health issues, crime, child protection and domestic violence issues all predicted being a frequent caller.

Conclusions: Collectively, frequent callers have a significant impact on crisis lines, and solutions need to be found for responding to them that are in everybody's best interests (i.e. the frequent callers themselves, other callers, telephone crisis supporters who staff crisis lines, and those who manage crisis lines). In striking this balance, the complex and multiple needs of frequent callers must be taken into account.

The repeated episodes of self-harm (RESH) score: A tool for predicting risk of future episodes of self-harm by hospital patients

Spittal MJ, Pirkis J, Miller M, Carter G, Studdert DM (Australia, USA)

Journal of Affective Disorders 161, 36-42, 2014

Background: Repetition of hospital-treated deliberate self-harm is common. Several recent studies have used emergency department data to develop clinical tools to assess risk of self-harm or suicide. Longitudinal, linked inpatient data is an alternative source of information.

Methods: We identified all individuals admitted to hospital for deliberate self-harm in two Australian states (~350 hospitals). The outcome of interest was a repeated episode of self-harm (non-fatal or fatal) within 6 months. Logistic regression was used to identify a set of predictors of repetition. A risk calculator (RESH: Repeated Episodes of Self-Harm) was derived directly from model coefficients.

Results: There were 84,659 episodes of self-harm during the study period. Four variables - number of prior episodes, time between episodes, prior psychiatric diagnoses and recent psychiatric hospital stay - strongly predicted repetition. The RESH score showed good discrimination (AUC=0.75) and had high specificity. Patients with scores of 0-3 had 14% risk of repeat episodes, whereas patients with scores of 20-25 had over 80% risk. We identified five thresholds where the RESH score could be used for prioritising interventions.

Limitations: The trade-off of a highly specific test is that the instrument has poor sensitivity. As a consequence, the RESH score cannot be used reliably for "ruling out" those who score below the thresholds.

Conclusions: The RESH score could be useful for prioritising patients to interventions to reduce readmission for deliberate self-harm. The five thresholds, representing the continuum from low to high risk, enable a stepped care model of overlapping or sequential interventions to be deployed to patients at risk of self-harm.

The association of suicide-related Twitter use with suicidal behaviour: A cross-sectional study of young internet users in Japan

Sueki H (Japan)
Journal of Affective Disorders 170, 155-160, 2014

Background: Infodemiology studies for suicide prevention have become increasingly common in recent years. However, the association between Twitter use and suicide has only been partially clarified. This study examined the association between suicide-related tweets and suicidal behaviour to identify suicidal young people on the Internet.

Methods: A cross-sectional survey was conducted using Internet survey panels (n=220,848) comprising users in their 20s, through a major Japanese Internet survey company. Final analyses included the data of 1000 participants.

Results: Of the participants (n=1000) used in the final analysis, 61.3% were women and the mean age was 24.9 years (SD=2.9, range=20-29). Logistic regression analyses showed that tweeting "want to die" and "want to commit suicide" was significantly related to suicidal ideation and behaviour. Lifetime suicide attempts, the most powerful predictor of future suicide out of all suicidal behaviours, were more strongly associated with tweeting "want to commit suicide" than tweeting "want to die". Having a Twitter account and tweeting daily were not associated with suicidal behaviour.

Limitations: An online panel survey has some inherent biases, such as coverage bias. Respondents were already registered as members of a particular Internet survey company in Japan, which limits the possibility of generalization.

Conclusions: Twitter logs may be used to identify suicidal young Internet users. This study provides a basis for the early identification of individuals at high risk for suicide.

The impact of suicidality-related internet use: A prospective large cohort study with young and middle-aged internet users

Sueki H, Yonemoto N, Takeshima T, Inagaki M (Japan)
PLoS ONE. Published online: 16 April 2014. doi: 10.1371/journal.pone.00948412014, 2014

Background: There has been no study that has allowed clear conclusions about the impact of suicide-related or mental health consultation-related internet use.

Aim: To investigate the impacts of suicide-related or mental health consultation-related internet use.

Methods: We conducted prospective observational longitudinal study with data collection at baseline screening (T0), 1 week after T0 (T1) and 7 weeks after T0 (T2). Participants with a stratified random sampling from 744,806 internet users were 20-49 years of age who employed the internet for suicide-related or mental health consultation-related reasons and internet users who did not. The main outcome was suicidal ideation. Secondary outcome measures comprised hopelessness, depression/anxiety, and loneliness.

Results: The internet users who had employed the internet for suicide-related or mental health consultation-related reasons at T0 (n = 2813), compared with those who had not (n = 2682), showed a significant increase in suicidal ideation (beta = 0.38, 95%CI: 0.20-0.55) and depression/anxiety (beta = 0.37, 95%CI: 0.12-0.61) from T1 to T2. Those who disclosed their own suicidal ideation and browsed for information about suicide methods on the web showed increased suicidal ideation (beta = 0.55, 95%CI: 0.23-0.88; beta = 0.45, 95% CI: 0.26-0.63, respectively). Although mental health consultation with an anonymous other online did not increase suicidal ideation, increased depression/anxiety was observed (beta = 0.34, 95%CI: -0.03-0.71).

Conclusions: An increased suicidal ideation was observed in the young and middle-aged who employed the internet for suicide-related or mental health consultation-related reasons. Mental health consultation via the internet was not useful, but those who did so showed worsened depression/anxiety.

Adult health outcomes of childhood bullying victimization: Evidence from a five-decade longitudinal British birth cohort

Takizawa R, Maughan B, Arseneault L (UK)

American Journal of Psychiatry 171, 777-784, 2014

Objective: The authors examined midlife outcomes of childhood bullying victimization.

Method: Data were from the British National Child Development Study, a 50-year prospective cohort of births in 1 week in 1958. The authors conducted ordinal logistic and linear regressions on data from 7,771 participants whose parents reported bullying exposure at ages 7 and 11 years, and who participated in follow-up assessments between ages 23 and 50 years. Outcomes included suicidality and diagnoses of depression, anxiety disorders, and alcohol dependence at age 45; psychological distress and general health at ages 23 and 50; and cognitive functioning, socioeconomic status, social relationships, and well-being at age 50.

Results: Participants who were bullied in childhood had increased levels of psychological distress at ages 23 and 50. Victims of frequent bullying had higher rates of depression (odds ratio=1.95, 95% CI=1.27-2.99), anxiety disorders (odds ratio=1.65, 95% CI=1.25-2.18), and suicidality (odds ratio=2.21, 95% CI=1.47-3.31) than their nonvictimized peers. The effects were similar to those of being placed in public or substitute care and an index of multiple childhood adversities, and the effects remained significant after controlling for known correlates of bullying victimization. Childhood bullying victimization was associated with a lack of social relationships, economic hardship, and poor perceived quality of life at age 50.

Conclusions: Children who are bullied and especially those who are frequently bullied continue to be at risk for a wide range of poor social, health, and economic outcomes nearly four decades after exposure. Interventions need to reduce bullying exposure in childhood and minimize long-term effects on victims' well-being; such interventions should cast light on causal processes.

Personality and suicide risk: The impact of economic crisis in Japan

Tanji F, Kakizaki M, Sugawara Y, Watanabe I, Nakaya N, Minami Y, Fukao A, Tsuji I (Japan)
Psychological Medicine. Published online: 18 July 2014. doi: 10.1017/S0033291714001688, 2014

Background: The interactive effect of personal factors and social factors upon suicide risk is unclear. We conducted prospective cohort study to investigate whether the impact of the economic crisis in 1997-1998 upon suicide risk differed according to Neuroticism and Psychoticism personality traits.

Methods: The Miyagi Cohort Study in Japan with a follow-up for 19 years from 1990 to 2008 has 29 432 subjects aged 40-64 years at baseline who completed a questionnaire about various health habits and the Japanese version of the Eysenck Personality Questionnaire - Revised Short Form in 1990.

Results: The suicide mortality rate increased from 4.6 per 100 000 person-years before 1998 to 27.8 after 1998. Although both Neuroticism and Psychoticism were significantly associated with an increased risk of mortality during the whole period from 1990 to 2008, the impact of the economic crisis upon suicide risk differed between the Neuroticism and Psychoticism personality traits. Compared with the lowest category, the hazard ratios (HRs) for the highest Neuroticism increased from 0.66 before 1998 to 2.45 after 1998. On the other hand, the HRs for the highest Psychoticism decreased from 7.85 before 1998 to 2.05 after 1998.

Conclusions: The impact of the 1997-1998 economic crisis upon suicide risk differed according to personality. Suicide risk increased among these with higher Neuroticism after the economic crisis, but this was not the case for other personality subscales.

Yearning to be heard: What veterans teach us about suicide risk and effective interventions

Thomas LPM, Palinkas LA, Meier EA, Iglewicz A, Kirkland T, Zisook S (USA)

Crisis 35, 161-167, 2014

Background: Patients with serious mental illness can be at higher risk for suicide. Most research has focused on determining the risk factors for suicide-related events using quantitative methodologies and psychological autopsies. However, fewer studies have examined patients' perspectives regarding the experience of suicidal events.

Aims: To better understand suicide experiences from the perspective of patients diagnosed with serious mental illness.

Method: This study purposively sampled and qualitatively interviewed 23 patients within the Veterans Affairs Hospital who were diagnosed with serious mental illness and who had attempted suicide. Using a phenomenological design, hermeneutic interviews included questions about the precursors, characteristics, and treatment of the suicide events, as well as patients' recommendations for care.

Results: Loneliness, isolation, depression, and hopelessness were commonly described as emotional precursors to the suicide events for all patients, while command hallucinations were reported among patients with schizophrenia-spectrum disorders. When evaluating whether treatments were effective, patients focused primarily on the level of empathy and compassion shown by their providers.

Conclusion: The most common recommendation for the improvement of care was to increase clinicians' empathy, compassion, and listening skills. Additionally, efforts to bolster social supports were highlighted as a means to diminish suicide events.

Surfing for suicide methods and help: Content analysis of websites retrieved with search engines in Austria and the United States

Till B, Niederkrotenthaler T (Austria)

Journal of Clinical Psychiatry 75, 886-892, 2014

Objective: The Internet provides a variety of resources for individuals searching for suicide-related information. Structured content-analytic approaches to assess intercultural differences in web contents retrieved with method-related and help-related searches are scarce.

Method: We used the 2 most popular search engines (Google and Yahoo/Bing) to retrieve US-American and Austrian search results for the term suicide, method-related search terms (eg, suicide methods, how to kill yourself, painless suicide, how to hang yourself), and help-related terms (eg, suicidal thoughts, suicide help) on February 11, 2013. In total, 396 websites retrieved with US search engines and 335 websites from Austrian searches were analyzed with content analysis on the basis of current media guidelines for suicide reporting. We assessed the quality of websites and compared findings across search terms and between the United States and Austria.

Results: In both countries, protective outweighed harmful website characteristics by approximately 2:1. Websites retrieved with method-related search terms (eg, how to hang yourself) contained more harmful (United States: P <.001, Austria: P <.05) and fewer protective characteristics (United States: P <.001, Austria: P <.001) compared to the term suicide. Help-related search terms (eg, suicidal thoughts) yielded more websites with protective characteristics (United States: P =.07, Austria: P <.01). Websites retrieved with US search engines generally had more protective characteristics (P <.001) than searches with Austrian search engines. Resources with harmful characteristics were better ranked than those with protective characteristics (United States: P <.01, Austria: P <.05).

Conclusions: The quality of suicide-related websites obtained depends on the search terms used. Preventive efforts to improve the ranking of preventive web content, particularly regarding method-related search terms, seem necessary.

Contact with child and adolescent psychiatric services among self-harming and suicidal adolescents in the general population: A cross sectional study

Tormoen AJ, Rossow I, Mork E, Mehlum L (Norway)
Child and Adolescent Psychiatry and Mental Health. Published online: 17 April 2014. doi: 10.1186/1753-2000-8-1318, 2014

Background: Studies have shown that adolescents with a history of both suicide attempts and non-suicidal self-harm report more mental health problems and other psychosocial problems than adolescents who report only one or none of these types of self-harm. The current study aimed to examine the use of child and adolescent psychiatric services by adolescents with both suicide attempts and non-suicidal self-harm, compared to other adolescents, and to assess the psychosocial variables that characterize adolescents with both suicide attempts and non-suicidal self-harm who report contact.

Methods: Data on lifetime self-harm, contact with child and adolescent psychiatric services, and various psychosocial risk factors were collected in a cross-sectional sample (response rate = 92.7 %) of 11,440 adolescents aged 14-17 years who participated in a school survey in Oslo, Norway.

Results: Adolescents who reported any self-harm were more likely than other adolescents to have used child and adolescent psychiatric services, with a particularly elevated likelihood among those with both suicide attempts and non-suicidal self-harm (OR = 9.3). This finding remained significant even when controlling for psychosocial variables. In adolescents with both suicide attempts and non-suicidal self-harm, symptoms of depression, eating problems, and the use of illicit drugs were associated with a higher likelihood of contact with child and adolescent psychiatric services, whereas a non-Western immigrant background was associated with a lower likelihood.

Conclusions: In this study, adolescents who reported self-harm were significantly more likely than other adolescents to have used child and adolescent psychiatric services, and adolescents who reported a history of both suicide attempts and non-suicidal self-harm were more likely to have used such services, even after controlling for other psychosocial risk factors. In this high-risk subsample, various psychosocial problems increased the probability of contact with child and adolescent psychiatric services, naturally reflecting the core tasks of the services, confirming that they represents an important area for interventions that aim to reduce self-harming behaviour. Such interventions should include systematic screening for early recognition of self-harming behaviours, and treatment programmes tailored to the needs of teenagers with a positive screen. Possible barriers to receive mental health services for adolescents with immigrant backgrounds should be further explored.

Passive suicide ideation: An indicator of risk among older adults seeking aging services?

Van Orden KA, O'Riley AA, Simning A, Podgorski C, Richardson TM, Conwell Y (USA)
Gerontologist. Published online: 8 April 2014. doi: 10.1093/geront/gnu026, 2014

Objectives: This study examines patterns of endorsements of active suicide ideation (SI), passive SI (synonymous with death ideation), and psychological distress (i.e., depressive and anxious symptomatology) in a sample of vulnerable older adults.

Methods: Data were collected via in-home interviews with aging services care management clients aged 60 years and older (n = 377). The Paykel scale for suicide measured the most severe level of suicidality over the past year, and the ninth item of the Patient Health Questionnaire (PHQ-9) measured current passive/active SI. The remaining items from the PHQ (i.e., PHQ-8) and the Goldberg Anxiety scale measured distress.

Results: Latent class analysis revealed a four-class model: a group with mild distress and no active SI, a group with high distress and no ideation, a group with mild distress and both passive and active SI, and a group with high distress and both passive and active SI.

Discussion: Results indicate that passive SI rarely presents in vulnerable older adults in the absence of significant risk factors for suicide (i.e., psychological distress or active SI). Thus, the desire for death and the belief that life is not worth living do not appear to be normative in late life.

Law enforcement suicide: A national analysis

Violanti JM, Robinson CF, Shen R (USA)

International Journal of Emergency Mental Health 15, 289-297, 2014

Previous research suggests that there is an elevated risk of suicide among workers within law enforcement occupations. The present study examined the proportionate mortality for suicide in law enforcement in comparison to the US working population during 1999, 2003-2004, and 2007, based on Centers for Disease Control and Prevention's National Institute for Occupational Safety and Health National Occupational Mortality Surveillance data. We analyzed data for all law enforcement occupations and focused on two specific law enforcement occupational categories-detectives/criminal investigators/ police and corrections officers. Suicides were also explored by race, gender and ethnicity. The results of the study showed proportionate mortality ratios (PMRs) for suicide were significantly high for all races and sexes combined (all law enforcement—PMR = 169, 95% CI = 150-191, p < 0.01, 264 deaths; detectives/criminal investigators/police—PMR = 182, 95% CI = 150-218, p < 0.01, 115 deaths; and corrections officers-PMR = 141, 95% CI = 111-178, p < 0.01, 73 deaths). Detectives/criminal investigators/police had the higher suicide risk (an 82% increase) compared to corrections officers (a 41% increase). When analyzed by race and sex, suicide PMRs for Caucasian males were significantly high for both occupations-detectives/ criminal investigators/police (PMR = 133; 95% CI = 108-162, p < 0.01; corrections officers—PMR = 134, 95% CI = 102-173, p < 0.01). A significantly high (PMR = 244, p < 0.01, 95% CI = 147-380) ratio was found among Hispanic males in the law enforcement combined category, and a similarly high PMR was found among Hispanic detectives/criminal investigators/police (PMR = 388, p < 0.01, 95% CI = 168-765). There were small numbers of deaths among female and African American officers. The results included significantly increased risk for suicide among detectives/criminal investigators/police and corrections officers, which suggests that additional study could provide better data to inform us for preventive action.

A CBT-based psychoeducational intervention for suicide survivors

Wittouck C, Van Autreve S, Portzky G, van Heeringen K (Belgium)

Crisis 35, 193-201, 2014

Background: Bereavement following suicide is associated with an increased vulnerability for depression, complicated grief, suicidal ideation, and suicide. There is, however, a paucity of studies of the effects of interventions in suicide survivors. *Aims:* This study therefore examined the effects of a cognitive behavioral therapy (CBT)-based psychoeducational intervention on depression, complicated grief, and suicide risk factors in suicide survivors. *Method:* In total, 83 suicide survivors were randomized to the intervention or the control condition in a cluster randomized controlled trial. Primary outcome measures included maladaptive grief reactions, depression, suicidal ideation, and hopelessness. Secondary outcome measures included grief-related cognitions and coping styles. *Results:* There was no significant effect of the intervention on the outcome measures. However, the intensity of symptoms of grief, depressive symptoms, and passive coping styles decreased significantly in the intervention group but not in the control group. *Conclusion:* The CBT-based psychoeducational intervention has no significant effect on the development of complicated grief reactions, depression, and suicide risk factors among suicide survivors. The intervention may, however, serve as supportive counseling for suicide survivors.

A Markov chain model for studying suicide dynamics: An illustration of the Rose Theorem

Yip P, So BK, Kawachi I, Zhang Y (Hong Kong, China, USA)

BMC Public Health 14, 625, 2014

Background: High-risk strategies would only have a modest effect on suicide prevention within a population. It is best to incorporate both high-risk and population-based strategies to prevent suicide. This study aims to compare the effectiveness of suicide prevention between high-risk and population-based strategies. *Methods:* A Markov chain illness and death model is proposed to determine suicide dynamic in a population and examine its effectiveness for reducing the number of suicides by modifying certain parameters of the model. Assuming a population with replacement, the suicide risk of the population was estimated by determining the final state of the Markov model. *Results:* The model shows that targeting the whole population for suicide prevention is more effective than reducing risk in the high-risk tail of the distribution of psychological distress (i.e. the mentally ill). *Conclusions:* The results of this model reinforce the essence of the Rose theorem that lowering the suicidal risk in the population at large may be more effective than reducing the high risk in a small population.

A study on the effect of exclusion period on the suicidal risk among the insured

Yip PSF, Chen F (Hong Kong, Australia)

Social Science and Medicine 110, 26-30, 2014

An exclusion period (usually from 12 months to 2 years) is usually found in life insurance policies as a precautionary measure to prohibit people from insuring their lives with the intent to kill themselves shortly thereafter. Several studies have been conducted to investigate the effect of exclusion periods on the risk of suicide among the insured in the US and Australia. However, while Hong Kong has experienced an increase in the number of suicides among the insured, little is known about the dynamic between the exclusion period and suicide in Asia. Here we make use of death claims data from one of the major life insurance companies in Hong Kong to ascertain the impact of a 12-month exclusion period on suicide risk. We also use utility functions derived from economic theory to better understand individual choices regarding suicide among the insured. More specifically, we sought to determine whether there is a greater risk of suicide immediately following the 12-month exclusion period. We also examined whether the risk of suicide claims was higher than that of other non-suicidal claims. The study period for this investigation was from January 1, 1997 to December 31, 2011, during which time there were 1935 claims based on 1243 deaths. Of these, 197 were suicide-related claims for 106 suicide deaths. The mean number of life policies held by suicidal claimants and non-suicidal claimants was 1.6 and 1.4, respectively. The average/median size of the claims (total payment made on all policies held by the insured life) was HK$665,800/426,600 and HK$497,700/276,200 for suicidal and non-suicidal deaths, respectively. The policy lifetime of the claims, or the number of days from policy issuance to suicide occurrence, ranged from 38 to 7561 days, with a mean of 2209 days, a median of 1941 days, and a standard deviation of 1544 days. The peak density of suicide claims occurred on day 1039 of the policy. Our results revealed that suicide claims tend to occur earlier than other claims and that there is a greater risk of suicide observed following the 12-month exclusion period. Some suggestions are made in terms of extending the exclusion period, which is anticipated to significantly reduce suicide at the global level.

A longitudinal moderated mediation model of nonsuicidal self-injury among adolescents

You J, Lin MP, Leung F (China)

Journal of Abnormal Child Psychology. Published online: 18 June 2014. doi: 10.1007/s10802-014-9901-x, 2014

This study tested a longitudinal moderated mediation model of the engagement in non suicidal self-injury (NSSI) based on Nock's (2009) integrated theoretical model of the development of NSSI. We assessed general predisposing factors (i.e. borderline personality disorder features), precipitating factors (i.e. negative emotions), and NSSI-specific vulnerability factors (i.e. behavioral impulsivity and self-criticism) among 3,600 Chinese secondary school adolescents (56.6 % females, aged between 12 and 18 years). Assessments were conducted for three times, 6 months apart. Results supported the longitudinal mediation model, such that negative emotions mediated the relation of borderline personality disorder features to NSSI. The moderating effects of behavioral impulsivity and self-criticism were both significant, indicating that adolescents with higher levels of both variables were more likely to engage in NSSI. Moreover, behavioral impulsivity made additional contribution to the prediction of future NSSI above and beyond the effects of other risk factors. Findings of this study may help to elucidate the diverse roles of different types of risk factors in the engagement in NSSI, and may also shed new light on our understanding about the nature of this behavior.

Why alternative teenagers self-harm: Exploring the link between non-suicidal self-injury, attempted suicide and adolescent identity

Young R, Sproeber N, Groschwitz RC, Preiss M, Plener PL (Canada)

BMC Psychiatry 14, 137-137, 2014

Background: The term 'self-harm' encompasses both attempted suicide and non-suicidal self-injury (NSSI). Specific adolescent subpopulations such as ethnic or sexual minorities, and more controversially, those who identify as 'Alternative' (Goth, Emo) have been proposed as being more likely to self-harm, while other groups such as 'Jocks' are linked with protective coping behaviours (for example exercise). NSSI has autonomic (it reduces negative emotions) and social (it communicates distress or facilitates group 'bonding') functions. This study explores the links between such aspects of self-harm, primarily NSSI, and youth subculture.

Methods: An anonymous survey was carried out of 452 15 year old German school students. Measures included: identification with different youth cultures, i. e. Alternative (Goth, Emo, Punk), Nerd (academic) or Jock (athletic); social background, e. g. socioeconomic status; and experience of victimisation. Self-harm (suicide and NSSI) was assessed using Self-harm Behavior Questionnaire and the Functional Assessment of Self-Mutilation (FASM).

Results: An "Alternative" identity was directly (r approximate to 0.3) and a "Jock" identity inversely (r approximate to -0.1) correlated with self-harm. "Alternative" teenagers self-injured more frequently (NSSI 45.5% vs. 18.8%), repeatedly self-injured, and were 4-8 times more likely to attempt suicide (even after adjusting for social background) than their non-Alternative peers. They were also more likely to self-injure for autonomic, communicative and social reasons than other adolescents.

Conclusions: About half of 'Alternative' adolescents' self-injure, primarily to regulate emotions and communicate distress. However, a minority self-injure to reinforce their group identity, i.e. 'To feel more a part of a group'.

Citation List

FATAL SUICIDAL BEHAVIOR

Epidemiology

Acar A (2014). Culture, corruption, suicide, happiness and global social media use: A cross-cultural perspective. *International Journal of Web Based Communities* 10, 357-400.

Adinkrah M (2014). Intimate partner femicide-suicides in Ghana: Victims, offenders, and incident characteristics. *Violence Against Women* 20, 1078-1096.

Afghah S, Aghahasani M, Noori-Khajavi M, Tavakoli E (2014). Survey of suicide attempts in Sari. *Iranian Journal of Psychiatry* 9, 89-95.

Ajdacic-Gross V, Tran US, Bopp M, Sonneck G, Niederkrotenthaler T, Kapusta ND, Rossler W, Seifritz E, Voracek M (2014). Understanding weekly cycles in suicide: An analysis of Austrian and Swiss data over 40 years. *Epidemiology and Psychiatric Sciences.* Published online: 23 April 2014. doi: 10.1017/S2045796014000195.

Akar T, Karapirli M, Akçan R, Demirel B, Akduman B, Dursun AZ, Sari S, Ozkök A (2014). Elderly deaths in Ankara, Turkey. *Archives of Gerontology and Geriatrics* 59, 398-402.

Ali NH, Zainun KA, Bahar N, Haniff J, Hamid AM, Bujang MAH, Mahmood MS (2014). Pattern of suicides in 2009: Data from the National Suicide Registry Malaysia. *Asia-Pacific Psychiatry* 6, 217-225.

Badiye A, Kapoor N, Ahmed S (2014). An empirical analysis of suicidal death trends in India: A 5 year retrospective study. *Journal of Forensic and Legal Medicine* 27, 29-34.

Bando DH, Lester D (2014). An ecological study on suicide and homicide in Brazil. *Ciencia e Saude Coletiva* 19, 1179-1189.

Bailey A, Istre GR, Nie C, Evans J, Quinton R, Stephens-Stidham S (2014). Truancy and injury-related mortality. *Injury Prevention.* Published online: 10 September 2014. doi: 10.1136/injuryprev-2014-041276.

Baxter AJ, Vos T, Scott KM, Ferrari AJ, Whiteford HA (2014). The global burden of anxiety disorders in 2010. *Psychological Medicine* 44, 2363-2374.

Beauchamp GA, Ho ML, Yin S (2014). Variation in suicide occurrence by day and during major American holidays. *Journal of Emergency Medicine* 46, 776-781.

Biswas DK, Biswas A, Das DK, Bhunia R, Ghosh D (2013). Socio-demographic profiles of post mortem cases in a sub-district, west Bengal, India. *Medico-Legal Update* 13, 32-37.

Bjorkenstam C, Johansson LA, Nordstrom P, Thiblin I, Fugelstad A, Hallqvist J, Ljung R (2014). Suicide or undetermined intent? A register-based study of signs of misclassification. *Population Health Metrics.* Published online: 17 April 2014. doi: 10.1186/1478-7954-12-11.

Bruno CM, Alessio B, Alberto B, Cristina C (2014). The injury pattern in fatal suicidal falls from a height: An examination of 307 cases. *Forensic Science International* 244, 57-62 .

Chan SMS, Chiu FKH, Lam CWL, Wong SMC, Conwell Y (2014). A multidimensional risk factor model for suicide attempts in later life. *Neuropsychiatric Disease and Treatment* 10, 1807-1817.

Chang SS, Chen YY, Yip PS, Lee WJ, Hagihara A, Gunnell D (2014). Regional changes in charcoal-burning suicide rates in East/Southeast Asia from 1995 to 2011: A time trend analysis. *PLoS Medicine.* Published online: 1 April 2014. doi: 10.1371/journal.pmed.1001622.

Chen J, Choi YJ, Mori K, Sawada Y, Sugano S (2014). An analysis of suicides in Japan, 1997-2007: Changes in incidence, persistence, and age profiles. *Social Indicators Research.* Published online: 27 April 2014. doi: 10.1007/s11205-014-0635-5.

Chen Q, Sjolander A, Runeson B, D'Onofrio BM, Lichtenstein P, Larsson H (2014). Drug treatment for attention-deficit/hyperactivity disorder and suicidal behaviour: Register based study. *BMJ.* Published online: 18 June 2014. doi: 10.1136/bmj.g3769.

Cheng J, Kumar S, Nelson E, Harris T, Coverdale J (2014). A national survey of medical student suicides. *Academic Psychiatry* 38, 538-541.

Cheung DYT, Spittal MJ, Williamson MK, Tung SJ, Pirkis J (2014). Predictors of suicides occurring within suicide clusters in Australia, 2004-2008. *Social Science and Medicine* 118, 135-142.

Choi YR, Cha ES, Chang SS, Khang YH, Lee WJ (2014). Suicide from carbon monoxide poisoning in South Korea: 2006-2012. *Journal of Affective Disorders* 167, 322-325.

Coope C, Gunnell D, Hollingworth W, Hawton K, Kapur N, Fearn V, Wells C, Metcalfe C (2014). Suicide and the 2008 economic recession: Who is most at risk? Trends in suicide rates in England and Wales 2001-2011. *Social Science and Medicine* 117, 76-85.

Cunningham R, Sarfati D, Peterson D, Stanley J, Collings S (2014). Premature mortality in adults using New Zealand psychiatric services. *New Zealand Medical Journal* 127, 31-41.

Dahmardehei M, Behmanesh Poor F, Mollashahi G, Moallemi S (2014). Epidemiological study of self-immolation at Khatamolanbia hospital of Zahedan. *International Journal of High Risk Behaviors and Addiction*. Published online: 10 March 2014. doi: 10.5812/ijhrba.13170.

Dedi G (2014). Gender differences in suicide in Serbia within the period 2006-2010. *Military-Medical and Pharmaceutical Review* 71, 265-270.

De Vogli R (2014). The financial crisis, health and health inequities in Europe: The need for regulations, redistribution and social protection. *International Journal for Equity in Health*. Published online: 25 July 2014. doi: 10.1186/s12939-014-0058-6.

Dinolova R, Zarkov Z, Okoliyski M, Hinkov H, Nakov V, Dimitrov P (2014). Prevalence of suicidal behavior among people with common mental disorders in Bulgaria. Results from the epidemiological study EPIBUL (2003-2007). *Bulgarian Journal of Public Health* 6, 74-82.

Elliott S, Evans J (2014). A 3-year review of new psychoactive substances in casework. *Forensic Science International* 243, 55-60.

Enginyurt O, Ozer E, Gumus B, Demir EY, Cankaya S (2014). Evaluation of suicide cases in Turkey, 2007-2012. *Medical Science Monitor* 20, 614-623.

Faria NM, Fassa AG, Meucci RD (2014). Association between pesticide exposure and suicide rates in Brazil. *NeuroToxicology*. Published online: 27 May 2014. doi: 10.1016/j.neuro.2014.05.003.

Fazeli S, Matin RK, Kakaei N, Pourghorban S, Moghadam MA, Faramani SS, Faramani RS (2014). Self-inflicted burn injuries in Kermanshah: A public health problem. *Journal of Health Scope* 3, e17780.

Ferrari AJ, Norman RE, Freedman G, Baxter AJ, Pirkis JE, Harris MG, Page A, Carnahan E, Degenhardt L, Vos T, Whiteford HA (2014). The burden attributable to mental and substance use disorders as risk factors for suicide: Findings from the global burden of disease study 2010. *PLoS ONE*. Published online: 2 April 2014. doi: 10.1371/journal.pone.0091936.

Fisher LB, Overholser JC, Dieter L (2014). Methods of committing suicide among 2,347 people in Ohio. *Death Studies*. Published online: 23 June 2014. doi: 10.1080/07481187.2013.851130.

Fraser SL, Geoffroy D, Chachamovich E, Kirmayer LJ (2014). Changing rates of suicide ideation and attempts among Inuit youth: A gender-based analysis of risk and protective factors. *Suicide and Life-Threatening Behavior*. Published online: 25 September 2014. doi: 10.1111/sltb.12122.

Gunnell D, Coope C, Fearn V, Wells C, Chang SS, Hawton K, Kapur N (2014). Suicide by gases in England and Wales 2001-2011: Evidence of the emergence of new methods of suicide. *Journal of Affective Disorders* 170, 190-195.

Hakim A, Khurshid R, Shah RAR, Mufti S, Krishan K, Singh Y, Afreen (2014). Pattern, profile and outcome of poisoning cases: A study at a large teaching hospital in north India. *JK Practitioner* 19, 36-40.

Hassanian-Moghaddam H, Zamani N, Rahimi M, Shadnia S, Pajoumand A, Sarjami S (2014). Acute adult and adolescent poisoning in Tehran, Iran; the epidemiologic trend between 2006 and 2011. *Archives of Iranian Medicine* 17, 534-538.

He M, Li W-C, Sun D-M, Ma K-J, Zhao Z-Q, Li B-X, Li L (2014). Epitome of China's unnatural deaths: A historically retrospective study of forensic autopsy cases in Shanghai Public Security Bureau from 1990 to 1999. *American Journal of Forensic Medicine and Pathology* 35, 218–221.

Hedlund J, Ahlner J, Kristiansson M, Sturup J (2014). A population-based study on toxicological findings in Swedish homicide victims and offenders from 2007 to 2009. *Forensic Science International* 244, 25-29.

Herne MA, Bartholomew ML, Weahkee RL (2014). Suicide mortality among American Indians and Alaska natives, 1999-2009. *American Journal of Public* Health 104, S336-S342.

Hiltunen L, Haukka J, Ruuhela R, Suominen K, Partonen T (2014). Local daily temperatures, thermal seasons, and suicide rates in Finland from 1974 to 2010. *Environmental Health and Preventive Medicine.* Published online: 3 May 2014. doi: 10.1007/s12199-014-0391-9.

Jhamad AR, Sikary AK, Millo T (2014). Analysis of custodial deaths in New Delhi: A 13 years study. *Journal of Indian Academy of Forensic Medicine* 36, 19-22.

Jones K, Mansfield CJ (2014). Premature mortality in North Carolina: Progress, regress, and disparities by county and race, 2000-2010. *North Carolina Medical Journal* 75, 159-168.

Jorm AF (2014). Why hasn't the mental health of Australians improved? The need for a national prevention strategy. *Australian and New Zealand Journal of Psychiatry* 48, 795-801.

Jung-Choi K, Khang YH, Cho HJ, Yun SC (2014). Decomposition of educational differences in life expectancy by age and causes of death among South Korean adults. *BMC Public Health* . Published online: 5 June 2014. doi: 10.1186/1471-2458-14-560.

Kafadar H, Kafadar S, Tokdemir M (2014). Suicides in adolescence: A twelve-year study from Eastern Turkey. *Journal of Forensic and Legal Medicine* 27, 6-8.

Kalesan B, Vasan S, Mobily ME, Villarreal MD, Hlavacek P, Teperman S, Fagan JA, Galea S (2014). State-specific, racial and ethnic heterogeneity in trends of firearm-related fatality rates in the USA from 2000 to 2010. *BMJ Open.* Published online: 14 August 2014. doi:10.1136/bmjopen-2014-005628.

Karami Joushin M, Saghafipour A, Noroozi M, Soori H, Khedmati Morasae E (2013). Epidemiology of accidents and traumas in Qom province in 2010. *Archives of Trauma Research* 2, 113-117.

Khajuria B (2013). Poisoning trend in militancy occupied state of India. *JK Science* 15, 122-124.

Kiadaliri AA, Saadat S, Shahnavazi H, Haghparast-Bidgoli H (2014). Overall, gender and social inequalities in suicide mortality in Iran, 2006-2010: A time trend province-level study. *BMJ Open.* Published online: 19 August 2014. doi:10.1136/bmjopen-2014-005227.

Knipe DW, Metcalfe C, Fernando R, Pearson M, Konradsen F, Eddleston M, Gunnell D (2014). Suicide in Sri Lanka 1975-2012: Age, period and cohort analysis of police and hospital data. *BMC Public Health.* Published online: 13 August 2014. doi: 10.1186/1471-2458-14-839.

Kõlves K, De Leo D (2014). Are immigrants responsible for the recent decline in Australian suicide rates? *Epidemiology and Psychiatric Sciences.* Published online: 2 May 2014. doi: 10.1017/S2045796014000122.

Kõlves K, De Leo D (2014). Regions with the highest suicide rates for children and adolescents-some observations. *Journal of Child And Adolescent Behavior.* Published online: 25 March 2014. doi: 10.4172/jcalb.1000e104.

Kõlves K, De Leo D (2014). Suicide rates in children aged 10-14 years worldwide: Changes in the past two decades. *British Journal of Psychiatry* 205, 283-285.

Kosenli O, Satar S, Ay MO, Kosenli A, Acikalin A, Kozaci N, Gulen M, Cokuk A (2014). Analysis of pharmaceutical poisonings in adults occurred in Adana region of Turkey in North Eastern Mediterranean. *Acta Medica Mediterranea* 30, 585-589.

Krawczyk N, Meyer A, Fonseca M, Lima J (2014). Suicide mortality among agricultural workers in a region with intensive tobacco farming and use of pesticides in Brazil. *Journal of Occupational and Environmental Medicine* 56, 993-1000.

Kristoffersen S, Lilleng PK, Mæhle BO, Morild I (2014). Homicides in Western Norway, 1985-2009, time trends, age and gender differences. *Forensic Science International*. Published online: 1 May 2014. doi: 10.1016/j.forsciint.2014.02.013.

Kumar RR, Punitha P (2014). Delayed causes of death in hanging: An autopsy study. *Journal of Punjab Academy of Forensic Medicine and Toxicology* 14, 32-35.

Kumar S, Verma AK, Ahmad I, Ali W, Singh US (2013). Profile of unnatural deaths- a study of autopsies at mortuary of King George's Medical University, Lucknow, India. *Medico-Legal Update* 13, 113-118.

Laanani M, Ghosn W, Jougla E, Rey G (2014). Impact of unemployment variations on suicide mortality in Western European countries (2000-2010). *Journal of Epidemiology and Community Health*. Published online: 18 June 2014. doi: 10.1136/jech-2013-203624.

Lahti A, Harju A, Hakko H, Riala K, Räsänen P (2014). Suicide in children and young adolescents: A 25-year database on suicides from Northern Finland. *Journal of Psychiatric Research* 58, 123-128.

Laszlo AM, Hulman A, Csicsman J, Bari F, Nyari TA (2014). The use of regression methods for the investigation of trends in suicide rates in Hungary between 1963 and 2011. *Social Psychiatry and Psychiatric Epidemiology*. Published online: 3 July 2014. doi: 10.1007/s00127-014-0926-9.

Law CK, Snider AM, De Leo D (2014). The influence of deprivation on suicide mortality in urban and rural Queensland: An ecological analysis. *Social Psychiatry and Psychiatric Epidemiology*. Published online: 12 June 2014. doi:10.1007/s00127-014-0905-1.

Law CK, Sveticic J, De Leo D (2014). Restricting access to a suicide hotspot does not shift the problem to another location. An experiment of two river bridges in Brisbane, Australia. *Australian and New Zealand Journal of Public Health* 38, 134-138.

Lee AY, Pridmore S (2014). Suicide and gender ratios in Tasmania (Australia) using the operationalized predicaments of suicide tool, and negative experiences. *Australasian Psychiatry* 22, 140-143.

Lovrecic M, Lovrecic B, Semerl JS, Maremmani AGI, Maremmani I (2013). The intentionality of fatal poisonings among illicit drug users, and predictors for intentional intoxication in Slovenia during the years 2002-2007. *Heroin Addiction and Related Clinical Problems* 15, 39-44.

Maron BJ, Haas TS, Murphy CJ, Ahluwalia A, Rutten-Ramos S (2014). Incidence and causes of sudden death in US College athletes. *Journal of the American College of Cardiology* 63, 1636-1643.

McMahon EM, Keeley H, Cannon M, Arensman E, Perry IJ, Clarke M, Chambers D, Corcoran P (2014). The iceberg of suicide and self-harm in Irish adolescents: A population-based study. *Social Psychiatry and Psychiatric Epidemiology*. Published online: 15 June 2014. doi: 10.1007/s00127-014-0907-z.

Moga M, Burtea V, Ifteni P (2014). Socioeconomic status and psychological factors involved in suicide. *Revista de Cercetare si Interventie Sociala* 45, 230-239.

Naidoo SS, Schlebusch L (2014). Sociodemographic characteristics of persons committing suicide in Durban, South Africa: 2006-2007. *African Journal of Primary Health Care and Family Medicine*. Published online: 24 February 2014. doi: 10.4102/phcfm.v6i1.568.

Najafi F, Beiki O, Ahmadijouybari T, Amini S, Moradinazar M, Hatemi M, Moradi M (2014). An assessment of suicide attempts by self-poisoning in the west of Iran. *Journal of Forensic and Legal Medicine* 27, 1-5.

Ngamini Ngui A, Apparicio P, Moltchanova E, Vasiliadis HM (2014). Spatial analysis of suicide mortality in Québec: Spatial clustering and area factor correlates. *Psychiatry Research* 220, 20-30.

Niedzwiedz C, Haw C, Hawton K, Platt S (2014). The definition and epidemiology of clusters of suicidal behavior: A systematic review. *Suicide and Life Threatening Behavior*. Pubished online: 7 April 2014. doi: 10.1111/sltb.12091.

Nielsen PR, Gheorghe A, Lynnerup N (2014). Forensic aspects of carbon monoxide poisoning by charcoal burning in Denmark, 2008-2012: An autopsy based study. *Forensic Science, Medicine, and Pathology* 10, 390-394.

Onyeka IN, Beynon CM, Hannila ML, Tiihonen J, Föhr J, Tuomola P, Kuikanmäki O, Tasa N, Paasolainen M, Kauhanen J (2014). Patterns and 14-year trends in mortality among illicit drug users in Finland: The HUUTI study. *International Journal of Drug Policy*. Published online: 30 July 2014. doi: 10.1016/j.drugpo.2014.07.008.

Ortega PA, Manrique RD, Tovilla Zarate CA, López Jaramillo C, Cuartas JM (2014). Clinical and epidemiological characteristics of suicides committed in Medellin, Colombia. *Revista Colombiana de Psiquiatria* 43, 106-112.

Park S, Ahn MH, Lee A, Hong JP (2014). Associations between changes in the pattern of suicide methods and rates in Korea, the US, and Finland. *International Journal of Mental Health Systems*. Published online: 4 June 2014. doi:10.1186/1752-4458-8-22.

Patel NS, Srivastava AK, Kumar A, Kiran Kumar JV, Nandwani S (2014). Trends of poisoning in Western Utter Pradesh a clinico-pathological study. *Journal of Indian Academy of Forensic Medicine* 36, 142-145.

Pawar CK, Bhullar DS, Oberoi SS, Aggarwal KK (2014). Profile of unnatural deaths in females: A retrospective study. *Journal of Indian Academy of Forensic Medicine* 36, 122-124.

Pedroso Zulueta TD (2013). Gender disparities in mortality: Challenges for health equity in Puerto Rico. *Acta Colombiana de Psicologi* 16, 103-114.

Peiris-John R, Kool B, Ameratunga S (2014). Fatalities and hospitalisations due to acute poisoning among New Zealand adults. *Internal Medicine Journal* 44, 273-281.

Peng TA, Lee CC, Lin JC, Shun CT, Shaw KP, Weng TI (2014). Fatal falls from height in Taiwan. *Journal of Forensic Sciences*. Published online: 16 April 2014. doi: 10.1111/1556-4029.12445.

Peonim V, Sujirachato K, Srisont S, Udnoon J, Worasuwannarak W (2014). Committed suicide: Forensic autopsy analysis at Ramathibodi hospital during year 2001-2010. *Journal of the Medical Association of Thailand* 97, 662-668.

Phillips JA (2014). A changing epidemiology of suicide? The influence of birth cohorts on suicide rates in the United States. *Social Science and Medicine* 114, 151-160.

Ploderl M, Fartacek C, Kunrath S, Pichler EM, Fartacek R, Datz C, Niederseer D (2014). Nothing like Christmas: Suicides during Christmas and other holidays in Austria. *European Journal of Public Health*. Published online: 22 September 2014. doi: 10.1093/eurpub/cku169.

Pobutsky A, Brown M, Nakao L, Reyes-Salvail F (2014). Results from the Hawaii domestic violence fatality review, 2000-2009. *Journal of Injury & Violence Research* 6, 79-90.

Pretorius K, Van Niekerk A (2014). Childhood psychosocial development and fatal injuries in Gauteng, South Africa. *Child: Care, Health and Development*. Published online: 15 April 2014. doi: 10.1111/cch.12140.

Puiguriguer Ferrando J, Nogué S, Echarte JL, Ferrer A, Dueñas A, García L, Córdoba F, Burillo-Putze G (2013). Hospital mortality due to acute poisoning: Exitox 2012. *Journal of the Spanish Society of Emergency Medicine* 25, 467-471.

Puttagunta R, Lomax ME, McGuinness JE, Coverdale J (2014). What is the prevalence of the experience of death of a patient by suicide among medical students and residents? A systematic review. *Academic Psychiatry* 38, 538–541.

Pyakurel R, Sharma N, Paudel D, Coghill A, Sinden L, Bost L, Larkin M, Burrus CJ, Roy K (2014). Cause of death in women of reproductive age in rural Nepal obtained through community-based surveillance: Is reducing maternal mortality the right priority for women's health programmes? *Health Care for Women International*. Published online: 28 May 2014. doi: 10.1080/07399332.2014.908193.

Qi X, Hu W, Page A, Tong S (2014). Dynamic pattern of suicide in Australia, 1986-2005: A descriptive-analytic study. *BMJ Open*. Published online: 29 July 2014. doi:10.1136/bmjopen-2014-005311.

Radeloff D, Lempp T, Herrmann E, Kettner M, Bennefeld-Kersten K, Freitag CM (2014). National total survey of German adolescent suicide in prison. *European Child & Adolescent Psychiatry*. Published online: 22 June 201. doi: 10.1007/s00787-014-0568-1.

Rane A, Nadkarni A (2014). Suicide in India: A systematic review. *Shanghai Archives of Psychiatry* 26, 69-80.

Rao BR, Basha VC, Reddy KS (2014). A study of ligature mark in deaths due to hanging in Warangal area, Andhra Pradesh. *Indian Journal of Forensic Medicine and Toxicology* 8, 85-88.

Razvodovsky YE (2013). Psychosocial distress as a risk factor of ischemic heart disease mortality. *Psychiatria Danubina* 25, 68-75.

Reques L, Giráldez-García C, Miqueleiz E, Belza MJ, Regidor E (2014). Educational differences in mortality and the relative importance of different causes of death: A 7-year follow-up study of Spanish adults. *Journal of Epidemiology and Community Health*. Published online: 14 August 2014. doi: 10.1136/jech-2014-204186.

Ruas F, Mendonca MC, Real FC, Vieira DN, Teixeira HM (2014). Carbon monoxide poisoning as a cause of death and differential diagnosis in the forensic practice: A retrospective study, 2000-2010. *Journal of Forensic and Legal Medicine* 24, 1-6.

Salvador-Carulla L, Bendeck M, Ferrer M, Andión O, Aragonès E, Casas M (2014). Cost of borderline personality disorder in Catalonia (Spain). *European Psychiatry* 8, 290-297.

Sane MR, Ananda K (2014). Unnatural deaths of adult females in South Bangalore: An autopsy study. *Journal of Indian Academy of Forensic Medicine* 36, 130-132.

Saurav C, Aayushi G, Behera C, Karthik K, Millo T, Gupta S (2014). Medico-legal autopsy of 1355 unclaimed dead bodies brought to a tertiary care hospital in Delhi, India (2006-2012). *Medico-Legal Journal* 82, 112-115.

Shah A, Zarate-Escudero S, Bhat R, De Leo D, Erlangsen A (2014). Suicide in centenarians: The international landscape. *International Psychogeriatrics* 26, 1703-1708.

Sheikhmoonesi F, Zarghami M (2014). Prevention of physicians' suicide. *Iranian Journal of Psychiatry and Behavioral Sciences* 8, 1-3.

Shibre T, Hanlon C, Medhin G, Alem A, Kebede D, Teferra S, Kullgren G, Jacobsson L, Fekadu A (2014). Suicide and suicide attempts in people with severe mental disorders in Butajira, Ethiopia: 10 year follow-up of a population-based cohort. *BMC Psychiatry*. Published online: 23 May 2014. doi: 10.1186/1471-244X-14-150.

Shinde SS, Nagarajaiah, Narayanaswamy JC, Viswanath B, Kumar NC, Gangadhar BN, Math SB (2014). Mortality among inpatients of a psychiatric hospital: Indian perspective. *Indian Journal of Psychological Medicine* 36, 142-146.

Sibia RS, Kumar SA, Bhullar DS, Pillai GR, Sharma H, Sandhu SS (2014). Poisoning trends at a tertiary hospital: A retrospective analysis. *Journal of Punjab Academy of Forensic Medicine and Toxicology* 14, 19-21.

Singh A, Harish D, Kumar A (2013). Aluminium phosphide, the most preferred poison: A 10 year retrospective study of deaths due to poisoning in a tertiary care center. *Journal of Punjab Academy of Forensic Medicine and Toxicology* 13, 74-79.

Sise RG, Calvo RY, Spain DA, Weiser TG, Staudenmayer KL (2014). The epidemiology of trauma-related mortality in the United States from 2002 to 2010. *Journal of Trauma and Acute Care Surgery* 76, 913-919.

Skerrett DM, Kõlves K, De Leo D (2014). Suicides among lesbian, gay, bisexual, and transgender populations in Australia: An analysis of the Queensland Suicide Register. *Asia Pacific Psychiatry*. Published online: 2 April 2014. doi: 10.1111/appy.12128.

Soole R, Kõlves K, De Leo D (2014). Factors related to childhood suicides: Analysis of the Queensland Child Death Register. *Crisis*. Published online: 22 September 2014. doi: 10.1027/0227-5910/a000267.

Sousa S, Santos L, Dinis-Oliveira RJ, Magalhaes T, Santos A (2014). Pedestrian fatalities resulting from train-person collisions. *Traffic Injury Prevention*. Published online: 9 October 2014. doi: 10.1111/appy.12128.

Spittal MJ, Forsyth S, Pirkis J, Alati R, Kinner SA (2014). Suicide in adults released from prison in Queensland, Australia: A cohort study. *Journal of Epidemiology and Community Health* 63, 993-998.

Sugano S, Matsuki Y (2014). Poisson analysis of suicide in Japan using municipal data. *Applied Economics Letters* 21, 723-726.

Sumarokov YA, Brenn T, Kudryavtsev AV, Nilssen O (2014). Suicides in the Indigenous and non-Indigenous populations in the Nenets Autonomous Okrug, Northwestern Russia, and associated socio-demographic characteristics. *International Journal of Circumpolar Health*. Published online: 6 May 2013. doi: 10.3402/ijch.v73.24308.

Sun S-H, Jia C-x (2014). Completed suicide with violent and non-violent methods in rural Shandong, China: A psychological autopsy study. *PLoS ONE*. Published online: 11 August, 2014. doi: 10.1371/journal.pone.0104333.

Suzuki H, Hikiji W, Tanifuji T, Abe N, Fukunaga T (2014). Child deaths from injury in the special wards of Tokyo, Japan (2006-2010): A descriptive study. *Journal of Epidemiology 24*, 178-182.

Toivanen S, Mellner C, Vinberg S (2014). Self-employed persons in Sweden - mortality differentials by industrial sector and enterprise legal form: A five-year follow-up study. *American Journal of Industrial Medicine*. Published online: 24 September 2014. doi: 10.1002/ajim.22387.

Torresani S, Toffol E, Scocco P, Fanolla A (2014). Suicide in elderly South Tyroleans in various residential settings at the time of death: A psychological autopsy study. *Psychogeriatrics* 14, 101-109.

Vassalini M, Verzeletti A, De Ferrari F (2014). Sharp force injury fatalities: A retrospective study (1982-2012) in Brescia (Italy). *Journal of Forensic Sciences*. Published online: 8 April 2014. doi: 10.1111/1556-4029.12487.

Verzeletti A, Russo MC, De Ferrari F (2014). Homicide-suicide in Brescia county (Northern Italy): A retrospective study from 1987 to 2012. *Journal of Forensic and Legal Medicine* 25, 62-66.

Vidanapathirana M (2014). Young tend to commit suicide, die of road traffic accidents or being killed by someone: An analysis of medico-legal deaths. *International Journal of Medical Toxicology and Forensic Medicine* 4, 42-48.

Webb RT, Lichtenstein P, Dahlin M, Kapur N, Ludvigsson JF, Runeson B (2014). Unnatural deaths in a national cohort of people diagnosed with diabetes. *Diabetes Care* 37, 2276-2283.

Westman J, Wahlbeck K, Laursen TM, Gissler M, Nordentoft M, Hällgren J, Arffman M, Osby U (2014). Mortality and life expectancy of people with alcohol use disorder in Denmark, Finland and Sweden. *Acta Psychiatrica Scandinavica.* Published online: 20 September 2014. doi: 10.1111/acps.12330.

Wong CA, Gachupin FC, Holman RC, Macdorman MF, Cheek JE, Holve S, Singleton RJ (2014). American Indian and Alaska native infant and pediatric mortality, United States, 1999-2009. *American Journal of Public Health* 104, S320-S328.

Ylijoki-Sørensen S, Boldsen JL, Boel LWT, Bøggild H, Lalu K, Sajantila A (2014). Autopsy rate in suicide is low among elderly in Denmark compared with Finland. *Forensic Science International* 244, 158-165.

Risk and protective factors

Ahmad N, Man CS, Ibrahim N, Rosman A (2014). Suicidal ideation among Malaysian adolescents. *Asia-Pacific Journal of Public Health* 26, 63S-69S.

Andres AR, Chakraborty B, Dasgupta P, Mitra S (2014). Realizing the significance of socio-economic triggers for mental health outcomes in India. *Journal of Behavioral and Experimental Economics* 50, 50-57.

Anestis MD, Khazem LR, Law KC (2014). How many times and how many ways: The impact of number of nonsuicidal self-injury methods on the relationship between nonsuicidal self-injury frequency and suicidal behavior. *Suicide and Life Threatening Behavior*. Published online: 16 September 2014. doi: 10.1111/sltb.12120.

Antonakakis N, Collins A (2014). The impact of fiscal austerity on suicide: On the empirics of a modern Greek tragedy. *Social Science and Medicine* 112, 39-50.

Austin AE, van den Heuvel C, Byard RW (2014). Body mass index and suicide. *American Journal of Forensic Medicine and Pathology* 35, 145-147.

Bakst S, Braun T, Hirshberg R, Zucker I, Shohat T (2014). Characteristics of suicide completers with a psychiatric diagnosis before death: A postmortem study of 98 cases. *Psychiatry Research* 220, 556-563.

Bartone PT (2013). A new taxonomy for understanding factors leading to suicide in the military. *International Journal of Emergency Mental Health* 15, 299-305.

Baumbach A, Gulis G (2014). Impact of financial crisis on selected health outcomes in Europe. *European Journal of Public Health* 24, 399-403.

Baumert J, Schneider B, Lukaschek K, Emeny RT, Meisinger C, Erazo N, Dragano N, Ladwig KH (2014). Adverse conditions at the workplace are associated with increased suicide risk. *Journal of Psychiatric Research* 57, 90-95.

Benedetti F, Riccaboni R, Poletti S, Radaelli D, Locatelli C, Lorenzi C, Pirovano A, Smeraldi E, Colombo C (2014). The serotonin transporter genotype modulates the relationship between early stress and adult suicidality in bipolar disorder. *Bipolar Disord*ers. Published online: 15 September 2014. doi: 10.1111/bdi.12250.

Bergen H, Hawton K, Webb R, Cooper J, Steeg S, Haigh M, Ness J, Waters K, Kapur N (2014). Alcohol-related mortality following self-harm: A multicentre cohort study. *JRSM Open*. Published online: 6 August 2014. doi: 10.1177/2054270414533326.

Berman AL, Sundararaman R, Price A, Au JS (2014). Suicide on railroad rights-of-way: A psychological autopsy study. *Suicide and Life-Threatening Behavior*. Published online: 20 June 2014. doi: 10.1111/sltb.12107.

Bernert RA, Turvey CL, Conwell Y, Joiner TE (2014). Association of poor subjective sleep quality with risk for death by suicide during a 10-year period: A longitudinal, population-based study of late life. *JAMA Psychiatry* 1, 1129-1137.

Bolton JM, Walld R, Chateau D, Finlayson G, Sareen J (2014). Risk of suicide and suicide attempts associated with physical disorders: A population-based, balancing score-matched analysis. *Psychological Medicine*. Published online: 17 July 2014. doi: 10.1017/S0033291714001639.

Borretzen MN, Bjerknes S, Saehle T, Skjelland M, Skogseid IM, Toft M, Dietrichs E (2014). Long-term follow-up of thalamic deep brain stimulation for essential tremor - patient satisfaction and mortality. *BMC Neurology*. Published online: 5 June 2014. doi: 10.1186/1471-2377-14-120.

Bourque F, Cunsolo Willox A (2014). Climate change: The next challenge for public mental health? *International Review Of Psychiatry* 26, 415-422.

Bozzay ML, Liu RT, Kleiman EM (2014). Gender and age differences in suicide mortality in the context of violent death: Findings from a multi-state population-based surveillance system. *Comprenensive Psychiatry* 55, 1077–1084.

Brandon M, Bailey S, Belderson P, Larsson B (2014). The role of neglect in child fatality and serious injury. *Child Abuse Review* 23, 235-245.

Breuer C (2014). Unemployment and suicide mortality: Evidence from regional panel data in Europe. *Health Economics.* Published online: 17 June 2014. doi: 10.1002/hec.3073.

Bruckner TA (2014). Invited commentary: Are there unrealized benefits of unemployment insurance among the employed? *American Journal of Epidemiology* 180, 53-55.

Cano-Langreo M, Cicirello-Salas S, López-López A, Aguilar-Vela M, Veiga-de Cabo J (2014). Current framework of suicide and suicidal ideation in health professionals. *Medicina y Seguridad del Trabajo* 60, 219-238.

Carli V (2014). Identifying inmates that will actually die by suicide. *Evidence Based Mental Health.* Published online: 26 September 2014. doi: 10.1136/eb-2014-101895

Carson HJ (2014). The medium, not the message: How tattoos correlate with early mortality. *American Journal of Clinical Pathology* 142, 99-103.

Carvalho AF, McIntyre RS, Dimelis D, Gonda X, Berk M, Nunes-Neto PR, Cha DS, Hyphantis TN, Angst J, Fountoulakis KN (2014). Predominant polarity as a course specifier for bipolar disorder: A systematic review. *Journal of Affective Disorders* 163, 56-64.

Chandley MJ, Szebeni A, Szebeni K, Crawford JD, Stockmeier CA, Turecki G, Kostrzewa RM, Ordway GA (2014). Elevated gene expression of glutamate receptors in noradrenergic neurons from the locus coeruleus in major depression. *The International Journal of Neuropsychopharmacology* 17, 1569-1578.

Chang WC, Chen ES, Hui CL, Chan SK, Lee EH, Chen EY (2014). Prevalence and risk factors for suicidal behavior in young people presenting with first-episode psychosis in Hong Kong: A 3-year follow-up study. *Social Psychiatry and Psychiatric Epidemiology.* Published online: 13 August 2014. doi: 10.1007/s00127-014-0946-5.

Chartier MJ, Finlayson G, Prior H, McGowan K-L, Chen H, Walld R, De Rocquigny J (2014). Are there mental health differences between Francophone and non-Francophone populations in Manitoba? *Canadian Journal of Psychiatry* 59, 366-375.

Cheung G, Casey J (2014). Few older people in New Zealand who commit suicide receive specialist psychogeriatric services. *Australasian Psychiatry* 22, 386 – 389.

Chopra A, Abulseoud OA, Sampson S, Lee KH, Klassen BT, Fields JA, Matsumoto JY, Adams AC, Stoppel CJ, Geske JR, Frye MA (2014). Mood stability in Parkinson disease following deep brain stimulation: A 6-month prospective follow-up study. *Psychosomatics* 55, 478-484.

Clouston SA, Rubin MS, Colen CG, Link BG (2014). Social inequalities in suicide: The role of selective serotonin reuptake inhibitors. *American Journal of Epidemiology.* Published online: 28 August 2014. doi: 10.1093/aje/kwu191.

Cochran SD, Mays VM (2014). Mortality risks among persons reporting same-sex sexual partners: Evidence from the 2008 general social survey-national death index data set. *American Journal of Public Health.* Published online: 17 July 2014. doi: 10.2105/AJPH.2014.301974.

Cole AB, Wingate LR, Slish ML, Tucker RP, Hollingsworth DW, O'Keefe VM (2013). Burdensomeness, depression, and suicide in a sample of American-Indian college students. *Ethnicity and Inequalities in Health and Social Care* 6, 77-86.

Cole TB, Bowling JM, Patetta MJ, Blazer DG (2014). Risk factors for suicide among older adults with cancer. *Aging and Mental Health* 18, 854-860.

Conner KR, Bossarte RM, He H, Arora J, Lu N, Tu XM, Katz IR (2014). Posttraumatic stress disorder and suicide in 5.9 million individuals receiving care in the veterans health administration health system. *Journal of Affective Disorders* 166, 1-5.

Costantini A, Pompili M, Innamorati M, Zezza MC, Di Carlo A, Sher L, Girardi P (2014). Psychiatric pathology and suicide risk in patients with cancer. *Journal of Psychosocial Oncology 32*, 383-395.

Crone C, DiMartini A (2014). Liver transplant for intentional acetaminophen overdose: A survey of transplant clinicians experiences with recommendations. *Psychosomatics.* Published online: 17 February 2014. doi: 10.1016/j.psym.2014.02.004.

Crowder MK, Kemmelmeier M (2014). Untreated depression predicts higher suicide rates in U.S. honor cultures. *Journal of Cross-Cultural Psychology* 45, 1145-1161.

Cylus J, Glymour MM, Avendano M (2014). Do generous unemployment benefit programs reduce suicide rates? A state fixed-effect analysis covering 1968-2008. *American Journal of Epidemiology* 180, 45-52.

Davison KM, Kaplan BJ (2014). Lipophilic statin use and suicidal ideation in a sample of adults with mood disorders. *Crisis* 35, 278-282.

de Bernier GL, Kim YR, Sen P (2014). A systematic review of the global prevalence of personality disorders in adult Asian populations. *Personality and Mental Health* 8, 264-275.

DeFina R, Hannon L (2014). The changing relationship between unemployment and suicide. *Suicide and Life Threatening Behavior.* Published online: 12 September 2014. doi: 10.1111/sltb.12116.

Delaveris GJM, Teige B, Rogde S (2014). Non-natural manners of death among users of illicit drugs: Substance findings. *Forensic Science International* 238, 16-21.

Diniz MdFHS, Moura LD, Kelles SMB, Diniz MTC (2013). Long-term mortality of patients submitted to Roux-en-Y gastric bypass in public health system: High prevalence of alcoholic cirrhosis and suicides. *Brazilian Archives of Digestive Surgery* 26, Suppl 1, 53-56.

Dogan KH, Demirci S, Deniz I (2014). Why do people hang themselves on trees? An evaluation of suicidal hangings on trees in Konya, Turkey, between 2001 and 2008. *Journal of Forensic Sciences*, Published online: 3 August 2014. doi: 10.1111/1556-4029.12589.

Dorsey ER, Brocht AFD, Nichols PE, Darwin KC, Anderson KE, Beck CA, Singh S, Biglan KM, Shoulson I (2013). Depressed mood and suicidality in individuals exposed to tetrabenazine in a large Huntington disease observational study. *Journal of Huntington's Disease* 2, 509-515.

Drescher MJ, Russell FM, Pappas M, Pepper DA (2014). Can emergency medicine practitioners predict disposition of psychiatric patients based on a brief medical evaluation? *European Journal of Emergency Medicine.* Published online: 6 June 2014. doi: 10.1097/MEJ.0000000000000131.

Du J, Sun H, Huang D, Jiang H, Zhong N, Xu D, Zhao Y, Lin S, Wang W, Du Z, Zhao M, Hser YI (2014). Use trajectories of amphetamine-type stimulants (ATS) in Shanghai, China. *Drug and Alcohol Dependence* 143, 44-50.

Duran S, Fistikci N, Keyvan A, Bilici M, Caliskan M (2014). ADHD in adult psychiatric outpatients: Prevalence and comorbidity. *Turkish Journal of Psychiatry* 25, 84-93.

Eke SM, Basoglu S, Bakar B, Oral G (2014). Maternal filicide in Turkey. *Journal of Forensic Sciences.* Published online: 28 July 2014. doi: 10.1111/1556-4029.12560.

Fabio Di Narzo A, Kozlenkov A, Roussos P, Hao K, Hurd Y, Lewis DA, Sibille E, Siever LJ, Koonin E, Dracheva S (2014). A unique gene expression signature associated with serotonin 2C receptor RNA editing in the prefrontal cortex and altered in suicide. *Human Molecular Genetics* 23, 4801-4813.

Feigelman W, Rosen Z, Gorman BS (2014). Exploring prospective predictors of completed suicides: Evidence from the general social survey. *Crisis* 35, 233-244.

Ferrara P, Ianniello F, Cutrona C, Quintarelli F, Vena F, Del Volgo V, Caporale O, Malamisura M, De Angelis M, Gatto A, Chiaretti A, Riccardi R (2014). A focus on recent cases of suicides among Italian children and adolescents and a review of literature. *Italian Journal of Pediatrics*. Published online: 15 July 2014. doi: 10.1186/s13052-014-0069-3.

Fischer G, Ameis N, Parzer P, Plener PL, Groschwitz R, Vonderlin E, Kölch M, Brunner R, Kaess M (2014). The German version of the self-injurious thoughts and behaviors interview (SITBI-G): A tool to assess non-suicidal self-injury and suicidal behavior disorder. *BMC psychiatry*. Published online: 18 September 2014. doi: 10.1186/s12888-014-0265-0.

Fleischhacker WW, Kane JM, Geier J, Karayal O, Kolluri S, Eng SM, Reynolds RF, Strom BL (2014). Completed and attempted suicides among 18,154 subjects with schizophrenia included in a large simple trial. *Journal of Clinical Psychiatry* 75, e184-e190.

Fountoulakis KN, Gonda X, Dome P, Theodorakis PN, Rihmer Z (2014). Possible delayed effect of unemployment on suicidal rates: The case of Hungary. *Annals of General Psychiatry*. Published online: 23 April 2014. doi:10.1186/1744-859X-13-12.

Fu KW, Chan C, Ip P (2014). Exploring the relationship between cyberbullying and unnatural child death: An ecological study of twenty-four European countries. *BMC Pediatrics*. Published online: 30 July 2014. doi: 10.1186/1471-2431-14-195.

Gallaway MS, Lagana-Riordan C, Dabbs CR, Bell MR, Bender AA, Fink DA, Forys-Donahue K, Pecko JA, Schmissrauter SC, Perales R, Coombs MA, Rattigan MR, Millikan AM (2014). A mixed methods epidemiological investigation of preventable deaths among U.S. Army soldiers assigned to a rehabilitative warrior transition unit. *Work*. Published online: 16 September 2014. doi: 10.3233/WOR-141928.

Grucza RA, Plunk AD, Krauss MJ, Cavazos-Rehg PA, Deak J, Gebhardt K, Chaloupka FJ, Bierut LJ (2014). Probing the smoking-suicide association: Do smoking policy interventions affect suicide risk? *Nicotine and Tobacco Research* 16, 1487-1494.

Guimarães PM, Passos SR, Calvet GA, Hökerberg YH, Lessa JL, Andrade CAd (2014). Suicide risk and alcohol and drug abuse in outpatients with HIV infection and Chagas disease. *Revista Brasileira de Psiquiatria*. Published online: 15 April 2014. doi: 10.1590/1516-4446-2013-1219.

Guintivano J, Brown T, Newcomer A, Jones M, Cox O, Maher BS, Eaton WW, Payne JL, Wilcox HC, Kaminsky ZA (2014). Identification and replication of a combined epigenetic and genetic biomarker predicting suicide and suicidal behaviors. *American Journal Of Psychiatry*. Published online: 31 October 2014. doi: 10.1176/appi.ajp.2014.14010008.

Gungormus Z, Tanriverdi D, Gundogan T (2014). The effect of religious belief on the mental health status and suicide probability of women exposed to violence. *Journal of Religion and Health*. Published online: 15 May 2014. doi: 10.1007/s10943-014-9877-4.

Han CSE, Oliffe JL, Ogrodniczuk JS (2013). Culture and suicide: Korean-Canadian immigrants' perspectives. *Ethnicity and Inequalities in Health and Social Care* 6, 30-42.

Hassett AL, Aquino JK, Ilgen MA (2014). The risk of suicide mortality in chronic pain patients. *Current Pain and Headache Reports* . Published online: 22 June 2014. doi: 10.1007/s11916-014-0436-1.

Hjelmeland H, Dieserud G, Dyregrov K, Knizek BL, Rasmussen ML (2014). Suicide and mental disorders. *Journal of the Norwegian Medical Association* 134, 1369-1370.

Hoffmire CA, Bossarte RM (2014). A reconsideration of the correlation between veteran status and firearm suicide in the general population. *Injury Prevention* 20 , 317-321.

Hooley JM, Franklin JC, Nock MK (2014). Chronic pain and suicide: Understanding the association. *Current Pain and Headache Reports.* Published online: 12 June 2014. doi: 10.1007/s11916-014-0435-2.

Houle JN, Light MT (2014). The home foreclosure crisis and rising suicide rates, 2005 to 2010. *American Journal of Public Health* 104, 1073-1079.

Hultcrantz M, Svensson T, Derolf AR, Kristinsson SY, Lindqvist EK, Ekbom A, Granath F, Bjorkholm M (2014). Incidence and risk factors for suicide and attempted suicide following a diagnosis of hematological malignancy. *Cancer Medicine.* Published online: 26 August 2014. doi: 10.1002/cam4.316.

Iannelli RJ, Finlayson AJR, Brown KP, Neufeld R, Gray R, Dietrich MS, Martin PR (2014). Suicidal behavior among physicians referred for fitness-for-duty evaluation. *General Hospital Psychiatry.* Published online: 28 June 2014. doi: 10.1016/j.genhosppsych.2014.06.008.

Isometsä E, Sund R, Pirkola S (2014). Post-discharge suicides of inpatients with bipolar disorder in Finland. *Bipolar Disorders.* Published online: 24 July 2014. doi: 10.1111/bdi.12237.

Jens B, Barbara S, Karoline L, Rebecca T. E, Christa M, Natalia E, Nico D, Karl-Heinz L (2014). Adverse conditions at the workplace are associated with increased suicide risk. *Journal of Psychiatric Research* 57, 90-95.

Jepsen PW, Butler B, Rasmussen S, Juel K, Bech P (2014). Predictive validity of neurotic disorders: A 50-year follow-up study. *Danish Medical Journal* 61, A4858.

Jha MK, Mazumder A, Garg A (2014). Suicide by medical students - a disturbing trend. *Journal of Punjab Academy of Forensic Medicine and Toxicology* 14, 40-42.

Ji N-J, Hong Y-P, Stack SJ, Lee W-Y (2014). Trends and risk factors of the epidemic of charcoal burning suicide in a recent decade among Korean people. *Journal of Korean Medical Science* 29, 1174-1177.

Jia CX, Wang LL, Xu AQ, Dai AY, Qin P (2014). Physical illness and suicide risk in rural residents of contemporary China. *Crisis* 35, 330-337.

Jimenez-Rodríguez I, Garcia-Leiva JM, Jimenez-Rodriguez BM, Condés-Moreno E, Rico-Villademoros F, Calandre EP (2014). Suicidal ideation and the risk of suicide in patients with fibromyalgia: A comparison with non-pain controls and patients suffering from low-back pain. *Neuropsychiatric Disease and Treatment* 10, 625-630.

Jokinen J (2014). Early antecedents of suicide: The role of prenatal and childhood risk factors. *Evidence-Based Mental Health.* Published online: 19 September 2014. doi: as 10.1136/eb-2014-101930.

Kaplan MS, Huguet N, McFarland BH, Caetano R, Conner KR, Giesbrecht N, Nolte KB (2014). Use of alcohol before suicide in the United States. *Annals of Epidemiology* 24, 588 – 592.

Kato K, Kimoto K, Kimoto K, Takahashi Y, Sato R, Matsumoto H (2014). Frequency and clinical features of patients who attempted suicide by hara-kiri in Japan. *Journal of Forensic Sciences* 59, 1303-1306.

Kelles SMB, Diniz MFHS, Machado CJ, Barreto SM (2014). Mortality rate after open Roux-in-Y gastric bypass: A 10-year follow-up. *Brazilian Journal of Medical and Biological Research* 47, 617-625.

Kennedy J, King L (2014). The political economy of farmers' suicides in India: Indebted cash-crop farmers with marginal landholdings explain state-level variation in suicide rates. *Globalization and Health.* Published online: 26 March 2014. doi: 10.1186/1744-8603-10-16.

Kim JI (2014). Association between social factors of health ageing and longevity: Determinants of the longevity index (LI) in OECD countries. *Ageing International* 39, 97-105.

Kinner SA, Degenhardt L, Coffey C, Hearps S, Spittal M, Sawyer SM, Patton GC (2014). Substance use and risk of death in young offenders: A prospective data linkage study. *Drug and Alcohol Review*. Published online: 25 July 2014. doi: 10.1111/dar.12179.

Kiosses DN, Szanto K, Alexopoulos GS (2014). Suicide in older adults: The role of emotions and cognition. *Current Psychiatry Reports*. Published online: 18 September 2014. doi: 10.1007/s11920-014-0495-3.

Kittirattanapaiboon P, Suttajit S, Junsirimongkol B, Likhitsathian S, Srisurapanont M (2014). Suicide risk among Thai illicit drug users with and without mental/alcohol use disorders. *Neuropsychiatric Disease and Treatment* 10, 453-458.

Komoto Y (2014). Factors associated with suicide and bankruptcy in Japanese pathological gamblers. *International Journal of Mental Health and Addiction* 12, 600-606.

Lahti M, Eriksson JG, Heinonen K, Kajantie E, Lahti J, Wahlbeck K, Tuovinen S, Pesonen AK, Mikkonen M, Osmond C, Barker DJ, Raikkonen K (2014). Late preterm birth, post-term birth, and abnormal fetal growth as risk factors for severe mental disorders from early to late adulthood. *Psychological Medicine*. Published online: 5 September 2014. doi: 10.1017/S0033291714001998.

Langan Martin J, McLean G, Park J, Martin DJ, Connolly M, Mercer SW, Smith DJ (2014). Impact of socioeconomic deprivation on rate and cause of death in severe mental illness. *BMC Psychiatry* 14, 261.

Larney S, Gisev N, Farrell M, Dobbins T, Burns L, Gibson A, Kimber J, Degenhardt L (2014). Opioid substitution therapy as a strategy to reduce deaths in prison: Retrospective cohort study. *BMJ Open*. Published online: 2 April 2014. doi: 10.1136/bmjopen-2013-004666.

Law YW, Yip PSF, Zhang Y, Caine ED (2014). The chronic impact of work on suicides and under-utilization of psychiatric and psychosocial services. *Journal of Affective Disorders* 168, 254-261.

Lee A-R, Ahn MH, Lee TY, Park S, Hong JP (2014). Rapid spread of suicide by charcoal burning from 2007 to 2011 in Korea. *Psychiatry Research* 219, 518-524.

Li J, Vestergaard M, Cnattingius S, Gissler M, Bech BH, Obel C, Olsen J (2014). Mortality after parental death in childhood: A nationwide cohort study from three Nordic countries. *PLoS Medicine* 11, 1679-1679.

Ljung T, Chen Q, Lichtenstein P, Larsson H (2014). Common etiological factors of attention-deficit/hyperactivity disorder and suicidal behavior: A population-based study in Sweden. *JAMA Psychiatry* 71, 958-964.

Logan JE, N AS, Reger MA, Gladden M, Smolenski DJ, Faye Floyd C, Gahm GA (2014). Precipitating circumstances of suicide among active duty U.S. army personnel versus U.S Civilians, 2005-2010. *Suicide and Life-Threatening Behavior*. Published online: 5 August 2014. doi: 10.1111/sltb.12111.

Lopez-Morinigo JD, Fernandes AC, Chang CK, Hayes RD, Broadbent M, Stewart R, David AS, Dutta R (2014). Suicide completion in secondary mental healthcare: A comparison study between schizophrenia spectrum disorders and all other diagnoses. *BMC Psychiatry* 14, 213.

Love S, Solomon GS (2014). Talking with parents of high school football players about chronic traumatic encephalopathy: A concise summary. *American Journal of Sports Medicine*. Published online: 6 June 2014. doi: 10.1177/0363546514535187.

Lukaschek K, Baumert J, Krawitz M, Erazo N, Förstl H, Ladwig K-H (2014). Determinants of completed railway suicides by psychiatric in-patients: Case-control study. *British Journal of Psychiatry* 205, 398-406.

Lyu J, Zhang J (2014). Characteristics of schizophrenia suicides compared with suicides by other diagnosed psychiatric disorders and those without a psychiatric disorder. *Schizophrenia Research* 155, 59-65.

Madianos MG, Alexiou T, Patelakis A, Economou M (2014). Suicide, unemployment and other socioeconomic factors: Evidence from the economic crisis in Greece. *The European Journal of Psychiatry* 28, 39-49.

Mauritz W, Brazinova A, Majdan M, Rehorcikova V, Leitgeb J (2014). Deaths due to traumatic brain injury in Austria between 1980 and 2012. *Brain Injury* 28, 1096-1101.

Mezuk B, Rock A, Lohman MC, Choi M (2014). Suicide risk in long-term care facilities: A systematic review. *International Journal of Geriatric Psychiatry*. Published online: 22 May 2014. doi: 10.1002/gps.4142.

Milner A, Morrell S, Lamontagne AD (2014). Economically inactive, unemployed and employed suicides in Australia by age and sex over a 10-year period: What was the impact of the 2007 economic recession? *International Journal of Epidemiology* 43, 1500-1507.

Milner A, Niven H, LaMontagne A (2014). Suicide by occupational skill level in the Australian construction industry: Data from 2001 to 2010. *Australian and New Zealand Journal of Public Health* 38, 281-28.

Mohammadi M, Moradi T, Bottai M, Reutfors J, Cao Y, Smedby KE (2014). Risk and predictors of attempted and completed suicide in patients with hematological malignancies. *Psycho-Oncology*. Published online: 30 April 2014. doi: 10.1002/pon.3561.

Mollan KR, Smurzynski M, Eron JJ, Daar ES, Campbell TB, Sax PE, Gulick RM, Na L, O'Keefe L, Robertson KR, Tierney C (2014). Association between efavirenz as initial therapy for HIV-1 infection and increased risk for suicidal ideation or attempted or completed suicide: An analysis of trial data. *Annals of Internal Medicine*. Published online: 1 July 2014. doi: 10.7326/M14-0293.

Moustgaard H, Joutsenniemi K, Myrskyla M, Martikainen P (2014). Antidepressant sales and the risk for alcohol-related and non-alcohol-related suicide in Finland-an individual-level population study. *PLoS ONE*. Published online: 3 June 2014. doi: 10.1371/journal.pone.0098405.

Munger Clary HM (2014). Anxiety and epilepsy: What neurologists and epileptologists should know. *European Journal of Orthopaedic Surgery and Traumatology*. Published online: 21 March 2014. doi: 10.1007/s11910-014-0445-9.

Nadaf A, Mugadlimath A, Chidananda PS, Manjunath KH (2014). Psychological autopsy study of suicides among elderly. *Journal of Indian Academy of Forensic Medicine* 36, 156-159.

Napoli AA, Wood JJ, Coumbis JJ, Soitkar AM, Seekins DW, Tilson HH (2014). No evident association between efavirenz use and suicidality was identified from a disproportionality analysis using the FAERS database. *Journal of the International AIDS Society*. Published online: 4 September 2014. doi: 10.7448/IAS.17.1.19214.

Narmadha MP, Nalini R, Ayyappan R, Murugesh N (2014). Analysis of organophosphates intoxication in a tertiary care hospital. *Research Journal of Pharmaceutical, Biological and Chemical Sciences* 5, 174-182.

Narvaez JCM, Jansen K, Pinheiro RT, Kapczinski F, Silva RA, Pechansky F, Magalhães PV (2014). Psychiatric and substance-use comorbidities associated with lifetime crack cocaine use in young adults in the general population. *Comprehensive Psychiatry* 55, 1369–1376.

Nedic Erjavec G, Nenadic Sviglin K, Nikolac Perkovic M, Muck-Seler D, Jovanovic T, Pivac N (2014). Association of gene polymorphisms encoding dopaminergic system components and platelet MAO-B activity with alcohol dependence and alcohol dependence-related phenotypes. *Progress in Neuro-Psychopharmacology & Biological Psychiatry* 54, 321-327.

Oberaigner W, Sperner-Unterweger B, Fiegl M, Geiger-Gritsch S, Haring C (2014). Increased suicide risk in cancer patients in Tyrol/Austria. *General Hospital Psychiatry* 36, 483-487.

Pandya C, Kutiyanawalla A, Turecki G, Pillai A (2014). Glucocorticoid regulates TrkB protein levels via c-Cbl dependent ubiquitination: A decrease in c-Cbl mRNA in the prefrontal cortex of suicide subjects. *Psychoneuroendocrinology* 45, 108-118.

Passos SM, Souza LD, Spessato BC (2014). High prevalence of suicide risk in people living with HIV: Who is at higher risk? *AIDS Care* 26, 1379-1382.

Phillips JA, Nugent CN (2014). Suicide and the great recession of 2007-2009: The role of economic factors in the 50 US states. *Social Science & Medicine* 116, 22-31.

Pompili M, Forte A, Lester D, Erbuto D, Rovedi F, Innamorati M, Amore M, Girardi P (2014). Suicide risk in type 1 diabetes mellitus: A systematic review. *Journal of Psychosomatic Research* 76, 352-360.

Pompili M, Innamorati M, Di Vittorio C, Baratta S, Masotti V, Badaracco A, Wong P, Lester D, Yip P, Girardi P, Amore M (2014). Unemployment as a risk factor for completed suicide: A psychological autopsy study. *Archives of Suicide Research* 18, 181-192.

Pompili M, Innamorati M, Lamis DA, Erbuto D, Venturini P, Ricci F, Serafini G, Amore M, Girardi P (2014). The associations among childhood maltreatment, "male depression" and suicide risk in psychiatric patients. *Psychiatry Research* 220, 571-578.

Popovi D, Benabarre A, Crespo JM, Goikolea JM, González-Pinto A, Gutiérrez-Rojas L, Montes JM, Vieta E (2014). Risk factors for suicide in schizophrenia: Systematic review and clinical recommendations. *Acta Psychiatrica Scandinavica* 130, 418-426.

Qi X, Hu W, Mengersen K, Tong S (2014). Socio-environmental drivers and suicide in Australia: Bayesian spatial analysis. *BMC Public Health* 14, 681-681.

Razvodovsky YE, Kandrychyn SV (2014). Spatial regularity in suicides and alcohol psychoses in Belarus. *Acta Medica Lituanica* 21, 57-64.

Reis C, Sinyor M, Schaffer A (2014). Medications without a patient: Potential lethal implications of pharmaceuticals left behind. *Crisis* 35, 283-285.

Rezaeian M (2014). Self-immolation among medical practitioners and medical students: More evidence is needed from developing countries. *Iranian Journal of Psychiatry and Behavioral Sciences* 8, 105-106.

Richa S, Fahed M, Khoury E, Mishara B (2014). Suicide in autism spectrum disorders. *Archives of Suicide Research*. Published online: 7 November 2014. doi: 10.1080/13811118.2013.824834.

Rocha S, Monteiro A, Linhares P, Chamadoira C, Basto MA, Reis C, Sousa C, Lima J, Rosas MJ, Massano J, Vaz R (2014). Long-term mortality analysis in Parkinson's disease treated with deep brain stimulation. *Parkinson's Disease*. Published online: 3 March 2014. doi: 10.1155/2014/717041.

Rostila M, Saarela J, Kawachi I (2014). Birth order and suicide in adulthood: Evidence from Swedish population data. *American Journal of Epidemiology* 179, 1450-1457.

Ruiz G, Wangmo T, Mutzenberg P, Sinclair J, Elger BS (2014). Understanding death in custody: A case for a comprehensive definition. *Journal of Bioethical Inquiry* 11, 387-398.

Rylander M, Valdez C, Nussbaum AM (2014). Does the legalization of medical marijuana increase completed suicide? *American Journal of Drug and Alcohol Abuse* 40, 269-273.

Sabzghabaee AM, Soleimani M, Farajzadegan Z, Hosseinpoor S, Mirhosseini SMM, Eizadi-Mood N (2013). Social risk factors and outcome analysis of poisoning in an Iranian referral medical center: A toxico-epidemiological approach. *Journal of Research In Pharmacy Practice* 2, 151-155.

Saini P, While D, Chantler K, Windfuhr K, Kapur N (2014). Assessment and management of suicide risk in primary care. *Crisis*. Published online: 18 September 2014. doi: 10.1027/0227-5910/a000277.

Schnieder TP, Trencevska I, Rosoklija G, Stankov A, Mann JJ, Smiley J, Dwork AJ (2014). Microglia of prefrontal white matter in suicide. *Journal of Neuropathology & Experimental Neurology* 73, 880-890.

Seemuller F, Meier S, Obermeier M, Musil R, Bauer M, Adli M, Kronmuller K, Holsboer F, Brieger P, Laux G, Bender W, Heuser I, Zeiler J, Gaebel W, Riedel M, Falkai P, Moller H-J (2014). Three-year long-term outcome of 458 naturalistically treated inpatients with major depressive episode: Severe relapse rates and risk factors. *European Archives of Psychiatry and Clinical Neuroscience* 264, 567-575.

Seguin M, Beauchamp G, Robert M, Dimambro M, Turecki G (2014). Developmental model of suicide trajectories. *British Journal of Psychiatry* 205, 120-126.

Selling D, Solimo A, Lee D, Horne K, Panove E, Venters H (2014). Surveillance of suicidal and nonsuicidal self-injury in the New York City jail system. *Journal of Correctional Health Care* 20, 163-167.

Sundquist K, Hamano T, Li X, Kawakami N, Shiwaku K, Sundquist J (2014). Linking social capital and mortality in the elderly: A Swedish national cohort study. *Experimental Gerontology* 55, 29-36.

Suzuki E, Kashima S, Kawachi I, Subramanian SV (2014). Prefecture-level economic conditions and risk of suicide in Japan: A repeated cross-sectional analysis 1975-2010. *European Journal of Public Health*. Published online: 7 March 2014. doi: 10.1093/eurpub/cku023.

Tanji F, Kakizaki M, Sugawara Y, Watanabe I, Nakaya N, Minami Y, Fukao A, Tsuji I (2014). Personality and suicide risk: The impact of economic crisis in Japan. *Psychological Medicine*. Published online: 18 July 2014. doi: 10.1017/S0033291714001688.

Ting TY (2014). Socio-economic correlates of suicidality in Hong Kong. *International Journal of Asia-Pacific Studies* 10, 97-110.

Tinney G, Gerlock AA (2014). Intimate partner violence, military personnel, veterans, and their families. *Family Court Review* 52, 400-416.

Toffolutti V, Suhrcke M (2014). Assessing the short term health impact of the great recession in the European Union: A cross-country panel analysis. *Preventive Medicine* 64, 54-62.

Torgler B, Schaltegger C (2014). Suicide and religion: New evidence on the differences between Protestantism and Catholicism. *Journal for the Scientific Study of Religion* 53, 316-340.

Tóth MD, Ádám S, Birkás E, Székely A, Stauder A, Purebl G (2014). Gender differences in deliberate self-poisoning in Hungary: Analyzing the effect of precipiting factor and their relation to depression. *Crisis* 35, 145-153.

Tsai AC, Lucas M, Okereke OI, O'Reilly EJ, Mirzaei F, Kawachi I, Ascherio A, Willett WC (2014). Suicide mortality in relation to dietary intake of n-3 and n-6 polyunsaturated fatty acids and fish: Equivocal findings from 3 large US cohort studies. *American Journal of Epidemiology* 179, 1458-1466.

Tsai AC, Lucas M, Sania A, Kim D, Kawachi I (2014). Social integration and suicide mortality among men: 24-year cohort study of U.S. health professionals. *Annals of Internal Medicine* 161, 85-95.

Twenge JM (2014). Time period and birth cohort differences in depressive symptoms in the U.S., 1982-2013. *Social Indicators Research*. Published online: 5 June 2014. doi: 10.1007/s11205-014-0647-1.

Usenko VS, Svirin SN, Shchekaturov YN, Ponarin ED (2014). Impact of some types of mass gatherings on current suicide risk in an urban population: Statistical and negative binominal regression analysis of time series. *BMC Public Health*. Published online: 4 April 2014. doi: 10.1186/1471-2458-14-308.

Verrotti A, Carrozzino D, Milioni M, Minna M, Fulcheri M (2014). Epilepsy and its main psychiatric comorbidities in adults and children. *Journal of the Neurological Sciences* 343, 23-29.

Violanti JM, Robinson CF, Shen R (2013). Law enforcement suicide: A national analysis. *International Journal of Emergency Mental Health* 15, 289-297.

Vuorio A, Laukkala T, Navathe P, Budowle B, Eyre A, Sajantila A (2014). Aircraft-assisted pilot suicides: Lessons to be learned. *Aviation Space and Environmental Medicine* 85, 841-846.

Vyssoki B, Kapusta ND, Praschak-Rieder N, Dorffner G, Willeit M (2014). Direct effect of sunshine on suicide. *JAMA Psychiatry* 71, 1231-1237.

Webb RT, Lichtenstein P, Larsson H, Geddes JR, Fazel S (2014). Suicide, hospital-presenting suicide attempts, and criminality in bipolar disorder: Examination of risk for multiple adverse outcomes. *Journal of Clinical Psychiatry* 75, e809-e816.

Wilchek-Aviad Y (2014). Meaning in life and suicidal tendency among immigrant (Ethiopian) youth and native-born Israeli youth. *Journal of Immigrant and Minority Health*. Published online: 1 May 2014. doi: 10.1007/s10903-014-0028-5.

Wilson-Mitchell K, Bennett J, Stennett R (2014). Psychological health and life experiences of pregnant adolescent mothers in Jamaica. *International Journal of Environmental Research and Public Health* 11, 4729-4744.

Wu YW, Chen CK, Wang LJ (2014). Is suicide mortality associated with meteorological and socio-economic factors? An ecological study in a city in Taiwan with a high suicide rate. *Psychiatria Danubina* 26, 152-158.

Yamauchi T, Inagaki M, Yonemoto N, Iwasaki M, Inoue M, Akechi T, Iso H, Tsugane S (2014). Death by suicide and other externally caused injuries after stroke in Japan (1990-2010): The Japan public health center-based prospective study. *Psychosomatic Medicine* 76, 452-459.

Yamauchi T, Inagaki M, Yonemoto N, Iwasaki M, Inoue M, Akechi T, Iso H, Tsugane S (2014). Death by suicide and other externally caused injuries following a cancer diagnosis: The Japan public health center-based prospective study. *Psycho-Oncology* 23, 1034-1041.

Yip PSF, Chen F (2014). A study on the effect of exclusion period on the suicidal risk among the insured. *Social Science and Medicine* 110, 26-30.

Younes N, Melchior M, Turbelin C, Blanchon T, Hanslik T, Chan Chee C (2014). Attempted and completed suicide in primary care: Not what we expected? *Journal of Affective Disorders* 170, 150-154.

Zamani SN, Bagheri M, Abbas Nejad M (2013). Investigation of the demographic characteristics and mental health in self-immolation attempters. *International Journal of High Risk Behaviors & Addiction* 2, 77-81.

Zuromski KL, Davis MT, Witte TK, Weathers F, Blevins C (2014). PTSD symptom clusters are differentially associated with components of the acquired capability for suicide. *Suicide and Life-Threatening Behavior*. Published online: 5 May 2014. doi: 10.1111/sltb.12098.

Prevention

Aleman A, Denys D (2014). A road map for suicide research and prevention. *Nature* 509, 421-423.

Allen J, Mohatt GV, Fok CCT, Henry D, Burkett R (2014). A protective factors model for alcohol abuse and suicide prevention among Alaska native youth. *American Journal of Community Psychology* 54, 125-139.

Asakura K, Craig SL (2014). "It gets better"... But how? Exploring resilience development in the accounts of LGBTQ adults. *Journal of Human Behavior in the Social Environment* 24, 253-266.

Berrouiguet S, Gravey M, Le Galudec M, Alavi Z, Walter M (2014). Post-acute crisis text messaging outreach for suicide prevention: A pilot study. *Psychiatry Research* 217, 154-157.

Bridge JA, Horowitz LM, Fontanella CA, Grupp-Phelan J, Campo JV (2014). Prioritizing research to reduce youth suicide and suicidal behavior. *American Journal of Preventive Medicine* 47, S229-S234.

Brown GK, Green KL (2014). A review of evidence-based follow-up care for suicide prevention: Where do we go from here? *American Journal of Preventive Medicine* 47, S209-S215.

Castro CA, Kintzle S (2014). Suicides in the military: The post-modern combat veteran and the Hemingway effect. *Current Psychiatry Reports* 16, 1-9.

Christensen H, Batterham PJ, O'Dea B (2014). E-health interventions for suicide prevention. *International Journal of Environmental Research and Public Health* 11, 8193-8212.

Claassen CA, Pearson JL, Khodyakov D, Satow PM, Gebbia R, Berman AL, Reidenberg DJ, Feldman S, Molock S, Carras MC, Lento RM, Sherrill J, Pringle B, Dalal S, Insel TR (2014). Reducing the burden of suicide in the U.S. The aspirational research goals of the national action alliance for suicide prevention research prioritization task force. *American Journal of Preventive Medicine*. Published online: 18 April 2014. doi: 10.1016/j.amepre.2014.01.004.

Conwell Y (2014). Suicide later in life: Challenges and priorities for prevention. *American Journal of Preventive Medicine* 47, S244-S250.

Crosby Budinger M, Cwik MF, Riddle MA (2014). Awareness, attitudes, and use of crisis hotlines among youth at-risk for suicide. *Suicide and Life-Threatening Behavior*. Published online: 5 August 2014. doi: 10.1111/sltb.12112.

Cwik MF, Barlow A, Goklish N, Larzelere-Hinton F, Tingey L, Craig M, Lupe R, Walkup J (2014). Community-based surveillance and case management for suicide prevention: An American Indian tribally initiated system. *American Journal of Public Health* 104, e18-e23.

Dlugacz HA (2014). Correctional mental health in the USA. *International Journal of Prisoner Health* 10, 3-26.

Ghahramanlou-Holloway M, Brown GK, Currier GW, Brenner L, Knox KL, Grammer G, Carreno-Ponce JT, Stanley B (2014). Safety planning for military (SAFE MIL): Rationale, design, and safety considerations of a randomized controlled trial to reduce suicide risk among psychiatric inpatients. *Contemporary Clinical Trials* 39, 113-123.

Gonzalez J, Trickett EJ (2014). Collaborative measurement development as a tool in CBPR: Measurement development and adaptation within the cultures of communities. *American Journal of Community Psychology* 54, 112-124.

Griffiths JJ, Zarate CA, Jr., Rasimas JJ (2014). Existing and novel biological therapeutics in suicide prevention. *American Journal of Preventative Medicine* 47, S195-S203.

Hegerl U, Rummel-Kluge C, Värnik A, Arensman E, Koburger N (2013). Alliances against depression - a community based approach to target depression and to prevent suicidal behaviour. *Neuroscience and Biobehavioral Reviews* 37, 2404-2409.

Hjelmeland H, Hagen J, Knizek BL (2014). Suicide prevention in mental health care - time for new ideas? *Tidsskr Nor Laegeforen* 134, 1222 .

Ikeda R, Hedegaard H, Bossarte R, Crosby AE, Hanzlick R, Roesler J, Seider R, Smith P, Warner M (2014). Improving national data systems for surveillance of suicide-related events. *American Journal of Preventive Medicine* 47, S122-S129.

Iacobucci G (2014). Who report says countries should do more to prevent suicides. *British Medical Journal* 349, g5461-g5461.

Jayaram G (2014). Inpatient suicide prevention: Promoting a culture and system of safety over 30 years of practice. *Journal of Psychiatric Practice* 20, 392-404 .

John A, Hawton K, Lloyd K, Luce A, Platt S, Scourfield J, Marchant AL, Jones PA, Dennis MS (2014). Printqual - a measure for assessing the quality of newspaper reporting of suicide. *Crisis*. Published online: 17 September 2014. doi: 10.1027/0227-5910/a000276.

King KA, Ossege J, Sorter MT, Strunk CM (2013). Emotionally troubled teens' help-seeking behaviors: an evaluation of surviving the Teens® suicide prevention and depression awareness program. *Journal of School Nursing* 30, 366-375.

Knox K (2014). Approaching suicide as a public health issue. *Annals of Internal Medicine* 161, 151-152.

Kröger C, Röpke S, Kliem S (2014). Reasons for premature termination of dialectical behavior therapy for inpatients with borderline personality disorder. *Behaviour Research and Therapy* 60, 46-52 .

Langille J (2014). Suicide prevention and postvention initiatives. *The Canadian Nurse* 110, 32-34 .

Love J, Zatzick D (2014). Screening and intervention for comorbid substance disorders, ptsd, depression, and suicide: A trauma center survey. *Psychiatric Services*. Published online: 1 July 201. doi: 10.1176/appi.ps.201300399.

Lynch FL (2014). Population health outcome models in suicide prevention policy. *American Journal of Preventive Medicine* 47, S137-S143.

Matarazzo BB, Homaifar BY, Wortzel HS (2014). Therapeutic risk management of the suicidal patient: Safety planning. *Journal of Psychiatric Practice* 20, 220-224.

Matthieu MM, Gardiner G, Ziegemeier E, Buxton M (2014). Using a service sector segmented approach to identify community stakeholders who can improve access to suicide prevention services for veterans. *Military Medicine* 179, 388-395.

Mohatt GV, Fok CC, Henry D, Allen J (2014). Feasibility of a community intervention for the prevention of suicide and alcohol abuse with Yup'ik Alaska Native youth: the Elluam Tungiinun and Yupiucimta Asvairtuumallerkaa studies. *American Journal of Community Psychology* 54, 153-169.

Nadorff MR, Ellis TE, Allen JG, Winer ES, Herrera S (2014). Presence and persistence of sleep-related symptoms and suicidal ideation in psychiatric inpatients. *Crisis*. Published online: 17 September 2014. doi: 10.1027/0227-5910/a000279.

Nakanishi M, Yamauchi T, Takeshima T (2014). National strategy for suicide prevention in Japan: The impact of a national fund on the progress of developing systems for suicide prevention and implementing initiatives among local authorities. *Psychiatry and the Clinical Neurosciences*. Published online: 10 July 2014. doi: 10.1111/pcn.12222.

Obando Medina C, Kullgren G, Dahlblom K (2014). A qualitative study on primary health care professionals' perceptions of mental health, suicidal problems and help-seeking among young people in Nicaragua. *BMC Family Practice* 15, 129.

Ogbuanu JN (2014). The problem of cultural stereotyping in the pastoral care of a suicidal person. *Acta Theologica* 34, 127-144.

O'Neill S, Corry CV, Murphy S, Brady S, Bunting BP (2014). Characteristics of deaths by suicide in Northern Ireland from 2005 to 2011 and use of health services prior to death. *Journal of Affective Disorders* 168C, 466-471.

Osborne K (2014). Mental health support needed to prevent suicides after discharge. *Nursing Standard* 28, 13.

Osteen PJ, Frey JJ, Ko J (2014). Advancing training to identify, intervene, and follow up with individuals at risk for suicide through research. *American Journal of Preventive Medicine* 47, S216-S221.

Otsuka K, Kawanishi C (2014). Suicide prevention activities of psychiatry-related professional societies: The promotion of suicide prevention in psychiatric care. *Psychiatria et Neurologia Japonica* 116, 677-682.

Pandya A (2014). Mental health as an advocacy priority in the lesbian, gay, bisexual, and transgender communities. *Journal of Psychiatric Practice* 20, 225-227.

Park AL, McCrone P, Knapp M (2014). Early intervention for first-episode psychosis: Broadening the scope of economic estimates. *Early Intervention in Psychiatry*. Published online: 17 April 2014. doi: 10.1111/eip.12149.

Pearson JL, Claassen CA, Booth CL (2014). Introduction to the suicide prevention research prioritization task force special supplement: The topic experts. *American Journal of Preventive Medicine* 47, S102-S105.

Pheister M, Kangas G, Thompson C, Lehrmann J, Berger B, Kemp J (2014). Suicide prevention and postvention resources: What psychiatry residencies can learn from the veteran's administration experience. *Academic Psychiatry* 38, 600-604.

Ramos MM, Fullerton L, Sapien R, Greenberg C, Bauer-Creegan J (2014). Rural-urban disparities in school nursing: Implications for continuing education and rural school health. *The Journal of Rural Health* 30, 265-274.

Raue PJ, Ghesquiere AR, Bruce ML (2014). Suicide risk in primary care: Identification and management in older adults. *Current Psychiatry Reports* 16, 466.

Robinson M, Braybrook D, Robertson S (2014). Influencing public awareness to prevent male suicide. *Journal of Public Mental Health* 13, 40-50.

Sarno M, Van Hasselt VB (2014). Suicide by cop: Implications for crisis (hostage) negotiations. *Journal of Criminal Psychology* 4, 143-154.

Sawyer JR (2014). Suicide prevention in healthcare. *Journal of Healthcare Protection Management* 30, 98-104.

Schilling EA, Lawless M, Buchanan L, Aseltine RH (2014). Signs of suicide shows promise as a middle school suicide prevention program. *Suicide and Life-Threatening Behavior*. Published online: 2 May 2014. doi: 10.1111/sltb.12097.

Shadick R, Akhter S (2014). Suicide prevention with diverse college students. *Journal of College Student Psychotherapy* 28, 117-131.

Sharpe TL, Jacobson Frey J, Osteen PJ, Bernes S (2014). Perspectives and appropriateness of suicide prevention gatekeeper training for MSW students. *Social Work in Mental Health* 12, 117-131.

Siegel M, Ross CS, King C (2014). Examining the relationship between the prevalence of guns and homicide rates in the USA using a new and improved state-level gun ownership proxy. *Injury Prevention* Published online: 16 April 2014. doi:10.1136/injuryprev-2014-041187.

Tingle J (2014). Preventing suicide in England: Saving lives. *British Journal of Nursing* 23, 236-237.

Toumbourou JW, Olsson CA, Rowland B, Renati S, Hallam B (2014). Health psychology intervention in key social environments to promote adolescent health. *Australian Psychologist* 49, 66-74.

Tsujii N, Akashi H, Mikawa W, Tsujimoto E, Niwa A, Adachi T, Shirakawa O (2014). Discrepancy between self- and observer-rated depression severities as a predictor of vulnerability to suicide in patients with mild depression. *Journal of Affective Disorders* 161, 144-149.

Vita A, De Peri L, Sacchetti E (2014). Lithium in drinking water and suicide prevention: A review of the evidence. *International Clinical Psychopharmacology*. Published online: 14 July 2014. doi: 10.1097/YIC.0000000000000048.

Wexler L, White J, Trainor B (2014). Why an alternative to suicide prevention gatekeeper training is needed for rural indigenous communities: Presenting an empowering community story-telling approach. *Critical Public Health*. Published online: 7 April 2014. doi: 10.1080/09581596.2014.904039.

White AM, Lu N, Cerulli C, Tu X (2014). Examining benefits of academic-community research team training: Rochester's suicide prevention training institutes. *Progress in Community Health* 8, 125-137.

White J (2014). Expanding and democratizing the agenda for preventing youth suicide: Youth participation, cultural responsiveness, and social transformation. *Canadian Journal of Community Mental Health* 33, 95-107.

Wu CY, Lin YY, Yeh MC, Huang LH, Chen SJ, Liao SC, Lee MB (2014). Effectiveness of interactive discussion group in suicide risk assessment among general nurses in Taiwan: A randomized controlled trial. *Nurse Education Today* 34, 1388-1394.

Wyman PA (2014). Developmental approach to prevent adolescent suicides: Research pathways to effective upstream preventive interventions. *American Journal of Preventive Medicine* 47, S251-S256.

Xavier B, Vargas MA (2014). Development and effectiveness of mindfullness based cognitive restructuring program on psychache and hopelessness as signals of suicidal ideation among adolescents. *Indian Journal of Positive Psychology* 5, 109-115.

Yip P, So BK, Kawachi I, Zhang Y (2014). A Markov chain model for studying suicide dynamics: An illustration of the Rose theorem. *BMC Public Health* 14, 625.

Zarghami A, Nazari P, Manouchehri A-A (2014). Suicide: Affected by the internet. *Yonsei Medical Journal* 55, 1161-1161.

Postvention and Bereavement

Abbott CH, Zakriski AL (2014). Grief and attitudes toward suicide in peers affected by a cluster of suicides as adolescents. *Suicide and Life-Threatening Behavior*. Published online: 8 May 2014. doi: 10.1111/sltb.12100.

Baddeley JL, Williams JL, Rynearson T, Correa F, Saindon C, Rheingold AA (2014). Death thoughts and images in treatment-seekers after violent loss. *Death Studies*. Published online: 8 October 2014. doi: 10.1080/07481187.2014.893274.

Cerel J, McIntosh JL, Neimeyer RA, Maple M, Marshall D (2014). The continuum of "survivor-ship": Definitional issues in the aftermath of suicide. *Suicide and Life-Threatening Behavior*. Published online: 7 April 2004. doi: 10.1111/sltb.12093.

Clark J (2014). Engaging in ritual after client suicide: The critical importance of linking objects for therapists. *Bereavement Care* 33, 70-76.

Fairman N, Montross Thomas LP, Whitmore S, Meier EA, Irwin SA (2014). What did I miss? A qualitative assessment of the impact of patient suicide on hospice clinical staff. *Journal of Palliative Medicine* 17, 832-836.

Krysinska K, Andriessen K, Corveleyn J (2014). Religion and spirituality in online suicide bereavement. *Crisis* 35, 349-356.

McKinnon JM, Chonody J (2014). Exploring the formal supports used by people bereaved through suicide: A qualitative study. *Social Work in Mental Health* 12, 231-248,

McLaughlin C, McGowan I, O'Neill S, Kernohan G (2014). The burden of living with and caring for a suicidal family member. *Journal of Mental Health* (23, 236-240.

Prabhakar D, Balon R, Anzia JM, Gabbard GO, Lomax JW, Bandstra BS, Eisen J, Figueroa S, Theresa G, Ruble M, Seritan AL, Zisook S (2014). Helping psychiatry residents cope with patient suicide. *Academic Psychiatry* 38, 593-597.

Omerov P, Steineck G, Nyberg T, Runeson B, Nyberg U (2014). Viewing the body after bereavement due to suicide: A population-based survey in Sweden. *PLoS ONE* 9, e101799.

Ratnarajah D, Maple M, Minichiello V (2014). Understanding family member suicide narratives by investigating family history. *Omega* 69, 41-57.

Wilks D (2014). Autobiographical case study: Using art and poetry therapy to process family member suicide. *Journal of Poetry Therapy* 27, 213-216.

Wittouck C, Van Autreve S, Portzky G, van Heeringen K (2014). A CBT-based psychoeducational intervention for suicide survivors. *Crisis* 35, 193-201.

NON FATAL SUICIDAL BEHAVIOR

Epidemiology

Al-Khafaji K, Loy J, Kelly A-M (2014). Characteristics and outcome of patients brought to an emergency department by police under the provisions (section 10) of the Mental Health Act in Victoria, Australia. *International Journal Of Law And Psychiatry* 37, 415-419.

Andover MS (2014). Non-suicidal self-injury disorder in a community sample of adults. *Psychiatry Research* 219, 305-310.

Angst J, Hengartner MP, Rogers J, Schnyder U, Steinhausen HC, Ajdacic-Gross V, Rössler W (2014). Suicidality in the prospective Zurich study: Prevalence, risk factors and gender. *European Archives of Psychiatry and Clinical Neuroscience* 264, 557-565.

Asami T, Okubo Y, Sekine M, Nomura T (2014). Eating disorders among patients incarcerated only for repeated shoplifting: A retrospective quasi-case-control study in a medical prison in Japan. *BMC Psychiatry* 14, 169.

Atay GM, Yaman GB, Demgrdag A, Akpinar A (2014). Outcomes of suicide attempters in the emergency unit of a university hospital. *Anatolian Journal of Psychiatry* 15, 124-131.

Aydin I, Karadas S, Gonullu H, Dulger AC (2014). Epidemiological analysis of poisoning cases in Van, Turkey. *Journal of the Pakistan Medical Association* 64, 560-562.

Bain J, Lal S, Baghel VS, Yedalwar V, Gupta R, Singh AK (2014). Decadorial of a burn center in central India. *Journal of Natural Science, Biology, and Medicine* 5, 116-122.

Bakhaidar M, Jan S, Farahat F, Attar A, Alsaywid B, Abuznadah W (2014). Pattern of drug overdose and chemical poisoning among patients attending an emergency department, western Saudi Arabia. *Journal of Community Health*. Published online: 14 June 2014. doi: 10.1007/s10900-014-9895-x.

Bahar MA, Pakyari M, Bahar R (2014). Burns in Tehran: Demographic, etiological, and clinical trends. *Asian Biomedicine* 8, 241-245.

Banerjee I, Tripathi SK, Roy AS (2014). Clinico-epidemiological profile of poisoned patients in emergency department: A two and half year's single hospital experience. *International Journal of Critical Illness and Injury Science* 4, 14-17.

Borschmann R, Coffey C, Moran P, Hearps S, Degenhardt L, Kinner SA, Patton G (2014). Self-harm in young offenders. *Suicide and Life-Threatening Behavior*. Published online: 29 April 2014. doi: 10.1111/sltb.12096.

Boza C, Nicholson Perry K (2014). Gender-related victimization, perceived social support, and predictors of depression among transgender Australians. *International Journal of Transgenderism* 15, 35-52.

Brunstein Klomek A, Lev-Wiesel R, Shellac E, Hadas A, Berger U, Horwitz M, Fennig S (2014). The relationship between self-injurious behavior and self-disclosure in adolescents with eating disorders. *Eating and Weight Disord*ers. Published online: 12 August 2014. doi: 10.1007/s40519-014-0145-0.

Cheatle MD, Wasser T, Foster C, Olugbodi A, Bryan J (2014). Prevalence of suicidal ideation in patients with chronic non-cancer pain referred to a behaviorally based pain program. *Pain Physician* 17, E359-E367.

Chen VC-H, Wang T-N, Liao Y-T, Lin TC, Stewart R, Lee CT-C (2014). Asthma and self-harm: A population-based cohort study in Taiwan. *Journal of Psychosomatic Research*. Published online: 6 September 2014. doi: 10.1016/j.jpsychores.2014.08.017. Chikhani M, Winter R (2014). Injury after non-judicial hanging. *Trauma* 16, 164-173.

Cordoba-Dona JA, San Sebastian M, Escolar-Pujolar A, Martinez-Faure JE, Gustafsson PE (2014). Economic crisis and suicidal behaviour: The role of unemployment, sex and age in Andalusia, southern Spain. *International Journal for Equity in Health* 13, 55.

Cross S, Bhugra D, Dargan PI, Wood DM, Greene SL, Craig TKJ (2014). Ethnic differences in self-poisoning across south London. *Crisis* 35, 268-272.

de Campos EV, Park M, Gomez DS, Ferreira MC, Azevedo LCP (2014). Characterization of critically ill adult burn patients admitted to a Brazilian intensive care unit. *Burns*. Published online: 2 June 2014. doi: 10.1016/j.burns.2014.03.022.

Diallo T, Maiga D, Maiga A, Sangho H, Coulibaly B, Hami H, Mokthari A, Soulaymani R, Dong X, Chen R, Wong E, Simon MA (2014). Suicidal ideation in an older U.S. Chinese population. *Journal of Aging Health* , 26, 1189-1208.

Dong XQ, Chen R, Chang ES, Simon MA (2014). The prevalence of suicide attempts among community-dwelling US Chinese older adults - findings from the Pine study. *Ethnicity and Inequalities in Health and Social Care* 7, 23-35.

Dong Y, Huang F, Hu G, Liu Y, Zheng R, Zhang Q, Mao X (2014). The prevalence of suicidal ideation among the elderly in China: A meta-analysis of 11 cross-sectional studies. *Comprehensive Psychiatry* 55, 1100-1105.

Etcheverry GB, Pereira EF, Cordeiro ML (2014). Depressive symptoms and suicidal ideation in adolescents accompanying a parent in recyclable trash collection. *The Spanish Journal of Psychology*. Published online: 15 April 2014. doi:10.1017/sjp.2014.13.

Fekadu A, Medhin G, Selamu M, Hailemariam M, Alem A, Giorgis TW, Breuer E, Lund C, Prince M, Hanlon C (2014). Population level mental distress in rural Ethiopia. *BMC Psychiatry* 14, 194.

Garcia-Nieto R, Carballo JJ, Hernando MD, de Leon-Martinez V, Baca-Garcia E (2014). Clinical correlates of non-suicidal self-injury (NSSI) in an outpatient sample of adolescents. *Archives of Suicide Research*. Published online: 25 Sep 2014. doi: 10.1080/13811118.2014.957447.

Ghrayeb FAW, Mohamed Rusli A, Mohd Ismail I, Rifai AA (2014). Prevalence of suicide ideation and attempt among Palestinian adolescents: A cross-sectional study. *World Journal of Medical Sciences* 10, 261-266.

Glenn JJ, Michel BD, Franklin JC, Hooley JM, Nock MK (2014). Pain analgesia among adolescent self-injurers. *Psychiatry Research*. Published online: 15 August 2014. doi:10.1016/j.psychres.2014.08.016.

Gmitrowicz A, Kostulski A, Kropiwnicki P, Zalewska-Janowska A (2014). Cutaneous deliberate self-harm in Polish school teenagers - an interdisciplinary challenge. *Acta Dermato-Venereologica* 94, 448-453.

Goodhew F, Van Hooff M, Sparnon A, Roberts R, Baur J, Saccone EJ, McFarlane A (2014). Psychiatric outcomes amongst adult survivors of childhood burns. *Burns* 40, 1079-1088.

Griffin E, Corcoran P, Cassidy L, O'Carroll A, Perry IJ, Bonner B (2014). Characteristics of hospital-treated intentional drug overdose in Ireland and Northern Ireland. *BMJ Open* 4. Published online; 29 July 2014. doi: 10.1136/bmjopen-2014-005557.

Gu J, Lau JTF, Li M, Li H, Gao Q, Feng X, Bai Y, Hao C, Hao Y (2014). Socio-ecological factors associated with depression, suicidal ideation and suicidal attempt among female injection drug users who are sex workers in China. *Drug and Alcohol Dependence* 114, 102-110.

Hammig B, Jozkowski K, Jones C (2014). Injury-related visits and comorbid conditions among homeless persons presenting to emergency departments. *Academic Emergency Medicine* 21, 449-455.

Handtke V, Wangmo T (2014). Ageing prisoners' views on death and dying: Contemplating end-of-life in prison. *Journal of Bioethical Inquiry* 11, 373-386.

Harada K, Eto N, Honda Y, Kawano N, Ogushi Y, Matsuo M, Nishimura R (2014). A comparison of the characteristics of suicide attempters with and without psychiatric consultation before their suicidal behaviours: A cross-sectional study. *BMC Psychiatry* 14, 146.

Hill SA, Brodrick P, Doherty A, Lolley J, Wallington F, White O (2014). Characteristics of female patients admitted to an adolescent secure forensic psychiatric hospital. *Journal of Forensic Psychiatry and Psychology* 25, 503-519.

Hodgson KJ, Shelton KH, van den Bree MBM (2014). Mental health problems in young people with experiences of homelessness and the relationship with health service use: A follow-up study. *Evidence-Based Mental Health* 17, 76-80.

Inder KJ, Handley TE, Johnston A, Weaver N, Coleman C, Lewin TJ, Slade T, Kelly BJ (2014). Determinants of suicidal ideation and suicide attempts: Parallel cross-sectional analyses examining geographical location. *BMC Psychiatry* 14, 208.

Kann L, Kinchen S, Shanklin SL, Flint KH, Kawkins J, Harris WA, Lowry R, Olsen EOM, McManus T, Chyen D, Whittle L, Taylor E, Demissie Z, Brener N, Thornton J, Moore J, Zaza S, Division of A, School Health NCfHIVA, Viral Hepatitis STD, Tb Prevention CDC (2014). Youth risk behavior surveillance - United States, 2013. *Morbidity and Mortality Weekly Report Surveillance Summaries* 63 S4, 1-168.

Kara H, Bayir A, Degirmenci S, Kayis SA, Akinci M, Ak A, Agacayak A, Azap M (2014). Causes of poisoning in patients evaluated in a hospital emergency department in Konya, Turkey. *Journal of the Pakistan Medical Association* 64, 1042-1048.

Kawashima Y, Yonemoto N, Inagaki M, Yamada M (2014). Prevalence of suicide attempters in emergency departments in Japan: A systematic review and meta-analysis. *Journal of Affective Disorders* 163, 33-39.

Kharsati N, Bhola P (2014). Patterns of non-suicidal self-injurious behaviours among college students in India. *International Journal of Social Psychiatry*. Published online: 27 May 2014. doi: 10.1177/0020764014535755.

Kimbrel NA, Johnson ME, Clancy C, Hertzberg M, Collie C, Van Voorhees EE, Dennis MF, Calhoun PS, Beckham JC (2014). Deliberate self-harm and suicidal ideation among male Iraq/Afghanistan-era veterans seeking treatment for PTSD. *Journal of Traumatic Stress* 27, 474-477.

Kokkevi A, Rotsika V, Botsis A, Kanavou E, Malliori M, Richardson C (2014). Adolescents' self-reported running away from home and suicide attempts during a period of economic recession in Greece. *Child & Youth Care Forum* 43, 691-704.

Kumar BKS, Krishnamurthy CN, Hariharan V, Lakshmi CMA (2014). A psychosociodemographic study of attempted suicide patients in Pesimsr: Hospital-based cross-sectional study. *Annals of Health and Health Sciences* 1, 108-112.

Kumar MR, Vignan Kumar GP, Babu PR, Kumar SS, Subrahmanyam BV, Veeraprasad M, Rammohan P, Srinivas M, Agrawal A (2014). A retrospective analysis of acute organophosphorus poisoning cases admitted to the tertiary care teaching hospital in south India. *Annals of African Medicine* 13, 71-75.

Limsuwan N (2014). Clinical presentations of bipolar disorder in children and adolescents. *Journal of the Medical Association of Thailand* 97, 179-183.

Martin MS, Dorken SK, Colman I, McKenzie K, Simpson AIF (2014). The incidence and prediction of self-injury among sentenced prisoners. *Canadian Journal of Psychiatry* 59, 259-267.

Messias E, Kindrick K, Castro J (2014). School bullying, cyberbullying, or both: Correlates of teen suicidality in the 2011 CDC youth risk behavior survey. *Comprehensive Psychiatry* 55, 1063–1068.

Mihai A, Ricean A, Voidazan S (2014). No significant difference in depression rate in employed and unemployed in a pair-matched study design. *Frontiers in Public Health* 2, 93.

Monirpoor N, Khoosfi H, Gholamy Zarch M, Tamaddonfard M, Tabatabaei Mir SF, Mohammad Alipour M, Karimi Y (2014). Vulnerability to substance abuse and the risk of suicide in students of region 12 of Islamic Azad university. *International Journal of High Risk Behaviors & Addiction*. Published online: 15 June 2014. doi: 10.5812/ijhrba.11229.

Morales YM, Guarnero PA (2014). Non-suicidal self-injury among adult males in a correctional setting. *Issues in Mental Health Nursing* 35, 628-634.

Mrazek DA, Hornberger JC, Altar CA, Degtiar I (2014). A review of the clinical, economic, and societal burden of treatment-resistant depression: 1996-2013. *Psychiatric Services* 65, 977-987.

Muñoz R, Borobia AM, Quintana M, Martínez-Virto AM, Frías J, Carcas Sansuan AJ (2013). Development and validation of a poisoning surveillance program with automatic case detection in a tertiary care hospital (SAT-HULP). *Journal of the Spanish Society of Emergency Medicine* 25, 423-429.

Pechuho SI, Sattar RA, Kumar S, Pechucho TA, Qureshi MA, Khanani MR (2014). Respiratory failure and thrombocytopenia in patients with organophosphorus insecticide poisoning. *Rawal Medical Journal* 39, 246-250.

Peltzer K, Pengpid S (2014). Physical fighting and social correlates among in-school adolescents in the Caribbean. *Mediterranean Journal of Social Sciences* 5, 531-538.

Perloe A, Esposito-Smythers C, Curby TW, Renshaw KD (2014). Concurrent trajectories of change in adolescent and maternal depressive symptoms in the Tordia study. *Journal of Youth and Adolescence* 43, 612-628.

Perry L, Adams RD, Bennett AR, Lupton DJ, Jackson G, Good AM, Thomas SH, Vale JA, Thompson JP, Bateman DN, Eddleston M (2014). National toxicovigilance for pesticide exposures resulting in health care contact - an example from the UK's national poisons information service. *Clinical Toxicology*, 52, 549-555.

Pluck G, Brooker C (2014). Epidemiological survey of suicide ideation and acts and other deliberate self-harm among offenders in the community under supervision of the probation service in England and Wales. *Criminal Behavious and Mental Health*. Published online: 8 April 2014. doi: 10.1002/cbm.1909.

Rahman A, Martin C, Graudins A, Chapman R (2014). Deliberate self-poisoning presenting to an emergency medicine network in south-east Melbourne: A descriptive study. *Emergency Medicine International* Published online: 12 June 2014. doi: 10.1155/2014/461841.

Rana HJ, Khan N (2014). Self-harm among women prisoners of Pakistan. *Journal of the Indian Academy of Applied Psychology* 40, 304-309.

Rhodes AE, Bethell J, Carlisle C, Rosychuk RJ, Lu H, Newton A (2014). Time trends in suicide-related behaviours in girls and boys. *Canadian Journal of Psychiatry* 59, 152-159.

Saraff PD, Pepper CM (2014). Functions, lifetime frequency, and variety of methods of non-suicidal self-injury among college students. *Psychiatry Research* 219, 298–304.

Selling DP, Solimo AMS, Lee DMS, Horne K, Panove EP, Venters HMDMS (2014). Surveillance of suicidal and nonsuicidal self-injury in the New York city jail system. *Journal of Correctional Health Care* 20, 163-167.

Senterre C, Levêque A, Di Pierdomenico L, Dramaix-Wilmet M, Pirson M (2014). Epidemiology of injuries in Belgium: Contribution of hospital data for surveillance. *BioMed Research International*. Published online: 28 April 2014. doi: 10.1155/2014/237486.

Shanmugavadivel D, Sands R, Wood D (2014). Common presenting problems for young people attending the emergency department. *Advances in Emergency Medicine*. Published online: 25 March 2014. doi: 10.1155/2014/536080.

Skeen S, Tomlinson M, Macedo A, Croome N, Sherr L (2014). Mental health of carers of children affected by HIV attending community-based programmes in South Africa and Malawi. *AIDS Care* 26 Suppl 1, S11-S20.

Stevenson JW, Minns AB, Smollin C, Albertson TE, Cantrell FL, Tomaszewski C, Clark RF (2014). An observational case series of dabigatran and rivaroxaban exposures reported to a poison control system. *American Journal of Emergency Medicine* 32, 1077-1084.

Stewart R, Das M, Ardagh M, Deely JM, Dodd S, Bartholomew N, Pearson S, Spearing R, Williams T, Than M (2014). The impact of alcohol-related presentations on a New Zealand hospital emergency department. *The New Zealand Medical Journal* 127, 23-39.

Stewart SL, Baiden P, Theall-Honey L (2014). Examining non-suicidal self-injury among adolescents with mental health needs, in Ontario, Canada. *Archives of Suicide Research* 18, 392-409.

Tsay ME, Klein-Schwartz W, Anderson B (2014). Toxicity and clinical outcomes of paliperidone exposures reported to US poison centers. *Clinical Toxicology* 52, 207-213.

Ursano RJ, Colpe LJ, Heeringa SG, Kessler RC, Schoenbaum M, Stein MB (2014). The army study to assess risk and resilience in servicemembers (Army STARRS). *Psychiatry* 77, 107-119.

Vaughn MG, Salas-Wright CP, Underwood S, Gochez-Kerr T (2014). Subtypes of non-suicidal self-injury based on childhood adversity. *Psychiatric Quarterly*. Published online: 15 August 2014. doi: 10.1007/s11126-014-9313-7.

Vawda N (2014). The prevalence of suicidal behaviour and associated risk factors in grade 8 learners in Durban. *South African Family Practice* 56, 37-42.

Wong MM, Yiu MG (2014). Consultation-liaison service in a regional hospital in Hong Kong. *East Asian Archives of Psychiatry* 24, 51-57.

Wood R (2014). Self-inflicted burn injuries in the Australian context. *Australasian Psychiatry* 22, 393-396.

Wolford-Clevenger C, Febres J, Elmquist J, Zapor H, Brasfield H, Stuart GL (2014). Prevalence and correlates of suicidal ideation among court-referred male perpetrators of intimate partner violence. *Psychological Services* Published online: 30 June 2014. doi: 10.1037/a0037338.

Wu YL, Yang HY, Wang J, Yao H, Zhao X, Chen J, Ding XX, Zhang HB, Bi P, Sun YH (2014). Prevalence of suicidal ideation and associated factors among HIV-positive MSM in Anhui, China. *International Journal of STD & AIDS*. Published online: 23 July 2014, doi: 10.1177/0956462414544722.

Zisman S, O'Brien A (2014). A retrospective cohort study describing six months of admissions under section 136 of the Mental Health Act; the problem of alcohol misuse. *Medicine, Science, and the Law*. Published online: 24 June 2014. doi: 10.1177/0025802414538247.

Risk and protective factors

Abdul-Hamid S, Denman C, Dudas RB (2014). Self-relevant disgust and self-harm urges in patients with borderline personality disorder and depression: A pilot study with a newly designed psychological challenge. *PLoS ONE* 9, e99696.

Abrutyn S, Mueller AS (2014). Are suicidal behaviors contagious in adolescence? Using longitudinal data to examine suicide suggestion. *American Sociological Review* 79, 211-227.

Adams DH, Zhang L, Millen BA, Kinon BJ, Gomez J-C (2014). Pomaglumetad methionil (LY2140023 monohydrate) and aripiprazole in patients with schizophrenia: A phase 3, multi-center, double-blind comparison. *Schizophrenia Research and Treatment* 2014, 758212.

Afifi TO, Macmillan HL, Boyle M, Taillieu T, Cheung K, Sareen J (2014). Child abuse and mental disorders in Canada. *Canadian Medical Association Journal*. Published online: 22 April 2014. doi: 10.1503/cmaj.131792.

Ainiyet B, Rybakowski JK (2014). Suicidal behaviour and lipid levels in unipolar and bipolar depression. *Acta Neuropsychiatrica* 26, 315-320.

Ainiyet B, Rybakowski JK (2014). Suicidal behavior in schizophrenia may be related to low lipid levels. *Medical Science Monitor* 20, 1486-1490.

Akkaya-Kalayci T, Popow C, Winkler D, Bingöl RH, Demir T, Ozlü Z (2014). The impact of migration and culture on suicide attempts of children and adolescents living in Istanbul. *International Journal of Psychiatry in Clinical Practice*. Published online: 8 September 2014. doi: 10.3109/13651501.2014.961929.

Alonzo D, Thompson RG, Stohl M, Hasin D (2014). The influence of parental divorce and alcohol abuse on adult offspring risk of lifetime suicide attempt in the United States. *American Journal Of Orthopsychiatry* 84, 316-320.

Alvarado-Esquivel C, Sánchez-Anguiano LF, Arnaud-Gil CA, Hernández-Tinoco J, Molina-Espinoza LF, Rábago-Sánchez E (2014). Socio-demographic, clinical and behavioral characteristics associated with a history of suicide attempts among psychiatric outpatients: A case control study in a northern Mexican city. *International Journal of Biomedical Science* 10, 61-68.

Amit BH, Krivoy A, Mansbach-Kleinfeld I, Zalsman G, Ponizovsky AM, Hoshen M, Farbstein I, Apter A, Weizman A, Shoval G (2014). Religiosity is a protective factor against self-injurious thoughts and behaviors in Jewish adolescents: Findings from a nationally representative survey. *European Psychiatry* 29, 509–513.

Amiya RM, Poudel KC, Poudel-Tandukar K, Pandey BD, Jimba M (2014). Perceived family support, depression, and suicidal ideation among people living with HIV/AIDS: A cross-sectional study in the Kathmandu Valley, Nepal. *PLoS ONE*. Published online: 6 March 2014. doi: 10.1371/journal.pone.0090959.

Amone POK, Lekhutlile T, Meiser-Stedman R, Ovuga E (2014). Mediators of the relation between war experiences and suicidal ideation among former child soldiers in northern Uganda: The WAYS study. *BMC Psychiatry* 14, 271.

Andrijic NL, Alajbegovic A, Zec SL, Loga S (2014). Suicidal ideation and thoughts of death in epilepsy patients. *Psychiatria Danubina* 26, 52-55.

Anestis MD, Kleiman EM, Lavender JM, Tull MT, Gratz KL (2014). The pursuit of death versus escape from negative affect: An examination of the nature of the relationship between emotion dysregulation and both suicidal behavior and non-suicidal self-injury. *Comprehensive Psychiatry* 55, 1820-1830.

Anestis MD, Pennings SM, Williams TJ (2014). Preliminary results from an examination of episodic planning in suicidal behavior. *Crisis* 35, 186-192.

Angeletti G, D'Onofrio M, Lai C, Tambelli R, Aceto P, Girardi P (2014). Behavioural, psychological, and temperamental predictors of risk suicide trend after brief psychodynamic psychotherapy. *European Review for Medical and Pharmacological Sciences* 18, 1001-1009.

Aoki Y, Okada M, Inokuchi R, Matsumoto A, Kumada Y, Yokoyama H, Ishida T, Saito I, Ito H, Sato H, Tomio J, Shinohara K, Thornicroft G (2014). Time-related changes in suicide attempts after the nuclear accident in Fukushima. *Social Psychiatry and Psychiatric Epidemiology*, 49,1911-1918.

Arbuthnott AE, Lewis SP, Bailey HN (2014). Rumination and emotions in nonsuicidal self-injury and eating disorder behaviors: A preliminary test of the emotional cascade model. *Journal of Clinical Psychology*. Published online: 8 July 2014. doi: 10.1002/jclp.22115.

Arenliu A, Kelmendi K, Haskuka M, Halimi T, Canhasi E (2014). Drug use and reported suicide ideation and attempt among Kosovar adolescents. *Journal of Substance Use* 19, 358-363.

Arens AM, Gaher RM, Simons JS, Dvorak RD (2014). Child maltreatment and deliberate self-harm: A negative binomial hurdle model for explanatory constructs. *Child Maltreatment*. Published online: 3 September 2014. doi: 10.1177/1077559514548315.

Armstrong G, Jorm AF, Samson L, Joubert L, Singh S, Kermode M (2014). Suicidal ideation and attempts among men who inject drugs in Delhi, India: Psychological and social risk factors. *Social Psychiatry and Psychiatric Epidemiology* 49, 1367-1377.

Auerbach RP, Kim JC, Chango JM, Spiro WJ, Cha C, Gold J, Esterman M, Nock MK (2014). Adolescent nonsuicidal self-injury: Examining the role of child abuse, comorbidity, and disinhibition. *Psychiatry Research* 220, 579-584.

Azorin JM, Belzeaux R, Fakra E, Kaladjian A, Hantouche E, Lancrenon S, Adida M (2014). Gender differences in a cohort of major depressive patients: Further evidence for the male depression syndrome hypothesis. *Journal of Affective Disorders* 167, 85-92.

Baetens I, Claes L, Onghena P, Grietens H, Van Leeuwen K, Pieters C, Wiersema JR, Griffith JW (2014). Non-suicidal self-injury in adolescence: A longitudinal study of the relationship between NSSI, psychological distress and perceived parenting. *Journal of Adolescence* 37, 817-826.

Bagge CL, Littlefield AK, Conner KR, Schumacher JA, Lee HJ (2014). Near-term predictors of the intensity of suicidal ideation: An examination of the 24 h prior to a recent suicide attempt. *Journal of Affective Disorders* 165, 53-58.

Bahk YC, Han E, Lee SH (2014). Biological rhythm differences and suicidal ideation in patients with major depressive disorder. *Journal of Affective Disorders* 168, 294-297.

Baiocco R, Ioverno S, Lonigro A, Baumgartner E, Laghi F (2014). Suicidal ideation among Italian and Spanish young adults: The role of sexual orientation. *Archives of Suicide Research*. Published online: 20 May 2014. doi: 10.1080/13811118.2013.833150.

Ballard ED, Cwik M, Storr CL, Goldstein M, Eaton WW, Wilcox HC (2014). Recent medical service utilization and health conditions associated with a history of suicide attempts. *General Hospital Psychiatry* 6, 437-441.

Bangs ME, Wietecha LA, Wang S, Buchanan AS, Kelsey DK (2014). Meta-analysis of suicide-related behavior or ideation in child, adolescent, and adult patients treated with atomoxetine. *Journal of Child and Adolescent Psychopharmacology* 24, 426-434.

Bannink R, Broeren S, van de Looij-Jansen PM, de Waart FG, Raat H (2014). Cyber and traditional bullying victimization as a risk factor for mental health problems and suicidal ideation in adolescents. *PLoS ONE* 9, e94026.

Barbui C, Patten SB (2014). Antidepressant dose and the risk of deliberate self-harm. *Epidemiology and Psychiatric Sciences* 23, 329-331.

Barnes JC, Meldrum RC (2014). The impact of sleep duration on adolescent development: A genetically informed analysis of identical twin pairs. *Journal of Youth and Adolescence.* Published online: 11 June 2014. doi: 10.1007/s10964-014-0137-4.

Barrocas AL, Giletta M, Hankin BL, Prinstein MJ, Abela JR (2014). Nonsuicidal self-injury in adolescence: Longitudinal course, trajectories, and intrapersonal predictors. *Journal of Abnormal Child Psychology,* Published online: 27 June 2014. doi: 10.1007/s10802-014-9895-4.

Barton JJ, Meade T, Cumming S, Samuels A (2014). Predictors of self-harm in male inmates. *Journal of Criminal Psychology* 4, 2-18.

Bashir F, Ara J, Kumar S (2014). Deliberate self poisoning at national poisoning control centre. *Journal of the Liaquat University of Medical and Health Sciences* 13, 3-8.

Batterham PJ, Fairweather-Schmidt AK, Butterworth P, Calear AL, Mackinnon AJ, Christensen H (2014). Temporal effects of separation on suicidal thoughts and behaviours. *Social Science & Medicine* 111, 58-63.

Battle CL, Weinstock LM, Howard M (2014). Clinical correlates of perinatal bipolar disorder in an interdisciplinary obstetrical hospital setting. *Journal of Affective Disorders* 158, 97-100.

Baus N, Fischer-Kern M, Naderer A, Klein J, Doering S, Pastner B, Leithner-Dziubas K, Plener PL, Kapusta ND (2014). Personality organization in borderline patients with a history of suicide attempts. *Psychiatry Research* 218,129-33.

Bay-Richter C, Linderholm KR, Lim CK, Samuelsson M, Traskman-Bendz L, Guillemin GJ, Erhardt S, Brundin L (2014). A role for inflammatory metabolites as modulators of the glutamate N-methyl-D-aspartate receptor in depression and suicidality. *Brain, Behavior, and Immunity.* Published online: 12 August 2014. doi: 10.1016/j.bbi.2014.07.012.

Bazrafshan M-R, Jahangir F, Mansouri A, Kashfi SH (2014). Coping strategies in people attempting suicide. *International Journal of High Risk Behaviors & Addiction* 3, e16265.

Bell J (2014). Harmful or helpful? The role of the internet in self-harming and suicidal behaviour in young people. *Mental Health Review Journal* 19, 61-71.

Bellis MA, Hughes K, Leckenby N, Jones L, Baban A, Kachaeva M, Povilaitis R, Pudule I, Qirjako G, Ulukol B, Raleva M, Terzic N (2014). Adverse childhood experiences and associations with health-harming behaviours in young adults: Surveys in eight Eastern European countries. *Bulletin of the World Health Organization* 92, 641-655.

Berkol TD, Yargiç I, Özyildirim I, Yazici O (2014). Comorbidity of adult attention deficit and hyperactivity disorder in bipolar patients: Prevalence, sociodemographic and clinical correlates. *Archives of Neuropsychiatry* 51, 97-102.

Berutti M, Nery FG, Sato R, Scippa A, Kapczinski F, Lafer B (2014). Association between family history of mood disorders and clinical characteristics of bipolar disorder: Results from the Brazilian bipolar research network. *Journal of Affective Disorders* 161, 104-108.

Bettmann JE, Tucker AR, Tracy J, Parry KJ (2014). An exploration of gender, client history, and functioning in wilderness therapy participants. *Residential Treatment for Children and Youth* 31, 155-170.

Bhaskaran J, Wang Y, Roos L, Sareen J, Skakum K, Bolton JM (2014). Method of suicide attempt and reaction to survival as predictors of repeat suicide attempts: A longitudinal analysis. *Journal of Clinical Psychiatry* 75, e802-e808.

Bifulco A, Schimmenti A, Moran P, Jacobs C, Bunn A, Rusu AC (2014). Problem parental care and teenage deliberate self-harm in young community adults. *Bulletin of the Menninger Clinic* 78, 95-114.

Bishop TM, Pigeon WR, Possemato K (2013). Sleep disturbance and its association with suicidal ideation in veterans. *Military Behavioral Health* 1, 81-84.

Björkenstam E, Weitoft GR, Lindholm C, Björkenstam C, Alexanderson K, Mittendorfer-Rutz E (2014). Associations between number of sick-leave days and future all-cause and cause-specific mortality: A population-based cohort study. *BMC Public Health* 14, 733.

Bland P (2014). Suicide risk increased in Asperger's syndrome. *Practitioner* 258, 8-9.

Blignaut RJ, Vergnani T, Jacobs JJ (2014). Correlates of sexual activity versus non-activity of incoming first-year students at a South African university. *African Journal of AIDS Research* 13, 81-91.

Blosnich JR, Gordon AJ, Bossarte RM (2014). Suicidal ideation and mental distress among adults with military service history: Results from 5 US states, 2010. *American Journal of Public Health* 104 Suppl 4, S595-S602.

Blosnich JR, Kopacz MS, McCarten J, Bossarte RM (2014). Mental health and self-directed violence among student service members/veterans in postsecondary education. *Journal of American College Health*. Published online: 11 June 2014. doi: 10.1080/07448481.2014.931282.

Blosnich JR, Mays VM, Cochran SD (2014). Suicidality among veterans: Implications of sexual minority status. *American Journal of Public Health* 104 Suppl 4, S535-S537.

Bolton S-L, Elias B, Enns MW, Sareen J, Beals J, Novins DK, Swampy Cree Suicide Prevention Team, AI-SUPERPFP TEAM (2014). A comparison of the prevalence and risk factors of suicidal ideation and suicide attempts in two American Indian population samples and in a general population sample. *Transcultural Psychiatry* 51, 3-22.

Borges G, Acosta I, Sosa AL (2014). Suicide ideation, dementia and mental disorders among community sample of older people in Mexico. *International Journal of Geriatric Psychiatry*. Published online: 1 May 2014. doi: 10.1002/gps.4134

Boricevic Marsanic V, Aukst Margetic B, Ozanic Bulic S, Duretic I, Kniewald H, Jukic T, Paradzik L (2014). Non-suicidal self-injury among psychiatric outpatient adolescent offspring of Croatian posttraumatic stress disorder male war veterans: Prevalence and psychosocial correlates. *International Journal of Social Psychiatry*. Published online: 9 July 2014. doi: 10.1177/0020764014541248.

Bostwick WB, Meyer I, Aranda F, Russell S, Hughes T, Birkett M, Mustanski B (2014). Mental health and suicidality among racially/ethnically diverse sexual minority youths. *American Journal of Public Health* 104, 1129-1136.

Bowes L, Wolke D, Joinson C, Lereya ST, Lewis G (2014). Sibling bullying and risk of depression, anxiety, and self-harm: A prospective cohort study. *Pediatrics*. Published online: 8 September 2014. doi: 10.1542/peds.2014-0832.

Braden A, Overholser J, Fisher L, Ridley J (2014). Life meaning is associated with suicidal ideation among depressed veterans. *Death Studies*. Published online: 24 Jul 2014. doi: 10.1080/07481187.2013.871604.

Braithwaite E, Gariepy G, Wiens-Kinkaid M, Elbejjani M, Fuhrer R (2014). Re: Hjorthoj et al.'s article: Risk of suicide according to level of psychiatric treatment: A nationwide nested case-control study, Soc Psychiatry Psychiatr Epidemiol. 2014. *Social Psychiatry and Psychiatric Epidemiology*. Published online: 3 August 2014. doi: 10.1007/s00127-014-0940-y.

Brewer-Smyth K (2014). Obesity, traumatic brain injury, childhood abuse, and suicide attempts in females at risk. *Rehabilitation Nursing* 39, 183-191.

Breyer BN, Kenfield SA, Blaschko SD, Erickson BA (2014). The association of lower urinary tract symptoms, depression and suicidal ideation: Data from the 2005-2006 and 2007-2008 national health and nutrition examination survey. *Journal of Urology* 191, 1333-1339.

Britton WB, Lepp NE, Niles HF, Rocha T, Fisher NE, Gold JS (2014). A randomized controlled pilot trial of classroom-based mindfulness meditation compared to an active control condition in sixth-grade children. *Journal of School Psychology* 52, 263-278.

Brodbeck J, Stulz N, Itten S, Regli D, Znoj H, Caspar F (2014). The structure of psychopathological symptoms and the associations with DSM-diagnoses in treatment seeking individuals. *Comprehensive Psychiatry* 55, 714-726.

Brown MJ, Cohen SA, Mezuk B (2014). Duration of US residence and suicidality among racial/ethnic minority immigrants. *Social Psychiatry and Psychiatric Epidemiology*. Published online: 10 August 2014. doi: 10.1007/s00127-014-0947-4.

Brownson C, Becker MS, Shadick R, Jaggars SS, Nitkin-Kaner Y (2014). Suicidal behavior and help seeking among diverse college students. *Journal of College Counseling* 17, 116-130.

Bruwer B, Govender R, Bishop M, Williams DR, Stein DJ, Seedat S (2014). Association between childhood adversities and long-term suicidality among South Africans from the results of the South African stress and health study: A cross-sectional study. *BMJ Open* 4, e004644.

Bryan CJ, Andreski SR, McNaughton-Cassill M, Osman A (2014). Agency is associated with decreased emotional distress and suicidal ideation in military personnel. *Archives of Suicide Research* 18, 241-250.

Bryan CJ, Bryan AO, May AM, Klonsky ED (2014). Trajectories of suicide ideation, nonsuicidal self-injury, and suicide attempts in a nonclinical sample of military personnel and veterans. *Suicide and Life-Threatening Behavior*. Published online: 25 September 2014. doi: 10.1111/sltb.12127.

Burk T, Edmondson AH, Whitehead T, Smith B (2014). Suicide risk factors among victims of bullying and other forms of violence: Data from the 2009 and 2011 Oklahma youth risk behavior surveys. *The Journal of the Oklahoma State Medical Association* 107, 335-342.

Caceda R, Moskovciak T, Prendes-Alvarez S, Wojas J, Engel A, Wilker SH, Gamboa JL, Stowe ZN (2014). Gender-specific effects of depression and suicidal ideation in prosocial behaviors. *PLoS ONE* 9, e108733.

Callan MJ, Kay AC, Dawtry RJ (2014). Making sense of misfortune: Deservingness, self-esteem, and patterns of self-defeat. *Journal of Personality and Social Psychology* 107, 142-162.

Camarena B, Fresán A, Sarmiento E (2014). Exploring personality features in patients with affective disorders and history of suicide attempts: A comparative study with their parents and control subjects. *Depression Research and Treatment*. Published online: 2 March 2014. doi: 10.1155/2014/291802.

Campos RC, Besser A, Abreu H, Parreira T, Blatt SJ (2014). Personality vulnerabilities in adolescent suicidality: The mediating role of psychological distress. *Bulletin of the Menninger Clinic* 78, 115-139.

Capron DW, Lamis DA, Schmidt NB (2014). Test of the depression distress amplification model in young adults with elevated risk of current suicidality. *Psychiatry Research* 219, 531-535.

Capuano A, Scavone C, Rafaniello C, Arcieri R, Rossi F, Panei P (2014). Atomoxetine in the treatment of attention deficit hyperactivity disorder and suicidal ideation. *Expert Opinion on Drug Safety* 13, 69-78.

Cardarelli R, Balyakina E, Malone K, Fulda KG, Ellison M, Sivernell R, Shabu T (2014). Suicide risk and mental health co-morbidities in a probationer population. *Community Mental Health Journal*. Published online: 29 July 2014. doi: 10.1007/s10597-014-9771-2.

Carlberg L, Schosser A, Calati R, Serretti A, Massat I, Papageorgiou K, Kocabas NA, Mendlewicz J, Zohar J, Montgomery SA, Souery D, Kasper S (2014). Association study of CREB1 polymorphisms and suicidality in MDD: Results from a European multicenter study on treatment resistant depression. *International Journal of Neuroscience*. Published online: 30 July 2014. doi: 10.3109/00207454.2014.936554.

Carney A (2014). Lesbian, gay, and bisexual adolescent suicidality: The impact of social stigma. *Kentucky Nurse* 62, 4.

Carvalho AF, Nunes-Neto PR, Castelo MS, Macêdo DS, Dimellis D, Soeiro-De-Souza MG, Soczynska JK, McIntyre RS, Hyphantis TN, Fountoulakis KN (2014). Screening for bipolar depression in family medicine practices: Prevalence and clinical correlates. *Journal of Affective Disorders* 162, 120-127.

Casadio P, Olivoni D, Ferrari B, Pintori C, Speranza E, Bosi M, Belli V, Baruzzi L, Pantieri P, Ragazzini G, Rivola F, Atti AR (2014). Personality disorders in addiction outpatients: Prevalence and effects on psychosocial functioning. *Substance Abuse* 8, 17-24.

Caselli RJ, Langbaum J, Marchant GE, Lindor RA, Hunt KS, Henslin BR, Dueck AC, Robert JS (2014). Public perceptions of presymptomatic testing for Alzheimer disease. *Mayo Clinic Proceedings* 89, 1389-1396.

Cater AK, Andershed AK, Andershed H (2014). Youth victimization in Sweden: Prevalence, characteristics and relation to mental health and behavioral problems in young adulthood. *Child Abuse & Neglect* 38, 1290-1302.

Cervantes RC, Goldbach JT, Varela A, Santisteban DA (2014). Self-harm among Hispanic adolescents: Investigating the role of culture-related stressors. *Journal of Adolescent Health* 55, 633-639.

Chabrol H, Melioli T, Goutaudier N (2014). Cannabis use and suicidal ideations in high-school students. *Addictive Behaviors* 39, 1766-1768.

Challet-Bouju G, Hardouin JB, Renard N, Legauffre C, Valleur M, Magalon D, Fatseas M, Chereau-Boudet I, Gorsane MA, Group JEU, Venisse JL, Grall-Bronnec M (2014). A gamblers clustering based on their favorite gambling activity. *Journal of Gambling Studies.* Published online: 6 September 2014. doi: 10.1007/s10899-014-9496-8.

Chan LF, Shamsul AS, Maniam T (2014). Are predictors of future suicide attempts and the transition from suicidal ideation to suicide attempts shared or distinct: A 12-month prospective study among patients with depressive disorders. *Psychiatry Research.* Published online: 6 September 2014. doi: 10.1016/j.psychres.2014.08.055,

Chan SMS, Chiu FKH, Lam CWL, Wong SMC, Conwell Y (2014). A multidimensional risk factor model for suicide attempts in later life. *Neuropsychiatric Disease and Treatment* 10, 1807-1817.

Chang EC, Kahle ER, Yu EA, Hirsch JK (2014). Understanding the relationship between domestic abuse and suicide behavior in adults receiving primary care: Does forgiveness matter? *Social Work* 59, 315-320.

Chang WC, Chen ESM, Hui CLM, Chan SKW, Lee EHM, Chen EYH (2014). The relationships of suicidal ideation with symptoms, neurocognitive function, and psychological factors in patients with first-episode psychosis. *Schizophrenia Research* 157, 12-18.

Chatzittofis A, Nordstrom P, Uvnas-Moberg K, Asberg M, Jokinen J (2014). CSF and plasma oxytocin levels in suicide attempters, the role of childhood trauma and revictimization. *Neuroendocrinology Letters* 35, 213-217.

Chau K, Kabuth B, Chau N (2014). Gender and family disparities in suicide attempt and role of socioeconomic, school, and health-related difficulties in early adolescence. *BioMed Research International.* Published online: 20 July 2014. doi: 10.1155/2014/314521.

Chen YJ, Tsai YF, Lee SH, Lee HL (2014). Protective factors against suicide among young-old Chinese outpatients. *BMC Public Health* 14, 372.

Cheref S, Lane R, Polanco-Roman L, Gadol E, Miranda R (2014). Suicidal ideation among racial/ethnic minorities: Moderating effects of rumination and depressive symptoms. *Cultural Diversity and Ethnic Minority Psychology.* Published online: 11 August 2014. doi: 10.1037/a0037139.

Chiang YH, Chen YJ, Yang CY (2013). The relationship between auditory hallucinations and suicide ideation in chronic schizophrenia patients. *Journal of Nursing and Healthcare Research* 9, 96-105.

Chittoria R, Mohapatra D, Friji M, Kumar S, Asokan A, Pandey S (2014). Camphor burns of the palm and non-suicidal self-injury: An uncommonly reported, but socially relevant issue. *Indian Journal of Plastic Surgery* 47, 252-255.

Choi I, Andrews G, Sharpe L, Hunt C (2014). Help-seeking characteristics of Chinese- and English-speaking Australians accessing internet-delivered cognitive behavioural therapy for depression. *Social Psychiatry and Psychiatric Epidemiology.* Published online: 6 September 2014. doi: 10.1007/s00127-014-0956-3.

Choi JH, Yu M, Kim KE (2014). Suicidal ideation in adolescents: A structural equation modeling approach. *Nursing & Health Sciences.* Published online: 19 June 2014. doi: 10.1111/nhs.12142.

Choi MH, Kim HS, Kim B, Lee JC, Park SJ, Jeong UH, Baek JH, Kim HJ, Lim DW, Chung SC (2014). Extraction and analysis of risk elements for Korean homecare patients with senile dementia. *The Journal of Behavioral Health Services & Research.* Published online: 22 July 2014. doi: 10.1007/s11414-014-9429-4.

Chopko BA, Palmieri PA, Facemire VC (2014). Prevalence and predictors of suicidal ideation among U.S. law enforcement officers. *Journal of Police and Criminal Psychology* 29. Published online: 6 February 2013. doi: 10.1007/s11896-013-9116-z.

Chou IC, Lin CC, Sung FC, Kao CH (2014). Attention-deficit hyperactivity disorder increases the risk of deliberate self-poisoning: A population-based cohort. *European Psychiatry* 29, 523-327.

Chowdhury AN, Banerjee S, Brahma A, Hazra A, Weiss MG (2013). Sociocultural context of suicidal behaviour in the Sundarban region of India. *Psychiatry Journal* 2013, 486081.

Chu J, Chi K, Chen K, Leino A (2014). Ethnic variations in suicidal ideation and behaviors: A prominent subtype marked by nonpsychiatric factors among Asian Americans. *Journal of Clinical Psychology* 70, 1211-1226.

Cicchetti D, Rogosch FA, Hecht KF, Crick NR, Hetzel S (2014). Moderation of maltreatment effects on childhood borderline personality symptoms by gender and oxytocin receptor and FK506 binding protein 5 genes. *Development and Psychopathology* 26, 831-849.

Class QA, Rickert ME, Larsson H, Lichtenstein P, D'Onofrio BM (2014). Fetal growth and psychiatric and socioeconomic problems: Population-based sibling comparison. *British Journal of Psychiatry.* Published online: 25 September 2014. doi: 10.1192/bjp.bp.113.143693.

Cohen JN, Stange JP, Hamilton JL, Burke TA, Jenkins A, Ong ML, Heimberg RG, Abramson LY, Alloy LB (2014). The interaction of affective states and cognitive vulnerabilities in the prediction of non-suicidal self-injury. *Cognition and Emotion.* Published online: 23 May 2014. doi: 10.1080/02699931.2014.918872.

Coleman C, Wileyto EP, Lenhart CM, Patterson F (2014). Multiple health risk behaviors in adolescents: An examination of youth risk behavior survey data. *American Journal of Health Education* 45, 271-277.

Conner KR, Bossarte RM, Lu N, Kaukeinen K, Chan G, Wyman P, Tu XM, Goldston DB, Houston RJ, Bucholz KK, Hesselbrock VM (2014). Parent and child psychopathology and suicide attempts among children of parents with alcohol use disorder. *Archives of Suicide Research* 18, 117-130.

Conner KR, Gamble SA, Bagge CL, He H, Swogger MT, Watts A, Houston RJ (2014). Substance-induced depression and independent depression in proximal risk for suicidal behavior. *Journal of Studies on Alcohol and Drugs* 75, 567-572.

Coohey C, Dirks-Bihun A, Renner LM, Baller R (2014). Strain, depressed mood and suicidal thoughts among maltreated adolescents in the United States. *Child Abuse and Neglect* 38, 1171-1179.

Coohey C, Easton SD, Kong J, Bockenstedt JKW (2014). Sources of psychological pain and suicidal thoughts among homeless adults. *Suicide and Life-Threatening Behavior*. Published online: 25 September 2014. doi: 10.1111/sltb.12126.

Copeland LA, McIntyre RT, Stock EM, Zeber JE, MacCarthy DJ, Pugh MJ (2014). Prevalence of suicidality among Hispanic and African American veterans following surgery. *American Journal of Public Health* 104 Suppl 4, S603-S608.

Correia CM, Gomes NP, Couto TM, Rodrigues AD, Erdmann AL, Diniz NMF (2014). Representations about suicide of women with history of domestic violence and suicide attempt. *Texto & Contexto - Enfermagem* 23, 118-125.

Courtet P, Jaussent I, Lopez-Castroman J, Gorwood P (2014). Poor response to antidepressants predicts new suicidal ideas and behavior in depressed outpatients. *European Neuropsychopharmacology* 24, 1650-1658.

Cox DW (2014). Gender differences in professional consultation for a mental health concern: A Canadian population study. *Canadian Psychology* 55, 68-74.

Cox Lippard ET, Johnston JAY, Blumberg HP (2014). Neurobiological risk factors for suicide: Insights from brain imaging. *American Journal of Preventive Medicine* 47, S152-S162.

Craig SL, Keane G (2014). The mental health of multiethnic lesbian and bisexual adolescent females: The role of self-efficacy, stress and behavioral risks. *Journal of Gay and Lesbian Mental Health* 18, 266-283.

Cramer RJ, Stroud CH, Fraser T, Graham J (2014). A trait-interpersonal analysis of suicide proneness among lesbian, gay, and bisexual community members. *Suicide and Life-Threatening Behavior*. Published online: 7 April 2014. doi: 10.1111/sltb.12092

Crow SJ, Swanson SA, le Grange D, Feig EH, Merikangas KR (2014). Suicidal behavior in adolescents and adults with bulimia nervosa. *Comprehensive Psychiatry* 55, 1534-1539.

Crowell SE, Baucom BR, Yaptangco M, Bride D, Hsiao R, McCauley E, Beauchaine TP (2014). Emotion dysregulation and dyadic conflict in depressed and typical adolescents: Evaluating concordance across psychophysiological and observational measures. *Biological Psychology* 98, 50-58.

Cruz D, Narciso I, Pereira C, Sampaio D (2014). Self-destructive symptomatic frames in clinical adolescents: Is the same different? *Journal of Research on Adolescence*. Published online: 13 June 2014. doi: 10.1111/jora.12152.

Cummings JR, Case BG, Ji X, Chae DH, Druss BG (2014). Racial/ethnic differences in perceived reasons for mental health treatment in US adolescents with major depression. *Journal of the American Academy of Child and Adolescent Psychiatry* 53, 980-990.

Dalley LP (2014). From asylums to jails: The prevailing impact on female offenders. *Women and Criminal Justice* 24, 209-228.

Damsa C, Lazignac C, Miller N, Maris S, Adam E, Rossignon K (2014). Lipid levels in dissociative disorders: Effects of psychodynamic psychotherapy. *The Psychiatric Quarterly* 85, 369-376.

da Silveira DX, Marques Fidalgo T, Di Pietro M, Santos JG, Oliveira LQ (2014). Is drug use related to the choice of potentially more harmful methods in suicide attempts? *Substance Abuse: Research and Treatment* 8, 41-43.

Davies LE, Oliver C (2014). The purported association between depression, aggression, and self-injury in people with intellectual disability: A critical review of the literature. *American Journal on Intellectual and Developmental Disabilities* 119, 452-471.

Davis TS, Mauss IB, Lumian D, Troy AS, Shallcross AJ, Zarolia P, Ford BQ, McRae K (2014). Emotional reactivity and emotion regulation among adults with a history of self-harm: Laboratory self-report and functional MRI evidence. *Journal of Abnormal Psycholology* 3, 499-509.

Davison KM, Kaplan BJ (2014). Lipophilic statin use and suicidal ideation in a sample of adults with mood disorders. *Crisis* 35, 278-282.

Davison KM, Marshall-Fabien GL, Gondara L (2014). Sex differences and eating disorder risk among psychiatric conditions, compulsive behaviors and substance use in a screened Canadian national sample. *General Hospital Psychiatry* 36, 411-414.

De Berardis D, Serroni N, Marini S, Rapini G, Carano A, Valchera A, Iasevoli F, Mazza M, Signorelli M, Aguglia E, Perna G, Martinotti G, Varasano PA, Pressanti GL, Di Giannantonio M (2014). Alexithymia, suicidal ideation, and serum lipid levels among drug-naive outpatients with obsessive-compulsive disorder. *Revista Brasileira de Psiquiatria* 36, 125-130.

De Luca S, Yan Y, Lytle M, Brownson C (2014). The associations of race/ethnicity and suicidal ideation among college students: A latent class analysis examining precipitating events and disclosure patterns. *Suicide and Life-Threatening Behavior* 44, 444-456.

Demirel H, Yesilbas D, Ozver I, Yuksek E, Sahin F, Aliustaoglu S, Emul M (2014). Psychopathy and facial emotion recognition ability in patients with bipolar affective disorder with or without delinquent behaviors. *Comprehensive Psychiatry* 55, 542-546.

Deutsch AR, Slutske WS (2014). A noncausal relation between casual sex in adolescence and early adult depression and suicidal ideation: A longitudinal discordant twin study. *The Journal of Sex Research*. Published online: 20 August 2014. doi: 10.1080/00224499.2014.942413.

Devries KM, Mak JY, Child JC, Falder G, Bacchus LJ, Astbury J, Watts CH (2014). Childhood sexual abuse and suicidal behavior: A meta-analysis. *Pediatrics*. Published online: 14 April 2014. doi: 10.1542/peds.2013-2166.

Dhingra K, Boduszek D, Palmer D, Shevlin M (2014). Psychopathy and self-injurious thoughts and behaviour: Application of latent class analysis. *Journal of Mental Health*. Published online: 29 April 2014. doi: 10.3109/09638237.2014.910645.

Dickerson Mayes S, Baweja R, Calhoun SL, Syed E, Mahr F, Siddiqui F (2014). Suicide ideation and attempts and bullying in children and adolescents. *Crisis* 35, 301-309.

Di Pierro R, Sarno I, Gallucci M, Madeddu F (2014). Nonsuicidal self-injury as an affect-regulation strategy and the moderating role of impulsivity. *Child and Adolescent Mental Health* 19, 259-264.

Dixon-Gordon KL, Gratz KL, McDermott MJ, Tull MT (2014). The role of executive attention in deliberate self-harm. *Psychiatry Research* 218, 113-117.

Dixon-Gordon KL, Tull MT, Gratz KL (2014). Self-injurious behaviors in posttraumatic stress disorder: An examination of potential moderators. *Journal of Affective Disorders* 166, 359-367.

Don Richardson J, Cyr KS, Nelson C, Elhai JD, Sareen J (2014). Sleep disturbances and suicidal ideation in a sample of treatment-seeking Canadian forces members and veterans. *Psychiatry Research* 218, 118-123.

Donath C, Graessel E, Baier D, Bleich S, Hillemacher T (2014). Is parenting style a predictor of suicide attempts in a representative sample of adolescents? *BMC Pediatrics* 14, 113.

Donskoy AL, Stevens R (2013). Starting from scratch: An exploration of the narratives of the first episode of self-wounding. *Ethnicity and Inequalities in Health and Social Care* 6, 62-76.

Drabble J, Bowles DP, Barker LA (2014). Investigating the role of executive attentional control to self-harm in a non-clinical cohort with borderline personality features. *Frontiers in Behavioral Neuroscience*. Published online: 20 August 2014. doi: 10.3389/fnbeh.2014.00274.

Du J, Sun H, Huang D, Jiang H, Zhong N, Xu D, Zhao Y, Lin S, Wang W, Du Z, Zhao M, Hser YI (2014). Use trajectories of amphetamine-type stimulants (ATS) in Shanghai, China. *Drug and Alcohol Dependence* 143, 44-50.

Dumais A, Cote G, Larue C, Goulet MH, Pelletier JF (2014). Clinical characteristics and service use of incarcerated males with severe mental disorders: A comparative case-control study with patients found not criminally responsible. *Issues in Mental Health Nursing* 35, 597-603.

Duong J, Bradshaw C (2014). Associations between bullying and engaging in aggressive and suicidal behaviors among sexual minority youth: The moderating role of connectedness. *Journal of School Health* 84, 636-645.

Eden KE, de Vries PJ, Moss J, Richards C, Oliver C (2014). Self-injury and aggression in tuberous sclerosis complex: Cross syndrome comparison and associated risk markers. *Journal of Neurodevelopmental Disorders* 6, 10.

Ellis AJ, Portnoff LC, Axelson DA, Kowatch RA, Walshaw P, Miklowitz DJ (2014). Parental expressed emotion and suicidal ideation in adolescents with bipolar disorder. *Psychiatry Research* 216, 213-216.

El-Ray LA, Abdou AA, Enaba DA (2014). Panic attacks and suicidality in bipolar patients. *Middle East Current Psychiatry* 21, 86-94.

Emmert-Aronson BO, Brown TA (2014). An IRT analysis of the symptoms of major depressive disorder. *Assessment.* Published online: 24 July 2014. doi: 10.1177/1073191114544470.

Emmert-Aronson BO, Moore MT, Brown TA (2014). Differential item functioning of the symptoms of major depression by race and ethnicity: An item response theory analysis. *Journal of Psychopathology and Behavioral Assessment* 36, 424-431.

Eneroth M, Sendén Gustafsson M, Løvseth LT, Schenck-Gustafsson K, Fridner A (2014). A comparison of risk and protective factors related to suicide ideation among residents and specialists in academic medicine. *BMC Public Health* 14, 271.

Erten E, Funda Uney A, Saatcioglu O, Ozdemir A, Fistikci N, Cakmak D (2014). Effects of childhood trauma and clinical features on determining quality of life in patients with bipolar I disorder. *Journal of Affective Disorders* 162, 107-113.

Ertl V, Pfeiffer A, Schauer-Kaiser E, Elbert T, Neuner F (2014). The challenge of living on: Psychopathology and its mediating influence on the readjustment of former child soldiers. *PLoS ONE* 9, e102786.

Evren C, Dalbudak E, Evren B, Can Y, Umut G (2014). The severity of attention deficit hyperactivity symptoms and its relationship with lifetime substance use and psychological variables among 10th grade students in Istanbul. *Comprehensive Psychiatry* 55, 1665-1670.

Evren C, Evren B, Bozkurt M (2014). Tobacco use among 10th grade students in Istanbul and related variables. *Asian Journal of Psychiatry* 8, 69-75.

Fang C-K, Chang M-C, Chen P-J, Lin C-C, Chen G-S, Lin J, Hsieh R-K, Chang Y-F, Chen H-W, Wu C-L, Lin K-C, Chiu Y-J, Li Y-C (2014). A correlational study of suicidal ideation with psychological distress, depression, and demoralization in patients with cancer. *Supportive Care in Cancer* 22, 3165-3174.

Fanning JR, Meyerhoff JJ, Lee R, Coccaro EF (2014). History of childhood maltreatment in intermittent explosive disorder and suicidal behavior. *Journal of Psychiatric Research* 56, 10-17.

Fassassi S, Vandeleur C, Aubry JM, Castelao E, Preisig M (2014). Prevalence and correlates of DSM-5 bipolar and related disorders and hyperthymic personality in the community. *Journal of Affective Disorders* 167, 198-205.

Fazel S, Wolf A, Palm C, Lichtenstein P (2014). Violent crime, suicide, and premature mortality in patients with schizophrenia and related disorders: A 38-year total population study in Sweden. *Lancet Psychiatry* 1, 44-54.

Fekadu A, Hanlon C, Gebre-Eyesus E, Agedew M, Solomon H, Teferra S, Gebre-Eyesus T, Baheretibeb Y, Medhin G, Shibre T, Workneh A, Tegegn T, Ketema A, Timms P, Thornicroft G, Prince M (2014). Burden of mental disorders and unmet needs among street homeless people in Addis Ababa, Ethiopia. *BMC Medicine* 12, 138.

Feixas G, Montesano A, Compan V, Salla M, Dada G, Pucurull O, Trujillo A, Paz C, Munoz D, Gasol M, Saul LA, Lana F, Bros I, Ribeiro E, Winter D, Carrera-Fernandez MJ, Guardia J (2014). Cognitive conflicts in major depression: Between desired change and personal coherence. *British Journal of Clinical Psychology* 53, 369-385.

Fergusson DM, Horwood LJ, Boden JM, Mulder RT (2014). Impact of a major disaster on the mental health of a well-studied cohort. *JAMA Psychiatry.*

Ferrer L, Kirchner T (2014). Suicidal tendency in a sample of adolescent outpatients with adjustment disorder: Gender differences. *Comprehensive Psychiatry* 55, 1342-1349.

Fink M (2014). What was learned: Studies by the consortium for research in ECT (CORE) 1997-2011. *Acta Psychiatrica Scandinavica* 129, 417-426.

Finley EP, Bollinger M, Noel PH, Amuan ME, Copeland LA, Pugh JA, Dassori A, Palmer R, Bryan C, Pugh MJ (2014). A national cohort study of the association between the polytrauma clinical triad and suicide-related behavior among US veterans who served in Iraq and Afghanistan. *American Journal of Public Health.* Published online: 17 July 2014. doi: 10.2105/AJPH.2014.301957.

Fino E, Iliceto P, Sabatello U, Petrucci F, Candilera G (2014). Self/other perception mediates between personality and suicidal ideation in young adults. *European Journal of Psychiatry* 28, 104-113.

Fisher AD, Ristori J, Bandini E, Giordano S, Mosconi M, Jannini EA, Greggio NA, Godano A, Manieri C, Meriggiola C, Ricca V, Dettore D, Maggi M, Italian Gn RHASOG (2014). Medical treatment in gender dysphoric adolescents endorsed by SIAMS-SIE-SIEDP-ONIG. *Journal of Endocrinological Investigation* 37, 675-687.

Flaskerud JH (2014). Depression in men: Issues for practice and research. *Issues in Mental Health Nursing* 35, 635-639.

Flood S, Foley FW, Zemon V, Picone M, Bongardino M, Quinn H (2014). Predictors of changes in suicidality in multiple sclerosis over time. *Disability and Rehabilitation* 36, 844-847.

Flowers KC, Walker RL, Thompson MP, Kaslow NJ (2014). Associations between reasons for living and diminished suicide intent among African-American female suicide attempters. *Journal of Nervous and Mental Disease* 202, 569-575.

Fok ML-Y, Stewart R, Hayes RD, Moran P (2014). Predictors of natural and unnatural mortality among patients with personality disorder: Evidence from a large UK case register. *PLoS ONE* 9, e100979.

Foroughipour M, Mokhber N, Azarpajooh MR, Taghavi M, Modarres Gharavi M, Akbarzadeh F, Ebrahimi A, Baghban Haghighi M (2013). Coping mechanisms, depression and suicidal risk among patients suffering from idiopathic epilepsy. *International Journal of High Risk Behaviors & Addiction* 1, 178-182.

Fragoso YD, Adoni T, Anacleto A, da Gama PD, Goncalves MVM, Matta APC, Parolin MFK (2014). Recommendations on diagnosis and treatment of depression in patients with multiple sclerosis. *Practical Neurology* 14, 206-209.

Franklin JC, Lee KM, Puzia ME, Prinstein MJ (2014). Recent and frequent nonsuicidal self-injury is associated with diminished implicit and explicit aversion toward self-cutting stimuli. *Clinical Psychological Science* 2, 306-318.

Franklin JC, Puzia ME, Lee KM, Prinstein MJ (2014). Low implicit and explicit aversion toward self-cutting stimuli longitudinally predict nonsuicidal self-injury. *Journal of Abnormal Psychology* 123, 463-469.

Fuller-Thomson E, Hamelin GP, Granger SJR (2013). Suicidal ideation in a population-based sample of adolescents: Implications for family medicine practice. *ISRN Family Medicine* 2013, 282378.

Furczyk K, Thome J (2014). Adult ADHD and suicide. *ADHD Attention Deficit and Hyperactivity Disorders* 6, 153-158.

Fursland A, Watson HJ (2014). Eating disorders: A hidden phenomenon in outpatient mental health? *The International Journal of Eating Disorders* 47, 422-425.

Gable RA, Park KL, Scott TM (2014). Functional behavioral assessment and students at risk for or with emotional disabilities: Current issues and considerations. *Education and Treatment of Children* 37, 111-135.

Gabriel F (2014). Sexting, selfies and self-harm: Young people, social media and the performance of self-development. *Media International Australia* 151, 104-112.

Gagné S, Vasiliadis HM, Préville M (2014). Gender differences in general and specialty outpatient mental health service use for depression. *BMC Psychiatry* 14,135.

Garcia-Nieto R, Blasco-Fontecilla H, de Leon-Martinez V, Baca-Garcia E (2014). Clinical features associated with suicide attempts versus suicide gestures in an inpatient sample. *Archives of Suicide Research* 18, 419-431.

Garcia-Williams AG, Moffitt L, Kaslow NJ (2014). Mental health and suicidal behavior among graduate students. *Academic Psychiatry* 38, 554-560.

Gassman-Pines A, Ananat EO, Gibson-Davis CM (2014). Effects of statewide job losses on adolescent suicide-related behaviors. *American Journal of Public Health* 104, 1964-1970.

Gauthier JM, Zuromski KL, Gitter SA, Witte TK, Cero IJ, Gordon KH, Ribeiro J, Anestis M, Joiner T (2014). The interpersonal-psychological theory of suicide and exposure to video game violence. *Journal of Social and Clinical Psychology* 33, 512-535.

Geoffroy PA, Bellivier F, Scott J, Etain B (2014). Seasonality and bipolar disorder: A systematic review, from admission rates to seasonality of symptoms. *Journal of Affective Disorders* 168, 210-233.

Geulayov G, Metcalfe C, Heron J, Kidger J, Gunnell D (2014). Parental suicide attempt and offspring self-harm and suicidal thoughts: Results from the Avon longitudinal study of parents and children (ALSPAC) birth cohort. *Journal of the American Academy of Child and Adolescent Psychiatry* 53, 509-517.

Ghaemi SN, Dalley S, Catania C, Barroilhet S (2014). Bipolar or borderline: A clinical overview. *Acta Psychiatrica Scandinavica* 130, 99-108.

Ghaziuddin N, Merchant C, Dopp R, King C (2014). A naturalistic study of suicidal adolescents treated with an SSRI: Suicidal ideation and behavior during 3-month post-hospitalization period. *Asian Journal of Psychiatry* 11, 13-19.

Giletta M, Calhoun CD, Hastings PD, Rudolph KD, Nock MK, Prinstein MJ (2014). Multi-level risk factors for suicidal ideation among at-risk adolescent females: The role of hypothalamic-pituitary-adrenal axis responses to stress. *Journal of Abnormal Child Psychology*. Published online: 24 June 2014. doi: 10.1007/s10802-014-9897-2.

Giner L, Jaussent I, Olie E, Beziat S, Guillaume S, Baca-Garcia E, Lopez-Castroman J, Courtet P (2014). Violent and serious suicide attempters: One step closer to suicide? *The Journal of Clinical Psychiatry* 75, e191-e197.

Gini G, Espelage DL (2014). Peer victimization, cyberbullying, and suicide risk in children and adolescents. *JAMA* 312, 545-546.

Gonzales D, Hajek P, Pliamm L, Nackaerts K, Tseng LJ, McRae TD, Treadow J (2014). Retreatment with varenicline for smoking cessation in smokers who have previously taken varenicline: A randomized, placebo-controlled trial. *Clinical Pharmacology & Therapeutics* 96, 390-396.

González-Castro TB, Juarez-Rojop I, Lopez-Narvaez ML, Tovilla-Zarate CA (2014). Association of TPH-1 and TPH-2 gene polymorphisms with suicidal behavior: A systematic review and meta-analysis. *BMC Psychiatry* 14, 196.

González-Castro TB, Nicolini H, Lanzagorta N, López-Narváez L, Genis A, Pool García S, Tovilla-Zárate CA (2014). The role of brain-derived neurotrophic factor (BDNF) Val66Met genetic polymorphism in bipolar disorder: A case-control study, comorbidities, and meta-analysis of 16,786 subjects. *Bipolar Disorders*. Published online: 8 July 2014. doi: 10.1111/bdi.12227.

Goodwin RD, Cohen GH, Tamburrino M, Calabrese JR, Liberzon I, Galea S (2014). Mental health service use in a representative sample of national guard soldiers. *Psychiatric Services* 65, 1347-1353.

Goodwin RD, Taha F (2014). Global health benefits of being raised in a rural setting: Results from the national comorbidity survey. *Psychiatry and the Clinical* Neurosciences 68, 395-403.

Gordon MS, Melvin GA (2014). Do antidepressants make children and adolescents suicidal? *Journal of Paediatrics and Child Health* 50, 847–854.

Gouveia-Pereira M, Abreu S, Martins C (2014). How do families of adolescents with suicidal ideation behave? *Psicologia: Reflexão e Crítica* 27, 171-178.

Grant JE, Derbyshire K, Leppink E, Chamberlain SR (2014). Suicidality in non-treatment seeking young adults with subsyndromal gambling disorder. *Psychiatric Quarterly* 85, 513-522.

Green B, Lowry TJ, Pathé M, McVie N (2014). Firesetting patterns, symptoms and motivations of insanity acquittees charged with arson offences. *Psychiatry, Psychology and Law* 21, 937-946.

Greenfield B, Henry M, Lis E, Slatkoff J, Guile JM, Dougherty G, Zhang X, Raz A, Eugene Arnold L, Daniel L, Mishara BL, Koenekoop RK, de Castro F (2014). Correlates, stability and predictors of borderline personality disorder among previously suicidal youth. *European Child & Adolescent Psychiatry*. Published online: 2 August 2014. doi: 10.1007/s00787-014-0589-9.

Grossbard JR, Malte CA, Saxon AJ, Hawkins EJ (2014). Clinical monitoring and high-risk conditions among patients with SUD newly prescribed opioids and benzodiazepines. *Drug and Alcohol Dependence* 142, 24-32.

Grudet C, Malm J, Westrin A, Brundin L (2014). Suicidal patients are deficient in vitamin D, associated with a pro-inflammatory status in the blood. *Psychoneuroendocrinology* 50, 210-219.

Gunn Iii JF, Lester D (2014). Sports participation and suicidal behaviour: Does sport type matter? *International Journal of Sport and Exercise Psychology* 12, 333-338.

Guo L, Deng J, He Y, Deng X, Huang J, Huang G, Gao X, Lu C (2014). Prevalence and correlates of sleep disturbance and depressive symptoms among Chinese adolescents: A cross-sectional survey study. *BMJ Open* 4, e005517.

Hah JM, Mackey S, Barelka PL, Wang CKM, Wang BM, Gillespie MJ, McCue R, Younger JW, Trafton J, Humphreys K, Goodman SB, Dirbas FM, Schmidt PC, Carroll IR (2014). Self-loathing aspects of depression reduce postoperative opioid cessation rate. *Pain Medicine* 15, 954-964.

Hahm HC, Chang STH, Tong HQ, Meneses MA, Yuzbasioglu RF, Hien D (2014). Intersection of suicidality and substance abuse among young Asian-American women: Implications for developing interventions in young adulthood. *Advances in Dual Diagnosis* 7, 90-104.

Hakim A, Khurshid R, Shah RAR, Mufti S, Krishan K, Singh Y, Afreen (2014). Pattern, profile and outcome of poisoning cases: A study at a large teaching hospital in north India. *JK Practitioner* 19, 36-40.

Harford TC, Yi Hy, Grant BF (2014). Associations between childhood abuse and interpersonal aggression and suicide attempt among U.S. adults in a national study. *Child Abuse and Neglect* 38, 1389-1398.

Haw C, Hawton K, Gunnell D, Platt S (2014). Economic recession and suicidal behaviour: Possible mechanisms and ameliorating factors. *International Journal of Social Psychiatry*. Published online: 4 June 2014. doi: 10.1177/0020764014536545.

He Q, Yang L, Shi S, Gao J, Tao M, Zhang K, Gao C, Yang L, Li K, Shi J, Wang G, Liu L, Zhang J, Du B, Jiang G, Shen J, Zhang Z, Liang W, Sun J, Hu J, Liu T, Wang X, Miao G, Meng H, Li Y, Hu C, Li Y, Huang G, Li G, Ha B, Deng H, Mei Q, Zhong H, Gao S, Sang H, Zhang Y, Fang X, Yu F, Yang D, Liu T, Chen Y, Hong X, Wu W, Chen G, Cai M, Song Y, Pan J, Dong J, Pan R, Zhang W, Shen Z, Liu Z, Gu D, Wang X, Liu Y, Liu X, Zhang Q, Li Y, Chen Y, Kendler KS, Wang X, Li Y, Flint J (2014). Smoking and major depressive disorder in Chinese women. *PLoS ONE* 9, e106287.

Henriksen CA, Mather AA, Mackenzie CS, Bienvenu OJ, Sareen J (2014). Longitudinal associations of obesity with affective disorders and suicidality in the Baltimore epidemiologic catchment area follow-up study. *Journal of Nervous and Mental Disease* 202, 379-385.

Herpertz-Dahlmann B, Schwarte R, Krei M, Egberts K, Warnke A, Wewetzer C, Pfeiffer E, Fleischhaker C, Scherag A, Holtkamp K, Hagenah U, Bühren K, Konrad K, Schmidt U, Schade-Brittinger C, Timmesfeld N, Dempfle A (2014). Day-patient treatment after short inpatient care versus continued inpatient treatment in adolescents with anorexia nervosa (ANDI): A multicentre, randomised, open-label, non-inferiority trial. *The Lancet* 383, 1222-1229.

Hewitt PL, Caelian CF, Chen C, Flett GL (2014). Perfectionism, stress, daily hassles, hopelessness, and suicide potential in depressed psychiatric adolescents. *Journal of Psychopathology and Behavioral Assessment* 36, 663–674.

Hidaka Y, Operario D, Tsuji H, Takenaka M, Kimura H, Kamakura M, Ichikawa S (2014). Prevalence of sexual victimization and correlates of forced sex in Japanese men who have sex with men. *PLoS ONE* 9, e95675.

Higson-Smith C (2014). Complicated grief in help-seeking torture survivors in sub-Saharan African contexts. *American Journal of Orthopsychiatry* 84, 487-495.

Hong JS, Kral MJ, Sterzing PR (2014). Pathways from bullying perpetration, victimization, and bully victimization to suicidality among school-aged youth: A review of the potential mediators and a call for further investigation. *Trauma Violence & Abuse*. Published online: 4 June 2014. doi: 10.1177/1524838014537904.

Hooley JM, St. Germain SA (2014). Nonsuicidal self-injury, pain, and self-criticism: Does changing self-worth change pain endurance in people who engage in self-injury? *Clinical Psychological Science* 2, 297-305.

Horton P (2014). 'I thought I was the only one': The misrecognition of LGBT youth in contemporary Vietnam. *Culture, Health & Sexuality* 16, 960-973.

Horwitz AG, Czyz EK, King CA (2014). Predicting future suicide attempts among adolescent and emerging adult psychiatric emergency patients. *Journal of Clinical Child & Adolescent Psychology*. Published online: 28 May 2014. doi: 10.1080/15374416.2014.910789.

Hottes TS, Ferlatte O, Gesink D (2014). Suicide and HIV as leading causes of death among gay and bisexual men: A comparison of estimated mortality and published research. *Critical Public Health*. Published online: 12 August 2014. doi: 10.1080/09581596.2014.946887.

Hovey JD, Morales LR, Hurtado G, Seligman LD (2014). Religion-based emotional social support mediates the relationship between intrinsic religiosity and mental health. *Archives of Suicide Research* 18, 376-391.

Huang YC, Wu YW, Chen CK, Wang LJ (2014). Methods of suicide predict the risks and method-switching of subsequent suicide attempts: A community cohort study in Taiwan. *Neuropsychiatric Disease and Treatment* 10, 711-718.

Huber CG, Smieskova R, Schroeder K, Studerus E, Harrisberger F, Aston J, Walter A, Walter M, Riecher-Rossler A, Borgwardt S (2014). Evidence for an agitated-aggressive syndrome pre-dating the onset of psychosis. *Schizophrenia Research* 157, 26-32.

Hunt CA, Reese JB, Hahn AP, Fauerbach JA (2014). Clinical and psychiatric characteristics of self-inflicted burn patients in the United States: Comparison with a nonintentional burn group. *Journal of Burn Care and Research.* Published online: 13 October 2013. doi: 10.1097/BCR.0000000000000100.

Husky M, Olié E, Guillaume S, Genty C, Swendsen J, Courtet P (2014). Feasibility and validity of ecological momentary assessment in the investigation of suicide risk. *Psychiatry Research* 220, 564-570.

Hutchinson PL, Ferrell N, Broussard M, Brown L, Chrestman SK (2014). Can school choice improve more than just academic achievement? An analysis of post-Katrina New Orleans. *Journal of School Health* 84, 221-232.

Ilie G, Mann RE, Boak A, Adlaf EM, Hamilton H, Asbridge M, Rehm J, Cusimano MD (2014). Suicidality, bullying and other conduct and mental health correlates of traumatic brain injury in adolescents. *PLoS ONE* 9, e94936.

Ishii T, Hashimoto E, Ukai W, Kakutani Y, Sasaki R, Saito T (2014). Characteristics of attempted suicide by patients with schizophrenia compared with those with mood disorders: A case-controlled study in northern Japan. *PLoS ONE* 9, e96272.

Isometsä, E (2014). Suicidal behaviour in mood disorders-who, when, and why? *Canadian Journal of Psychiatry* 59, 120-130.

Jager-Hyman S, Cunningham A, Wenzel A, Mattei S, Brown GK, Beck AT (2014). Cognitive distortions and suicide attempts. *Cognitive Therapy and Research* 38, 369-374.

Jakubczyk A, Klimkiewicz A, Krasowska A, Kopera M, Sławi ska-Ceran A, Brower KJ, Wojnar M (2014). History of sexual abuse and suicide attempts in alcohol-dependent patients. *Child Abuse and Neglect* 38, 1560-1568.

James LM, Strom TQ, Leskela J (2014). Risk-taking behaviors and impulsivity among veterans with and without PTSD and mild TBI. *Military Medicine* 179, 357-363.

Janelidze S, Suchankova P, Ekman A, Erhardt S, Sellgren C, Samuelsson M, Westrin A, Minthon L, Hansson O, Traskman-Bendz L, Brundin L (2014). Low IL-8 is associated with anxiety in suicidal patients: Genetic variation and decreased protein levels. *Acta Psychiatrica Scandinavica.* Published online: 24 September 2014. doi: 10.1111/acps.12339.

Jang J-M, Park J-I, Oh K-Y, Lee K-H, Kim MS, Yoon M-S, Ko S-H, Cho H-C, Chung Y-C (2014). Predictors of suicidal ideation in a community sample: Roles of anger, self-esteem, and depression. *Psychiatry Research* 216, 74-81.

Jardri R, Bartels-Velthuis AA, Debbane M, Jenner JA, Kelleher I, Dauvilliers Y, Plazzi G, Demeulemeester M, David CN, Rapoport J, Dobbelaere D, Escher S, Fernyhough C (2014). From phenomenology to neurophysiological understanding of hallucinations in children and adolescents. *Schizophrenia Bulletin* 40 Suppl 4, S221-S232.

Jegannathan B, Dahlblom K, Kullgren G (2014). 'Plue plun' male, 'kath klei' female: gender differences in suicidal behavior as expressed by young people in Cambodia. *International Journal of Culture and Mental Health* 7, 326-338.

Jenkins AL, Singer J, Conner BT, Calhoun S, Diamond G (2014). Risk for suicidal ideation and attempt among a primary care sample of adolescents engaging in nonsuicidal self-injury. *Suicide and Life-Threatening Behavior.* Published online: 10 April 2014. doi: 10.1111/sltb.12094.

Jensen L, Pagsberg A, Dalhoff K (2014). Methylphenidate misuse in adult patients and the impact of therapeutic use. *Human & Experimental Toxicology*, doi: 10.1177/0960327114543935.

Jeon HJ, Park JI, Fava M, Mischoulon D, Sohn JH, Seong S, Park JE, Yoo I, Cho MJ (2014). Feelings of worthlessness, traumatic experience, and their comorbidity in relation to lifetime suicide attempt in community adults with major depressive disorder. *Journal of Affective Disorders* 166, 206-212.

Juengst SB, Kumar RG, Arenth PM, Wagner AK (2014). Exploratory associations with tumor necrosis factor- , disinhibition and suicidal endorsement after traumatic brain injury. *Brain, Behavior, and Immunity* 41, 134-143.

Juodis M, Starzomski A, Porter S, Woodworth M (2014). A comparison of domestic and non-domestic homicides: Further evidence for distinct dynamics and heterogeneity of domestic homicide perpetrators. *Journal of Family Violence* 29, 299-313.

Kaess M, Durkee T, Brunner R, Carli V, Parzer P, Wasserman C, Sarchiapone M, Hoven C, Apter A, Balazs J, Balint M, Bobes J, Cohen R, Cosman D, Cotter P, Fischer G, Floderus B, Iosue M, Haring C, Kahn JP, Musa GJ, Nemes B, Postuvan V, Resch F, Saiz PA, Sisask M, Snir A, Varnik A, Ziberna J, Wasserman D (2014). Pathological internet use among European adolescents: Psychopathology and self-destructive behaviours. *European Child and Adolescent Psychiatry* 23, 1093-1102.

Kaiser BN, McLean KE, Kohrt BA, Hagaman AK, Wagenaar BH, Khoury NM, Keys HM (2014). Reflechi twòp - thinking too much: Description of a cultural syndrome in Haiti's central plateau. *Culture, Medicine and Psychiatry* 38, 448-472.

Kaley S, Mancino MJ, Messias E (2014). Sadness, suicide, and drug misuse in Arkansas: Results from the youth risk behavior survey 2011. *The Journal of the Arkansas Medical Society* 110, 185-186.

Kang EH, Hyun MK, Choi SM, Kim JM, Kim GM, Woo JM (2014). Twelve-month prevalence and predictors of self-reported suicidal ideation and suicide attempt among Korean adolescents in a web-based nationwide survey. *Australian & New Zealand Journal of Psychiatry*. Published online: 13 August. doi: 10.1177/0004867414540752.

Karsberg S, Armour C, Elklit A (2014). Patterns of victimization, suicide attempt, and posttraumatic stress disorder in Greenlandic adolescents: A latent class analysis. *Social Psychiatry and Psychiatric Epidemiology* 49, 1389-1399.

Keenan K, Hipwell AE, Stepp SD, Wroblewski K (2014). Testing an equifinality model of non-suicidal self-injury among early adolescent girls. *Development and Psychopathology* 26, 851-862.

Keilp JG, Beers SR, Burke AK, Melhem NM, Oquendo MA, Brent DA, Mann JJ (2014). Neuropsychological deficits in past suicide attempters with varying levels of depression severity. *Psychological Medicine* 44, 2965-2974.

Keilp JG, Wyatt G, Gorlyn M, Oquendo MA, Burke AK, John Mann J (2014). Intact alternation performance in high lethality suicide attempters. *Psychiatry Research* 30,129-36.

Kelleher I, Devlin N, Wigman JTW, Kehoe A, Murtagh A, Fitzpatrick C, Cannon M (2014). Psychotic experiences in a mental health clinic sample: Implications for suicidality, multimorbidity and functioning. *Psychological Medicine* 44, 1615-1624.

Kene P, Hovey JD (2014). Predictors of suicide attempt status: Acquired capability, ideation, and reasons. *Psychiatric Quarterly* 85, 427-437.

Keuroghlian AS, Shtasel D, Bassuk EL (2014). Out on the street: A public health and policy agenda for lesbian, gay, bisexual, and transgender youth who are homeless. *The American Journal of Orthopsychiatry* 84, 66-72.

Khalifeh H, Moran P, Borschmann R, Dean K, Hart C, Hogg J, Osborn D, Johnson S, Howard LM (2014). Domestic and sexual violence against patients with severe mental illness. *Psychological Medicine.* Published online: 4 September 2014. doi:10.1017/S0033291714001962.

Khazaeipour Z, Norouzi-Javidan A, Kaveh M, Mehrabani FK, Kazazi E, Emami-Razavi SH (2014). Psychosocial outcomes following spinal cord injury in Iran. *Journal of Spinal Cord Medicine* 37, 338-345.

Khazanov GK, Cui L, Merikangas KR, Angst J (2014). Treatment patterns of youth with bipolar disorder: Results from the national comorbidity survey-adolescent supplement (NCS-A). *Journal of Abnormal Child Psychology.* Published online: 24 June 2014. doi: 10.1007/s10802-014-9885-6.

Kim J, Kim K (2014). Gender differences in health-related quality of life of Korean patients with chronic obstructive lung disease. *Public Health Nursing.* Published online: 22 May 2014. doi: 10.1111/phn.12129.

Kim J-M, Stewart R, Kim S-W, Kang H-J, Kim S-Y, Lee J-Y, Bae K-Y, Shin I-S, Yoon J-S (2014). Interactions between a serotonin transporter gene, life events and social support on suicidal ideation in Korean elders. *Journal of Affective Disorders* 160, 14-20.

Kim KL, Galvan T, Puzia ME, Cushman GK, Seymour KE, Vanmali R, Jones RN, Spirito A, Dickstein DP (2014). Psychiatric and self-injury profiles of adolescent suicide attempters versus adolescents engaged in nonsuicidal self-injury. *Suicide and Life-Threatening Behavior.* Published online: 24 July 2014. doi: 10.1111/sltb.12110.

Kim SY, Park SP (2014). Suicidal ideation and risk factors in Korean migraine patients. *Journal of Clinical Neuroscience* 21, 1699-1704.

Kim YJ (2014). The role of self-esteem in the relationship between depression and suicidal ideation of Korean adolescents. *Life Science Journal* 11, 494-498.

Kimbrel NA, Calhoun PS, Elbogen EB, Brancu M, Workgroup VAM-AMR, Beckham JC (2014). The factor structure of psychiatric comorbidity among Iraq/Afghanistan-era veterans and its relationship to violence, incarceration, suicide attempts, and suicidality. *Psychiatry Research* 220, 397-403.

Kitagawa Y, Shimodera S, Togo F, Okazaki Y, Nishida A, Sasaki T (2014). Suicidal feelings interferes with help-seeking in bullied adolescents. *PLoS ONE* 9, e106031.

Kleiman EM, Ammerman B, Look AE, Berman ME, McCloskey MS (2014). The role of emotion reactivity and gender in the relationship between psychopathology and self-injurious behavior. *Personality and Individual Differences* 69, 150-155.

Knight A, Weiss P, Morales K, Gerdes M, Gutstein A, Vickery M, Keren R (2014). Depression and anxiety and their association with healthcare utilization in pediatric lupus and mixed connective tissue disease patients: A cross-sectional study. *Pediatric Rheumatology Online Journal.* Published online: 10 September 2014. doi: 10.1186/1546-0096-12-42.

Ko A, Swampillai B, Timmins V, Scavone A, Collinger K, Goldstein BI (2014). Clinical characteristics associated with lithium use among adolescents with bipolar disorder. *Journal of Child and Adolescent Psychopharmacology* 24, 382-389.

Ko MJ, Lee EY, Kim K (2014). Relationship between socioeconomic position and suicide attempts among the Korean adolescents. *Journal of Korean Medical Science* 29, 1287-1292.

Kohyama J (2014). The possible long-term effects of early-life circadian rhythm disturbance on social behavior. *Expert Review of Neurotherapeutics* 14, 745-755.

Konkan R, Erku GH, Güçlü O, enormanci Ö, Aydin E, Ülgen MC, Sungur MZ (2014). Coping strategies in patients who had suicide attempts. *Archives of Neuropsychiatry* 51, 46-51.

Kowalski RM, Giumetti GW, Schroeder AN, Lattanner MR (2014). Bullying in the digital age: A critical review and meta-analysis of cyberbullying research among youth. *Psychological Bulletin* 140, 1073-1137.

Koyawala N, Stevens J, McBee-Strayer SM, Cannon EA, Bridge JA (2014). Sleep problems and suicide attempts among adolescents: A case-control study. *Behavioral Sleep Medicine.* Published online: 21 March 2014. doi: 10.1080/15402002.2014.888655.

Krzyzanowska M, Steiner J, Brisch R, Mawrin C, Busse S, Braun K, Jankowski Z, Bernstein HG, Bogerts B, Gos T (2014). Ribosomal DNA transcription in the dorsal raphe nucleus is increased in residual but not in paranoid schizophrenia. *European Archives of Psychiatry and Clinical Neuroscience.* Published online: 5 August 2014. doi: 10.1007/s00406-014-0518-4.

Kuroki Y (2014). Risk factors for suicidal behaviors among Filipino Americans: A data mining approach. *American Journal of Orthopsychiatry.* Published online: 11 August 2014. doi: 10.1037/ort0000018.

Kurumaji A, Narushima K, Ooshima K, Yukizane T, Takeda M, Nishikawa T (2014). Clinical course of the bipolar II disorder in a Japanese sample. *Journal of Affective Disorders* 168, 363-366 ,

Kvitland LR, Melle I, Aminoff SR, Lagerberg TV, Andreassen OA, Ringen PA (2014). Cannabis use in first-treatment bipolar I disorder: Relations to clinical characteristics. *Early Intervention in Psychiatry.* Published online: 17 April 2014. doi: 10.1111/eip.12138.

Kwon O-Y, Park S-P (2014). Depression and anxiety in people with epilepsy. *Journal of Clinical Neurology* 10, 175-188.

Lamis DA, Ballard ED, Patel AB (2014). Loneliness and suicidal ideation in drug-using college students. *Suicide and Life Threatening Behavior.* Published online: 22 April 2014. doi: 10.1111/sltb.12095.

Lamis DA, Kaslow NJ (2014). Mediators of the daily hassles-suicidal ideation link in African American women. *Suicide and Life-Threatening Behavior.* Published online: 5 May 2014. doi: 10.1111/sltb.12099.

Lamis DA, Saito M, Osman A, Klibert J, Malone PS, Langhinrichsen-Rohling J (2014). Hopelessness and suicide proneness in U.S. and Japanese college students: Depressive symptoms as a potential mediator. *Journal of Cross-Cultural Psychology* 45, 805-820.

Lara E, Olaya B, Garin N, Ayuso-Mateos JL, Miret M, Moneta V, Haro JM (2014). Is cognitive impairment associated with suicidality? A population-based study. *European Neuropsychopharmacology.* Published online: 10 August 2014. doi: 10.1016/j.euroneuro.2014.08.010.

Larson BK, Eisenberg ME, Resnick MD (2014). Engagement in risk behaviors among adolescents who misuse prescription drugs: Evidence for subgroups of misusers. *Journal of Substance Use* 19, 334-339.

Lee DJ, Liverant GI, Lowmaster SE, Gradus JL, Sloan DM (2014). PTSD and reasons for living: Associations with depressive symptoms and alcohol use. *Psychiatry Research* 219, 550-555.

Lee J, Lee WY, Noh M, Khang YH (2014). Does a geographical context of deprivation affect differences in injury mortality? A multilevel analysis in South Korean adults residing in metropolitan cities. *Journal of Epidemiology and Community Health* 68, 457-465.

Lee K, Namkoong K, Choi W-J, Park JY (2014). The relationship between parental marital status and suicidal ideation and attempts by gender in adolescents: Results from a nationally representative Korean sample. *Comprehensive Psychiatry* 55, 1093-1099.

Lee S-H, Park Y-C, Yoon S, Kim J-I, Hahn SW (2014). Clinical implications of loudness dependence of auditory evoked potentials in patients with atypical depression. *Progress in Neuro-Psychopharmacology & Biological Psychiatry* 54, 7-12.

Leeners B, Rath W, Block E, Goerres G, Tschudin S (2014). Risk factors for unfavorable pregnancy outcome in women with adverse childhood experiences. *Journal of Perinatal Medicine* 42, 171-178.

Leon AC, Fiedorowicz JG, Solomon DA, Li C, Coryell WH, Endicott J, Fawcett J, Keller MB (2014). Risk of suicidal behavior with antidepressants in bipolar and unipolar disorders. *Journal of Clinical Psychiatry* 75, 720-727.

Le Strat Y, Le Foll B, Dubertret C (2014). Major depression and suicide attempts in patients with liver disease in the United States. *Liver International.* Published online: 23 June 2014. doi: 10.1111/liv.12612.

Lester D (2014). Participation in sports teams and suicidal behavior: An analysis of the 1995 national college health risk behavior survey. *Perceptual and Motor Skills* 119, 38-41.

Lev-Wiesel R, Zohar G (2014). The role of dissociation in self-injurious behavior among female adolescents who were sexually abused. *Journal of Child Sexual Abuse* 23, 824-839.

Levi-Belz Y, Zerach G, Solomon Z (2014). Suicide ideation and deliberate self-harm among ex-prisoners of war. *Archives of Suicide Research.* Published online: 10 July 2014. doi: 10.1080/13811118.2013.845123.

Levine SZ, Goldberg Y, Yoffe R, Pugachova I, Reichenberg A (2014). Suicide attempts in a national population of twins concordant for psychoses. *European Neuropsychopharmacology* 24, 1203–1209.

Lewis AJ, Bertino MD, Bailey CM, Skewes J, Lubman DI, Toumbourou JW (2014). Depression and suicidal behavior in adolescents: A multi-informant and multi-methods approach to diagnostic classification. *Frontiers in Psychology* 5, 766.

Li GQ (2013). Research on seafarer physical and psychological evaluation model and physical activity intervention measures. *Information Technology Journal* 12, 7821-7826.

Lijffijt M, Rourke ED, Swann AC, Zunta-Soares GB, Soares JC (2014). Illness-course modulates suicidality-related prefrontal gray matter reduction in women with bipolar disorder. *Acta Psychiatrica Scandinavica* 130, 374-87.

Lim M, Kim SW, Nam YY, Moon E, Yu J, Lee S, Chang JS, Jhoo JH, Cha B, Choi JS, Ahn YM, Ha K, Kim J, Jeon HJ, Park JI (2014). Reasons for desiring death: Examining causative factors of suicide attempters treated in emergency rooms in Korea. *Journal of Affective Disorders* 168, 349-356.

Lin F-G, Lin J-D, Hsieh Y-H, Chang C-Y (2014). Quarrelsome family environment as an enhanced factor on child suicidal ideation. *Research in Developmental Disabilities* 35, 3245-3253.

Liu DW, Fairweather-Schmidt AK, Roberts RM, Burns R, Anstey KJ (2014). Does resilience predict suicidality? A lifespan analysis. *Arch Suicide Res* ,

Liu RT, Case BG, Spirito A (2014). Injection drug use is associated with suicide attempts but not ideation or plans in a sample of adolescents with depressive symptoms. *Journal of Psychiatric Research* 56, 65-71.

Liu RT, Frazier EA, Cataldo AM, Simon VA, Spirito A, Prinstein MJ (2014). Negative life events and non-suicidal self-injury in an adolescent inpatient sample. *Archives of Suicide Research* 18, 251-258.

Lopez-Castroman J, Guillaume S, Olié E, Jaussent I, Baca-Garcia E, Courtet P (2014). The additive effect on suicidality of family history of suicidal behavior and early traumatic experiences. *Archives of Suicide Research.* Published online: 26 September 2014. doi: 10.1080/13811118.2014.957449.

Lopez-Castroman J, Jaussent I, Beziat S, Guillaume S, Baca-Garcia E, Genty C, Olié E, Courtet P (2014). Increased severity of suicidal behavior in impulsive aggressive patients exposed to familial adversities. *Psychological Medicine* 44, 3059-3068.

Lucassen MF, Clark TC, Denny SJ, Fleming TM, Rossen FV, Sheridan J, Bullen P, Robinson EM (2014). What has changed from 2001 to 2012 for sexual minority youth in New Zealand? *Journal of Paediatrics and Child Health*. Published online: 10 September 2014. doi: 10.1111/jpc.12727.

MacGregor EK, Grunebaum MF, Galfalvy HC, Melhem N, Burke AK, Brent DA, Oquendo MA, Mann JJ (2014). Depressed parents' attachment: Effects on offspring suicidal behavior in a longitudinal family study. *Journal of Clinical Psychiatry* 75, 879-885.

Maciejewski DF, Creemers HE, Lynskey MT, Madden PA, Heath AC, Statham DJ, Martin NG, Verweij KJ (2014). Overlapping genetic and environmental influences on nonsuicidal self-injury and suicidal ideation: Different outcomes, same etiology? *JAMA Psychiatry* 71, 699-705.

Mackelprang JL, Bombardier CH, Fann JR, Temkin NR, Barber JK, Dikmen SS (2014). Rates and predictors of suicidal ideation during the first year after traumatic brain injury. *American Journal of Public Health* 104, e100-e107.

Mak KK, Ho CS, Chua V, Ho RC (2014). Ethnic differences in suicide behavior in Singapore. *Transcultural Psychiatry*. Published online: 25 July 2014. doi: 10.1177/1363461514543545.

Mandhouj O, Aubin HJ, Amirouche A, Perroud NA, Huguelet P (2014). Spirituality and religion among French prisoners: An effective coping resource? *International Journal of Offender Therapy and Comparative Criminology* 58, 821-834.

Marinova P, Koychev I, Laleva L, Kancheva L, Tsvetkov M, Bilyukov R, Vandeva D, Felthouse A, Koychev G (2014). Nightmares and suicide: Predicting risk in depression. *Psychiatria Danubina* 26, 159-164.

Mars B, Heron J, Crane C, Hawton K, Kidger J, Lewis G, MacLeod J, Tilling K, Gunnell D (2014). Differences in risk factors for self-harm with and without suicidal intent: Findings from the ALSPAC cohort. *Journal of Affective Disorders* 168, 407-414.

Marshal MP, Dermody SS, Shultz ML, Sucato GS, Stepp SD, Chung T, Burton CM, Markovic N, Hipwell AE (2013). Mental health and substance use disparities among urban adolescent lesbian and bisexual girls. *Journal of the American Psychiatric Nurses Association* 19, 271-279.

Martin G, Thomas H, Andrews T, Hasking P, Scott JG (2014). Psychotic experiences and psychological distress predict contemporaneous and future non-suicidal self-injury and suicide attempts in a sample of Australian school-based adolescents. *Psychological Medicine*. Published online: 17 July 2014. doi: 10.1017/S0033291714001615.

Mash HB, Fullerton CS, Ramsawh HJ, Ng TH, Wang L, Kessler RC, Stein MB, Ursano RJ (2014). Risk for suicidal behaviors associated with alcohol and energy drink use in the US army. *Social Psychiatry and Psychiatric Epidemiology* 49, 1379-1387.

Mayes SD, Calhoun SL, Baweja R, Feldman L, Syed E, Gorman AA, Montaner J, Annapareddy J, Gupta N, Bello A, Siddiqui F (2014). Suicide ideation and attempts are associated with co-occurring oppositional defiant disorder and sadness in children and adolescents with adhd. *Journal of Psychopathology and Behavioral Assessment*. Published online: 10 August 2014. doi: 10.1007/s10862-014-9451-0.

Mayes SD, Fernandez-Mendoza J, Baweja R, Calhoun S, Mahr F, Aggarwal R, Arnold M (2014). Correlates of suicide ideation and attempts in children and adolescents with eating disorders. *Eating Disorders* 22, 352-366.

Maynard BR, Salas-Wright CP, Vaughn MG (2014). High school dropouts in emerging adulthood: Substance use, mental health problems, and crime. *Community Mental Health Journal*. Published online: 17 July 2014. doi: 10.1007/s10597-014-9760-5.

McClatchey IS, Wimmer JS (2014). Coping with parental death as seen from the perspective of children who attended a grief camp. *Qualitative Social Work* 13, 221-236.

McLaren S, Gomez R, Gill P, Chesler J (2014). Marital status and suicidal ideation among Australian older adults: The mediating role of sense of belonging. *International Psychogeriatrics.* Published online: 7 August 2014. doi: 10.1017/S1041610214001501.

McLaughlin KA, Aldao A, Wisco BE, Hilt LM (2014). Rumination as a transdiagnostic factor underlying transitions between internalizing symptoms and aggressive behavior in early adolescents. *Journal of Abnormal Psychology* 123, 13-23.

McLean CP, Morris SH, Conklin P, Jayawickreme N, Foa EB (2014). Trauma characteristics and posttraumatic stress disorder among adolescent survivors of childhood sexual abuse. *Journal of Family Violence* 29, 559-566.

Meyer IH, Teylan M, Schwartz S (2014). The role of help-seeking in preventing suicide attempts among lesbians, gay men, and bisexuals. *Suicide and Life Threatening Behavior.* Published online: 14 May 2014. doi: 10.1111/sltb.12104.

Meyer N, Voysey M, Holmes J, Casey D, Hawton K (2014). Self-harm in people with epilepsy: A retrospective cohort study. *Epilepsia* 55, 1355-1365.

Miletic V, Lukovic JA, Ratkovic N, Aleksic D, Grgurevic A (2014). Demographic risk factors for suicide and depression among Serbian medical school students. *Social Psychiatry and Psychiatric Epidemiology.* Published online: 10 September 2014. doi: 10.1007/s00127-014-0950-9.

Miller M, Swanson SA, Azrael D, Pate V, Sturmer T (2014). Antidepressant dose, age, and the risk of deliberate self-harm. *JAMA Internal Medicine* 174, 899-909.

Min J-A, Lee C-U, Chae J-H (2014). Resilience moderates the risk of depression and anxiety symptoms on suicidal ideation in patients with depression and/or anxiety disorders. *Comprensive Psychiatry.* Published online: 4 August 2014. doi:10.1016/j.comppsych.2014.07.022.

Minzenberg MJ, Lesh TA, Niendam TA, Yoon JH, Rhoades RN, Carter CS (2014). Frontal cortex control dysfunction related to long-term suicide risk in recent-onset schizophrenia. *Schizophrenia Research* 157, 19-25.

Miranda R, Ortin A, Scott M, Shaffer D (2014). Characteristics of suicidal ideation that predict the transition to future suicide attempts in adolescents. *Journal of Child Psychology and Psychiatry* 55, 1288-1296.

Miret M, Caballero FF, Huerta-Ramirez R, Moneta MV, Olaya B, Chatterji S, Haro JM, Ayuso-Mateos JL (2014). Factors associated with suicidal ideation and attempts in Spain for different age groups. Prevalence before and after the onset of the economic crisis. *Journal of Affective Disorders.* Published online: 1 April 2014. doi: 10.1016/j.jad.2014.03.045.

Mitsui N, Asakura S, Shimizu Y, Fujii Y, Toyomaki A, Kako Y, Tanaka T, Kitagawa N, Inoue T, Kusumi I (2014). The association between suicide risk and self-esteem in Japanese university students with major depressive episodes of major depressive disorder. *Neuropsychiatric Disease and Treatment* 10, 811-816.

Moberg T, Stenbacka M, Jönsson EG, Nordström P, Åsberg M, Jokinen J (2014). Risk factors for adult interpersonal violence in suicide attempters. *BMC Psychiatry* 14, 195.

Monfrim X, Gazal M, De Leon PB, Quevedo L, Souza LD, Jansen K, Oses JP, Pinheiro RT, Silva RA, Lara DR, Ghisleni G, Spessato B, Kaster MP (2014). Immune dysfunction in bipolar disorder and suicide risk: Is there an association between peripheral corticotropin-releasing hormone and interleukin-1beta? *Bipolar Disorders* 16, 741-747.

Moran P, Coffey C, Romaniuk H, Degenhardt L, Borschmann R, Patton GC (2014). Substance use in adulthood following adolescent self-harm: A population-based cohort study. *Acta Psychiatrica Scandinavica.* Published online: 23 June 2014. doi: 10.1111/acps.12306.

Muenzenmaier K, Schneeberger AR, Castille DM, Battaglia J, Seixas AA, Link B (2014). Stressful childhood experiences and clinical outcomes in people with serious mental illness: A gender comparison in a clinical psychiatric sample. *Journal of Family Violence* 29, 419-429.

Mullins N, Perroud N, Uher R, Butler AW, Cohen-Woods S, Rivera M, Malki K, Euesden J, Power RA, Tansey KE, Jones L, Jones I, Craddock N, Owen MJ, Korszun A, Gill M, Mors O, Preisig M, Maier W, Rietschel M, Rice JP, Muller-Myhsok B, Binder EB, Lucae S, Ising M, Craig IW, Farmer AE, McGuffin P, Breen G, Lewis CM (2014). Genetic relationships between suicide attempts, suicidal ideation and major psychiatric disorders: A genome-wide association and polygenic scoring study. *American Journal of Medical Genetics Part B: Neuropsychiatric Genetics* 165, 428-437.

Musci RJ, Hart SR, Ialongo N (2014). Internalizing antecedents and consequences of binge-eating behaviors in a community-based, urban sample of African American females. *Prevention Science* 15, 570-578.

Narishige R, Kawashima Y, Otaka Y, Saito T, Okubo Y (2014). Gender differences in suicide attempters: A retrospective study of precipitating factors for suicide attempts at a critical emergency unit in Japan. *BMC Psychiatry* 14, 144.

Nery FG, Miranda-Scippa A, Nery-Fernandes F, Kapczinski F, Lafer B (2014). Prevalence and clinical correlates of alcohol use disorders among bipolar disorder patients: Results from the Brazilian bipolar research network. *Comprehensive Psychiatry* 55, 1116-1121.

Newton-John TRO (2014). Negotiating the maze: Risk factors for suicidal behavior in chronic pain patients. *Current Pain and Headache Reports* Published online: 5 August 2014. doi: 10.1007/s11916-014-0447-y.

O'Connor RC, Rasmussen S, Hawton K (2014). Adolescent self-harm: A school-based study in Northern Ireland. *Journal of Affective Disorders* 159, 46-52.

O'Connor RC, Smyth R, Williams JMG (2014). Intrapersonal positive future thinking predicts repeat suicide attempts in hospital-treated suicide attempters. *Journal of Consulting and Clinical Psychology*. Published online: 1 September 2014. doi: 10.1037/a0037846.

O'Connor RC, Williams JMG (2014). The relationship between positive future thinking, brooding, defeat and entrapment. *Personality and Individual Differences* 70, 29-34.

O'Donoghue B, Lyne JP, Fanning F, Kinsella A, Lane A, Turner N, O'Callaghan E, Clarke M (2014). Social class mobility in first episode psychosis and the association with depression, hopelessness and suicidality. *Schizophrenia Research* 157, 8-11.

Ogundipe OA, Olagunju AT, Adeyemi JD (2014). Suicidal ideation among attendees of a West African HIV clinic. *Archives of Suicide Research*. Published online: 24 July 2014. *doi:* 10.1080/13811118.2014.915776.

Okado Y, Bierman KL (2014). Differential risk for late adolescent conduct problems and mood dysregulation among children with early externalizing behavior problems. *Journal of Abnormal Child Psychology*. Published online: 3 September 2014. doi: 10.1007/s10802-014-9931-4.

Oliver LN, Fines P, Bougie E, Kohen D (2014). Intentional injury hospitalizations in geographical areas with a high percentage of Aboriginal-identity residents, 2004/2005 to 2009/2010. *Chronic Diseases and Injuries in Canada* 34, 82-93.

Orri M, Paduanello M, Lachal J, Falissard B, Sibeoni J, Revah-Levy A (2014). Qualitative approach to attempted suicide by adolescents and young adults: The (neglected) role of revenge. *PLoS ONE* 9, e96716.

Ortíz-Gómez LD, López-Canul B, Arankowsky-Sandoval G (2014). Factors associated with depression and suicide attempts in patients undergoing rehabilitation for substance abuse. *Journal of Affective Disorders* 169, 10-14.

Osterman K, Bjorkqvist K, Wahlbeck K (2014). Twenty-eight years after the complete ban on the physical punishment of children in Finland: Trends and psychosocial concomitants. *Aggressive Behavior* 40, 568-581.

Ozdilek B, Gultekin BK (2014). Suicidal behavior among Turkish patients with Parkinson's disease. *Neuropsychiatric Disease and Treatment* 10, 541-545.

Pan PM, Salum GA, Gadelha A, Moriyama T, Cogo-Moreira H, Graeff-Martins AS, Rosario MC, Polanczyk GV, Brietzke E, Rohde LA, Stringaris A, Goodman R, Leibenluft E, Bressan RA (2014). Manic symptoms in youth: Dimensions, latent classes, and associations with parental psychopathology. *Journal of the American Academy of Child and Adolescent Psychiatry* 53, 625-634.e622.

Panagioti M, Gooding PA, Tarrier N (2014). A prospective study of suicidal ideation in posttraumatic stress disorder: The role of perceptions of defeat and entrapment. *Journal of Clinical Psychology*. Published online: 9 June 2014. doi: 10.1002/jclp.22103.

Paquette-Smith M, Weiss J, Lunsky Y (2014). History of suicide attempts in adults with Asperger syndrome. *Crisis* 35, 273-277.

Park JE, Lee JY, Jeon HJ, Han KH, Sohn JH, Sung SJ, Cho MJ (2014). Age-related differences in the influence of major mental disorders on suicidality: A Korean nationwide community sample. *Journal of Affective Disorders* 162, 96-101.

Park S-C, Kim J-M, Jun T-Y, Lee M-S, Kim J-B, Jeong S-H, Park YC (2013). Prevalence and clinical correlates of insomnia in depressive disorders: The CRESCEND study. *Psychiatry Investigation* 10, 373-381.

Park S-C, Lee H-Y, Sakong J-K, Jun T-Y, Lee M-S, Kim J-M, Kim J-B, Yim H-W, Park YC (2014). Distinctive clinical correlates of psychotic major depression: The CRESCEND study. *Psychiatry Investigation* 11, 281-289.

Park SM (2014). Health status and suicidal ideation in Korean elderly: The role of living arrangement. *Journal of Mental Health* 23, 94-98.

Park YM, Ko YH, Lee MS, Lee HJ, Kim L (2014). Type-d personality can predict suicidality in patients with major depressive disorder. *Psychiatry Investigation* 11, 232-236.

Park YM, Lee BH, Lee SH (2014). The association between serum lipid levels, suicide ideation, and central serotonergic activity in patients with major depressive disorder. *Journal of Affective Disorders* 159, 62-65.

Pavony MT, Lenzenweger MF (2014). Somatosensory processing and borderline personality disorder: Pain perception and a signal detection analysis of proprioception and exteroceptive sensitivity. *Personality Disorders: Theory, Research, and Treatment* 5, 164-171.

Peñas-Lledó E, Guillaume S, Naranjo MEG, Delgado A, Jaussent I, Blasco-Fontecilla H, Courtet P, Llerena A (2014). A combined high CYP2D6-CYP2C19 metabolic capacity is associated with the severity of suicide attempt as measured by objective circumstances. *Pharmacogenomics Journal*. Published online: 12 August 2014. doi: 10.1038/tpj.2014.42.

Peng H, Wu K, Li J, Qi H, Guo S, Chi M, Wu X, Guo Y, Yang Y, Ning Y (2014). Increased suicide attempts in young depressed patients with abnormal temporal-parietal-limbic gray matter volume. *Journal of Affective Disorders* 165, 69-73.

Penning SL, Collings SJ (2014). Perpetration, revictimization, and self-injury: Traumatic reenactments of child sexual abuse in a nonclinical sample of South African adolescents. *Journal of Child Sexual Abuse* 23, 708-726.

Pereira A, Conwell Y, Gitlin MJ, Dworkin RH (2014). Suicidal ideation and behavior associated with antidepressant medications: Implications for the treatment of chronic pain. *Pain*. Published online: 27 August 2014. doi: 10.1016/j.pain.2014.08.022.

Perez-Rodriguez MM, Baca-Garcia E, Oquendo MA, Wang S, Wall MM, Liu SM, Blanco C (2014). Relationship between acculturation, discrimination, and suicidal ideation and attempts among US Hispanics in the national epidemiologic survey of alcohol and related conditions. *Journal of Clinical Psychiatry* 75, 399-407.

Perich T, Mitchell PB, Loo C, Hadzi-Pavlovic D, Roberts G, Green M, Frankland A, Lau P, Corry J (2014). Cognitive styles and clinical correlates of childhood abuse in bipolar disorder. *Bipolar Disorders* 16, 600-607.

Perugi G, Medda P, Swann AC, Reis J, Rizzato S, Mauri M (2014). Phenomenological subtypes of severe bipolar mixed states: A factor analytic study. *Comprehensive Psychiatry* 55, 799-806.

Peter T, Taylor C (2014). Buried above ground: A university-based study of risk/protective factors for suicidality among sexual minority youth in Canada. *Journal of LGBT Youth* 11, 125-149.

Petersen L, Sorensen TIA, Andersen PK, Mortensen PB, Hawton K (2014). Y genetic and familial environmental effects on suicide attempts: A study of Danish adoptees and their biological and adoptive siblings. *Journal of Affective Disorders* 155, 273-277.

Pfennig A, Bschor T, Falkai P, Bauer M (2013). Clinical practice guideline: The diagnosis and treatment of bipolar disorder: Recommendations from the current S3 guideline. *Deutsches Arzteblatt International* 110, 92-100.

Phillips G, 2nd, Hightow-Weidman LB, Fields SD, Giordano TP, Outlaw AY, Halpern-Felsher B, Wohl AR (2014). Experiences of community and parental violence among HIV-positive young racial/ethnic minority men who have sex with men. *AIDS Care* 26, 827-834.

Pietrzak RH, El-Gabalawy R, Tsai J, Sareen J, Neumeister A, Southwick SM (2014). Typologies of posttraumatic stress disorder in the U.S. adult population. *Journal of Affective Disorders* 162, 102-106.

Pincus D, Eberle K, Walder CS, Kemp AS, Lenjav M, Sandman CA (2014). The role of self-injury in behavioral flexibility and resilience. *Nonlinear Dynamics, Psychology, and Life Sciences* 18, 277-296.

Pjescic KD, Nenadovic MM, Jasovic-Gasic M, Trajkovic G, Kostic M, Ristic-Dimitrijevic R (2014). Influence of psycho-social factors on the emergence of depression and suicidal risk in patients with schizophrenia. *Psychiatria Danubina* 26, 226-230.

Pompili M, Innamorati M, Gonda X, Erbuto D, Forte A, Ricci F, Lester D, Akiskal HS, Vazquez GH, Rihmer Z, Amore M, Girardi P (2014). Characterization of patients with mood disorders for their prevalent temperament and level of hopelessness. *Journal of Affective Disorders* 166, 285-291.

Pompili M, Lester D, Forte A, Seretti ME, Erbuto D, Lamis DA, Amore M, Girardi P (2014). Bisexuality and suicide: A systematic review of the current literature. *Journal of Sexual Medicine* 11, 1903-1913.

Ponte C, Almeida V, Fernandes L (2014). Suicidal ideation, depression and quality of life in the elderly: Study in a gerontopsychiatric consultation. *The Spanish Journal of Psychology*. Published online: 15 April 2014. doi: 10.1017/sjp.2014.15.

Pottie K, Dahal G, Georgiades K, Premji K, Hassan G (2014). Do first generation immigrant adolescents face higher rates of bullying, violence and suicidal behaviours than do third generation and native born? *Journal of Immigrant and Minority Health*. Published online: 24 September 2014. doi: 10.1007/s10903-014-0108-6.

Preyde M, Vanderkooy J, Chevalier P, Heintzman J, Warne A, Barrick K (2014). The psychosocial characteristics associated with NSSI and suicide attempt of youth admitted to an inpatient psychiatric unit. *Journal of the Canadian Academy of Child and Adolescent Psychiatry* 23, 100-110.

Pridmore S (2014). Mental disorder and suicide: A faulty connection. *Australian and New Zealand Journal of Psychiatry*. Published online: 19 August 2014. doi: 10.1177/0004867414548904.

Puggioni R (2014). Speaking through the body: Detention and bodily resistance in Italy. *Citizenship Studies* 18, 562-577.

Qin B, Zhang Y, Zhou X, Cheng P, Liu Y, Chen J, Fu Y, Luo Q, Xie P (2014). Selective serotonin reuptake inhibitors versus tricyclic antidepressants in young patients: A meta-analysis of efficacy and acceptability. *Clinical Therapeutics* 36, 1087-1095.

Quirk SW, Wier D, Martin SM, Christian A (2014). The influence of parental rejection on the development of maladaptive schemas, rumination, and motivations for self-injury. *Journal of Psychopathology and Behavioral Assessment*. Published online: 2 September 2014. doi: 10.1007/s10862-014-9453-y.

Quiroga CV, Walton B (2014). Needs and strengths associated with acute suicidal ideation and behavior in a sample of adolescents in mental health treatment: Youth and family correlates. *Residential Treatment for Children and Youth* 31, 171-187.

Raffi F, Pozniak AL, Wainberg MA (2014). Has the time come to abandon efavirenz for first-line antiretroviral therapy? *Journal of Antimicrobial Chemotherapy* 69, 1742-1747.

Rahman S, Alexanderson K, Jokinen J, Mittendorfer-Rutz E (2014). Risk factors for suicidal behaviour in individuals on disability pension due to common mental disorders - a nationwide register-based prospective cohort study in Sweden. *PLoS ONE* 9, e98497.

Raines AM, Capron DW, Bontempo AC, Dane BF, Schmidt NB (2014). Obsessive compulsive symptom dimensions and suicide: The moderating role of anxiety sensitivity cognitive concerns. *Cognitive Therapy and Research* 38, 660–669.

Rajapakse T, Griffiths K, Christensen H, Cotton S (2014). A comparison of non-fatal self-poisoning among males and females, in Sri Lanka. *BMC Psychiatry* 14, 22.

Raleva M, Jordanova Peshevska D, Filov I, Sethi D, Novotni A, Bonevski D, Hamza KH (2014). Childhood abuse, household dysfunction and the risk of attempting suicide in secondary school and university students in the Republic of Macedonia. *Macedonian Journal of Medical Sciences* 7, 375-379.

Ramberg M, Stanley B, Ystgaard M, Mehlum L (2014). Depressed suicide attempters with post-traumatic stress disorder. *Archives of Suicide Research*. Published online: 24 July 2014. doi: 10.1080/13811118.2014.915777.

Ramsawh HJ, Fullerton CS, Mash HBH, Ng THH, Kessler RC, Stein MB, Ursano RJ (2014). Risk for suicidal behaviors associated with PTSD, depression, and their comorbidity in the U.S. army. *Journal of Affective Disorders* 161, 116-122.

Ran MS, Zhang Z, Fan M, Li RH, Li YH, Ou GJ, Jiang Z, Tong YZ, Fang DZ (2014). Risk factors of suicidal ideation among adolescents after Wenchuan earthquake in China. *Asian Journal of Psychiatry*. Published online: 5 July 2014. doi: 10.1016/j.ajp.2014.06.016.

Rani RA, Razali R, Hod R, Mohamad K, Rani SAM, Yahya WNNW, Sahathevan R, Remli R, Law ZK, Ibrahim NM, Tan HJ (2014). Suicidal ideation amongst epilepsy patients in a tertiary centre. *Neurology Asia* 19, 129-136.

Rasool IA, Payton JL (2014). Tongues of fire: Women's suicide and self-injury by burns in the Kurdistan region of Iraq. *Sociological Review* 62, 237-254.

Raudino A, Carr VJ, Bush R, Saw S, Burgess P, Morgan VA (2014). Patterns of service utilisation in psychosis: Findings of the 2010 Australian national survey of psychosis. *Australian and New Zealand Journal of Psychiatry* 48, 341-351.

Read J, Cartwright C, Gibson K (2014). Adverse emotional and interpersonal effects reported by 1829 New Zealanders while taking antidepressants. *Psychiatry Research* 216, 67-73.

Rebok F, Teti GL, Fantini AP, Cárdenas-Delgado C, Rojas SM, Derito MNC, Daray FM (2014). Types of borderline personality disorder (BPD) in patients admitted for suicide-related behavior. *Psychiatric Quarterly*. Published online: 2 September 2014. doi: 10.1007/s11126-014-9317-3.

Recklitis CJ, Zhou ES, Zwemer EK, Hu JC, Kantoff PW (2014). Suicidal ideation in prostate cancer survivors: Understanding the role of physical and psychological health outcomes. *Cancer* 120, 3393-3400.

Reisner SL, Biello K, Perry NS, Gamarel KE, Mimiaga MJ (2014). A compensatory model of risk and resilience applied to adolescent sexual orientation disparities in nonsuicidal self-injury and suicide attempts. *American Journal of Orthopsychiatry* 84, 545-556.

Rhoades H, Winetrobe H, Rice E (2014). Prescription drug misuse among homeless youth. *Drug and Alcohol Dependence* 138, 229-233.

Richard-Devantoy S, Szanto K, Butters MA, Kalkus J, Dombrovski AY (2014). Cognitive inhibition in older high-lethality suicide attempters. *International Journal of Geriatric Psychiatry*. Published online: 12 May 2014. doi: 10.1002/gps.4138.

Richards D, Sanabria AS (2014). Point-prevalence of depression and associated risk factors. *Journal of Psychology: Interdisciplinary and Applied* 148, 305-326.

Ridgway R, Tang C, Lester D (2014). Membership in fraternities and sororities, depression, and suicidal ideation. *Psychological Reports* 114, 966-970.

Rieger SJ, Peter T, Roberts LW (2014). Give me a reason to live! Examining reasons for living across levels of suicidality. *Journal of Religion and Health*. Published online: 10 une 2014. doi: 10.1007/s10943-014-9893-4.

Rodav O, Levy S, Hamdan S (2014). Clinical characteristics and functions of non-suicide self-injury in youth. *European Psychiatry* 29, 503-508.

Rogers MJ, Follingstad DR (2014). Women's exposure to psychological abuse: Does that experience predict mental health outcomes? *Journal of Family Violence*. Published online: 22 July 2014. doi: 10.1007/s10896-014-9621-6.

Rojas SM, Bujarski S, Babson KA, Dutton CE, Feldner MT (2014). Understanding PTSD comorbidity and suicidal behavior: Associations among histories of alcohol dependence, major depressive disorder, and suicidal ideation and attempts. *Journal of Anxiety Disorders* 28, 318-325.

Rombold F, Lauterbach E, Felber W, Mueller-Oerlinghausen B, Ahrens B, Bronisch T, Kilb B, Lewitzka U, Richter K, Broocks A, Heuser I, Hohagen F, Quante A (2014). Adjunctive lithium treatment in the prevention of suicidal behavior in patients with depression and comorbid personality disorders. *International Journal of Psychiatry in Clinical Practice* 18, 300-303.

Rosellini AJ, Coffey SF, Tracy M, Galea S (2014). A person-centered analysis of posttraumatic stress disorder symptoms following a natural disaster: Predictors of latent class membership. *Journal of Anxiety Disorders* 28, 16-24.

Ross LE, Bauer GR, MacLeod MA, Robinson M, MacKay J, Dobinson C (2014). Mental health and substance use among bisexual youth and non-youth in Ontario, Canada. *PLoS ONE* 9, e101604.

Runfola CD, Allison KC, Hardy KK, Lock J, Peebles R (2014). Prevalence and clinical significance of night eating syndrome in university students. *Journal of Adolescent Health* 55, 41-48.

Rusow JA, Fletcher JB, Le H, Reback CJ (2014). Associations between sexual abuse and negative health consequences among high-risk men who have sex with men. *Journal of Gay and Lesbian Social Services* 26, 244-257.

Russell PSS, Nair MKC, Chandra A, Subramaniam VS, Bincymol K, George B, Samuel B (2013). ADad 9: Suicidal behavior in anxiety disorders among adolescents in a rural community population in India. *Indian Journal of Pediatrics* 80, S175-S180.

Sala R, Goldstein BI, Wang S, Blanco C (2014). Childhood maltreatment and the course of bipolar disorders among adults: Epidemiologic evidence of dose-response effects. *Journal of Affective Disorders* 165, 74-80.

Sampasa-Kanyinga H, Roumeliotis P, Xu H (2014). Associations between cyberbullying and school bullying victimization and suicidal ideation, plans and attempts among Canadian schoolchildren. *PLoS ONE* 9, e102145.

Sánchez-García S, García-Peña C, González-Forteza C, Jiménez-Tapia A, Gallo JJ, Wagner FA (2014). Depressive symptoms among adolescents and older adults in Mexico city. *Social Psychiatry and Psychiatric Epidemiology* 49, 953-960.

Sanchez-Gistau V, Baeza I, Arango C, Gonzalez-Pinto A, de la Serna E, Parellada M, Graell M, Paya B, Llorente C, Castro-Fornieles J (2014). The affective dimension of early-onset psychosis and its relationship with suicide. *Journal of Child Psychology and Psychiatry*. Published online: 26 September 2014. doi: 10.1111/jcpp.12332.

Sansone RA, Wiederman MW (2014). Sex and age differences in symptoms in borderline personality symptomatology. *International Journal of Psychiatry in Clinical Practice* 18, 145-149.

Sauer C, Arens EA, Stopsack M, Spitzer C, Barnow S (2014). Emotional hyper-reactivity in borderline personality disorder is related to trauma and interpersonal themes. *Psychiatry Research* 220, 468-476.

Schilders MR, Ogloff JRP (2014). Review of point-of-reception mental health screening outcomes in an Australian prison. *Journal of Forensic Psychiatry and Psychology* 25, 480-494.

Schroeder SR, Marquis JG, Reese RM, Richman DM, Mayo-Ortega L, Oyama-Ganiko R, LeBlanc J, Brady N, Butler MG, Johnson T, Lawrence L (2014). Risk factors for self-injury, aggression, and stereotyped behavior among young children at risk for intellectual and developmental disabilities. *American Journal on Intellectual and Developmental Disabilities* 119, 351-370.

Scourfield J, Evans R (2014). Why might men be more at risk of suicide after a relationship breakdown? Sociological insights. *American Journal of Men's Health* Published online: 26 August 2014. doi: 10.1177/1557988314546395.

Seaman EL, Levy MJ, Lee Jenkins J, Godar CC, Seaman KG (2014). Assessing pediatric and young adult substance use through analysis of prehospital data. *Prehospital and Disaster Medicine* 29, 468-472.

Seidel RW, Kilgus MD (2014). Agreement between telepsychiatry assessment and face-to-face assessment for emergency department psychiatry patients. *Journal of Telemedicine and Telecare* 20, 59-62.

Seil KS, Desai MM, Smith MV (2014). Sexual orientation, adult connectedness, substance use, and mental health outcomes among adolescents: Findings from the 2009 New York City youth risk behavior survey. *American Journal of Public Health* 104, 1950-1956.

Selim Reza AM, Feroz AHM, Nurul Islam SM, Nazmul Karim M, Golam Rabbani M, Sha Halam M, Mujibur Rahman AKM, Ridwanur Rahman M, Ahmed HU, Bhowmik AD, Zillur Rahman Khan M, Sarkar M, Alam MT, Jalal Uddin MM (2013). Risk factors of suicide and para suicide in rural Bangladesh. *Journal of Medicine* 14, 123-129.

Seo HJ, Jung YE, Jeong S, Kim JB, Lee MS, Kim JM, Yim HW, Jun TY (2014). Personality traits associated with suicidal behaviors in patients with depression: The CRESCEND study. *Comprehensive Psychiatry* 55, 1085-1092.

Shakya DR (2014). Common stressors among suicide attempters as revealed in a psychiatric service of eastern Nepal. *Journal of Traumatic Stress Disorders and Treatment*. Published online: 30 June 2014. doi: 10.4172/2324-8947.1000129.

Sheikhmoonesi F, Khademloo M, Pazhuheshgar S (2014). Patients discharged against medical advice from a psychiatric hospital in Iran: A prospective study. *Global Journal of Health Science* 6, 213-218.

Shelef L, Fruchter E, Mann JJ, Yacobi A (2014). Correlations between interpersonal and cognitive difficulties: Relationship to suicidal ideation in military suicide attempters. *European Psychiatry* 29, 498-502.

Shepardson RL, Funderburk JS (2014). Implementation of universal behavioral health screening in a university health setting. *Journal of Clinical Psychology in Medical Settings* 21, 253-266.

Sher L (2014). Men's mental health and suicide. *Psychiatria Danubina* 26, 298.

Sher L, Grunebaum MF, Sullivan GM, Burke AK, Cooper TB, Mann JJ, Oquendo MA (2014). Association of testosterone levels and future suicide attempts in females with bipolar disorder. *Journal of Affective Disorders* 166, 98-102.

Shin SH, Ko SJ, Yang YJ, Oh HS, Jang MY, Choi JM (2014). Comparison of boys' and girls' families for actor and partner effect of stress, depression and parent-adolescent communication on middle school students' suicidal ideation: Triadic data analysis. *Journal of Korean Academy of Nursing* 44, 317-327.

Simó-Pinatella D, Font-Roura J, Alomar-Kurz E, Giné C, Matson JL (2014). Functional variables of challenging behavior in individuals with intellectual disabilities. *Research in Developmental Disabilities* 35, 2635-2643.

Slavtcheva-Petkova V, Nash VJ, Bulger M (2014). Evidence on the extent of harms experienced by children as a result of online risks: Implications for policy and research. *Information Communication and Society* 18, 48-62.

Slijepcevic MK, Jukic V, Novalic D, Zarkovic-Palijan T, Milosevic M, Rosenzweig I (2014). Alcohol abuse as the strongest risk factor for violent offending in patients with paranoid schizophrenia. *Croatian Medical Journal* 55, 156-162.

Smith HP, Power J (2014). Themes underlying self-injurious behavior in prison: Gender convergence and divergence. *Journal of Offender Rehabilitation* 53, 273-299.

Smith NB, Steele AM, Weitzman ML, Trueba AF, Meure AE (2014). "I'm disgusting": Investigating the role of self-disgust in nonsuicidal self-injury. *Archives of Suicide Research*. Published online: 10 July 2014. doi: 10.1080/13811118.2013.850135.

Smith TJ, White A, Hadden L, Young AJ, Marriott BP (2014). Associations between mental health disorders and body mass index among military personnel. *American Journal of Health Behavior* 38, 529-540.

Soehner AM, Kaplan KA, Harvey AG (2014). Prevalence and clinical correlates of co-occurring insomnia and hypersomnia symptoms in depression. *Journal of Affective Disorders* 167, 93-97.

Soloff P, White R, Diwadkar VA (2014). Impulsivity, aggression and brain structure in high and low lethality suicide attempters with borderline personality disorder. *Psychiatry Research: Neuroimaging* 222, 131-139.

Soloff PH, Chiappetta L, Mason NS, Becker C, Price JC (2014). Effects of serotonin-2a receptor binding and gender on personality traits and suicidal behavior in borderline personality disorder. *Psychiatry Research: Neuroimaging* 222, 140-148.

Soltaninejad A, Fathi-Ashtiani A, Ahmadi K, Mirsharafoddini HS, Nikmorad A, Pilevarzadeh M (2014). Personality factors underlying suicidal behavior among military youth. *Iranian Red Crescent Medical Journal* 16, e12686.

Song Y, Ji C-Y, Agardh A (2014). Sexual coercion and health-risk behaviors among urban Chinese high school students. *Global Health Action* 7, 24418.

Stone LB, Liu RT, Yen S (2014). Adolescent inpatient girls' report of dependent life events predicts prospective suicide risk. *Psychiatry Research* 219, 137-142.

Storch EA, Bussing R, Jacob ML, Nadeau JM, Crawford E, Mutch PJ, Mason D, Lewin AB, Murphy TK (2014). Frequency and correlates of suicidal ideation in pediatric obsessive-compulsive disorder. *Child Psychiatry & Human Development.* Published online: 29 March 2014. doi: 10.1007/s10578-014-0453-7.

Strandheim A, Bjerkeset O, Gunnell D, Bjornelv S, Holmen TL, Bentzen N (2014). Risk factors for suicidal thoughts in adolescence a prospective cohort study: The Young-HUNT study. *BMJ Open* 4, e005867.

Stratta P, Capanna C, Carmassi C, Patriarca S, Di Emidio G, Riccardi I, Collazzoni A, Dell'Osso L, Rossi A (2014). The adolescent emotional coping after an earthquake: A risk factor for suicidal ideation. *Journal of Adolescence* 37, 605-611.

Sueki H (2014). The association of suicide-related twitter use with suicidal behaviour: A cross-sectional study of young internet users in Japan. *Journal of Affective Disorders* 170, 155-160.

Sueki H, Yonemoto N, Takeshima T, Inagaki M (2014). The impact of suicidality-related internet use: A prospective large cohort study with young and middle-aged internet users. *PloS ONE* 9, e94841.

Sunderland M, Carragher N, Buchan H, Batterham PJ, Slade T (2014). Comparing profiles of mental disorder across birth cohorts: Results from the 2007 Australian national survey of mental health and wellbeing. *Australian and New Zealand Journal of Psychiatry* 48, 452-463.

Symons FJ, Gilles E, Tervo R, Wendelschafer-Crabb G, Panoutsopoulou I, Kennedy W (2014). Skin and self-injury: A possible link between peripheral innervation and immune function? *Developmental Medicine & Child Neurology.* Published online: 3 September 2014. doi: 10.1111/dmcn.12580.

Szabo ST, Kilts JD, Naylor JC, Youssef NA, Strauss JL, Morey RA, Brancu M, Hamer RM, Bradford DW, Marx CE, Grp VAM-AMW (2014). Amino acids as biomarker candidates for suicidality in male OEF/OIF veterans: Relevance to NMDA receptor modulation and nitric oxide signaling. *Military Medicine* 179, 486-491.

Szanto K, Clark L, Hallquist M, Vanyukov P, Crockett M, Dombrovski AY (2014). The cost of social punishment and high-lethality suicide attempts in the second half of life. *Psychology and Aging* 29, 84-94.

Tachibana A, Kitamura H, Shindo M, Honma H, Someya T (2014). Psychological distress in an earthquake-devastated area with pre-existing high rate of suicide. *Psychiatry Research* 219, 336-340.

Takizawa R, Maughan B, Arseneault L (2014). Adult health outcomes of childhood bullying victimization: Evidence from a five-decade longitudinal British birth cohort. *American Journal of Psychiatry* 171, 777-784.

Taliaferro LA, Muehlenkamp JJ (2014). Factors associated with current versus lifetime self-injury among high school and college students. *Suicide and Life-Threatening Behavior.* Published online: 28 August 2014. doi: 10.1111/sltb.12117.life threat.

Taliaferro LA, Muehlenkamp JJ (2014). Risk factors associated with self-injurious behavior among a national sample of undergraduate college students. *Journal of American College Health.* Published online: 21 November 2013. doi: 10.1080/07448481.2014.953166.

Tammariello AE, Gallahue NK, Ellard KA, Woldesemait N, Jacobsen KH (2012). Parental involvement and mental health among Thai adolescents. *Advances in School Mental Health Promotion* 5, 236-245.

Tang D (2014). Perspectives on same-sex sexualities and self-harm amongst service providers and teachers in Hong Kong. *Sex Education* 14, 444-456.

Tanner AK, Hasking P, Martin G (2014). Non-suicidal self-injury and firesetting: Shared and unique correlates among school-based adolescents. *Journal of Youth and Adolescence*. Published online: 30 March 2014. doi: I 10.1007/s10964-014-0119-6.

Taraz M, Taraz S, Dashti-Khavidaki S (2014). Association between depression and inflammatory/anti-inflammatory cytokines in chronic kidney disease and end-stage renal disease patients: A review of literature. *Hemodialysis International*. Published online: 15 July 2014. doi: :10.1111/hdi.12200.

Taylor MR, Boden JM, Rucklidge JJ (2014). The relationship between ADHD symptomatology and self-harm, suicidal ideation, and suicidal behaviours in adults: A pilot study. *ADHD Attention Deficit and Hyperactivity Disorders*. Published online: 8 May 2014. doi: 10.1007/s12402-014-0139-9.

Thomas A, Hammond WP, Kohn-Wood LP (2014). Chill, be cool man: African American men, identity, coping, and aggressive ideation. *Cultural Diversity and Ethnic Minority Psychology*. Published online: 4 August 2014. doi: 10.1037/a0037545.

Thomas LPM, Palinkas LA, Meier EA, Iglewicz A, Kirkland T, Zisook S (2014). Yearning to be heard: What veterans teach us about suicide risk and effective interventions. *Crisis* 35, 161-167.

Thompson JM, Zamorski MA, Sweet J, VanTil L, Sareen J, Pietrzak RH, Hopman WH, MacLean MB, Pedlar D (2014). Roles of physical and mental health in suicidal ideation in Canadian armed forces regular force veterans. *Canadian Journal of Public Health* 105, e109-e115.

Tidemalm D, Haglund A, Karanti A, Landén M, Runeson B (2014). Attempted suicide in bipolar disorder: Risk factors in a cohort of 6086 patients. *PLoS ONE* 9, e94097.

Till B, Tran US, Voracek M, Sonneck G, Niederkrotenthaler T (2014). Associations between film preferences and risk factors for suicide: An online survey. *PLoS ONE* 9, e102293.

Tingey L, Cwik MF, Goklish N, Larzelere-Hinton F, Lee A, Suttle R, Walkup JT, Barlow A (2014). Risk pathways for suicide among native American adolescents. *Qualitative Health Research* 24, 1518-1526.

Tondo L, Visioli C, Preti A, Baldessarini RJ (2014). Bipolar disorders following initial depression: Modeling predictive clinical factors. *Journal of Affective Disorders* 167, 44-49.

Tormoen AJ, Rossow I, Mork E, Mehlum L (2014). Contact with child and adolescent psychiatric services among self-harming and suicidal adolescents in the general population: A cross sectional study. *Child and Adolescent Psychiatry and Mental Health* 8, 13.

Toth MD, Adam S, Birkas E, Szekely A, Stauder A, Purebl G (2014). Gender differences in deliberate self-poisoning in Hungary: Analyzing the effect of precipitating factors and their relation to depression. *Crisis* 35, 145-153.

Trinanes Y, Gonzalez-Villar A, Gomez-Perretta C, Carrillo-de-la-Pena MT (2014). Suicidality in chronic pain: Predictors of suicidal ideation in fibromyalgia. *Pain Practice*. Published online: 1 April 2014. doi: 10.1111/papr.12186.

Tsai J, Harpaz-Rotem I, Pilver CE, Wolf EJ, Hoff RA, Levy KN, Sareen J, Pietrzak RH (2014). Latent class analysis of personality disorders in adults with posttraumatic stress disorder: Results from the national epidemiologic survey on alcohol and related conditions. *Journal of Clinical Psychiatry* 75, 276-284.

Tseng FY, Yang HJ (2014). Internet use and web communication networks, sources of social support, and forms of suicidal and nonsuicidal self-injury among adolescents: Different patterns between genders. *Suicide and Life-Threatening Behavior*. Published online: 25 September 2014. doi: 10.1111/sltb.12.

Tucker RP, O'Keefe VM, Cole AB, Rhoades-Kerswill S, Hollingsworth DW, Helle AC, DeShong HL, Mullins-Sweatt SN, Wingate LR (2014). Mindfulness tempers the impact of personality on suicidal ideation. *Personality and Individual Differences* 68, 229-233.

Tucker RP, Wingate LR (2014). Basic need satisfaction and suicidal ideation: A self-determination perspective on interpersonal suicide risk and suicidal thinking. *Archives of Suicide Research* 18, 282-294.

Tucker RP, Wingate LR, Slish ML, O'Keefe VM, Cole AB, Hollingsworth DW (2014). Rumination, suicidal ideation, and the mediating effect of self-defeating humor. *Europe's Journal of Psychology* 10, 492-504.

Turner BJ, Arya S, Chapman AL (2014). Nonsuicidal self-injury in Asian versus Caucasian university students: Who, how, and why? *Suicide and Life-Threatening Behavior*. Published online: 26 August 2014. doi: 10.1111/sltb.12113.

Turunen E, Hiilamo H (2014). Health effects of indebtedness: A systematic review. *BMC Public Health* 14, 489.

Upthegrove R, Ross K, Brunet K, McCollum R, Jones L (2014). Depression in first episode psychosis: The role of subordination and shame. *Psychiatry Research* 217, 177-184.

van den Berg JF, Hermes JSJ, van den Brink W, Blanken P, Kist N, Kok RM (2014). Physical and mental health and social functioning in older alcohol-dependent inpatients: The role of age of onset. *European Addiction Research* 20, 226-232.

van Loo HM, Cai T, Gruber MJ, Li J, de Jonge P, Petukhova M, Rose S, Sampson NA, Schoevers RA, Wardenaar KJ, Wilcox MA, Al-Hamzawi AO, Andrade LH, Bromet EJ, Bunting B, Fayyad J, Florescu SE, Gureje O, Hu C, Huang Y, Levinson D, Medina-Mora ME, Nakane Y, Posada-Villa J, Scott KM, Xavier M, Zarkov Z, Kessler RC (2014). Major depressive disorder subtypes to predict long-term course. *Depression and Anxiety* 31, 765-777.

Van Meter A, Genzlinger J, Youngstrom EA (2014). Temperament and bis-bas: Cross-cultural indicators of suicidality and self-injury in young adults. *Bipolar Disorders* 16, 42-43.

Van Orden KA, O'Riley AA, Simning A, Podgorski C, Richardson TM, Conwell Y (2014). Passive suicide ideation: An indicator of risk among older adults seeking aging services? *Gerontologist*. Published online: 8 April 2014. doi: :10.1093/geront/gnu026.

Van Orden KA, Wiktorsson S, Duberstein P, Berg AI, Fässberg MM, Waern M (2014). Reasons for attempted suicide in later life. *American Journal of Geriatric Psychiatry*. Published online: 23 July 2014. doi: 10.1016/j.jagp.2014.07.003.

Venta A, Mellick W, Schatte D, Sharp C (2014). Preliminary evidence that thoughts of thwarted belongingness mediate the relations between level of attachment insecurity and depression and suicide-related thoughts in inpatient adolescents. *Journal of Social and Clinical Psychology* 33, 428-447.

Victor SE, Klonsky ED (2014). Correlates of suicide attempts among self-injurers: A meta-analysis. *Clinical Psychology Review* 34, 282-297.

Vivar R, Moron G, Padilla M, Alarcon RD (2014). Homicidal/violent thoughts, suicidal ideation and violent behavior in adolescents with social phobia in metropolitan Lima, Peru. *Asia-Pacific Psychiatry* 6, 252-258.

Vogel I, van de Looij-Jansen PM, Mieloo CL, Burdorf A, de Waart F (2014). Risky music listening, permanent tinnitus and depression, anxiety, thoughts about suicide and adverse general health. *PLoS ONE* 9, e98912.

Voon D, Hasking P, Martin G (2014). Change in emotion regulation strategy use and its impact on adolescent nonsuicidal self-injury: A three-year longitudinal analysis using latent growth modeling. *Journal of Abnormal Psychology* 123, 487-498.

Voon D, Hasking P, Martin G (2014). Emotion regulation in first episode adolescent non-suicidal self-injury: What difference does a year make? *Journal of Adolescence* 37, 1077-1087.

Wai CM, Talib MA, Yaacob SN, Jo-Pei T, Awang H, Hassan S, Ismail Z (2014). Hope and its relation to suicidal risk behaviors among Malaysian adolescents. *Asian Social Science* 10, 67-71.

Waldö ML, Santillo AF, Gustafson L, Englund E, Passant U (2014). Somatic complaints in frontotemporal dementia. *American Journal of Neurodegenerative Diseases* 3, 84-92.

Walker RL, Salami TK, Carter SE, Flowers K (2014). Perceived racism and suicide ideation: Mediating role of depression but moderating role of religiosity among African American adults. *Suicide and Life-Threatening Behavior* 44, 548-559.

Wallen GR, Minniti CP, Krumlauf M, Eckes E, Allen D, Oguhebe A, Seamon C, Darbari DS, Hildesheim M, Yang L, Schulden JD, Kato GJ, Taylor JG (2014). Sleep disturbance, depression and pain in adults with sickle cell disease. *BMC Psychiatry* 14, 207.

Wan YH, Xu SJ, Chen J, Hu CL, Tao FB (2014). Longitudinal effects of psychological symptoms on non-suicidal self-injury: A difference between adolescents and young adults in China. *Social Psychiatry and Psychiatric Epidemiology.* Published online: 29 June 2014. doi: 10.1007/s00127-014-0917-x.

Wang J, Dey M, Soldati L, Weiss MG, Gmel G, Mohler-Kuo M (2014). Psychiatric disorders, suicidality, and personality among young men by sexual orientation. *European Psychiatry* 29, 514-522.

Watson HJ, Egan SJ, Limburg K, Hoiles KJ (2014). Normative data for female adolescents with eating disorders on the children's depression inventory. *International Journal of Eating Disorders* 47, 666-670.

Weinstein A, Klein LD, Dannon PN (2014). A comparison of the status, legal, economic, and psychological characteristics of types of adult male gamblers. *Journal of Gambling Studies.* Published online: 17 May 2014. doi: 10.1007/s10899-014-9462-5.

Weitz E, Hollon SD, Kerkhof A, Cuijpers P (2014). Do depression treatments reduce suicidal ideation? The effects of CBT, IPT, pharmacotherapy, and placebo on suicidality. *Journal of Affective Disorders* 167, 98-103.

Wigg CMD, Filgueiras A, Gomes MdM (2014). The relationship between sleep quality, depression, and anxiety in patients with epilepsy and suicidal ideation. *Arquivos de Neuro-Psiquiatria* 72, 344-348.

Wilberforce M, Tucker S, Brand C, Abendstern M, Jasper R, Stewart K, Challis D (2014). Community mental health teams for older people: Variations in case mix and service receipt (II). *International Journal of Geriatric Psychiatry.* Published online: 9 September 2014. doi: 10.1002/gps.4190.

Winer ES, Nadorff MR, Ellis TE, Allen JG, Herrera S, Salem T (2014). Anhedonia predicts suicidal ideation in a large psychiatric inpatient sample. *Psychiatry Research* 218, 124-128.

Winsler A, Deutsch A, Vorona RD, Payne PA, Szklo-Coxe M (2014). Sleepless in Fairfax: The difference one more hour of sleep can make for teen hopelessness, suicidal ideation, and substance use. *Journal of Youth and Adolescence.* Published online: 2 September 2014. doi: 10.1007/s10964-014-0170-3.

Wiste A, Robinson EB, Milaneschi Y, Meier S, Ripke S, Clements CC, Fitzmaurice GM, Rietschel M, Penninx BW, Smoller JW, Perlis RH (2014). Bipolar polygenic loading and bipolar spectrum features in major depressive disorder. *Bipolar Disorders* 16, 608-616.

Wolff J, Esposito-Smythers C, Becker S, Seaboyer L, Rizzo C, Lichtenstein D, Spirito A (2014). Social-cognitive moderators of the relationship between peer victimization and suicidal ideation among psychiatrically hospitalized adolescents. *Journal of Aggression, Maltreatment and Trauma* 23, 268-285.

Wolff JC, Frazier EA, Esposito-Smythers C, Becker SJ, Burke TA, Cataldo A, Spirito A (2014). Negative cognitive style and perceived social support mediate the relationship between aggression and NSSI in hospitalized adolescents. *Journal of Adolescence* 37, 483-491.

Wong PWC, Kwok NCF, Tang JYC, Blaszczynski A, Tse S (2014). Suicidal ideation and familicidal-suicidal ideation among individuals presenting to problem gambling services: A retrospective data analysis. *Crisis* 35, 219-232.

Yao Ys, Chang Ww, Jin Yl, Chen Y, He Lp, Zhang L (2014). Life satisfaction, coping, self-esteem and suicide ideation in Chinese adolescents: A school-based study. *Child: Care, Health and Development* 40, 747-752.

Yates SC, Arya D (2014). Nothing in between: A multi-faith response to the paper on religion and suicide. *British Journal of Psychiatry* 205, 163.

Yenilmez E, Kumsar NA, Kütük EK, Dilbaz N (2014). Comparison between clinical features and residual depressive symptoms of patients with bipolar depressive and unipolar depressive disorder in remission. *African Journal of Psychiatry*. Published online: 26 April 2014. doi: 10.4172/1994-8220.1000119.

Yoon JH, Won JU, Lee W, Jung PK, Roh J (2014). Occupational noise annoyance linked to depressive symptoms and suicidal ideation: A result from nationwide survey of Korea. *PLoS ONE* 9, e105321.

You Z, Chen M, Yang S, Zhou Z, Qin P (2014). Childhood adversity, recent life stressors and suicidal behavior in Chinese college students. *PloS ONE* 9, e101612.

Young R, Sproeber N, Groschwitz RC, Preiss M, Plener PL (2014). Why alternative teenagers self-harm: Exploring the link between non-suicidal self-injury, attempted suicide and adolescent identity. *BMC Psychiatry* 14, 137.

Yusainy C, Lawrence C (2014). Relating mindfulness and self-control to harm to the self and to others. *Personality and Individual Differences* 64, 78-83.

Zamorski MA, Boulos D (2014). The impact of the military mission in Afghanistan on mental health in the Canadian armed forces: A summary of research findings. *European Journal of Psychotraumatology*. Published online: 14 August 2014. doi: 10.3402/ejpt.v5.23822.

Zampieri MAJ, Tognola WA, Galego JCB (2014). Patients with chronic headache tend to have more psychological symptoms than those with sporadic episodes of pain. *Arquivos de Neuro-Psiquiatria* 72, 598-602.

Zangeneh M (2014). Frequency of attempted suicide methods and the fetal outcomes in pregnant women in Kermanshah. *Journal of Women's Health Care*. Published online: 24 May 2014. doi: doi: 10.4172/2167-0420.1000164.

Zeller M, Yuval K, Nitzan-Assayag Y, Bernstein A (2014). Self-compassion in recovery following potentially traumatic stress: Longitudinal study of at-risk youth. *Journal of Abnormal Child Psychology*. Published online: 20 September 2014. doi: 10.1007/s10802-014-9937-y.

Zetterqvist M, Lundh L-G, Svedin CG (2014). A cross-sectional study of adolescent non-suicidal self-injury: Support for a specific distress-function relationship. *Child and Adolescent Psychiatry and Mental Health* 8, 23-23.

Zhang X, Wu L-T (2014). Suicidal ideation and substance use among adolescents and young adults: A bidirectional relation? *Drug and Alcohol Dependence* 142, 63-73.

Zhou ES, Hu JC, Kantoff PW, Recklitis CJ (2014). Identifying suicidal symptoms in prostate cancer survivors using brief self-report. *Journal of Cancer Survivorship*. Published online: 19 August 2014. doi: 10.1007/s11764-014-0385-z.

Ziglinas P, Menger DJ, Georgalas C (2014). The body dysmorphic disorder patient: To perform rhinoplasty or not? *European Archives of Oto-Rhino-Laryngology* 271, 2355-2358.

Zoghbi AW, Al Jurdi RK, Deshmukh PR, Chen DC, Xiu MH, Tan YL, Yang FD, Zhang XY (2014). Cognitive function and suicide risk in Han Chinese inpatients with schizophrenia. *Psychiatry Research* 220, 188-192.

Prevention

Anastasia TT, Humphries-Wadsworth T, Pepper CM, Pearson TM (2014). Family centered brief intensive treatment: A pilot study of an outpatient treatment for acute suicidal ideation. *Suicide and Life-Threatening Behavior.* Published online: 28 August 2014. doi: 10.1111/sltb.12114.

Andover MS, Schatten HT, Morris BW, Miller IW (2014). Development of an intervention for nonsuicidal self-injury in young adults: An open pilot trial. *Cognitive and Behavioral Practice.* Published online: 17 June 2014. doi:10.1016/j.cbpra.2014.05.003.

Ballard ED, Ionescu DF, Vande Voort JL, Niciu MJ, Richards EM, Luckenbaugh DA, Brutsché NE, Ameli R, Furey ML, Zarate CA (2014). Improvement in suicidal ideation after ketamine infusion: Relationship to reductions in depression and anxiety. *Journal of Psychiatric Research* 58, 161-166.

Berger E, Hasking P, Reupert A (2014). Response and training needs of school staff towards student self-injury. *Teaching and Teacher Education* 44, 25-34.

Berger E, Hasking P, Reupert A (2014). "We're working in the dark here": Education needs of teachers and school staff regarding student self-injury. *School Mental Health* 6, 201-212.

Bratsis ME (2014). Preventing teen suicide. *The Science Teacher* 81, 14.

Brondani MA, Ramanula D, Pattanaporn K (2014). Tackling stress management, addiction, and suicide prevention in a predoctoral dental curriculum. *Journal of Dental Education* 78, 1286-1293.

Bush NE, Dobscha SK, Crumpton R, Denneson LM, Hoffman JE, Crain A, Cromer R, Kinn JT (2014). A virtual hope box smartphone app as an accessory to therapy: Proof-of-concept in a clinical sample of veterans. *Suicide and Life-Threatening Behavior.* Published online: 15 May 2014. doi: 10.1111/sltb.12103.

Collinson M, Owens D, Blenkiron P, Burton K, Graham L, Hatcher S, House A, Martin K, Pembroke L, Protheroe D, Tubeuf S, Farrin A (2014). MIDSHIPS: Multicentre intervention designed for self-harm using interpersonal problem-solving: Protocol for a randomised controlled feasibility study. *Trials* 15, 163.

Coppens E, Van Audenhove C, Iddi S, Arensman E, Gottlebe K, Koburger N, Coffey C, Gusmão R, Quintão S, Costa S, Székely A, Hegerl U (2014). Effectiveness of community facilitator training in improving knowledge, attitudes, and confidence in relation to depression and suicidal behavior: Results of the OSPI-Europe intervention in four European countries. *Journal of Affective Disorders* 165, 142-150.

Diderich HM, Verkerk PH, Oudesluys-Murphy AM, Dechesne M, Buitendijk SE, Fekkes M (2014). Missed cases in the detection of child abuse based on parental characteristics in the emergency department (the Hague Protocol). *Journal of Emergency Nursing.* Pulished online: 29 July 2014. doi:10.1016/j.jen.2014.05.016.

Farrelly S, Brown G, Szmukler G, Rose D, Birchwood M, Marshall M, Waheed W, Thornicroft G (2014). Can the therapeutic relationship predict 18 month outcomes for individuals with psychosis? *Psychiatry Research* 220, 585-591.

Gibson J, Booth R, Davenport J, Keogh K, Owens T (2014). Dialectical behaviour therapy-informed skills training for deliberate self-harm: A controlled trial with 3-month follow-up data. *Behaviour Research and Therapy* 60, 8-14.

Hayes A, Senior J, Fahy T, Shaw J (2014). Actions taken in response to mental health screening at reception into prison. *Journal of Forensic Psychiatry and Psychology* 25, 371-379.

Hicks CF, Ward MJ, Platt SL (2014). Adolescents' and young adults' perspectives on their emergency care. *Pediatric Emergency Care* 30, 529-533.

Hjelmeland H, Hagen J, Knizek BL (2014). Suicide prevention in mental health care - time for new ideas? *Journal of the Norwegian Medical Association* 134, 1222.

Humensky JL, Gil R, Coronel B, Cifre R, Mazzula S, Lewis-Fernández R (2013). Life is precious: Reducing suicidal behavior in Latinas. *Ethnicity and Inequalities in Health and Social Care* 6, 54-61.

Hoyer D (2014). Addressing suicide risk in emergency department patients. *Journal of the American Medical Association* 312, 297-298.

Jacob N, Scourfield J, Evans R (2014). Suicide prevention via the internet. *Crisis* 35, 261-267.

Kerr DCR, DeGarmo DS, Leve LD, Chamberlain P (2014). Juvenile justice girls' depressive symptoms and suicidal ideation 9 years after multidimensional treatment foster care. *Journal of Consulting and Clinical Psychology* 82, 684-693.

Kumar D, Nizamie SH, Abhishek P, Prasanna LT (2014). Identification of suicidal ideations with the help of projective tests: A review. *Asian Journal of Psychiatry*. Published online: 4 August 2014. doi:10.1016/j.ajp.2014.07.004.

Lara MA, Tiburcio M, Aguilar Abrego A, Sanchez-Solis A (2014). A four-year experience with a web-based self-help intervention for depressive symptoms in Mexico. *American Journal of Public Health* 35, 399-406.

Large MM, Ryan CJ (2014). 'Heed not the oracle': Risk assessment has no role in preventing suicide in schizophrenia. *Acta Psychiatrica Scandinavica* 130, 415–417.

Latimer EA, Gariepy G, Greenfield B (2014). Cost-effectiveness of a rapid response team intervention for suicidal youth presenting at an emergency department. *Canadian Journal of Psychiatry* 59, 310-318.

Lewis SP, Mahdy JC, Michal NJ, Arbuthnott AE (2014). Googling self-injury: The state of health information obtained through online searches for self-injury. *JAMA Pediatrics* 168, 443-449.

Lynn CJ, Acri MC, Goldstein L, Bannon W, Beharie N, McKay MM (2014). Improving youth mental health through family-based prevention in family homeless shelters. *Children and Youth Services Review* 44, 243-248.

McKinnon I, Grubin D (2014). Evidence-based risk assessment screening in police custody: The HELP-PC study in London, UK. *Policing* 8, 174-182.

Mohanraj R, Kumar S, Manikandan S, Kannaiyan V, Vijayakumar L (2014). A public health initiative for reducing access to pesticides as a means to committing suicide: Findings from a qualitative study. *International Review of Psychiatry* 26, 445-452.

Obando Medina C, Kullgren G, Dahlblom K (2014). A qualitative study on primary health care professionals' perceptions of mental health, suicidal problems and help-seeking among young people in Nicaragua. *BMC Family Practice* 15, 129.

Osteen PJ, Jacobson JM, Sharpe TL (2014). Suicide prevention in social work education: How prepared are social work students? *Journal of Social Work Education* 50, 349-364.

Oulanova O, Moodley R, Seguin M (2014). From suicide survivor to peer counselor: Breaking the silence of suicide bereavement. *Omega* 69, 151-168.

Perry Y, Petrie K, Buckley H, Cavanagh L, Clarke D, Winslade M, Hadzi-Pavlovic D, Manicavasagar V, Christensen H (2014). Effects of a classroom-based educational resource on adolescent mental health literacy: A cluster randomised controlled trial. *Journal of Adolescence* 37, 1143-1151.

Poduska JM, Kurki A (2014). Guided by theory, informed by practice: Training and support for the good behavior game, a classroom-based behavior management strategy. *Journal of Emotional and Behavioral Disorders* 22, 83-94.

Rice SM, Hickie IB, Yung AR, Mackinnon A, Berk M, Davey C, Hermens DF, Hetrick SE, Parker AG, Schäfer MR, McGorry PD, Amminger GP (2014). Youth depression alleviation: The fish oil youth depression study (YoDA-F): A randomized, double-blind, placebo-controlled treatment trial. *Early Intervention in Psychiatry* . Published online: 13 August 2014. doi: 10.1111/eip.12166.

Ridani R, Shand FL, Christensen H, McKay K, Tighe J, Burns J, Hunter E (2014). Suicide prevention in Australian Aboriginal communities: A review of past and present programs. *Suicide and Life-Threatening Behavior*. Published online: 16 September 2014. doi: 10.1111/sltb.12121.

Robinson J, Hetrick S, Cox G, Bendall S, Yuen HP, Yung A, Pirkis J (2014). Can an internet-based intervention reduce suicidal ideation, depression and hopelessness among secondary school students: Results from a pilot study. *Early Intervention in Psychiatry*. Published online: 31 March 2014. doi: 10.1111/eip.12137.

Robinson J, Hetrick S, Cox G, Bendall S, Yung A, Pirkis J (2014). The safety and acceptability of delivering an online intervention to secondary students at risk of suicide: Findings from a pilot study. *Early Intervention in Psychiatry*. Published online: 31 March 2014. doi: 10.1111/eip.12136.

Robinson J, Hetrick S, Cox G, Bendall S, Yung A, Yuen HP, Templer K, Pirkis J (2014). The development of a randomised controlled trial testing the effects of an online intervention among school students at risk of suicide. *BMC Psychiatry* 14, 155.

Ross AM, Kelly CM, Jorm AF (2014). Re-development of mental health first aid guidelines for non-suicidal self-injury: A Delphi study. *BMC Psychiatry* 14, 236.

Schilling EA, Lawless M, Buchanan L, Aseltine RH (2014). "Signs of Suicide" shows promise as a middle school suicide prevention program. *Suicide and Life-Threatening Behavior*. Published online: 2 May 2014. doi: 10.1111/sltb.12097.

Silverman MM (2014). Suicide risk assessment and suicide risk formulation: Essential components of the therapeutic risk management model. *Journal of Psychiatric Practice* 20, 373-378.

Spirito A, Wolff JC, Seaboyer LM, Hunt J, Esposito-Smythers C, Nugent N, Zlotnick C, Miller I (2014). Concurrent treatment for adolescent and parent depressed mood and suicidality: Feasibility, acceptability, and preliminary findings. *Journal of Child and Adolescent Psychopharmacology*. Published online: 14 May 2014. doi: 10.1089/cap.2013.0130.

Spittal MJ, Fedyszyn I, Middleton A, Bassilios B, Gunn J, Woodward A, Pirkis J (2014). Frequent callers to crisis helplines: Who are they and why do they call? *Australian and New Zealand Journal of Psychiatry*. Published online: 27 June 2014. doi: 10.1177/0004867414541154.

Strunk CM, King KA, Vidourek RA, Sorter MT (2014). Effectiveness of the Surviving the Teens® suicide prevention and depression awareness program. An impact evaluation utilizing a comparison group. *Health Education & Behavior* 41, 605-13.

Taylor C (2014). Birth of the suicidal subject: Nelly Arcan, Michel Foucault, and voluntary death. *Culture, Theory and Critique*. Published online: 23 July 2014. doi: 10.1080 /14735784.2014.937820.

Van den Bosch LM, Sinnaeve R, Hakkaart-van Roijen L, van Furth EF (2014). Efficacy and cost-effectiveness of an experimental short-term inpatient dialectical behavior therapy (DBT) program: Study protocol for a randomized controlled trial. *Trials* 15, 152.

Care and support

Ahmedani BK, Vannoy S (2014). National pathways for suicide prevention and health services research. *American Journal of Preventive Medicine* 47, S222-S228.

Alesiani R, Boccalon S, Giarolli L, Blum N, Fossati A (2014). Systems training for emotional predictability and problem solving (STEPPS): Program efficacy and personality features as predictors of drop-out - an Italian study. *Comprehensive Psychiatry* 55, 920-927.

Annemans L, Brignone M, Druais S, De Pauw A, Gauthier A, Demyttenaere K (2014). Cost-effectiveness analysis of pharmaceutical treatment options in the first-line management of major depressive disorder in Belgium. *Pharmacoeconomics* 32, 479-493.

Asarnow JR, Berk M, Hughes JL, Anderson NL (2014). The safety program: A treatment-development trial of a cognitive-behavioral family treatment for adolescent suicide attempters. *Journal of Clinical Child and Adolescent Psychology.* Published online: 25 September 2014. doi: 10.1080/15374416.2014.940624.

Asarnow JR, Miranda J (2014). Improving care for depression and suicide risk in adolescents: Innovative strategies for bringing treatments to community settings. *Annual Review of Clinical Psychology* 10, 275-303.

Atkinson SD, Prakash A, Zhang Q, Pangallo BA, Bangs ME, Emslie GJ, March JS (2014). A double-blind efficacy and safety study of duloxetine flexible dosing in children and adolescents with major depressive disorder. *Journal of Child and Adolescent Psychopharmacology* 24, 180-189.

Bartlett A, Somers N, Fiander M, Harty MA (2014). Pathways of care of women in secure hospitals: Which women go where and why. *British Journal of Psychiatry* 205, 298-306.

Bennewith O, Evans J, Donovan J, Paramasivan S, Owen-Smith A, Hollingworth W, Davies R, O'Connor S, Hawton K, Kapur N, Gunnell D (2014). A contact-based intervention for people recently discharged from inpatient psychiatric care: A pilot study. *Archives of Suicide Reserarch* 18, 131-143.

Bickerton A, Ward J, Southgate M, Hense T (2014). The safety first assessment intervention: A whole family approach for young people with high risk mental health presentations. *Australian and New Zealand Journal of Family Therapy* 35, 150-168.

Carlson WL, Ong TD (2014). Suicide in later life: Failed treatment or rational choice? *Clinics in Geriatric Medicine* 30, 553-576.

Chapman R, Martin C (2014). Perceptions of Australian emergency staff towards patients presenting with deliberate self-poisoning: A qualitative perspective. *International Emergency Nursing* 22, 140-145.

Chen Q, Sjolander A, Runeson B, D'Onofrio BM, Lichtenstein P, Larsson H (2014). Drug treatment for attention-deficit/hyperactivity disorder and suicidal behaviour: Register based study. *BMJ* 348, g3769.

Cherukuri H, Pramoda K, Rohini D, Thunga G, Vijaynarayana K, Sreedharan N, Varma M, Pandit V (2014). Demographics, clinical characteristics and management of herbicide poisoning in tertiary care hospital. *Toxicology International* 21, 209-213.

Chmiel C, Rosemann T, Senn O (2014). Demand and characteristics of a psychiatric 24-hour emergency service performed by mandatory rotation of licensed psychiatrists in Swiss primary care. *Patient Preference and Adherence* 8, 383-390.

Christensen H, Calear AL, Van Spijker B, Gosling J, Petrie K, Donker T, Fenton K (2014). Psychosocial interventions for suicidal ideation, plans, and attempts: A database of randomised controlled trials. *BMC Psychiatry* 14, 86.

Dahmani S, Delivet H, Hilly J (2014). Emergence delirium in children: An update. *Current Opinion in Anaesthesiology* 27, 309-315 .

Davidson KM, Brown TM, James V, Kirk J, Richardson J (2014). Manual-assisted cognitive therapy for self-harm in personality disorder and substance misuse: A feasibility trial. *The Psychiatric Bulletin* 38, 108-111.

Davis TS, Mauss IB, Lumian D, Troy AS, Shallcross AJ, Zarolia P, Ford BQ, McRae K (2014). Emotional reactivity and emotion regulation among adults with a history of self-harm: Laboratory self-report and functional MRI evidence. *Journal of Abnormal Psychology* 123, 499-509.

Demyttenaere K, Desaiah D, Raskin J, Cairns V, Brecht S (2014). Suicidal thoughts and reasons for living in hospitalized patients with severe depression: Post-hoc analyses of a double-blind randomized trial of duloxetine. *Primary Care Companion to the Journal of Clinical Psychiatry.* Published online: 1 May 2014. doi :10.4088/PCC.13m01591.

Denckla CA, Bailey R, Jackson C, Tatarakis J, Chen CK (2014). A novel adaptation of distress tolerance skills training among military veterans: Outcomes in suicide-related events. *Cognitive and Behavioral Practice.* Published online: 13 April 2014. doi: 10.1016/j.cbpra.2014.04.001.

Denneson LM, Corson K, Helmer DA, Bair MJ, Dobscha SK (2014). Mental health utilization of new-to-care Iraq and Afghanistan veterans following suicidal ideation assessment. *Psychiatry Research* 217 147-153.

Downs N, Feng W, Kirby B, McGuire T, Moutier C, Norcross W, Norman M, Young I, Zisook S (2014). Listening to depression and suicide risk in medical students: The healer education assessment and referral (HEAR) program. *Academic Psychiatry* 38, 547-553.

Emslie GJ, Prakash A, Zhang Q, Pangallo BA, Bangs ME, March JS (2014). A double-blind efficacy and safety study of duloxetine fixed doses in children and adolescents with major depressive disorder. *Journal of Child and Adolescent Psychopharmacology* 24, 170-179.

Eren N, Öğünç NE, Keser V, Bikmaz S, Sahin D, Saydam B (2014). Psychosocial, symptomatic and diagnostic changes with long-term psychodynamic art psychotherapy for personality disorders. *Arts in Psychotherapy* 41, 375-385.

Fischer S, Peterson C (2014). Dialectical behavior therapy for adolescent binge eating, purging, suicidal behavior, and non-suicidal self-injury: A pilot study. *Psychotherapy.* Published online: 28 April 2014. doi: 10.1037/a0036065.

Fond G, Loundou A, Rabu C, Macgregor A, Lancon C, Brittner M, Micoulaud-Franchi JA, Richieri R, Courtet P, Abbar M, Roger M, Leboyer M, Boyer L (2014). Ketamine administration in depressive disorders: A systematic review and meta-analysis. *Psychopharmacology*, 231, 3663-3676.

Foster A, Chaudhary N, Murphy J, Lok B, Waller J, Buckley PF (2014). The use of simulation to teach suicide risk assessment to health profession trainees-rationale, methodology, and a proof of concept demonstration with a virtual patient. *Academic Psychiatry.* Published online: 16 July 2014. doi: 10.1007/s40596-014-0185-9.

Gauthier JM, Zuromski KL, Gitter SA, Witte TK, Cero IJ, Gordon KH, Ribeiro J, Anestis M, Joiner T (2014). The interpersonal-psychological theory of suicide and exposure to video game violence. *Journal of Social and Clinical Psychology* 33, 512-535.

George MS, Raman R, Benedek DM, Pelic CG, Grammer GG, Stokes KT, Schmidt M, Spiegel C, DeAlmeida N, Beaver KL, Borckardt JJ, Sun X, Jain S, Stein MB (2014). A two-site pilot randomized 3 day trial of high dose left prefrontal repetitive transcranial magnetic stimulation (RTMS) for suicidal inpatients. *Brain Stimulation* 7, 421-431.

Gjelsvik B, Heyerdahl F, Lunn D, Hawton K (2014). Change in access to prescribed medication following an episode of deliberate self-poisoning: A multilevel approach. *PLoS ONE* 9. Published online: 22 May 2014. doi: 10.1371/journal.pone.0098086.

Gleeson JF, Lederman R, Wadley G, Bendall S, McGorry PD, Alvarez-Jimenez M (2014). Safety and privacy outcomes from a moderated online social therapy for young people with first-episode psychosis. *Psychiatric Services* 65, 546-550.

Glenn CR, Franklin JC, Nock MK (2014). Evidence-based psychosocial treatments for self-injurious thoughts and behaviors in youth. *Journal of Clinical Child amd Adolescent Psychology*. Published online: 25 September 2014. doi: 10.1080/15374416.2014.945211.

Govender RD, Schlebusch L, Esterhuizen T (2014). Brief suicide preventive intervention in newly diagnosed HIV-positive persons. *African Journal of Psychiatry* 17, 543-547.

Grimholt TK, Haavet OR, Jacobsen D, Sandvik L, Ekeberg O (2014). Perceived competence and attitudes towards patients with suicidal behaviour: A survey of general practitioners, psychiatrists and internists. *BMC Health Services Research*, 14, 208.

Gudmundsdottir RM, Thome M (2014). Evaluation of the effects of individual and group cognitive behavioural therapy and of psychiatric rehabilitation on hopelessness of depressed adults: A comparative analysis. *Journal of Psychiatric and Mental Health Nursing*. Published online: 20 May 2014. doi: 10.1111/jpm.12157.

Hashimoto M, Maekawa M, Katakura M, Hamazaki K, Matsuoka Y (2014). Possibility of polyunsaturated fatty acids for the prevention and treatment of neuropsychiatric illnesses. *Journal of Pharmacological Sciences* 124, 294-300.

Hashmi A, Shad M, Rhoades HM, Parsaik AK (2014). Involuntary detention: Do psychiatrists clinically justify continuing involuntary hospitalization? *Psychiatric Quarterly* 85, 285-293.

Heisel MJ, Talbot NL, King DA, Tu XM, Duberstein PR (2014). Adapting interpersonal psychotherapy for older adults at risk for suicide. *American Journal of Geriatric Psychiatry*. Published online: 29 March 2014. doi: 10.1016/j.jagp.2014.03.010.

Horowitz LM, Bridge JA, Pao M, Boudreaux ED (2014). Screening youth for suicide risk in medical settings: Time to ask questions. *American Journal of Preventive Medicine* 47, S170-S175.

Huang HH, Fan JS, Chen YC, Yen DHT (2014). Coordination between medical care providers and information technology resources in the management of patients with suicide attempts attending the emergency department. *Journal of the Chinese Medical Association* 77, 275-276.

Husain N, Afsar S, Ara J, Fayyaz H, Rahman RU, Tomenson B, Hamirani M, Chaudhry N, Fatima B, Husain M, Naeem F, Chaudhry IB (2014). Brief psychological intervention after self-harm: Randomised controlled trial from Pakistan. *British Journal of Psychiatry* 204, 462-470.

James E, Larzelere MM (2014). Behavioral interventions for office-based care: Depressive disorders. *FP Essentials* 418, 26-29.

James S, Freeman KR, Mayo D, Riggs ML, Morgan JP, Schaepper MA, Montgomery SB (2014). Does insurance matter? Implementing dialectical behavior therapy with two groups of youth engaged in deliberate self-harm. *Administration and Policy in Mental Health*. Published online: 9 September 2014. doi: 10.1007/s10488-014-0588-7.

Karatzias T, Ferguson S, Chouliara Z, Gullone A, Cosgrove K, Douglas A (2014). Effectiveness and acceptability of group psychoeducation for the management of mental health problems in survivors of child sexual abuse (CSA). *International Journal of Group Psychotherapy* 64, 492-514.

Kemp AH, Outhred T, Saunders S, Brunoni AR, Nathan PJ, Malhi GS (2014). Impact of escitalopram on vagally mediated cardiovascular function in healthy participants: Implications for understanding differential age-related, treatment emergent effects. *Psychopharmacology* 231, 2281-2290.

Kim JH, Park JY, Song YS (2014). Traumatic penile injury: From circumcision injury to penile amputation. *BioMed Research International*. Published online: 28 August 2014. doi:10.1155/2014/375285.

Kishi Y, Otsuka K, Akiyama K, Yamada T, Sakamoto Y, Yanagisawa Y, Morimura H, Kawanishi C, Higashioka H, Miyake Y, Thurber S (2014). Effects of a training workshop on suicide prevention among emergency room nurses. *Crisis*. Published online: 29 August 2014. doi: 10.1027/0227-5910/a000268.

Krüger A, Kleindienst N, Priebe K, Dyer AS, Steil R, Schmahl C, Bohus M (2014). Non-suicidal self-injury during an exposure-based treatment in patients with posttraumatic stress disorder and borderline features. *Behaviour Research and Therapy* 61, 163-141.

Kvarstein EH, Pedersen G, Urnes O, Hummelen B, Wilberg T, Karterud S (2014). Changing from a traditional psychodynamic treatment programme to mentalization-based treatment for patients with borderline personality disorder - does it make a difference? *Psychology and Psychotherapy*. Published online: 15 July 2014. doi: 10.1111/papt.12036.

Lin CJ, Lu HC, Sun FJ, Fang CK, Wu SI, Liu SI (2014). The characteristics, management, and aftercare of patients with suicide attempts who attended the emergency department of a general hospital in northern Taiwan. *Journal of the Chinese Medical Association* 77, 317-324.

Liu S, Ali S, Rosychuk RJ, Newton AS (2014). Characteristics of children and youth who visit the emergency department for a behavioural disorder. *Journal of the Canadian Academy of Child and Adolescent Psychiatry* 23, 111-117.

Loch AA (2014). Discharged from a mental health admission ward: Is it safe to go home? A review on the negative outcomes of psychiatric hospitalization. *Psychology Research and Behavior Management* 7, 137-145.

Macaron G, Fahed M, Matar D, Bou-Khalil R, Kazour F, Nehme-Chlela D, Richa S (2014). Anxiety, depression and suicidal ideation in Lebanese patients undergoing hemodialysis. *Community Mental Health Journal* 50, 235-238.

Madadi P, Persaud N (2014). Suicide by means of opioid overdose in patients with chronic pain. *Current Pain and Headache Reports* 18, 460.

Margolis RL (2014). Tetrabenazine, depression and suicide: Good news. *Journal of Huntington's Disease* 3, 137-138.

Mauer S, Vergne D, Ghaemi SN (2014). Standard and trace-dose lithium: A systematic review of dementia prevention and other behavioral benefits. *Australian and New Zealand Journal of Psychiatry* 48, 809-818.

Maund E, Tendal B, Hrobjartsson A, Jorgensen KJ, Lundh A, Schroll J, Gotzsche PC (2014). Benefits and harms in clinical trials of duloxetine for treatment of major depressive disorder: Comparison of clinical study reports, trial registries, and publications. *BMJ* 348, g3510.

Maund E, Tendal B, Hrobjartsson A, Lundh A, Gotzsche PC (2014). Coding of adverse events of suicidality in clinical study reports of duloxetine for the treatment of major depressive disorder: Descriptive study. *BMJ*. Published online: 4 June 2014. doi: 10.1136/bmj.g3555

Mehlum L, Tørmoen AJ, Ramberg M, Haga E, Diep LM, Laberg S, Larsson BS, Stanley BH, Miller AL, Sund AM, Grøholt B (2014). Dialectical behavior therapy for adolescents with repeated suicidal and self-harming behavior-a randomized trial. *Journal of the American Academy of Child and Adolescent Psychiatry* 53, 1082-1091.

Meltzer-Brody S, Brandon AR, Pearson B, Burns L, Raines C, Bullard E, Rubinow D (2014). Evaluating the clinical effectiveness of a specialized perinatal psychiatry inpatient unit. *Archives of Womens Mental Health* 17, 107-113.

Mewton L, Andrews G (2014). Cognitive behaviour therapy via the internet for depression: A useful strategy to reduce suicidal ideation. *Journal of Affective Disorders* 170, 78-84.

Middleton A, Gunn J, Bassilios B, Pirkis J (2014). Systematic review of research into frequent callers to crisis helplines. *Journal of Telemedicine and Telecare* 20, 89-98.

Montross Thomas LP, Palinkas LA, Meier EA, Iglewicz A, Kirkland T, Zisook S (2014). Yearning to be heard. *Crisis 35,* 161-167.

Neves MG, Leanza F (2014). Mood disorders in adolescents. Diagnosis, treatment, and suicide assessment in the primary care setting. *Primary Care* 41, 587-606.

Ojengbede OA, Baba Y, Morhason-Bello IO, Armah M, Dimiti A, Buwa D, Kariom M (2014). Group psychological therapy in obstetric fistula care: A complementary recipe for the accompanying mental ill health morbidities? *African Journal of Reproductive Health* 18, 155-159.

Owen-Smith A, Bennewith O, Donovan J, Evans J, Hawton K, Kapur N, O'Connor S, Gunnell D (2014). "When you're in the hospital, you're in a sort of bubble.". *Crisis* 35, 154-160.

Parker GF (2014). DSM-5 and psychotic and mood disorders. *Journal of the American Academy of Psychiatry and the Law* 42, 182-190.

Perboell PW, Hammer NM, Oestergaard B, Konradsen H (2014). Danish emergency nurses' attitudes towards self-harm - a cross-sectional study. *International Emergency Nursing.* Published online: 23 July 2014. doi: 10.1016/j.ienj.2014.07.003.

Plener PL, Sukale T, Groschwitz RC, Pavlic E, Fegert JM (2014). "Stop cutting - rock!". *Psychotherapeut* 59, 24-30.

Price RB, Iosifescu DV, Murrough JW, Chang LC, Al Jurdi RK, Iqbal SZ, Soleimani L, Charney DS, Foulkes AL, Mathew SJ (2014). Effects of ketamine on explicit and implicit suicidal cognition: A randomized controlled trial in treatment-resistant depression. *Depression and Anxiety* 31, 335-343.

Reiss N, Lieb K, Arntz A, Shaw IA, Farrell J (2014). Responding to the treatment challenge of patients with severe BPD: Results of three pilot studies of inpatient schema therapy. *Behavioural and Cognitive Psychotherapy* 42, 355-367.

Sahlem GL, Kalivas B, Fox JB, Lamb K, Roper A, Williams EN, Williams NR, Korte JE, Zuschlag ZD, El Sabbagh S, Guille C, Barth KS, Uhde TW, George MS, Short EB (2014). Adjunctive triple chronotherapy (combined total sleep deprivation, sleep phase advance, and bright light therapy) rapidly improves mood and suicidality in suicidal depressed inpatients: An open label pilot study. *Journal of Psychiatric Research.* Published online: 3 September 2014. doi: 10.1016/j.jpsychires.2014.08.015.

Salter EK (2014). The desire to die: Making treatment decisions for suicidal patients who have an advance directive. *The Journal of Clinical Ethics* 25, 43-49.

Scheckel MM, Nelson KA (2014). An interpretive study of nursing students' experiences of caring for suicidal persons. *Journal of Professional Nursing* 30, 426-435.

Shah R, Franks P, Jerant A, Feldman M, Duberstein P, EF YG, Hinton L, Strohecker L, Kravitz RL (2014). The effect of targeted and tailored patient depression engagement interventions on patient-physician discussion of suicidal thoughts: A randomized control trial. *Journal of General Internal Medicine* 29, 1148-54.

Siegel M, Beresford CA, Bunker M, Verdi M, Vishnevetsky D, Karlsson C, Teer O, Stedman A, Smith KA (2014). Preliminary investigation of lithium for mood disorder symptoms in children and adolescents with autism spectrum disorder. *Journal of Child and Adolescent Psychopharmacology* , 24, 399-402.

Silverman MM, Berman AL (2014). Training for suicide risk assessment and suicide risk formulation. *Academic Psychiatry* 38, 526-537.

Slepian ML, Bogart KR, Ambady N (2014). Thin-slice judgments in the clinical context. *Annual Review of Clinical Psychology* 10, 131-153.

Stephens RJ, White SE, Cudnik M, Patterson ES (2014). Factors associated with longer length of stay for mental health emergency department patients. *Journal of Emergency Medicine* 47, 412-419.

Straub J, Sproeber N, Plener PL, Fegert JM, Bonenberger M, Koelch MG (2014). A brief cognitive-behavioural group therapy programme for the treatment of depression in adolescent outpatients: A pilot study. *Child and Adolescent Psychiatry and Mental Health* 8, 9.

Tormoen AJ, Groholt B, Haga E, Brager-Larsen A, Miller A, Walby F, Stanley B, Mehlum L (2014). Feasibility of dialectical behavior therapy with suicidal and self-harming adolescents with multi-problems: Training, adherence and retention. *Archives of Suicide Research* 18, 432-444.

Tsai M, Ogrodniczuk JS, Sochting I, Mirmiran J (2014). Forecasting success: Patients' expectations for improvement and their relations to baseline, process and outcome variables in group cognitive-behavioural therapy for depression. *Clinical Psychology & Psychotherapy* 21, 97-107.

Warnez S, Alessi-Severini S (2014). Clozapine: A review of clinical practice guidelines and prescribing trends. *BMC Psychiatry* 14, 102.

Weiland TJ, Cotter A, Jelinek GA, Phillips G (2014). Suicide risk assessment in Australian emergency departments: Assessing clinicians' disposition decisions. *Psychiatry Journal* 2014, e943574.

Weisler R, Montgomery SA, Earley WR, Szamosi J, Eriksson H (2014). Extended release quetiapine fumarate in patients with major depressive disorder: Suicidality data from acute and maintenance studies. *Journal of Clinical Psychiatry* 75, 520-527.

Whiteside U, Richards J, Steinfeld B, Simon G, Caka S, Tachibana C, Stuckey S, Ludman E (2014). Online cognitive behavioral therapy for depressed primary care patients: A pilot feasibility project. *The Permanente Journal* 18, 21-27.

Williams A, Larocca R, Chang T, Trinh NH, Fava M, Kvedar J, Yeung A (2014). Web-based depression screening and psychiatric consultation for college students: A feasibility and acceptability study. *International Journal of Telemedicine and Applications*. Published online: 30 March 2014. doi:10.1155/2014/580786.

Williams CL, Cooper WO, Balmer LS, Dudley JA, Gideon PS, Deranieri MM, Stratton SM, Callahan ST (2014). Evaluation and disposition of Medicaid-insured children and adolescents with suicide attempts. *Academic Pediatrics*. Published online: 16 June 2014. doi: 10.1016/j.acap.2014.04.005.

Williams JMG, Crane C, Barnhofer T, Brennan K, Duggan DS, Fennell MJV, Hackmann A, Krusche A, Muse K, Von Rohr IR, Shah D, Crane RS, Eames C, Jones M, Radford S, Silverton S, Sun Y, Weatherley-Jones E, Whitaker CJ, Russell D, Russell IT (2014). Mindfulness-based cognitive therapy for preventing relapse in recurrent depression: A randomized dismantling trial. *Journal of Consulting and Clinical Psychology* 82, 275.

Yen S, Fuller AK, Solomon J, Spirito A (2014). Follow-up treatment utilization by hospitalized suicidal adolescents. *Journal of Psychiatric Practice* 20, 353-362.

Case Reports

Advenier A-S, de la Grandmaison GL (2014). Traumatic rupture of deep neck structures in hanging: Two case reports. *American Journal of Forensic Medicine and Pathology* 35, 189-192.

Aesch B, Lefrancq T, Destrieux C, Saint-Martin P (2014). Fatal gunshot wound to the head with lack of immediate incapacitation. *American Journal of Forensic Medicine and Pathology* 35, 86-88.

Allison-Roan V (2014). Tales of a 43 year-old runaway. *Life Writing* 11, 333-347.

Altay S, Ilhan E, Satilmis S, Tayyareci G (2014). Mortal suicidal acetazolamide intoxication in a young female. *Anatolian Journal of Cardiology* 14, 408-409.

Alunni V, Grevin G, Buchet L, Quatrehomme G (2014). Forensic aspect of cremations on wooden pyre. *Forensic Science International* 241, 167-172.

Akpinar A, Demirda A (2014). Dissociative identity disorder presenting as a suicide attempt or drug overdose: A case report. *Erciyes Medical Journal* 36, 38-39.

Al-Abri SA, Anderson IB, Pedram F, Colby JM, Olson KR (2014). Massive naproxen overdose with serial serum levels. *Journal of Medical Toxicology*. Published online: 23 April 2014. doi: 10.1007/s13181-014-0396-1.

Alatas E, Bulut SD, Berkol TD, Alatas G (2014). Repetetively cutting own oral mucosa as a self-harming behavior: A case report. *Dusunen Adam* 27, 173-177.

Alex R, Mathew M, Arul S, Kundavaram A (2014). Overdose of mycophenolate mofetil managed in a secondary care hospital in south India. *Indian Journal of Pharmacology* 46, 337-338.

Atay IM (2014). A pica case associated with suicide-bereavement. *Anatolian Journal of Psychiatry* 15, S39-S42.

Badrane N, Askour M, Berechid K, Abidi K, Dendane T, Zeggwagh AA (2014). Severe oral and intravenous insecticide mixture poisoning with diabetic ketoacidosis: A case report. *BMC Research Notes* 7, 485-485.

Bakovic M, Petrovecki V, Strinovi D, Mayer D (2014). Shot through the heart: Firepower and potential lethality of air weapons. *Journal of Forensic Sciences*. Published online: 20 May 2014. doi: 10.1111/1556-4029.12486.

Banerjee P, Ali Z, Levine B, Fowler DR (2014). Fatal caffeine intoxication: A series of eight cases from 1999 to 2009. *Journal of Forensic Sciences* 59, 865-868.

Behera C, Karthik K, Singh H, Deepak P, Jhamad AR, Bhardwaj D (2014). Suicide pact by drowning with bound wrists: A case of medico-legal importance. *The Medico-Legal Journal* 82, 29-31.

Bharadwaj RS (2014). The complex clinical picture of benzodiazepine misuse. *General Hospital Psychiatry* 36, e5-e6.

Bhoi SB, Tumram NK, Shinde DK, Chandekar KS (2013). Delayed death after attempted suicide by hanging. *Journal of Punjab Academy of Forensic Medicine and Toxicology* 13, 86-87.

Bhullar DS, Aggarwal KK, Aggarwal AD, Goyal A, Sangwan C (2013). Death due to constriction of neck: A case report. *Journal of Punjab Academy of Forensic Medicine and Toxicology* 13, 93-96.

Bjorkenstam C, Bjorkenstam E, Hjern A, Boden R, Reutfors J (2014). Suicide in first episode psychosis: A nationwide cohort study. *Schizophrenia Research* 157, 1-7.

Bonsignore A, Sblano S, Pozzi F, Ventura F, Dell'Erba A, Palmiere C (2014). A case of suicide by ingestion of caffeine. *Forensic Science, Medicine, and Pathology* 10, 448-451.

Breitstein J, Penix B, Roth BJ, Baxter T, Mysliwiec V (2014). Intensive sleep deprivation and cognitive behavioral therapy for pharmacotherapy refractory insomnia in a hospitalized patient. *Journal of Clinical Sleep Medicine* 10, 689-690 .

Byard RW, Charlwood C (2014). Commemorative tattoos as markers for anniversary reactions and suicide. *Journal of Forensic and Legal Medicine* 24, 15-17.

Can SS, Udurlu GK, Cakmak S (2014). Dandy Walker variant and bipolar I disorder with graphomania. *Psychiatry Investigation* 11, 336-339.

Cantrell FL, Ogera P, Mallett P, McIntyre IM (2014). Fatal oral methylphenidate intoxication with postmortem concentrations. *Journal of Forensic Sciences* 59, 847-849.

Chao C-T (2014). Concurrent salmonella mycotic abdominal aneurysm and empyema thoracis: A rare coincidence. *Medical Principles and Practice* 23, 482-484.

Chaudhary SC, Sawlani KK, Atam V, Khemraj (2014). Takotsubo cardiomyopathy. *Journal of Association of Physicians of India* 62, 427-429.

Chaudhary SC, Sawlani KK, Yathish BE, Singh A, Kumar S, Parihar A (2014). Pyopneumothorax following kerosene poisoning. *Toxicology International* 21, 112-114.

Chiriac A, Foia L, Birsan C, Goriuc A, Solovan C (2014). Cutaneous factitia in elderly patients: Alarm signal for psychiatric disorders. *Clinical Interventions in Aging* 9, 421-424.

Colon-Rivera HA, Oldham MA (2014). The mind with a radio of its own: A case report and review of the literature on the treatment of musical hallucinations. *General Hospital Psychiatry* 36, 220-224.

Cuesta Martín M, Gómez Irwing L (2013). Attempted suicide by ingestion of potassium permanganate in solution. *Emergencias* 25, 502-503.

Das S, Hamide A, Mohanty MK, Muthusamy R (2014). Fatal cleistanthus collinus toxicity: A case report and review of literature. *Journal of Forensic Sciences* 59, 1441-1447.

Dimitriadis K, Pfefferkorn T, Noachtar S (2014). Severe depression as the sole symptom of affective focal status epilepticus. *BMJ Case Reports*. Published online: 4 May 2014. doi: 10.1136/bcr-2013-201149.

Dogan E, Guzel A, Ciftci T, Aycan I, Celik F, Cetin B, Kavak GO (2014). Zinc phosphide poisoning. *Case Reports in Critical Care*. Published online: 30 June 2014. doi:10.1155/2014/589712.

Efrimescu C-I, Yagoub E, Doyle R (2013). Intentional insulin overdose associated with minimal hypoglycemic symptoms in a non-diabetic patient. *Maedica* 8, 365-369.

Ellard R, Ahmed A, Shah R, Bewley A (2014). Suicide and depression in a patient with psoriasis receiving adalimumab: The role of the dermatologist. *Clinical and Experimental Dermatology* 39, 624-627.

Fentanes E (2014). Eating seeds from the 'be still' tree, yet having lucky nut poisoning: A case of acute yellow oleander poisoning. *BMJ Case Reports*. Published online: 4 June 2014. doi: 10.1136/bcr-2013-200392.

Ganzevoort RR, Nadeau JG (2014). Reading Robert and beyond: Narrative analysis of the story of a sexually abused Catholic man. *Verbum et Ecclesia*. Published online: 6 August 2014. doi: 10.4102/ve.v35i2.868.

Garg A, Panda S, Dalvi P, Mehra S, Ray S, Singh VK (2014). Severe suicidal digoxin and propranolol toxicity with insulin overdose. *Indian Journal of Critical Care* 18, 173-175.

Gebhardtova A, Vavrinec P, Vavrincova-Yaghi D, Seelen M, Dobisova A, Flassikova Z, Cikova A, Henning RH, Yaghi A (2014). A case of severe chlorite poisoning successfully treated with early administration of methylene blue, renal replacement therapy, and red blood cell transfusion: Case report. *Medicine* 93, e60.

Ghosh S (2014). Atypical manifestations of organophosphorus poisoning following subcutaneous injection of dichlorvos with suicidal intention. *Indian Journal of Critical Care Medicine* 18, 244-246.

Gierowski JK, Skupién E (2014). Murder or suicide? The dilemmas of a complex expert opinion. *Problems of Forensic Sciences* 97, 62-72.

Grazier MR, Armenian P, Vohra R (2014). Illicit distribution of prescription drugs: Report of inadvertent chloroquine toxicity and a market survey of businesses serving ethnic minority populations in central California. *Annals of Pharmacotherapy*. Published online: 19 May 2014. doi: 10.1177/1060028014535908.

Grosse Perdekamp M, Glardon M, Kneubuehl BP, Bielefeld L, Nadjem H, Pollak S, Pircher R (2014). Fatal contact shot to the chest caused by the gas jet from a muzzle-loading pistol discharging only black powder and no bullet: Case study and experimental simulation of the wounding effect. *International Journal of Legal Medicine*. Published online: 14 August 2014. doi: 10.1007/s00414-014-1064-3.

Hadzik B, Grass H, Mayatepek E, Daldrup T, Hoehn T (2014). Fatal non-accidental alpha-lipoic acid intoxication in an adolescent girl. *Klinische Pädiatrie* 226, 292-294.

Hagiwara S, Kaneko M, Murata M, Ikegami T, Oshima K (2014). A survival case of severe liver failure caused by acetylsalicylic acid that was treated with living donor liver transplantation. *Hippokratia* 18, 71-73.

Hsiao PJ, Chen TY, Chiu CC, Wu TJ, Chan JS, Wu CC, Chen JS (2014). Delayed high anion gap metabolic acidosis after a suicide attempt: Case report. *Clinica Chimica Acta* 436, 329-331.

Hugar BS, Praveen S, Hosahally JS, Kainoor S, Shetty AR (2014). Gastrointestinal hemorrhage in aluminum phosphide poisoning. *Journal of Forensic Sciences*. Published online: 7 August 2014. doi: 10.1111/1556-4029.12588.

Inckle K (2014). Strong and silent: Men, masculinity, and self-injury. *Men and Masculinities* 17, 3-21.

Isik Y, Soyoral L, Karadas S, Emre H, Cegin MB, Goktas U (2013). Effectivity of one session charcoal hemoperfusion treatment in severe carbamazepine poisoning. *Iranian Red Crescent Medical Journal* 15, 749-751.

Jain A, Yadav J, Kumar G, Dubey BP (2014). Fatal cut-throat injury labeled as suicide after meticulous autopsy: Case report. *Journal of Indian Academy of Forensic Medicine* 36, 206-208.

Johnson B, Nichols S (2014). Crying and suicidal, but not depressed. Pseudobulbar affect in multiple sclerosis successfully treated with valproic acid: Case report and literature review. *Palliative and Support Care*. Published online: 11 June 2014. doi: http://dx.doi.org/10.1017/S1478951514000376.

Johnson T, Rovner B, Haller J (2014). Suicide and visual loss: A case report reflecting the need for recognition and management in ophthalmological settings. *Seminars in Ophthalmology* 29, 202-204.

Joo SH, Jeong JH, Hong SC (2014). A case report of suicidal behavior related to subclinical hyperthyroidism. *Neuropsychiatric Disease and Treatment* 10, 641-643.

Jung-Choi K, Khang YH, Cho HJ, Yun SC (2014). Decomposition of educational differences in life expectancy by age and causes of death among South Korean adults. *BMC Public Health* 14, 560.

Katsuma A, Hinoshita F, Masumoto S, Hagiwara A, Kimura A (2014). Acute renal failure following exposure to metallic mercury. *Clinical Nephrology* 82, 73-76.

Kern AM, Akerman SC, Nordstrom BR (2014). Opiate dependence in schizophrenia: Case presentation and literature review. *Journal of Dual Diagnosis* 10, 52-57.

Kii Y, Mizuma M (2014). Rehabilitation approaches to dysphagia that was developed for a patient who attempted to commit suicide by hanging: A case report. *European Journal of Physical and Rehabilitation Medicine* 50, 185-188.

Kiliçoğlu AG, Ipek H, Mutlu C, Doğan H, Avci A, Erdoğan A (2014). 3240 mg long acting methylphenidate intake for suicide attempt. *Anatolian Journal of Psychiatry* 15, S1-S3.

Kim JB, Jang J-W, Kim JH (2014). Reversible leukoencephalopathy in sodium monofluoroacetate intoxication. *Neurology* 82, 1190-1191.

King PR (2014). Cognitive-behavioral intervention in a case of self-mutilation. *Clinical Case Studies* 13, 181-189.

Kobayashi T, Kato S, Takeuchi M (2014). Considering patients' mental capacity when giving them bad news may help their well-being: A case of suicide attempt after being informed of lung cancer diagnosis. *Case Reports in Psychiatry.* Published online: 21 May 2014. doi:10.1155/2014/645769.

Koizumi T, Imamura N, Aruga N, Watanabe H, Nakagawa T, Masuda R, Iwazaki M (2014). Successful treatment of penetrating chest injury caused by a crossbow. *The Tokai Journal of Experimental and Clinical Medicine* 39, 64-68.

Koning JC, Gage EG, Sarhan M, Gaudin D, McGinnis R, Atallah JN (2014). Exacerbation of major depression in a patient with a peripheral nerve stimulator. *Journal of Anesthesia and Clinical Research* 5, 2.

Korkut E, Saritas A, Aydin Y, Korkut S, Kandis H, Baltaci D (2013). Suicidal ingestion of potassium permanganate. *World Journal of Emergency Medicine* 4, 73-74.

Kuroe Y, Naito H, Sugiyama J, Kawanishi S, Morimoto N, Hagioka S (2014). Acute methemoglobinemia caused by suicidal ingestion of liquid fertilizer. *Clinical Toxicology* 52, 819-819.

Lardi C, Schmit G, Burkhardt S, Mangin P, Palmiere C (2014). Philemon and Baucis deaths: Case reports and postmortem biochemistry contribution. *Journal of Forensic Sciences* 59, 1133-1138.

Latasiewicz M, Chang-Sotomayor M, Alonso-Caldarelli C, Farias-Plazas F, Leszczynska A, Gonzalez-Candial M (2014). Bilateral self-inflicted infectious dacryoadenitis. *Orbit.* Published online: 10 September 2014. doi:10.3109/01676830.2014.950292.

Lee S, Kim H, Lee S, Kim Y, Lee D, Ju J, Myung H (2014). Detection of a suicide by hanging based on a 3-d image analysis. *IEEE Sensors Journal* 14, 2934-2935.

Lee YH, Ahn HC, Sohn YD, Ahn JY, Park SM, Hong CK, Hwang SY, Na JU, Shin DH, Jo IJ, Song KJ, Sim MS (2014). Clinical experience of therapeutic hypothermia in cases of near-hanging and recovered from cardiac arrest due to hanging. *Hong Kong Journal of Emergency Medicine* 21, 316-321.

Link LH, Bindels AJGH, Brassé BP, Intven FA, Grouls RJE, Roos AN (2014). Severe colchicine intoxication; always lethal?!? *Netherlands Journal of Critical Care* 18, 19-21.

Łukasik-Głebocka M, Sommerfeld K, Han A, Grzegorowski A, Barałkiewicz D, Gaca M, Zieli ska-Psuja B (2014). Barium determination in gastric contents, blood and urine by inductively coupled plasma mass spectrometry in the case of oral barium chloride poisoning. *Journal of Analytical Toxicology* 38, 380-382.

Malbora B, Polat E, Akyuz SG (2014). Hemophagocytic lymphohistiocytosis and pelger-huët anomaly associated with colchicines intoxication. *Hematology Reports* 6, 25-26 .

Malla G, Basnet B, Vohra R, Lohani SP, Yadav A, Dhungana V (2013). Parenteral organophosphorus poisoning in a rural emergency department: A case report. *BMC Research Notes* 6, 524.

Manjula M, Chandrashekar C (2014). Filicide as a part of extended suicide: An experience of psychotherapy with the survivor. *Indian Journal of Psychiatry* 56, 194-196.

Mannou H, Ikemura M, Nakagawa Y, Nata M, Inoue H (2014). An autopsy case of serotonin toxicity resulting from suicidal administrations of fluvoxamine and lithium. Case report. *Romanian Journal of Legal Medicine* 22, 59-62.

Margiotta G, Gabbrielli M, Carnevali E, Alberti T, Carlini L, Lancia M, Bacci M (2014). Genetic identification by using short tandem repeats analysis in a case of suicide by self-incineration: A case report. *The American Journal of Forensic Medicine and Pathology* 35, 172-175.

Marusic S, Obreli Neto PR, Vuletic V, Kirin M (2014). Peripheral mononeuropathy associated with valproic acid poisoning in an adult patient. *International Journal of Clinical Pharmacology and Therapeutics* 52, 802-804.

McConnell LK, Lee WW, Black DW, Shriver EM (2014). Beauty is in the eye of the beholder: Body dysmorphic disorder in ophthalmic plastic and reconstructive surgery. *Ophthalmic Plastic and Reconstructive Surgery*. Published online: 14 May 2014. doi: 10.1097/IOP0000000000000019.

McIntyre IM, Mallett P, Burton CG, Morhaime J (2014). Acute benztropine intoxication and fatality. *Journal of Forensic Sciences*. Published online: 3 April 2014. doi: 10.1111/1556-4029.12489.

Meijer KA, Russo RR, Adhvaryu DV (2014). Smoking synthetic marijuana leads to self-mutilation requiring bilateral amputations. *Orthopedics* 37, e391-e394.

Melez IE, Avsar A, Baspinar B, Melez DO, Sahin F, Ozdes T (2014). Simultaneous homicide-suicide: A case report of double drowning. *Journal of Forensic Sciences* 59, 1432-1435.

Mikami K, Onishi Y, Matsumoto H (2014). Attempted suicide of an adolescent with autism spectrum disorder. *International Journal of Psychiatry in Medicine* 47, 263-271.

Mills AT, Davidson ME, Young P (2014). Concealed paracetamol overdose treated as hellp syndrome in the presence of postpartum liver dysfunction. *International Journal of Obstetric Anesthesia* 23, 189-193.

Mishra SN, Jena M, Mishra S, Rath A, Sahu MC (2014). Suicide as temporal lobe epilepsy phenomena: A rare case report. *International Journal of Pharmaceutical Sciences Review and Research* 26, 63-66.

Mizutani K, Nishimura K, Ichihara A, Ishigooka J (2014). Dissociative disorder due to graves' hyperthyroidism: A case report. *General Hospital Psychiatry* 36, 450.e1-450.e2.

Moreschi C, Da Broi U, Cividino S, Gubiani R, Pergher G (2014). Neck injury patterns resulting from the use of petrol and electric chainsaws in suicides. Report on two cases. *Journal of Forensic and Legal Medicine* 25, 14-20 .

Morioka D, Ohkubo F, Amikura Y (2014). Self-mutilation by a patient with borderline personality disorder. *Aesthetic Plastic Surgery* 38, 812-814.

Mukherjee S, Sen S, Ghosal M, Tripathi S (2014). Selective serotonin reuptake inhibitor associated suicidal ideation: A case report. *International Journal of Basic and Clinical Pharmacology* 3, 738-738.

Naha K, Suryanarayana J, Aziz RA, Shastry BA (2014). Amlodipine poisoning revisited: Acidosis, acute kidney injury and acute respiratory distress syndrome. *Indian Journal of Critical Care Medicine* 18, 467-469.

Nishiyori Y, Nishida M, Shioda K, Suda S, Kato S (2014). Unilateral hippocampal infarction associated with an attempted suicide: A case report. *Journal of Medical Case Reports* 8, 219.

Northcut TB, Kienow A (2014). The trauma trifecta of military sexual trauma: A case study illustrating the integration of mind and body in clinical work with survivors of mst. *Clinical Social Work Journal* 42, 247-259.

Özer Ü, Yüksel G, Erkoç N (2014). Traumatic grief presented with self-injury and suicide attempt: A case report. *Anatolian Journal of Psychiatry* 15, S21-S24.

Paulzen M, Henkel K, Tauber S, Reich A, Eap CB, Grunder G (2014). Plasma levels and cerebrospinal fluid penetration of venlafaxine in a patient with a nonfatal overdose during a suicide attempt. *Journal of Clinical Psychopharmacology* 34, 398-399.

Pesic D, Peljto A, Lukic B, Milovanovic M, Svetozarevic S, Lecic Tosevski D (2014). Cerebellar cognitive affective syndrome presented as severe borderline personality disorder. *Case Reports in Medicine*. Published online: 11 March 2014. doi:10.1155/2014/894263.

Petrea S, Brezean I (2014). Self harm through foreign bodies ingestion - a rare cause of digestive perforation. *Journal of Medicine and Life* 7, 67-74.

Phatake R, Desai S, Lodaya M, Deshpande S, Tankasali N (2014). Posterior reversible encephalopathy syndrome in a patient of organophosphate poisoning. *Indian Journal of Critical Care Medicine* 18, 250-252 .

Pipyrou S (2014). Narrating death: Affective reworking of suicide in rural Greece. *Social Anthropology* 22, 189-199.

Pompili M, Innamorati M, Di Vittorio C, Baratta S, Masotti V, Badaracco A, Wong P, Lester D, Yip P, Girardi P, Amore M (2014). Unemployment as a risk factor for completed suicide: A psychological autopsy study. *Archives of Suicide Research* 18, 181-192.

Poulos CK, Thorne TA (2013). A unique case of attempted two-gun suicide with one firearm discharge and two muzzle imprints. *Academic Forensic Pathology* 3, 250-253.

Prasad R, Horton JK, Chastain PD, II, Gassman NR, Freudenthal BD, Hou EW, Wilson SH (2014). Suicidal cross-linking of PARP-1 to AP site intermediates in cells undergoing base excision repair. *Nucleic Acids Research* 42, 6337-6351.

Qureshi PN, Schofield M, Maneta E, Coffey DBJ (2014). Misdiagnosis and a suicide attempt: The importance of accurate evaluation and treatment. *Journal of Child and Adolescent Psychopharmacology* 24, 407-410.

Ramón Del Río D, Satústegui Dordá PJ, Pueyo Enrique C, Valero Orós MP (2014). Transcutaneous intubation after a suicide attempt as an alternative method to control the airway. *Emergencias* 26, 320-321.

Ranga Rao GSRKG, Jakkam S, Prasad GKV (2014). Atypical ligature mark of hanging mimicking ligature strangulation: A case study. *Journal of Indian Academy of Forensic Medicine* 36, 218-219.

Rasmus SM, Charles B, Mohatt GV (2014). Creating Qungasvik (a Yup'ik intervention "toolbox"): case examples from a community-developed and culturally-driven intervention. *American Journal of Community Psychology* 54, 140-152.

Ring HC, Miller IM, Benfeldt E, Jemec GB (2014). Artefactual skin lesions in children and adolescents: Review of the literature and two cases of factitious purpura. *International Journal of Dermatology*. Published online: 16 April 2014. doi: 10.1111/ijd.12493.

Romano M, Zorzoli F, Bertona R, Villani R (2013). Takotsubo cardiomyopathy as an early complication of drug-induced suicide attempt. *Case Reports in Medicine*. Published online: 14 November 2013. doi:10.1155/2013/946378.

Sabahi AR, Amini-Ranjbar Z, Sharifi A, Kheradmand A (2014). Enucleation of eye using finger following cannabis consumption: A case report. *Addiction & Health* 6, 81-84.

Sabatini D, Truscelli G, Ciccaglioni A, Gaudio C, Grassi MC (2014). Bidirectional tachycardia after an acute intravenous administration of digitalis for a suicidal gesture. *Case Reports in Psychiatry*. Published online: 24 August 2014. doi:10.1155/2014/109167.

Sakurai K, Morita S, Otsuka H, Sugita M, Taira T, Nakagawa Y, Inokuchi S (2014). Non-traumatic bilateral orbital subperiosteal hematoma in a person who attempted suicide by hanging. *Tokai Journal of Experimental and Clinical Medicine* 39, 103-105.

Sarkar S, Nandi M, Mondal R, Mandal SK (2014). Organophosphorus-induced extrapyramidal intermediate syndrome in an adolescent suicide attempt survivor. *Journal of Neurosciences in Rural Practice* 5, 276-278.

Schepers R, van der Voort PHJ, van Werven EW, Uges DRA, Franssen EJF (2014). Legal issues in patient management of intoxicated patients: A case of auto-intoxication by intravenous pentobarbital injection. *Netherlands Journal of Critical Care* 18, 22-24.

Schipper EM, de Graaff LCG, Koch BCP, Brkic Z, Wilms EB, Alsma J, Schuit SCE (2014). A new challenge: Suicide attempt using nicotine fillings for electronic cigarettes. *British Journal of Clinical Pharmacology*. Published online: 12 August 2014. doi: 10.111/bcp.12495.

Shrum JM, Byers B, Parhar K (2014). Thyroid storm following suicide attempt by hanging. *BMJ Case Reports*. Published online: 9 July 2014. doi: 10.1136/bcr-2014-204589.

Singh P, Maldonado-Duran JM (2014). Drug-induced QT prolongation as a result of an escitalopram overdose in a patient with previously undiagnosed congenital long QT syndrome. *Case Reports in Medicine*. Published online: 1 July 2014. doi: 10.1155/2014/917846.

Sloan ME, Iskric A, Low NC (2014). Psychopharmacology for the clinician. *Journal of Psychiatry & Neuroscience* 39, e34-e35.

Song HR, Woo YS, Wang H-R, Jun T-Y, Bahk W-M (2014). How does antiepileptic drug induce suicidality? A case associated with levitracetam use. *General Hospital Psychiatry* 36, 360.e361-362.

Striebel JM, Kalapatapu RK (2014). The anti-suicidal potential of buprenorphine: A case report. *International Journal of Psychiatry in Medicine* 47, 169-174.

Takacs R, Makkos Z, Kassai-Farkas A, Pusztai A, Ungvari GS, Gazdag G (2014). Lamotrigine in the treatment of psychotic depression associated with hereditary coproporphyria - case report and a brief review of the literature. *Neuropsychopharmacologia Hungarica* 16, 43-46.

Taneja AK, Rosemberg LA, Kaup AO (2014). Foot drop after a suicide attempt. *Skeletal Radiology* 43, 1149-1150.

Tattoli L, Schmid S, Tsokos M (2014). Three rounds as "tandem bullets": Unusual findings in a case of a suicidal gunshot to the head. *Forensic Science, Medicine, and Pathology*. Published online: 6 August 2014. doi: 10.1007/s12024-014-9591-2.

Verma R, Mina S, Sachdeva A (2014). Auto cannibalism in mental retardation. *Journal of Pediatric Neurosciences* 9, 60-62.

Viero A, Giraudo C, Cecchetto G, Muscovich C, Favretto D, Puglisi M, Fais P, Viel G (2014). An unusual case of "dyadic-death" with a single gunshot. *Forensic Science International*. Published online: 15 August 2014. doi: 10.1016/j.forsciint.2014.08.001.

White M, Zacharin MR, Werther GA, Cameron FJ (2014). Intravenous glucagon in a deliberate insulin overdose in an adolescent with type 1 diabetes mellitus. *Pediatric Diabetes*. Published online: 17 September 2014. doi: 10.1111/pedi.12210.

Wiles DA, Russell JL, Olson KR, Walson PD, Kelley M (2014). Massive lindane overdose with toxicokinetics analysis. *Journal of Medical Toxicology*. Published online: 8 May 2014. doi: 10.1007/s13181-014-0403-6.

Williams JR, Aghion DM, Doberstein CE, Cosgrove RG, Asaad WF (2014). Penetrating brain injury after suicide attempt with speargun: Case study and review of literature. *Frontiers in Neurology* 5, 13.

Willner N, Schiff E (2014). A case of suicide attempt with zolpidem - will zolpidem show up on standard urine toxicology screening? *Excli Journal* 13, 454-456.

Wollersen H, Erdmann F, Dettmeyer RB, Hennemann K, Spencer V (2013). Three unusual cases of co poisoning with each two victims. *Toxichem Krimtech* 80, 335-338.

Yilmaz A, Uyanık E, Balci engül MC, Yaylaci S, Karcioglu O, Serinken M (2014). Self-cannibalism: The man who eats himself. *Western Journal of Emergency Medicine* 15, 701-702.

Yonguc T, Bozkurt IH, Ors B, Kozacioglu Z, Arslan B, Yonguc NG (2014). Penile fracture with bilateral corporeal rupture without urethral involvement. *Cuaj-Canadian Urological Association Journal* 8, E51-E53.

Zakhari R (2014). Ethylene glycol poisoning: Resolution of cranial nerve deficit. *Journal for Nurse Practitioners* 10, 616-619.

Miscellaneous

Aas M, Etain B, Bellivier F, Henry C, Lagerberg T, Ringen A, Agartz I, Gard S, Kahn JP, Leboyer M, Andreassen OA, Melle I (2014). Additive effects of childhood abuse and cannabis abuse on clinical expressions of bipolar disorders. *Psychological Medicine* 44, 1653-1662.

Abbing-Karahagopian V, Kurz X, Vries Fd, van Staa TP, Alvarez Y, Hesse U, Hasford J, Dijk Lv, de Abajo FJ, Weil JG, Grimaldi-Bensouda L, Egberts ACG, Reynolds RF, Klungel OH (2014). Bridging differences in outcomes of pharmacoepidemiological studies: Design and first results of the protect project. *Current Clinical Pharmacology* 9, 130-138.

Abrutyn S, Mueller AS (2014). Reconsidering Durkheim's assessment of Tarde: Formalizing a Tardian theory of imitation, contagion, and suicide suggestion. *Sociological Forum* 29, 698-719.

Adams N (2013). Developing a suicide precaution procedure. *Medsurg Nursing* 22, 383-386.

Adedoyin AC, Salter SN (2013). Mainstreaming black churches into suicide prevention among adolescents: A literature review. *Ethnicity and Inequalities in Health and Social Care* 6, 43-53.

Afridi HK, Yousaf M, Mateen A, Malik AR, Aziz K (2014). In strangulation deaths: Forensic significance of hyoid bone fracture. *Pakistan Journal of Medical and Health Sciences* 8, 376-378.

Agrawal A (2014). Re: Farmers' suicides in the Vidarbha region of Maharashtra, India: A qualitative exploration of their causes. *Journal of Injury and Violence Research* 6, 53-53.

Aligeti S, Quinones M, Salazar R (2014). Rapid resolution of suicidal behavior and depression with single low-dose ketamine intravenous push even after 6 months of follow-up. *Journal of Clinical Psychopharmacology* 34, 533-535.

Allen J, Mohatt GV (2014). Introduction to ecological description of a community intervention: Building prevention through collaborative field based research. *American Journal of Community Psychology* 54, 83-90.

Amone POK, Lekhutlile T, Meiser-Stedman R, Ovuga E (2014). Mediators of the relation between war experiences and suicidal ideation among former child soldiers in northern Uganda: The WAYS study. *BMC Psychiatry*. Published online: 24 September 2014. doi: 10.1186/s12888-014-0271-2.

Anderson HD, Valuck RJ (2013). Provider contact and antidepressant fills prior to suicide attempt: A retrospective case series of 32,000 attempters. *Pharmacoepidemiology and Drug Safety* 22, 453.

Ando S, Yasugi D, Matsumoto T, Kanata S, Kasai K (2014). Serious outcomes associated with overdose of medicines containing barbituratesfor treatment of insomnia. *Psychiatry and the Clinical Neurosciences* 68, 721.

Andreasson K, Krogh J, Rosenbaum B, Gluud C, Jobes DA, Nordentoft M (2014). The dias trial: Dialectical behavior therapy versus collaborative assessment and management of suicidality on self-harm in patients with a recent suicide attempt and borderline personality disorder traits - study protocol for a randomized controlled trial. *Trials* 15, 194.

Andriessen K (2014). Suicide bereavement and postvention in major suicidology journals. *Crisis* 35, 338-348.

Andriessen K, Krysinska K, Stack S (2014). Predictors of article impact in suicidology: The bereavement literature, a research note. *Suicide and Life-Threatening Behavior*. Published online: 27 May 2014. doi: 10.1111/sltb.12106.

Anestis MD, Soberay KA, Gutierrez PM, Hernandez TD, Joiner TE (2014). Reconsidering the link between impulsivity and suicidal behavior. *Personaliy and Social Psychology Review*. Published online: 26 June 2014. doi: 10.1177/1088868314535988.

Anglemyer A (2014). Guns, suicide, and homicide [1]. *Annals of Internal Medicine* 160, 876.

Anonymous (2014). Doing more to prevent suicide. *The Lancet* 384, 638.

Apter A (2014). Adolescent self-harm: New horizons? *Journal of the American Academy of Child and Adolescent Psychiatry* 53, 1048-1049.

Arenliu A, Kelmendi K, Haskuka M, Halimi T, Canhasi E (2014). Drug use and reported suicide ideation and attempt among Kosovar adolescents. *Journal of Substance Use* 19, 358-363.

Asherson P, Young AH, Eich-Hochli D, Moran P, Porsdal V, Deberdt W (2014). Differential diagnosis, comorbidity, and treatment of attention-deficit/hyperactivity disorder in relation to bipolar disorder or borderline personality disorder in adults. *Current Medical Researh and Opinion* 30,1657-1672.

Atal DK, Das S, Gautam P (2014). Importance of suicide note: In Indian context. *Medico-Legal Update* 14, 1-5.

Badrane N, Abadi F, Soulaymani A, Rhalem N, Bencheikh RS (2014). Suicide attempt and suicide by medication poisoning in children and adolescents: Moroccan poison control centre data. *Clinical Toxicology* 52, 417-418.

Baker C, Brown B (2014). Suicide, self-harm and survival strategies in contemporary heavy metal music: A cultural and literary analysis. *Journal of Medical Humanities.* Published online: 29 March 2014. doi: 10.1007/s10912-014-9274-8.

Bailin A, Milanaik R, Adesman A (2014). Health implications of new age technologies for adolescents: A review of the research. *Current Opinion in Pediatrics* 26, 605-619.

Ballard ED, Ionescu DF, Voort JLV, Slonena EE, Franco-Chaves JA, Zarate CA, Grillon C (2014). Increased fear-potentiated startle in major depressive disorder patients with lifetime history of suicide attempt. *Journal of Affective Disorders* 162, 34-38.

Balon R, Coverdale JH, Beresin EV, Louie AK, Roberts LW (2014). Improving psychiatric education related to suicide. *Academic Psychiatry* 38, 521-524.

Barber CW, Miller MJ (2014). Reducing a suicidal person's access to lethal means of suicide: A research agenda. *American Journal of Preventive Medicine* 47, S264-S274.

Bar-On V (2014). It cuts both ways: An analysis of the psychological discourse on self-injury from a linguistic point of view. *Psychoanalytic Review* 101, 701-734.

Bassilios B, Harris M, Middleton A, Gunn J, Pirkis J (2014). Characteristics of people who use telephone counseling: Findings from secondary analysis of a population-based study. *Administration and Policy in Mental Health.* Published online: 19 September 2014. doi:10.1007/s10488-014-0595-8.

Bastian B, Jetten J, Hornsey MJ, Leknes S (2014). The positive consequences of pain: A biopsychosocial approach. *Personality and Social Psychology Review* 18, 256-279.

Beauchaine TP, Crowell SE, Hsiao RC (2014). Post-dexamethasone cortisol, self-inflicted injury, and suicidal ideation among depressed adolescent girls. *Journal of Abnormal Child Psychology.* Published online: 11 September 2014. doi: 10.1007/s10802-014-9933-2.

Bebarta VS, Hensley MD, Borys DJ (2014). Acute methotrexate ingestions in adults: A report of serious clinical effects and treatments. *Journal of Toxicology.* Published online: 16 April 2014. doi:10.1155/2014/214574.

Behera C, Karthik K, Dogra T, Lalwani S, Millo T, Singh S (2014). E-suicide note: A newer trend and its medico-legal implications in India. *Medico-Legal Journal* 82, 80-82.

Beier JM, Mutimer D (2014). Pathologizing subjecthoods: Pop culture, habits of thought, and the unmaking of resistance politics at Guantanamo Bay. *International Political Sociology* 8, 311-323.

Bein LA, Petrik ML, Saunders SM, Wojcik JV (2014). Discrepancy between parents and children in reporting of distress and impairment: Association with critical symptoms. *Clinical Child Psychology and Psychiatry.* Published online: 23 April 2014. doi: 10.1177/1359104514532185.

Beland S-G, Tournier M, Brabant M-J, Greenfield B, Lynd L, Moride Y (2013). Development and validation of an algorithm to ascertain non-hospitalized suicide attempts using administrative claims data. *Pharmacoepidemiology and Drug Safety* 22, 380.

Bennett DC, Kerig PK, Chaplo SD, McGee AB, Baucom BR (2014). Validation of the five-factor model of PTSD symptom structure among delinquent youth. *Psychological Trauma* 6, 438-447.

Berent D, Macander M, Szemraj J, Orzechowska A, Galecki P (2014). Vascular endothelial growth factor a gene expression level is higher in patients with major depressive disorder and not affected by cigarette smoking, hyperlipidemia or treatment with statins. *Acta Neurobiologiae Experimentalis* 74, 82-90.

Berk M, Adrian M, McCauley E, Asarnow J, Avina C, Linehan M (2014). Conducting research on adolescent suicide attempters: Dilemmas and decisions. *Behavior Therapist* 37, 65-69.

Bernert RA, Hom MA, Roberts LW (2014). A review of multidisciplinary clinical practice guidelines in suicide prevention: Toward an emerging standard in suicide risk assessment and management, training and practice. *Academic Psychiatry* 38, 585-592.

Bhatia MS, Rathi A, Kaur N (2014). Confounders in studies of suicide by occupation. *British Journal of Psychiatry* 204, 402-405.

Bland P (2014). Identifying which patients are at risk of suicide. *Practitioner* 258, 7.

Bland P (2014). Suicide risk increased in Asperger's syndrome. *Practitioner* 258, 8-9.

Bonnell AG (2014). Explaining suicide in the imperial German army. *German Studies Review* 37, 275-295.

Booth CL (2014). Experiences and wisdom behind the numbers: Qualitative analysis of the national action alliance for suicide prevention's research prioritization task force stakeholder survey. *American Journal of Preventive Medicine* 47, S106-S114.

Boscarino JA, Hoffman SN, Adams RE, Figley CR, Solhkhah R (2014). Mental health outcomes among vulnerable residents after Hurricane Sandy: Implications for disaster research and planning. *American Journal of Disaster Medicine* 9, 107-120.

Boudreaux ED, Horowitz LM (2014). Suicide risk screening and assessment: Designing instruments with dissemination in mind. *American Journal of Preventive Medicine* 47, S163-S169.

Bowers L, Alexander J, Bilgin H, Botha M, Dack C, James K, Jarrett M, Jeffery D, Nijman H, Owiti JA, Papadopoulos C, Ross J, Wright S, Stewart D (2014). Safewards: The empirical basis of the model and a critical appraisal. *Journal of Psychiatric and Mental Health Nursing* 21, 354-364.

Bowers L, Wright S, Stewart D (2014). Patients subject to high levels of coercion: Staff's understanding. *Issues in Mental Health Nursing* 35, 364-371.

Boyce P (2014). Spectrum disorders, social stressors and suicide: The impact on service utilisation. *Australian and New Zealand Journal of Psychiatry* 48, 299-301.

Brady CF (2014). Presentation and treatment of complicated obsessive-compulsive disorder. *The Journal of Clinical Psychiatry* 75, e07.

Bremer J (2014). Purple and turquoise ribbons. *American Journal of Psychiatry* 171, 916-917.

Brenner L, Bahraini N, Homaifar B, Forster J, Monteith L, Dorsey-Holliman B (2014). Executive dysfunction and suicide in veterans with and without a history of traumatic brain injury. *Brain Injury* 28, 737-738.

Brent DA, Gibbons R (2014). Initial dose of antidepressant and suicidal behavior in youth: Start low, go slow. *JAMA Internal Medicine* 174, 909-911.

Brooker C, Denney D, Sirdifield C (2014). Mental disorder and probation policy and practice: A view from the UK. *International Journal of Law and Psychiatry* 37, 484-489.

Brown GK, Jager-Hyman S (2014). Evidence-based psychotherapies for suicide prevention: Future directions. *American Journal of Preventative Medicine* 47, S186-194.

Brown RP, Imura M, Osterman LL (2014). Gun culture: Mapping a peculiar preference for firearms in the commission of suicide. *Basic and Applied Social Psychology* 36, 164-175.

Bruni AT, Velho JA, Ferreira ASL, Tasso MJ, Ferrari RS, Yoshida RL, Dias MS, Leite VBP (2014). Analysis of the procedures used to evaluate suicide crime scenes in Brazil: A statistical approach to interpret reports. *Journal of Forensic and Legal Medicine* 26, 29-38.

Bryan CJ, Corso KA, Macalanda J (2014). An evidence-based approach to managing suicidal patients in the patient-centered medical home. *Cognitive and Behavioral Practice* 21, 269-281.

Bryan CJ, David Rudd M, Wertenberger E, Etienne N, Ray-Sannerud BN, Morrow CE, Peterson AL, Young-McCaughon S (2014). Improving the detection and prediction of suicidal behavior among military personnel by measuring suicidal beliefs: An evaluation of the suicide cognitions scale. *Journal of Affective Disorders* 159, 15-22.

Bryant L, Garnham B (2014). Economies, ethics and emotions: Farmer distress within the moral economy of agribusiness. *Journal of Rural Studies* 34, 304-312.

Bschor T (2014). Lithium in the treatment of major depressive disorder. *Drugs* 74, 855-62.

Buller AM, Devries KM, Howard LM, Bacchus LJ (2014). Associations between intimate partner violence and health among men who have sex with men: A systematic review and meta-analysis. *PLoS Medicine*. Published online: 04 March 2014. doi: 10.1371/journal.pmed.1001609.

Burgi N (2014). Societies without citizens: The anomic impacts of labor market restructuring and the erosion of social rights in Europe. *European Journal of Social Theory* 17, 290-306.

Burns B (2014). Mental health: Debunking myths around suicide. *Nursing New Zealand (Wellington, NZ : 1995)* 20, 35.

Buryi P, Gilbert S (2014). Effects of college education on demonstrated happiness in the United States. *Applied Economics Letters*. Published online: 25 Jun 2014. doi:10.1080/13504851.2014.920470.

Caceda R, Durand D, Cortes E, Prendes-Alvarez S, Moskovciak T, Harvey PD, Nemeroff CB (2014). Impulsive choice and psychological pain in acutely suicidal depressed patients. *Psychosomatic Medicine* 76, 445-451.

Calear AL, Batterham PJ, Christensen H (2014). Predictors of help-seeking for suicidal ideation in the community: Risks and opportunities for public suicide prevention campaigns. *Psychiatry Research* 219, 525-530.

Can A, Schulze TG, Gould TD (2014). Molecular actions and clinical pharmacogenetics of lithium therapy. *Pharmacology Biochemistry and Behavior* 123, 3-16.

Caplan R (2014). Antiepileptic drugs and suicide: The light at the end of the tunnel. *Epilepsy Currents* 14, 125-126.

Carpenter LM, Hubbard GB (2014). Cyberbullying: Implications for the psychiatric nurse practitioner. *Journal of Child and Adolescent Psychiatric Nursing* 27, 142-148.

Carrà G, Bartoli F, Crocamo C, Brady KT, Clerici M (2014). Attempted suicide in people with co-occurring bipolar and substance use disorders: Systematic review and meta-analysis. *Journal of Affective Disorders* 167, 125-135.

Castro CA (2014). The US framework for understanding, preventing, and caring for the mental health needs of service members who served in combat in Afghanistan and Iraq: A brief review of the issues and the research. *European Journal of Psychotraumatology*. Published online: 14 August 2014. doi: 10.3402/ejpt.v5.24713.

Cave R, DiMaio VJ, Molina DK (2014). Homicide or suicide? Gunshot wound interpretation: A Bayesian approach. *American Journal of Forensic Medicine and Pathology* 35, 118-23.

Chan J, Natekar A, Einarson A, Koren G (2014). Risks of untreated depression in pregnancy. *Canadian Family Physician* 60, 242-243.

Chandler A (2014). Narrating the self-injured body. *Medical Humanities.* Published online: 8 May 2014. doi:10.1136/medhum-2013-010488.

Chappell D (2014). Firearms regulation, violence and the mentally ill: A contemporary Antipodean appraisal. *International Journal of Law and Psychiatry* 37, 399-408.

Cheatle MD (2014). Assessing suicide risk in patients with chronic pain and depression. *Journal of Family Practice* 63, S6-S11.

Chen Y-Y, Yip PSF, Chan CH, Fu K-W, Chang S-S, Lee WJ, Gunnell D (2014). The impact of a celebrity's suicide on the introduction and establishment of a new method of suicide in South Korea. *Archives of Suicide Research* 18, 221-226.

Cheng Q, Li H, Silenzio V, Caine ED (2014). Suicide contagion: A systematic review of definitions and research utility. *PLoS ONE* 9, e108724-e108724.

Chesney E, Goodwin GM, Fazel S (2014). Risks of all-cause and suicide mortality in mental disorders: A meta-review. *World Psychiatry* 13, 153-160.

Chinthapalli K (2014). Cortisol levels predict depression in teenage boys, study shows. *BMJ* 348, g1654.

Christensen H, Batterham PJ, Mackinnon AJ, Donker T, Soubelet A (2014). Predictors of the risk factors for suicide identified by the interpersonal-psychological theory of suicidal behaviour. *Psychiatry Research.* 219, 290–297.

Christensen H, Petrie K (2014). Online mental health programs promising tools for suicide prevention. *Medicine Today* 15, 66-68.

Christiansen E, Larsen KJ, Agerbo E, Bilenberg N, Stenager E (2014). Risk factors and study designs used in research of youths' suicide behaviour-an epidemiological discussion with focus on level of evidence. *Nordic Journal of Psychiatry* 68, 513-23.

Claassen CA, Harvilchuck-Laurenson JD, Fawcett J (2014). Prognostic models to detect and monitor the near-term risk of suicide: State of the science. *American Journal of Preventive Medicine* 47, S181-S185.

Cleaver K, Meerabeau L, Maras P (2014). Attitudes towards young people who self-harm: Age, an influencing factor. *Journal of Advanced Nursing.* Published online: 23 May 2014. doi: 10.1111/jan.12451.

Cohen AB (2014). Overliving. *Hastings Center Report* 44, 5.

Colpe LJ, Pringle BA (2014). Data for building a national suicide prevention strategy: What we have and what we need. *American Journal of Preventive Medicine* 47, S130-S136.

Conner KR, Bagge CL, Goldston DB, Ilgen MA (2014). Alcohol and suicidal behavior: What is known and what can be done. *American Journal of Preventive Medicine* 47, S204-S208.

Conus P, Macneil C, McGorry PD (2014). Public health significance of bipolar disorder: Implications for early intervention and prevention. *Bipolar Disorders* 16, 548-556.

Cook CC (2014). Suicide and religion. *British Journal of Psychiatry* 204, 254-255.

Cook CCH (2014). The clinical implications of church attendance and suicide reply. *British Journal of Psychiatry* 205, 248-249.

Cook S, Turner NE, Ballon B, Paglia-Boak A, Murray R, Adlaf EM, Ilie G, den Dunnen W, Mann RE (2014). Problem gambling among ontario students: Associations with substance abuse, mental health problems, suicide attempts, and delinquent behaviours. *Journal of Gambling Studies.* Published online: 1 July 2014. doi: 10.1007/s10899-014-9483-0.

Cornette MM, Schlotthauer AE, Berlin JS, Clark DC, French LM, Miller ML, Pfeiffer HM (2014). The public health approach to reducing suicide: Opportunities for curriculum development in psychiatry residency training programs. *Academic Psychiatry* 38, 575-584.

Courtet P, Lopez-Castroman J, Jaussent I, Gorwood PA (2014). Antidepressant dosage and suicidal ideation. *JAMA Internal Medicine*. Published online: 22 September 2014. doi: 10.1001/jamainternmed.2014.4509.

Cox Lippard ET, Johnston JA, Blumberg HP (2014). Neurobiological risk factors for suicide: Insights from brain imaging. *American Journal of Preventative Medicine* 47, S152-162.

Culver A (2014). Letter to the editor: Specificity of electrodermal reactivity testing for suicidal propensity in thorell et al. *Journal of Psychiatric Research* 55, 133.

Curran G, Ravindran A (2014). Lithium for bipolar disorder: A review of the recent literature. *Expert Review of Neurotherapeutics* 14, 1079-1098.

Czyz EK, Bohnert AS, King CA, Price AM, Kleinberg F, Ilgen MA (2014). Self-efficacy to avoid suicidal action: Factor structure and convergent validity among adults in substance use disorder treatment. *Suicide and Life-Threatening Behavior*. Published online: 12 May 2014. doi: 10.1111/sltb.12101.

D'Souza P, Jago C (2014). Spotlight on depression: A pharma matters report. *Drugs of Today* 50, 251-267.

Darracq MA, Toy JM, Chen T, Mo C, Cantrell FL (2014). A retrospective review of isolated gliptin-exposure cases reported to a state poison control system. *Clinical Toxicology* 52, 226-230.

Davidsen AH, Poulsen S, Waaddegaard M, Lindschou J, Lau M (2014). Feedback versus no feedback in improving patient outcome in group psychotherapy for eating disorders (F-EAT): Protocol for a randomized clinical trial. *Trials* 15, 138.

Davis Molock S, Heekin JM, Matlin SG, Barksdale CL, Gray E, Booth CL (2014). The baby or the bath water? Lessons learned from the national action alliance for suicide prevention research prioritization task force literature review. *American Journal of Preventive Medicine* 47, S115-S121.

Dazzi T, Gribble R, Wessely S, Fear NT (2014). Does asking about suicide and related behaviours induce suicidal ideation? What is the evidence? *Psychological Medicine*. Published online: 07 July 2014. doi:10.1017/S0033291714001299.

De Beurs DP, de Vries AL (2014). Applying computer adaptive testing to optimize online assessment of suicidal behavior: A simulation study. *Journal of Medical Internet Research* 16, e207.

De Oliveira GN, Lessa JMK, Gonçalves AP, Portela EJ, Sander JW, Teixeira AL (2014). Screening for depression in people with epilepsy: Comparative study among neurological disorders depression inventory for epilepsy (NDDI-E), hospital anxiety and depression scale depression subscale (HADS-D), and beck depression inventory (BDI). *Epilepsy and Behavior* 34C, 50-54.

Dean B, Tawadros N, Seo MS, Jeon WJ, Everall I, Scarr E, Gibbons A (2014). Lower cortical serotonin 2a receptors in major depressive disorder, suicide and in rats after administration of imipramine. *The International Journal of Neuropsychopharmacology* 17, 895-906.

Deneke DE, Schultz H, Fluent TE (2014). Screening for depression in the primary care population. *Primary Care* 41, 399-420.

Deringer E, Caligor E (2014). Supervision and responses of psychiatry residents to adverse patient events. *Academic Psychiatry*. Published online: 5 June 2014. doi: 10.1007/s40596-014-0151-6.

Di Bona L, Saxon D, Barkham M, Dent-Brown K, Parry G (2014). Predictors of patient nonattendance at improving access to psychological therapy services demonstration sites. *Journal of Affective Disorders* 169, 157-164.

Diderich HM, Dechesne M, Fekkes M, Verkerk PH, Buitendijk SE, Oudesluys-Murphy AM (2014). What parental characteristics can predict child maltreatment at the emergency department? Considering expansion of the Hague Protocol. *European Journal of Emergency Medicine*. Published online: 2 June 2014. doi: 10.1097/MEJ.0000000000000174.

Dodds L, Robinson KM, Daking L, Paul L (2014). The concept of 'intent' within Australian coronial data: Factors affecting the national coronial information system's classification of mortality attributable to intentional self-harm. *Health Information Management Journal.* 02 June 2014. doi: 10.1097/MEJ.0000000000000174.

Dracheva S, Di Narzo AF, Kozlenkov A, Roussos P, Hao K, Hurd Y, Sibille E, Koonin E (2014). Unique gene expression signature associated with serotonin 2C receptor (5-HT2CR) RNA editing in the prefrontal cortex and altered in suicide. *Human Molecular Genetics* 23, 4801-4813.

Drescher MJ, Russell FM, Pappas M, Pepper DA (2014). Can emergency medicine practitioners predict disposition of psychiatric patients based on a brief medical evaluation? *European Journal of Emergency Medicine.* Published online: 6 June 2014. doi: 10.1097/MEJ.0000000000000131.

Duberstein PR, Jerant AF (2014). Suicide prevention in primary care: Optimistic humanism imagined and engineered. *Journal of General Internal Medicine* 2, 827-829.

Dyer A, Mayer-Eckhard L, White AJ, Alpers GW (2014). The role of scar origin in shaping men's body image. *American Journal of Men's Health.* Published online: 30 April 2014. doi: 10.1177/1557988314531446.

Eberlein CK, Frieling H, Kohnlein T, Hillemacher T, Bleich S (2014). Suicide attempt by poisoning using nicotine liquid for use in electronic cigarettes. *American Journal of Psychiatry.* Published online: 1 August 2014. doi: 10.1176/appi.ajp.2014.14030277.

Eggertson L (2014). Nunavut extends implementation of suicide prevention plan. *Canadian Medical Association Journal* 186, e226.

Eggertson L (2014). Opal fuel reduces gas-sniffing and suicides in Australia. *Canadian Medical Association Journal* 186, e229-e230.

Eisenwort B, Till B, Hinterbuchinger B, Niederkrotenthaler T (2014). Sociable, mentally disturbed women and angry, rejected men: Cultural scripts for the suicidal behavior of women and men in the Austrian print media. *Sex Roles* 71, 246-260.

Ellisdon AM, Zhang Q, Henstridge MA, Johnson TK, Warr CG, Law RHP, Whisstock JC (2014). High resolution structure of cleaved serpin 42 da from drosophila melanogaster. *BMC Structural Biology.* Published online: 24 April 2014. doi:10.1186/1472-6807-14-14.

Fan-Ko S, Chun-Ying C, Wei-Jen C, Ruey-Hsia W, Hui-Man H, Hung-Yen L (2014). Development and psychometric testing of the suicide caring competence scale (SCCS) for family caregivers in Taiwan. *Archives of Psychiatric Nursing* 28, 284-289.

Fanaj N, Melonashi E (2014). A systematic evidence review on suicide in Kosovo. *Sage Open.* Published online: 26 March 2014. doi: 10.1177/2158244014528717.

Fang Q, Freedenthal S, Osman A (2014). Validation of the suicide resilience inventory-25 with American and Chinese college students. *Suicide and Life-Threatening Behavior.* Published online: 11 June 2014. doi: 10.1111/sltb.12108.

Faqeih EA, Al-Owain M, Colak D, Kenana R, Al-Yafee Y, Al-Dosary M, Al-Saman A, Albalawi F, Al-Sarar D, Domiaty D, Daghestani M, Kaya N (2014). Novel homozygous deaf1 variant suspected in causing white matter disease, intellectual disability, and microcephaly. *American Journal of Medical Genetics, Part A* 164, 1565-1570.

Fishbain DA, Lewis JE, Gao J (2014). The pain suicidality association: A narrative review. *Pain Medicine.* Published online: 4 July 2014. doi: 10.1111/pme.12463.

Fischer G, Ameis N, Parzer P, Plener PL, Groschwitz R, Vonderlin E, Kolch M, Brunner R, Kaess M (2014). The German version of the self-injurious thoughts and behaviors interview (SITBI-G): A tool to assess non-suicidal self-injury and suicidal behavior disorder. *BMC Psychiatry.* Published online:18 September 2014. doi:10.1186/s12888-014-0265-0.

Fitzpatrick SJ (2014). Re-moralizing the suicide debate. *Journal of Bioethical Inquiry* 11, 223-232.

Fitzpatrick SJ (2014). Stories worth telling: Moral experiences of suicidal behavior. *Narrative Inquiry in Bioethics* 4, 147-160.

Flaskerud JH (2014). Suicide culture. *Issues in Mental Health Nursing* 35, 403-405.

Forrest AD (2014). Confounders in studies of suicide by occupation. *British Journal of Psychiatry* 204, 402-405.

Fountoulakis KN (2014). Suicide rates and the economic crisis in Europe. *Dusunen Adam: The Journal of Psychiatry and Neurological Sciences* 27, 1-5.

Galasi ski D, Ziółkowska J (2013). Experience of suicidal thoughts: A discourse analytic study. *Communication and Medicine* 10, 117-127.

Gale SD, Brown BL, Berrett A, Erickson LD, Hedges DW (2014). Association between latent toxoplasmosis and major depression, generalised anxiety disorder and panic disorder in human adults. *Folia Parasitologica* 61, 285-292.

Gallaway MS, Lagana-Riordan C, Fink DS, Pecko JA, Barczyk AN, Brannen SJ, Milliken AM (2014). An epidemiological assessment of reintegration and behavioral health risk at Joint Base Lewis-Mccord, Washington. *Military Medicine* 179, 594-601.

Gauthier S, Reisch T, Bartsch C (2014). Self-burning - a rare suicide method in Switzerland and other industrialised nations - a review. *Burns.* Published online: 29 April 2014. doi: 10.1016/j.burns.2014.02.007.

Gee T (2014). Losing a child to suicide: A personal and professional reflection. *Illness Crisis and Loss* 22, 269-272.

Ghaemi SN, Dalley S (2014). The bipolar spectrum: Conceptions and misconceptions. *The Australian and New Zealand Journal of Psychiatry* 48, 314-324.

Ghahramanlou-Holloway M, Tucker J, Neely LL, Carreno-Ponce JT, Ryan K, Holloway K, George B (2014). Suicide risk among military women. *Psychiatric Annals* 44, 189-193.

Ghoncheh R, Koot HM, Kerkhof AJFM (2014). Suicide prevention e-learning modules designed for gatekeepers. *Crisis* 35, 176-185.

Gies J, Martino S (2014). Uncovering Ed: A qualitative analysis of personal blogs managed by individuals with eating disorders. *Qualitative Report* 19, 1-15.

Gilliver SC, Sundquist J, Li X, Sundquist K (2014). Recent research on the mental health of immigrants to Sweden: A literature review. *European Journal of Public Health* 24 Suppl 1, 72-79.

Gilman SE, Bromet EJ, Cox KL, Colpe LJ, Fullerton CS, Gruber MJ, Heeringa SG, Lewandowski-Romps L, Millikan-Bell AM, Naifeh JA, Nock MK, Petukhova MV, Sampson NA, Schoenbaum M, Stein MB, Ursano RJ, Wessely S, Zaslavsky AM, Kessler RC, Army SC (2014). Sociodemographic and career history predictors of suicide mortality in the United States army 2004-2009. *Psychological Medicine* 44, 2579-2592.

Girolami A, Bertozzi I, Tasinato V, Sambado L, Treleani M (2014). Bleeding manifestations apparently unrelated to coagulation or other organic disorders: A tentative classification and diagnostic clues. *Hematology* 19, 293-298.

Glenn CR, Franklin JC, Nock MK (2014). Evidence-based psychosocial treatments for self-injurious thoughts and behaviors in youth. *Journal of Clinical Child and Adolescent Psychology.* Published online: 25 September 2014. doi:10.1080/15374416.2014.945211.

Glenn CR, Nock MK (2014). Improving the short-term prediction of suicidal behavior. *American Journal of Preventive Medicine* 47, S176-S180.

Glowa-Kollisch S, Lim S, Summers C, Cohen L, Selling D, Venters H (2014). Beyond the bridge: Evaluating a novel mental health program in the New York City jail system. *American Journal of Public Health* 104, 2212-2218.

Goldney RD (2014). Suicide research: Interesting and/or clinically useful? *Australasian Psychiatry* 22, 109-111.

Goldney RD (2014). The importance of mental disorders in suicide. *Australian and New Zealand Journal of Psychiatry.* Published online: 19 August 2014. doi:10.1177/0004867414549200.

González-Rodríguez A, Molina-Andreu O, Navarro Odriozola V, Gastó Ferrer C, Penadés R, Catalán R (2014). Suicidal ideation and suicidal behaviour in delusional disorder: A clinical overview. *Psychiatry Journal.* Published online: 30 January 2014. doi:10.1155/2014/834901.

Gottfried E, Bodell L, Carbonell J, Joiner T (2014). The clinical utility of the MMPI-2-RF suicidal/death ideation scale. *Psychological Assessment.* Published online: 28 July 2014. doi: 10.1037/pas0000017.

Graham R (2014). Diabetes and self-harm: Understanding and addressing the problem. *Practical Diabetes* 31, 138-140.

Gray K (2014). Harm concerns predict moral judgments of suicide: Comment on Rottman, Kelemen and Young (2014). *Cognition* 133, 329-31.

Grzanka PR, Mann ES (2014). Queer youth suicide and the psychopolitics of "it gets better". *Sexualities* 17, 369-393.

Gupta MA (2014). Suicide attempt and externalizing behaviours in posttraumatic stress disorder (PTSD): Possible role of the activating effect of antidepressants. *Australian and New Zealand Journal of Psychiatry.* Published online: 12 June 2014. doi: 10.1177/0004867414538676.

Gvion Y, Levi-Belz Y, Apter A (2014). Suicide in Israel - an update. *Crisis* 35, 141-144 .

Gyles C (2014). Veterinarian suicides. *The Canadian Veterinary Journal* 55, 715-718 .

Habibi M, Khawaja NG, Moradi S, Dehghani M, Fadaei Z (2014). University student depression inventory: Measurement model and psychometric properties. *Australian Journal of Psychology* 66, 149-157.

Haggerty G, Blanchard M, Baity MR, Defife JA, Stein MB, Siefert CJ, Sinclair SJ, Zodan J (2014). Clinical validity of a dimensional assessment of self- and interpersonal functioning in adolescent inpatients. *Journal of Personality Assessment.* Published online: 10 July 2014. doi: 10.1080/00223891.2014.930744.

Haggerty G, Forlenza N, Poland C, Ray S, Zodan J, Mehra A, Goyal A, Baity MR, Siefert CJ, Sobin S, Leite D, Sinclair SJ (2014). Assessing overall functioning with adolescent inpatients. *Journal of Nervous and Mental Disease.* 25 September 2014. doi: 10.1097/NMD.0000000000000200.

Halabi ZG (2013). The unbearable heaviness of being: The suicide of the intellectual in Rabi Jabir's Ralf Rizqallah through the looking glass. *Journal of Arabic Literature* 44, 53-82.

Hancocks S (2014). Taking a life. *British Dental Journal* 216, 47.

Haneef S, Iqbal P, Hussain T, Abbasi MH, Tariq A, Barkat H (2014). Spectrum of firearm autopsy cases brought to autopsy lab of Allama Iqbal medical college Lahore. *Pakistan Journal of Medical and Health Sciences* 8, 365-368.

Harlow AF, Bohanna I, Clough A (2014). A systematic review of evaluated suicide prevention programs targeting indigenous youth. *Crisis.* Published online: 13 August 2014. doi:10.1186/1471-2458-13-463.

Hegerl U, Mergl R (2014). Depression and suicidality in COPD: Understandable reaction or independent disorders? *European Respiratory Journal* 44, 734-743.

Heit OF, Silva RF, Franco A (2014). Improving traditional dental autopsies in postmortem examinations of intraoral gunshot wounds. *Journal of Forensic and Legal Medicine* 23, 87-90 .

Hemenway D (2014). Guns, suicide, and homicide: Response. *Annals of Internal Medicine* 160, 877 .

Henry SG, Feng B, Franks P, Bell RA, Tancredi DJ, Gottfeld D, Kravitz RL (2014). Methods for assessing patient-clinician communication about depression in primary care: What you see depends on how you look. *Health Services Research* 49, 1684-1700.

Higgins J (2014). Integrated services and suicide prevention training: A case study of one community mental health agency. *Professional Case Management* 19, 137-142.

Howe AS, Leung T, Bani-Fatemi A, Souza R, Tampakeras M, Zai C, Kennedy JL, Strauss J, De Luca V (2014). Lack of association between dopamine- hydroxylase gene and a history of suicide attempt in schizophrenia: Comparison of molecular and statistical haplotype analyses. *Psychiatric Genetics* 24, 110-115.

Hsu PC, Groer M, Beckie T (2014). New findings: Depression, suicide, and toxoplasma gondii infection. *Journal of the American Association of Nurse Practitioners.* Published online: 8 April 2014. doi: 10.1002/2327-6924.12129.

Hughes S, Cohen D, Jaggi R (2014). Differences in reporting serious adverse events in industry sponsored clinical trial registries and journal articles on antidepressant and antipsychotic drugs: A cross-sectional study. *BMJ Open* 4, e005535.

Hundekari IA, Surykar AN, Dongre NN, Rathi DB (2012). Acute poisoning with organophosphorus pesticide: Patients admitted to a hospital in Bijapur, Karnataka. *Journal of Krishna Institute of Medical Sciences University* 1, 38-47 .

Huprich SK, Paggeot AV, Samuel DB (2014). Comparing the personality disorder interview for DSM-IV (PDI-IV) and SCID-II borderline personality disorder scales: An item-response theory analysis. *Journal of Personality Assessment.* Published online: 9 September 2014. doi:10.1080/00223891.2014.946606.

Icick R, Peoc'h K, Ksouda K, Bloch V, Laplanche JL, Lépine JP, Bellivier F, Vorspan F (2014). OPRM1 polymorphism and lifetime suicide attempts among stabilized, methadone-maintained outpatients. *Psychiatry Research* 218, 259-260.

Isaza JP, Muñoz F, Avila A (2014). Clustering analysis of a Colombian toxicological database. *Human and Ecological Risk Assessment* 20, 1058-1076.

Jacob N, Scourfield J, Evans R (2014). Suicide prevention via the internet. *Crisis* 35, 261-267.

Jeffrey Allen S, Kristi L. M, B. Christopher F (2014). Documented suicides within the British Army during the Crimean War 1854-1856. *Military Medicine* 179, 721-723.

Jiao Y, Phillips MR, Sheng Y, Wu G, Li X, Xiong W, Wang L (2014). Cross-sectional study of attitudes about suicide among psychiatrists in Shanghai. *BMC Psychiatry* 14, 87.

Johnson RH (2014). Touch of the healer: Defining core behaviors of oncologists that affect the mental health of patients with cancer. *Cancer* 20, 2233–2236.

Juodis M, Starzomski A, Porter S, Woodworth M (2014). What can be done about high-risk perpetrators of domestic violence? *Journal of Family Violence* 29, 381-390 .

Kancírová M, Kudela K (2014). The relationship between suicide incidents in Slovakia and the Czech Republic and heliophysical parameters: Empirical results. *Journal of Astrobiology and Outreach* 2, 116.

Karam EG, Sampson N, Itani L, Andrade LH, Borges G, Chiu WT, Florescu S, Horiguchi I, Zarkov Z, Akiskal H (2014). Under-reporting bipolar disorder in large-scale epidemiologic studies. *Journal of Affective Disorders* 159, 147-154 .

Karen M, Hope T, Jera S, Gerald R. H, Sarah S. K (2014). A comparison of risk factors associated with suicide ideation/attempts in American Indian and white youth in Montana. *Archives of Suicide Research.* Published online: 10 Jul 2014. doi:10.1080/13811118.2013.840254.

Karim J, Shah SH (2014). Ability emotional intelligence predicts quality of life beyond personality, affectivity, and cognitive intelligence. *Applied Research in Quality of Life* 9, 733-747.

Kaschka W, Thorell LH, Hodgkinson S, Steyer J, Straub R, Wolfersdorf M, Jandl M (2014). Strong evidence for an association between electrodermal hyporeactivity and suicide propensity in bipolar disorder. *Bipolar Disorders* 16, 73-74 .

Kaufmann JK (2014). History of a suicide: My sister's unfinished life. *Contemporary Psychoanalysis* 50, 284-289.

Kellogg KJ, Kaur S, Blank WC (2014). Suicide in corrections: An overview. *Disease-a-Month* 60, 215-220.

Kelly BD, Foley SR (2013). Love, spirituality, and regret: Thematic analysis of last statements from death row, Texas (2006-2011). *Journal of the American Academy of Psychiatry and the Law* 41, 540-550.

Kennedy AJ, Maple MJ, McKay K, Brumby SA (2014). Suicide and accidental death in Australia's rural farming communities: A review of the literature. *Rural and Remote Health* 14, 2517-2517.

Kennedy B, Ibrahim JE, Bugeja L, Ranson D (2014). Causes of death determined in medicolegal investigations in residents of nursing homes: A systematic review. *Journal of the American Geriatrics Society* 62, 1513-1526.

Keshavarz H, Fitzpatrick-Lewis D, Streiner DL, Maureen R, Ali U, Shannon HS, Raina P (2013). Screening for depression: A systematic review and meta-analysis. *Canadian Medical Association Open Access Journal* 1, E159-167.

Khaled A (2014). Application of proteomics in diagnosis of ADHD, schizophrenia, major depression, and suicidal behavior. *Advances in Protein Chemistry and Structural Biology* 95, 283-315.

Kiadaliri AA, Saadat S, Shahnavazi H, Haghparast-Bidgoli H (2014). Overall, gender and social inequalities in suicide mortality in Iran, 2006-2010: A time trend province-level study. *BMJ Open* 4, e005227.

Kiernan F, Rahman F (2014). Characteristics of patients admitted to the intensive care unit following self-poisoning and their impact on resource utilisation. *Irish Journal of Medical Science* 183, 391-395.

Kim J-M, Stewart R, Kim S-W, Kang H-J, Kim S-Y, Lee J-Y, Bae K-Y, Shin I-S, Yoon J-S (2014). Interactions between a serotonin transporter gene, life events and social support on suicidal ideation in Korean elders. *Journal of Affective Disorders* 160, 14-20.

Kim K, Park J-I (2014). Attitudes toward suicide among college students in South Korea and the United States. *International Journal of Mental Health Dystems* 8, e17.

Kim Y (2014). Understanding the life experiences of older adults in Korea following a suicide attempt. *Qualitative Health Research* 24, 1391-1399.

Kinahan JC, MacHale S (2014). The surgeon and self-harm: At the cutting edge. *Surgeon.* Published online: 14 April 2014. doi: 10.1016/j.surge.2014.03.002.

Kleiman EM, Liu RT (2014). Nothing in between: A multi-faith response to the paper on religion and suicide reply. *British Journal of Psychiatry* 205, 163-164.

Kleiman EM, Liu RT (2014). Religious service attendance as a protective factor against suicide reply. *British Journal of Psychiatry* 204, 404-405.

Kleiman EM, Riskind JH, Stange JP, Hamilton JL, Alloy LB (2014). Cognitive and interpersonal vulnerability to suicidal ideation: A weakest link approach. *Behavior Therapy* 45, 778–790.

Klein A, Schröder C, Heinemann A, Püschel K (2014). Homicide or suicide? Xylophagia: A possible explanation for extraordinary autopsy findings. *Forensic Science, Medicine, and Pathology* 10, 437-442.

Kloor K (2014). The GMO-suicide myth. *Issues in Science and Technology* 30, 65-70

Koopersmith EG, Tarpey CM (2014). Do no harm: Physicians' duties toward suicidal patients. *Medical Economics* 91, 30-31.

Kopacz MS, Silver E, Bossarte RM (2014). A position article for applying spirituality to suicide prevention. *Journal of Spirituality in Mental Health* 16, 133-146.

Koyama A, Fukunaga R, Abe Y, Nishi Y, Fujise N, Ikeda M (2014). Item non-response on self-reported depression screening questionnaire among community-dwelling elderly. *Journal of Affective Disorders* 162, 30-33.

Kronfol Z, Saleh M, Al-Ghafry M (2014). Mental health issues among migrant workers in Gulf cooperation council countries: Literature review and case illustrations. *Asian Journal of Psychiatry* 10, 109-113.

Krischel M (2014). German urologists under national socialism. *World Journal of Urology* 32, 1055-1060.

Kryczka T, Chrapusta SJ, Szaflik JP, Szaflik J, Midelfart A (2014). Impact of donor health on corneal biochemistry - an unexpected caveat from a pilot study. *Annals of Transplantation* 19, 129-137.

Large M, Mullin K, Gupta P, Harris A, Nielssen O (2014). Systematic meta-analysis of outcomes associated with psychosis and co-morbid substance use. *Australian and New Zealand Journal of Psychiatry* 48, 418-432 ,

Large M, Ryan C (2014). Suicide risk assessment: Myth and reality. *International Journal of Clinical Practice* 68, 679-681.

Large MM, Ryan CJ (2014). Disturbing findings about the risk of suicide and psychiatric hospitals. *Social Psychiatry and Psychiatric Epidemiology* 49, 1353-1355.

Large MM, Ryan CJ (2014). Suicide risk assessment and risk of suicide in schizophrenia. *Psychiatric Services* 65, 564.

Large MM, Ryan CJ (2014). Suicide risk categorisation of psychiatric inpatients: What it might mean and why it is of no use. *Australasia Psychiatry*. Published online: 28 May 2014. doi: 10.1177/1039856214537128.

Latalova K, Kamaradova D, Prasko J (2014). Suicide in bipolar disorder: A review. *Psychiatria Danubina* 26, 108-114.

Latimer S, Meade T, Tennant A (2014). Development of item bank to measure deliberate self-harm behaviours: Facilitating tailored scales and computer adaptive testing for specific research and clinical purposes. *Psychiatry Research* 217, 240-247.

Laursen TM, Nordentoft M, Mortensen PB (2014). Excess early mortality in schizophrenia. *Annual Review of Clinical Psychology* 10, 425-448.

Le J (2013). The 20-minute clinic visit: It's sometimes easier for physicians to bring up what families cannot. *Minnesota Medicine* 96, 26-27.

Leah C (2014). Our encounters with suicide. *British Journal of Social Work* 44, 474-475.

Lee AY, Pridmore S (2014). Absence of seasonality of suicide in Tasmania (Australia). *Australasian Psychiatry* 22, 204-206.

LeFevre ML (2014). Screening for suicide risk in adolescents, adults, and older adults in primary care: U.S. preventive services task force recommendation statement. *Annals of Internal Medicine* 160, 719-726 .

Lemieux AM, Saman DM, Lutfiyya MN (2014). Men and suicide in primary care. *Disease-a-Month* 60, 155-161.

Lester D (2014). Murder-suicide in workplace violence. *Psychological Reports.* 115, 28-31.

Lewis DS, Anderson KH, Feuchtinger J (2014). Suicide prevention in neurology patients: Evidence to guide practice. *The Journal of Neuroscience Nursing* 46, 241-248.

Lewis KC, Meehan KB, Tillman JG, Cain NM, Wong PC, Clemence AJ, Stevens J (2014). Impact of object relations and impulsivity on persistent suicidal behavior. *Journal of the American Psychoanalytic Association* 62, 485-492.

Lewis SP, Michal NJ (2014). Start, stop, and continue: Preliminary insight into the appeal of self-injury e-communities. *Journal of Health Psychology*. Published online: 3 April 2014. doi: 10.1177/1359105314527140.

Librero J, Segura A, Beatriz L-V (2014). Suicides, hurricanes and economic crisis. *European Journal of Public Health* 24, 183.

Linden S, Bussing R, Gerhard T, Shuster JJ, Winterstein AG (2013). Risk of suicide and suicide attempt associated with atomoxetine compared to central nervous system stimulant treatment. *Pharmacoepidemiology and Drug Safety* 22, 175-176.

Links PS, Prakash A (2014). Strategic issues in the psychotherapy of patients with narcissistic pathology. *Journal of Contemporary Psychotherapy* 44, 97-107.

Lintern S (2014). Hospital nurses left to look after children who have self-harmed. *Nursing times* 110, 6.

Liu NH, Contreras O, Munoz RF, Leykin Y (2014). Assessing suicide attempts and depression among Chinese speakers over the internet. *Crisis* 35, 322-329.

Lloyd-Williams M, Payne S, Reeve J, Dona RK (2014). Thoughts of self-harm and depression as prognostic factors in palliative care patients. *Journal of Affective Disorders* 166, 324-329.

Lord VB (2014). Police responses in officer-involved violent deaths: Comparison of suicide by cop and non-suicide by cop incidents. *Police Quarterly* 17, 79-100.

Lux C, Schyma C, Madea B, Courts C (2014). Identification of gunshots to the head by detection of RNA in backspatter primarily expressed in brain tissue. *Forensic Science International* 237, 62-69.

Mackelprang JL, Karle J, Reihl KM, Cash REG (2014). Suicide intervention skills: Graduate training and exposure to suicide among psychology trainees. *Training and Education in Professional Psychology* 8, 136-142.

Malhi GS, Coulston CM, Fritz K, Lampe L, Bargh DM, Ablett M, Lyndon B, Sapsford R, Theodoros M, Woolfall D, van der Zypp A, Hopwood M, Mitchell AJ (2014). Unlocking the diagnosis of depression in primary care: Which key symptoms are GPs using to determine diagnosis and severity? *Australian and New Zealand Journal of Psychiatry* 48, 542-547.

Maloney J, Pfuhlmann B, Arensman E, Coffey C, Gusmao R, Postuvan V, Scheerder G, Sisask M, van der Feltz-Cornelis CM, Hegerl U, Schmidtke A (2014). How to adjust media recommendations on reporting suicidal behavior to new media developments. *Archives of Suicide Research* 18, 156-169.

Manchia M, Hajek T, O'Donovan C (2014). Genetic risk of suicidal behavior in bipolar spectrum disorder: Analysis of 737 pedigrees. *Bipolar Disorders* 15, 496-506.

Mandal P, Prakash S (2014). Methodological considerations in studying psycho-social aspects of suicide. *Indian Journal of Psychiatry* 56, 208-209.

Manuela S, Sibley CG (2014). Exploring the hierarchical structure of Pacific identity and wellbeing. *Social Indicators Research* 118, 969-985.

Marcinko D, Jaksic N, Skocic M, Franic T (2013). Mentalization and psychopharmacotherapy in patients with personality and eating disorders. *Psychiatria Danubina* 25, 320-323 .

Marcus P (2013). Assessing suicide risk in individuals who have had intimate partner violence. *Journal of the American Psychiatric Nurses Association* 19, 28.

Mars B, Burrows S, Hjelmeland H, Gunnell D (2014). Suicidal behaviour across the African continent: A review of the literature. *BMC Public Health* 14, 606.

Martin CA, Chapman R, Rahman A, Graudins A (2014). A retrospective descriptive study of the characteristics of deliberate self-poisoning patients with single or repeat presentations to an Australian emergency medicine network in a one year period. *BMC Emergency Medicine* 14, 21.

Matsubayashi T, Sawada Y, Ueda M (2014). Does the installation of blue lights on train platforms shift suicide to another station?: Evidence from Japan. *Journal of Affective Disorders* 169, 57-60.

Maussion G, Yang J, Suderman M, Diallo A, Nagy C, Arnovitz M, Mechawar N, Turecki G (2014). Functional DNA methylation in a transcript specific 3'UTR region of TRKB associates with suicide. *Epigenetics*. Published online: 27 Oct 2014. doi: 10.4161/epi.29068.

McCrory PV (2014). Dentist suicides: Professional investigations. *British Dental Journal* 216, 436-437.

McCarthy M (2014). Suicide rates double among US soldiers between 2004 and 2009, research shows. *Britich Medical Journal* 348, g1987.

McLaughlin S, Bonner G, Canning C (2014). Improving confidence in suicide risk assessment. *Nursing Times* 110, 16-18.

Michaels MS, Chu C, Silva C, Schulman BE, Joiner T (2014). Considerations regarding online methods for suicide-related research and suicide risk assessment. *Suicide and Life-Threatening Behavior*. Published online: 27 May 2014. doi: 10.1111/sltb.12105.

Michaelsen K, Shankar C (2014). Suicide: Who is to blame? *Journal of the American Academy of Psychiatry and the Law* 42, 109-111.

Michailakis D, Schirmer W (2014). Social work and social problems: A contribution from systems theory and constructionism. *International Journal of Social Welfare* 23, 431-442.

Michel K (2014). Will new insights into neural networks help us improve our models of suicidal behavior? *Crisis* 35, 215-218.

Miguel-Hidalgo JJ, Wilson BA, Hussain S, Meshram A, Rajkowska G, Stockmeier CA (2014). Reduced connexin 43 immunolabeling in the orbitofrontal cortex in alcohol dependence and depression. *Journal of Psychiatric Research* 55, 101-109.

Miller C, Bauer MS (2014). Excess mortality in bipolar disorders. *Current Psychiatry Reports* 16, 1-7.

Miller PK (2013). Depression, sense and sensitivity: On pre-diagnostic questioning about self-harm and suicidal inclination in the primary care consultation. *Communication and Medicine* 10, 37-49.

Milner A (2014). Confounders in studies of suicide by occupation reply. *British Journal of Psychiatry* 204, 402-403.

Milner A, Page K, Spencer-Thomas S, Lamotagne AD (2014). Workplace suicide prevention: A systematic review of published and unpublished activities. *Health Promottion International*. Published online: 25 September 2014. doi: 10.1093/heapro/dau085.

Minshawi NF, Hurwitz S, Fodstad JC, Biebl S, Morriss DH, McDougle CJ (2014). The association between self-injurious behaviors and autism spectrum disorders. *Psychology Research and Behavior Management* 7, 125-136.

Mohamadi K, Ahmadi K, Ashtiani AF, Fallah PA, Ebadi A, Yahaghi E (2014). Indicators of mental health in various Iranian populations. *Iranian Red Crescent Medical Journal* 16, e14292.

Mollison E, Chaplin E, Underwood L, McCarthy J (2014). A review of risk factors associated with suicide in adults with intellectual disability. *Advances in Mental Health and Intellectual Disabilities* 8, 302-308.

Morgan AJ, Reavley NJ, Jorm AF (2014). Beliefs about mental disorder treatment and prognosis: Comparison of health professionals with the Australian public. *The Australian and New Zealand Journal of Psychiatry* 48, 442-451.

Morioka D, Ohkubo F (2014). Borderline personality disorder and aesthetic plastic surgery. *Aesthetic Plastic Surgery* 38, 1169-1176.

Mosurinjohn S (2014). Popular journalism, religious morality, and the Canadian imaginary: Queers and immigrants as threats to the public sphere. *Journal of Religion and Popular Culture* 26, 244-258 ,

Mugisha J, Hjelmeland H, Kinyanda E, Knizek BL (2014). The internal dialogue between the individual and the community: A discourse analysis of public views on suicide among the Baganda, Uganda. *International Journal of Culture and Mental Health* 7, 122-136.

Münster DN (2014). Farmers' suicides as public death: Politics, agency and statistics in a suicide-prone district (south India). *Modern Asian Studies.* Published online: 27 May 2014. doi: 10.1017/S0026749X14000225.

Mushquash C, Weaver B, Mazmanian D (2014). Reporting sensitivity and specificity for suicide risk instruments: A comment on Thorell et al. (2013). *Journal of Psychiatric Research.* Published Online: 26 March 2014. doi: 10.1016/j.jpsychires.2014.03.014.

Mushquash CJ, Weaver B, Mazmanian D (2014). Corrigendum to "reporting sensitivity and specificity for suicide risk instruments: A comment on thorell et al. (2013)" [j psychiat res 54 (2014) 144-145] (doi:10.1016/j.Jpsychires.2014.03.014). *Journal of Psychiatric Research.* Published Online: 31 July 2014. doi: 10.1016/j.jpsychires.2014.07.010

Nadorff MR, Lambdin KK, Germain A (2014). Pharmacological and non-pharmacological treatments for nightmare disorder. *International Review of Psychiatry* 26, 225-236.

Nagy C, Suderman M, Yang J, Szyf M, Mechawar N, Ernst C, Turecki G (2014). Astrocytic abnormalities and global DNA methylation patterns in depression and suicide. *Molecular Psychiatry.* Published online: 25 March 2014. doi: 10.1038/mp.2014.21.

Nazir A, Ichinomiya T, Miyamura N, Sekiya Y, Kinosada Y (2014). Identification of suicide-related events through network analysis of adverse event reports. *Drug Safety* 37, 609-616.

Nebhinani M, Nebhinani N, Tamphasana L, Gaikwad AD (2014). Nursing students' attitude toward suicide attempters. *Journal of Neurosciences in Rural Practice* 5, 207-208.

Nebhinani N (2014). Religious service attendance as a protective factor against suicide. *British Journal of Psychiatry* 204, 404.

Niciu MJ, Ionescu DF, Richards EM, Zarate CA, Jr. (2014). Glutamate and its receptors in the pathophysiology and treatment of major depressive disorder. *Journal of Neural Transmission* 121, 907-924.

Nilsson A (2014). Objective and reasonable? Scrutinising compulsory mental health interventions from a non-discrimination perspective. *Human Rights Law Review* 14, 459-485.

Niederkrotenthaler T, Reidenberg DJ, Till B, Gould MS (2014). Increasing help-seeking and referrals for individuals at risk for suicide by decreasing stigma: The role of mass media. *American Journal of Preventive Medicine* 47, S235-243.

Niederkrotenthaler T, Tinghög P, Alexanderson K, Dahlin M, Wang M, Beckman K, Gould M, Mittendorfer-Rutz E (2014). Future risk of labour market marginalization in young suicide attempters-a population-based prospective cohort study. *International Journal of Epidemiology* 43, 1520-1530.

Nielssen O, Large M (2014). High rates of suicide attempt in early-onset psychosis are associated with depression, anxiety and previous self-harm. *Evidence Based Mental Health.* Published online: 9 July 2014. doi:10.1136/eb-2014-101806.

Nordentoft M, Laursen TM (2014). Was risk of suicide underestimated? *JAMA Psychiatry* 71, 716.

O'Connor N, Allan J, Scott C (2014). Debate: Clinical risk categorization is valuable in the prevention of suicide and severe violence? Yes. *Australasian Psychiatry* 22, 7-9.

O'Connor RC, Williams JMG (2014). The relationship between positive future thinking, brooding, defeat and entrapment. *Personality and Individual Differences* 70, 29-34.

O'Dowd A (2014). Economic recession may have caused 10 000 extra suicides. *BMJ* 348, g3809.

Oldham J (2014). The problem of suicide, continued. *Journal of Psychiatric Practice* 20, 327.

Olfson M, Marcus SC, Bridge JA (2014). Addressing suicide risk in emergency department patients. *JAMA* 312, 297-298.

Omar H, Tejerina-Arreal M, Crawford MJ (2014). Are recommendations for psychological treatment of borderline personality disorder in current UK guidelines justified? Systematic review and subgroup analysis. *Personality and Mental Health* 8, 228-237.

Onkay Ho A (2014). Suicide: Rationality and responsibility for life. *Canadian Journal of Psychiatry* 59, 141-147.

Oquendo MA (2014). Suicidal behavior: Strategies for prevention at the individual and population levels. *Journal of Clinical Psychiatry* 75, 877-878.

Oquendo MA, Baca-Garcia E (2014). Suicidal behavior disorder as a diagnostic entity in the DSM-5 classification system: Advantages outweigh limitations. *World Psychiatry* 13, 128-130.

O'Shea LE, Dickens GL (2014). Short-term assessment of risk and treatability (START): Systematic review and meta-analysis. *Psychological Assessessment* 26, 990-1002.

O'Shea LE, Picchioni MM, Mason FL, Sugarman PA, Dickens GL (2014). Predictive validity of the HCR-20 for inpatient self-harm. *Comprehensive Psychiatry* 55, 1937–1949.

Osuch E, Ford K, Wrath A, Bartha R, Neufeld R (2014). Functional MRI of pain application in youth who engaged in repetitive non-suicidal self-injury vs. psychiatric controls. *Psychiatry Research* 223, 104-112.

Ougrin D (2014). Commentary: Self-harm: A global health priority - reflections on Brunner et al. (2014). *Journal of Child Psychology and Psychiatry* 55, 349-351.

Owens C, Roberts S, Taylor J (2014). Utility of local suicide data for informing local and national suicide prevention strategies. *Public Health* 128, 424–429.

Pagnini F, Phillips D, Langer E (2014). A mindful approach with end-of-life thoughts. *Frontiers in Psychology*. Published online: 21 February 2014. doi: 10.3389/fpsyg.2014.00138.

Pajak K, Trzebi ski J (2014). Escaping the world: Linguistic indicators of suicide attempts in poets. *Journal of Loss and Trauma*. Published online: 3 Jun 2014. doi: 10.1080/15325024.2013.794663.

Palmer BS, Bennewith O, Simkin S, Cooper J, Hawton K, Kapur N, Gunnell D (2014). Factors influencing coroners' verdicts: An analysis of verdicts given in 12 coroners' districts to researcher-defined suicides in England in 2005. *Journal of Public Health*. Published online: 10 Apr 2014. doi: 10.1093/pubmed/fdu024

Palmer RN (2014). Editorial: Suicide notes. *Medico-Legal Journal* 82, 47.

Papworth J (2014). Dentist suicides: Speculation and myths. *British Dental Journal* 216, 376.

Paraschakis A, Michopoulos I, Douzenis A, Christodoulou C, Lykouras L, Koutsaftis F (2014). Switching suicide methods in order to achieve lethality: A study of Greek suicide victims. *Death Studies* 38, 438-442.

Park H, Choi H, Suarez ML, Zhao Z, Park C, Wilkie DJ (2014). Predictors of valid engagement with a video streaming web study among Asian American and non-Hispanic white college students. *Computers, Informatics, Nursing* 32, 156-165.

Park N, Peterson C (2014). Suicide in happy places revisited: The geographical unit of analysis matters. *Applied Psychology: Health and Well-Being* 6, 318–323.

Park S-C, Choi J, Kim J-M, Jun T-Y, Lee M-S, Kim J-B, Yim H-W, Park YC (2014). Is the psychotic depression assessment scale a useful diagnostic tool?: The CRESCEND study. *Journal of Affective Disorders* 166, 79-85.

Parry J (2014). Falling suicide rates in China mask emerging upward trends. *BMJ* 348, g4486.

Patel V, Weobong B, Nadkarni A, Weiss HA, Anand A, Naik S, Bhat B, Pereira J, Araya R, Dimidjian S, Hollon SD, King M, McCambridge J, McDaid D, Murthy P, Velleman R, Fairburn CG, Kirkwood B (2014). The effectiveness and cost-effectiveness of lay counsellor-delivered psychological treatments for harmful and dependent drinking and moderate to severe depression in primary care in India: Premium study protocol for randomized controlled trials. *Trials* 15, 101.

Patra BN, Khandelwal SK, Chadda RK, Ramakrishnan L (2014). A controlled study of serum lipid profiles in Indian patients with depressive episode. *Indian Journal of Psychological Medicine* 36, 129-133.

Patry MW, Magaletta PR (2014). Measuring suicidality using the personality assessment inventory: A convergent validity study with federal inmates. *Assessment.* Published online: 19 June 2014. doi: 10.1177/1073191114539381

Pedersen CG (2014). Suicide risk assessment and risk of suicide in schizophrenia: In reply. *Psychiatric Services* 65, 564.

Peiris-John R, Kool B, Ameratunga S (2014). Fatalities and hospitalisations due to acute poisoning among New Zealand adults. *Internal Medicine Journal* 44, 273-281.

Pena JM, Manguno-Mire GM (2013). Scylla and Charybdis: Dual roles and undetected risks in campus mental health assessments. *Journal of the American Academy of Psychiatry and the Law* 41, 532-539.

Persoon-Gundy J (2014). Dream of a suicide. *Annals of Internal Medicine* 160, 498.

Picazo-Zappino J (2014). Suicide among children and adolescents: A review. *Actas Espanolas De Psiquiatria* 42, 125-132

Pikala M, Bryla M, Bryla P, Maniecka-Bryla I (2014). Years of life lost due to external causes of death in the Lodz Province, Poland. *PLoS ONE.* Published online: 8 May 2014. doi: 10.1371/journal.pone.0096830.

Pinholt EM, Mitchell JD, Butler JH, Kumar H (2014). "Is there a gun in the home?" Assessing the risks of gun ownership in older adults. *Journal of the American Geriatrics Society* 62, 1142-1146.

Pires MCdC, Silva TdPSd, Passos MPd, Sougey EB, Bastos Filho OC (2014). Risk factors of suicide attempts by poisoning: Review. *Trends in Psychiatry and Psychotherapy* 36, 63-74.

Ploderl M, Tremblay P (2014). Complementing remarks to Skerrett et al. (2014) "Suicides among lesbian, gay, bisexual, and transgender populations in Australia: An analysis of the Queensland Suicide Register". *Asia-Pacific Psychiatry* 6, 350-351.

Poole R (2014). The clinical implications of church attendance and suicide. *British Journal of Psychiatry* 205, 248.

Powell R (2014). Is preventive suicide a rational response to a presymptomatic diagnosis of dementia? *Journal of Medical Ethics* 40, 511-512.

Punzi G, Ursini G, Shin JH, Kleinman JE, Hyde TM, Weinberger DR (2014). Increased expression of MARCKS in post-mortem brain of violent suicide completers is related to transcription of a long, noncoding, antisense RNA. *Molecular Psychiatry* 19, 1057-1059.

Quinlivan L, Cooper J, Steeg S, Davies L, Hawton K, Gunnell D, Kapur N (2014). Scales for predicting risk following self-harm: An observational study in 32 hospitals in England. *BMJ Open* 4, e004732.

Rae M (2014). Train nurses to be part of a suicide prevention strategy. *Nursing Standard* 28, 33.

Rahu K, Bromet EJ, Hakulinen T, Auvinen A, Uuskula A, Rahu M (2014). Non-cancer morbidity among Estonian Chernobyl cleanup workers: A register-based cohort study. *BMJ Open* 4, e004516.

Ramadas S, Kuttichira P, John CJ, Isaac M, Kallivayalil RA, Sharma I, Asokan TV, Mallick A, Mallick NN, Andrade C (2014). Position statement and guideline on media coverage of suicide. *Indian Journal of Psychiatry* 56, 107-110.

Randall B (2014). Death certification: A primer. Part II - the cause of death statement. *South Dakota Medicine* 67, 231-235.

Rasmussen ML, Dieserud G, Dyregrov K, Haavind H (2014). Warning signs of suicide among young men. *Nordic Psychology*. Published online: 6 June 2014. doi: 10.1080/19012276.2014.921576.

Raza MS, Yasir Jaffery SA, Khan FA (2014). Flexor zone 5 cut injuries: Emergency management and outcome. *Journal of the College of Physicians and Surgeons Pakistan* 24, 194-197,

Razack S (2014). "It happened more than once": Freezing deaths in Saskatchewan. *Canadian Journal of Women and the Law* 26, 51-80.

Read J, Cartwright C, Gibson K (2014). Adverse emotional and interpersonal effects reported by 1829 New Zealanders while taking antidepressants. *Psychiatry Research* 216, 67-73.

Reavley NJ, Jorm AF (2014). Associations between beliefs about the causes of mental disorders and stigmatising attitudes: Results of a national survey of the Australian public. *Australian and New Zealand Journal of Psychiatry* 48, 764-771.

Reavley NJ, Mackinnon AJ, Morgan AJ, Jorm AF (2014). Stigmatising attitudes towards people with mental disorders: A comparison of Australian health professionals with the general community. *The Australian and New Zealand Journal of Psychiatry* 48, 433-441.

Reddy AK, Baker MS, Sobel RK, Whelan DA, Carter KD, Allen RC (2014). Survivors of self-inflicted gunshot wounds to the head: Characterization of ocular injuries and health care costs. *JAMA Ophthalmology*, 132, 730-736.

Reeves A, McKee M, Stuckler D (2014). Economic suicides in the great recession in Europe and North America. *British Journal of Psychiatry*. Published online: 12 June 2014. doi: 10.1192/bjp.bp.114.144766.

Reinhard MJ, Bloeser KJ (2014). Enhanced survey methods to clinically assess suicide risk. *Psychiatric Services* 65, 1179.

Reneflot A, Evensen M (2014). Systematic literature review unemployment and psychological distress among young adults in the Nordic countries: A review of the literature. *International Journal of Social Welfare* 23, 3-15.

Ressler KJ, Schoomaker EB (2014). Commentary on "The army study to assess risk and resilience in servicemembers (Army STARRS)": Army STARRS: A Framingham-like study of psychological health risk factors in soldiers. *Psychiatry* 77, 120-129.

Retamero C, Walsh L, Otero-Perez G (2014). Use of the film The Bridge to augment the suicide curriculum in undergraduate medical education. *Academic Psychiatry* 38, 605-610.

Rezaeian M (2014). Integrating social epidemiological methods into self-immolation studies. *Burns* 40, 361-362.

Rezaeian M (2014). The trend of indexed papers in PubMed covering different aspects of self-immolation. *Acta Medica Iranica* 52, 158-162.

Rhee P, Joseph B, Pandit V, Aziz H, Vercruysse G, Kulvatunyou N, Friese RS (2014). Increasing trauma deaths in the United States. *Annals of Surgery* 260, 13-21.

Ricci S, Massoni F, Schiffino L, Pelosi M, Salesi M (2014). Foreign bodies ingestion: What responsibility? *Journal of Forensic and Legal Medicine* 23, 5-8.

Richard-Devantoy S, Berlim MT, Jollant F (2014). Suicidal behaviour and memory: A systematic review and meta-analysis. *World Journal of Biological Psychiatry* Published online: 12 August 2014. doi: 10.3109/15622975.2014.925584.

Richardson JS, Mark TL, McKeon R (2014). The return on investment of postdischarge follow-up calls for suicidal ideation or deliberate self-harm. *Psychiatric Services* 65, 1012-1019.

Riechers RG, Ruff SE, Ruff RL (2014). Suicidality and injury of the prefrontal cortex in multiple incidents of mild traumatic brain injury. *JAMA Psychiatry* 71, 94.

Riemann G, Weisscher N, Goossens PJJ, Draijer N, Apenhorst-Hol M, Kupka RW (2014). The addition of STEPPS in the treatment of patients with bipolar disorder and comorbid borderline personality features: A protocol for a randomized controlled trial. *BMC Psychiatry* 14, 172.

Roberts M, Lamont E (2014). Suicide: An existentialist reconceptualization. *Journal of Psychiatric and Mental Health Nursing.* Published online: 4 May 2014. doi: 10.1111/jpm.12155.

Robinson P, Barrett B, Bateman A, Hakeem A, Hellier J, Lemonsky F, Rutterford C, Schmidt U, Fonagy P (2014). Study protocol for a randomized controlled trial of mentalization based therapy against specialist supportive clinical management in patients with both eating disorders and symptoms of borderline personality disorder. *BMC Psychiatry* 14, 51.

Rottman J, Kelemen D, Young L (2014). Purity matters more than harm in moral judgments of suicide: Response to Gray (2014). *Cognition* 133, 332-334.

Rozatkar AR (2014). Stigma of suicide. *Journal of Neurosciences in Rural Practice* 5, 206-207.

Rui Q, Wang Y, Liang S, Liu Y, Wu Y, Wu Q, Nuamah I, Gopal S (2014). Relapse prevention study of paliperidone extended-release tablets in Chinese patients with schizophrenia. *Progress in Neuro-Psychopharmacology and Biological Psychiatry* 53, 45-53.

Sachmann M, Johnson CMH (2014). The relevance of long-term antecedents in assessing the risk of familicide-suicide following separation. *Child Abuse Review* 23, 130-141.

Sadanandan A (2014). Political economy of suicide: Financial reforms, credit crunches and farmer suicides in India. *Journal of Developing Areas* 48, 287-307.

Said M (2014). Suicide and shame in southern Sri Lanka: Networks of dependency. *South Asia Research* 34, 19-30.

Sakinofsky I (2014). Preventing suicide among inpatients. *Canadian Journal of Psychiatry* 59, 131-140.

Saldana SN, Keeshin BR, Wehry AM, Blom TJ, Sorter MT, DelBello MP, Strawn JR (2014). Antipsychotic polypharmacy in children and adolescents at discharge from psychiatric hospitalization. *Pharmacotherapy* 34, 836-844.

Sareen J, Isaak C, Katz LY, Bolton J, Enns MW, Stein MB (2014). Promising strategies for advancement in knowledge of suicide risk factors and prevention. *American Journal of Preventive Medicine* 47, S257-S263.

Sarkar S, Balhara YPS (2014). Diabetes mellitus and suicide. *Indian Journal of Endocrinology and Metabolism* 18, 468-474.

Savage A, McConnell D, Emerson E, Llewellyn G (2014). Disability-based inequity in youth subjective well-being: Current findings and future directions. *Disability and Society* 29, 877-892.

Schmitt A, Falkai P (2014). Suicide ideation, stability of symptoms and effects of aerobic exercise in major depression. *European Archives of Psychiatry and Clinical Neuroscience* 264, 555-556.

Schwarz JK (2014). Hospice care for patients who choose to hasten death by voluntarily stopping eating and drinking. *Journal of Hospice and Palliative Nursing* 16, 126-131.

Segers M, Rawana J (2014). What do we know about suicidality in autism spectrum disorders? A systematic review. *Autism Research* 7, 507–521.

Seguin M, Bordeleau V, Drouin MS, Castelli-Dransart DA, Giasson F (2014). Professionals' reactions following a patient's suicide: Review and future investigation. *Archives of Suicide Research* 18, 340-362.

Serafini G, Pompili M, Innamorati M, Temple EC, Amore M, Borgwardt S, Girardi P (2013). The association between cannabis use, mental illness, and suicidal behavior: What is the role of hopelessness? *Frontiers in Psychiatry* 4, 125.

Shin J, Lee H, Kim J, Kim J, Choi S, Jeung K, Cho I, Cha G, Kim G, Han C, Lee D, Park K, Suh G, Hwang S (2014). Outcomes of hanging-induced cardiac arrest patients who underwent therapeutic hypothermia: A multicenter retrospective cohort study. *Resuscitation* 85, 1047-1051.

Silva AC, de Oliveira Ribeiro NP, de Mello Schier AR, Pereira VM, Vilarim MM, Pessoa TM, Arias-Carrion O, Machado S, Nardi AE (2014). Caffeine and suicide: A systematic review. *CNS Neurological Disorders Drug Targets* 13, 937-944.

Silverman MM, Pirkis JE, Pearson JL, Sherrill JT (2014). Reflections on expert recommendations for U.S. research priorities in suicide prevention. *American Journal of Preventive Medicine* 47, S97-S101.

Simon RI (2014). Passive suicidal ideation: Still a high-risk clinical scenario. *Current Psychiatry* 13, 13-15.

Simou E, Koutsogeorgou E (2014). Effects of the economic crisis on health and healthcare in Greece in the literature from 2009 to 2013: A systematic review. *Health Policy* 115, 111-119.

Sinclair SJ, Smith M, Chung WJ, Liebman R, Stein MB, Antonius D, Siefert CJ, Haggerty G, Blais MA (2014). Extending the validity of the personality assessment inventory's (PAI) level of care index (LOCI) in multiple psychiatric settings. *Journal of Personality Assessment.* Published online: 7 August 2014. doi: 10.1080/00223891.2014.941441.

Sklaroff RB (2014). Guns, suicide, and homicide [2]. *Annals of Internal Medicine* 160, 876-877.

Sloan ME, Iskric A, Low NC (2014). The treatment of bipolar patients with elevated impulsivity and suicide risk. *Journal of Psychiatry and Neuroscience* 39, e34-e35.

Smith CP, Freyd JJ (2014). Institutional betrayal. *The American Psychologist* 69, 575-587.

Sodhi-Berry N, Knuiman M, Alan J, Morgan VA, Preen DB (2014). Pre-sentence mental health service use predicts post-sentence mortality in a population cohort of first-time adult offenders. *Social Psychiatry and Psychiatric Epidemiology.* Published online: 1 July 2014. doi: 10.1007/s00127-014-0919-8.

Sokolowski M, Wasserman J, Wasserman D (2014). An overview of the neurobiology of suicidal behaviors as one meta-system. *Molecular Psychiatry.* Published online: 2 September 2014. doi: 10.1038/mp.2014.101.

Spallek J, Reeske A, Norredam M, Nielsen SS, Lehnhardt J, Razum O (2014). Suicide among immigrants in Europe-a systematic literature review. *European Journal of Public Health.* Published online: 5 August 2014. doi: 10.1093/eurpub/cku121.

Spittal MJ, Pirkis J, Miller M, Carter G, Studdert DM (2014). The repeated episodes of self-harm (RESH) score: A tool for predicting risk of future episodes of self-harm by hospital patients. *Journal of Affective Disorders* 161, 36-42.

Sprinks J (2014). Social engagement crucial to tackling loneliness in old age. *Nursing Older People* 26, 8-9.

Stevens JR, Jarrahzadeh T, Brendel RW, Stern TA (2014). Strategies for the prescription of psychotropic drugs with black box warnings. *Psychosomatics* 55, 123-133.

Sulkowski ML, Michael K (2014). Meeting the mental health needs of homeless students in schools: A multi-tiered system of support framework. *Children and Youth Services Review* 44, 145-151.

Swanson JW, McGinty EE, Fazel S, Mays VM (2014). Mental illness and reduction of gun violence and suicide: Bringing epidemiologic research to policy. *Annals of Epidemiology.* Published online: 29 April 2014. doi: 10.1016/j.annepidem.2014.03.004.

Syme KL, Hagen EH (2014). Testing theories of suicide in 245 cultures. *American Journal of Physical Anthropology* 153, 251.

Talisa VB, Boyle L, Crafa D, Kaufmann WE (2014). Autism and anxiety in males with fragile x syndrome: An exploratory analysis of neurobehavioral profiles from a parent survey. *American Journal of Medical Genetics Part A* 164, 1198-1203.

Tarrier N, Kelly J, Maqsood S, Snelson N, Maxwell J, Law H, Dunn G, Gooding P (2014). The cognitive behavioural prevention of suicide in psychosis: A clinical trial. *Schizophrenic Research* 156, 204-210

Tattoli L, Buschmann CT, Tsokos M (2014). Remarkable findings in suicidal hanging. *Forensic Science, Medicine, and Pathology* 10, 639-642.

Thapa TB (2014). Living with diabetes: Lay narratives as idioms of distress among the low-caste Dalit of Nepal. *Medical Anthropology* 33, 428-440.

Thombs BD, Razykov I, Hudson M, Baron M (2014). Screening strategy of depression in patients with systemic sclerosis with special reference to suicide: Comment on the article by Razykov et al reply. *Arthritis Care and Research* 66, 497.

Thompson WK, Gershon A, O'Hara R, Bernert RA, Depp CA (2014). The prediction of study-emergent suicidal ideation in bipolar disorder: A pilot study using ecological momentary assessment data. *Bipolar Disorders* 16, 669–677.

Thorell LH, Wolfersdorf M, Straub R, Steyer J, Hodgkinson S, Kaschka WP, Jandl M, Wahlin K (2014). A paradox in suicide statistics in estimating specificity of tests for suicide - reply to Mushquash and co-workers and Culver. *Journal of Psychiatric Research* 54, 142-143.

Till B, Niederkrotenthaler T (2014). Surfing for suicide methods and help: Content analysis of websites retrieved with search engines in Austria and the United States. *Journal of Clinical Psychiatry* 75, 886-892.

Todt M, Ast F, Wolff-Maras R, Roesler B, Germerott T (2014). Suicide by drowning: A forensic challenge. *Forensic Science International* 240, e22-e24.

Tonelli LH (2014). Neuroinflammation in suicide: Too little may be just as bad as too much. *Acta Psychiatrica Scandinavica*. Published online: 24 September 2014. doi: 10.1111/acps.12340.

Topiwala A, Chouliaras L, Ebmeier KP (2014). Prescribing selective serotonin reuptake inhibitors in older age. *Maturitas* 77, 118-123.

Torres-Platas SG, Cruceanu C, Chen GG, Turecki G, Mechawar N (2014). Evidence for increased microglial priming and macrophage recruitment in the dorsal anterior cingulate white matter of depressed suicides. *Brain, Behavior, and Immunity* 42, 50–59.

Townsend E (2014). Self-harm in young people. *Evidence Based Mental Health* 17, 97-99.

Tran L, Crane MF, Phillips JK (2014). The distinct role of performing euthanasia on depression and suicide in veterinarians. *Journal of Occupational Health Psychology* 19, 123-132.

Trevino K, Abbott C, Fisch M, Friedlander R, Duberstein P, Prigerson H (2014). Patient-oncologist alliance as protection against suicidal ideation in young adults with advanced cancer. *Psycho-Oncology* 23, 52-53.

Turecki G (2014). Epigenetics and suicidal behavior research pathways. *American Journal of Preventive Medicine* 47, S144-S151.

Turegano-Fuentes F, Perez-Diaz D, Sanz-Sanchez M, Alfici R, Ashkenazi I (2014). Abdominal blast injuries: Different patterns, severity, management, and prognosis according to the main mechanism of injury. *European Journal of Trauma and Emergency Surgery* 40, 451-460.

Ursano RJ, Colpe LJ, Heeringa SG, Kessler RC, Schoenbaum M, Stein MB (2014). The army study to assess risk and resilience in servicemembers (Army STARRS). *Psychiatry* 77, 107-119.

Vakkalanka P, Rushton WF, Hardison LS, Bishop MC, Haverstick DM, Holstege CP (2014). Evaluation of the initiation of urine drug screens intended for use in transfer patients. *The American Journal of Emergency Medicine* 32, 1037-1040.

van Loo HM, Cai T, Gruber MJ, Li J, de Jonge P, Petukhova M, Rose S, Sampson NA, Schoevers RA, Wardenaar KJ, Wilcox MA, Al-Hamzawi AO, Andrade LH, Bromet EJ, Bunting B, Fayyad J, Florescu SE, Gureje O, Hu C, Huang Y, Levinson D, Medina-Mora ME, Nakane Y, Posada-Villa J, Scott KM, Xavier M, Zarkov Z, Kessler RC (2014). Major depressive disorder subtypes to predict long-term course. *Depression and Anxiety* 31, 765-777.

van Veen M, van Weeghel I, Koekkoek B, Braam AW (2014). Structured assessment of suicide risk in a psychiatric emergency service: Psychometric evaluation of the nurses' global assessment of suicide risk scale (NGASR). *International Journal of Social Psychiatry*. Published online 24 July 2014. doi: 10.1177/0020764014543311.

Veysey S (2014). People with a borderline personality disorder diagnosis describe discriminatory experiences. *Kotuitui* 9, 20-35.

Vilhauer RP (2014). Depictions of auditory verbal hallucinations in news media. *International Journal of Social Psychiatry*. Published online: 27 May 2014, doi: 10.1177/0020764014535757.

Vlachadis N, Vlachadi M, Iliodromiti Z, Kornarou E, Vrachnis N (2014). Greece's economic crisis and suicide rates: Overview and outlook. *Journal of Epidemiology and Community Health*. Published online: 12 July 2014. doi: 10.1136/jech-2014-204407.

Volavka J (2013). Violence in schizophrenia and bipolar disorder. *Psychiatria Danubina* 25, 24-33.

von Wolff A, Jansen M, Hoelzel LP, Westphal A, Haerter M, Kriston L (2014). Generalizability of findings from efficacy trials for chronic depression: An analysis of eligibility criteria. *Psychiatric Services* 65, 897-904.

Wachtel S, Vocks S, Edel MA, Nyhuis P, Willutzki U, Teismann T (2014). Validation and psychometric properties of the German capability for suicide questionnaire. *Comprehensive Psychiatry* 55, 1292-1302.

Wambui H (2014). Suicidal intent. *Nursing Standard* 28, 61.

Warden S, Spiwak R, Sareen J, Bolton JM (2014). The SAD PERSONS scale for suicide risk assessment: A systematic review. *Archives of Suicide Research* 18, 313-326.

Whisenhunt JL, Chang CY, Brack GL, Orr J, Adams LG, Paige MR, McDonald CPL, O'Hara C (2014). Professional counselors' conceptualizations of the relationship between suicide and self-injury. *Journal of Mental Health Counseling* 36, 263-282.

Whitlock J, Exner-Cortens D, Purington A (2014). Assessment of nonsuicidal self-injury: development and initial validation of the Non-Suicidal Self-Injury-Assessment Tool (NSSI-AT).*Psychological Assessment* 26, 935-946.

Widger T (2014). Reading Sri Lanka's suicide rate. *Modern Asian Studies* 48, 791-825.

Williams K (2013). School nurse feasibility, reliability, and validity test of the SARA and SLICE ® tools for self-harm. *Journal of the American Psychiatric Nurses Association* 19, 29.

Winsper C, Tang NKY (2014). Linkages between insomnia and suicidality: Prospective associations, high-risk subgroups and possible psychological mechanisms. *International Review of Psychiatry* 26, 189-204.

Wise J (2014). Schizophrenia is associated with increased rates of violence and suicide, Swedish study finds. *BMJ* 348, g3690.

Wong PW, Kwok NC, Tang JY, Blaszczynski A, Tse S (2014). Suicidal ideation and familicidal-suicidal ideation among individuals presenting to problem gambling services. *Crisis* 35, 219-232.

Yen Y-C, Huang C-K, Tai C-M (2014). Psychiatric aspects of bariatric surgery. *Current Opinion in Psychiatry* 27, 374-379

Yoon JH, Ahn YS (2014). Cause-specific mortality due to malignant and non-malignant disease in Korean foundry workers. *PLoS ONE*. Published online: 5 February 2014. doi: 10.1371/journal.pone.0088264.

Yoshimatsu K, Palmer B (2014). Depression in patients with borderline personality disorder. *Harvard Review of Psychiatry* 22, 266-273.

You J, Lin MP, Leung F (2014). A longitudinal moderated mediation model of nonsuicidal self-injury among adolescents. *Journal of Abnormal Child Psychology.* Published online: 18 June 2014. doi: 10.1007/s10802-014-9901-x.

Zai CC, Zai GC, Tiwari AK, Manchia M, de Luca V, Shaikh SA, Strauss J, Kennedy JL (2014). Association study of GABRG2 polymorphisms with suicidal behaviour in schizophrenia patients with alcohol use disorder. *Neuropsychobiology* 69, 154-158.

Zajdel J, Zajdel R (2014). Should a doctor stop rendering medical services? Part II - analysis of medico-legal conduct in cases of uncertainties regarding informed consent in minors. The Polish perspective. *Annals of Agricultural and Environmental Medicine* 21, 388-393.

Zarghami A, Nazari P, Manouchehri AA (2014). Suicide: Affected by the internet. *Yonsei Medical Journal* 55, 1161.

Zarrilli F, Amato F, Keller S, Florio E, Carli V, Stuppia L, Sarchiapone M, Chiariotti L, Castaldo G, Tomaiuolo R (2014). Tropomyosin-related kinase B receptor polymorphisms and isoforms expression in suicide victims. *Psychiatry Research* 220, 725–726.

Zhang J, Lv J (2014). Psychological strains and depression in Chinese rural populations. *Psychology, Health and Medicine* 19, 365-373.

Zimmerman M, Martinez J, Young D, Chelminski I, Dalrymple K (2014). Differences between patients with borderline personality disorder who do and do not have a family history of bipolar disorder. *Comprehensive Psychiatry* 55, 1491–1497.

www.ingramcontent.com/pod-product-compliance
Lightning Source LLC
Chambersburg PA
CBHW080234270326
41926CB00020B/4234